Give Sorrow Words

Give Sorrow Words

MARYSE HOLDER'S LETTERS FROM MEXICO

Introduction by KATE MILLETT

Grove Press, Inc./New York

First Edition 1979
First Printing 1979
ISBN: 0-394-50621-9
Grove Press ISBN: 0-8021-0185-2
Library of Congress Catalog Card Number: 78-74551

Library of Congress Cataloging in Publication Data

Holder, Maryse.
    Give sorrow words.

    1. Holder, Maryse. 2. Victims of crimes—Biography.
I. Title.
HV6250.4.W65H643   301.41'2'0924   78-74551
ISBN 0-394-50621-9

Manufactured in the United States of America

Distributed by Random House, Inc., New York

GROVE PRESS, INC., 196 West Houston Street, New York, N.Y. 10014

Give sorrow words: the grief that does not speak
Whispers the o'er-fraught heart and bids it break.
      —*Macbeth*, Act IV, Scene 3

ACKNOWLEDGMENTS

I wish to give my special thanks to the following people for their help in the publication of this book: Laurie Sucher, "the magic connection"; Susan Axelrod, who "authored" the group; Tom Paino, for his marvelous letter and many helpful suggestions and ideas; Augusta Walker, for her sympathetic ear and help at a difficult time; Bonnie Leeds, for her genuine interest; Iris Ludwig, for her interest and help; Carol Goldner, for her interest and help; Harriet Yarowsky, for saving one letter for twenty years; Selma Yampolsky, for her invaluable help and contributions; and of course Stanley Kline, without whom none of this would have come to pass. I wish to give my very special thanks to Kate Millett for the very special role she played. And finally, I wish to thank the editor at Grove Press who worked with us, Kent E. Carroll, for the creative role he played in helping to make this book a reality.

—EDITH JONES

Ω

INTRODUCTION

These pages are the account of a woman on her way to death, a death not only imposed but sought after. That the author is a young American writer who was murdered was the first information I heard. And that her friends were trying to publish her letters. Friends of mine who were friends of her friends—that loyal band staying by her single relic, the one publishable document of her life, its explanation—entreated me to read it. The thing was so poignant I couldn't refuse. What I found was a sister, an adventuress, a madwoman, daring as an early Henry Miller, self-destructive as Janis, the voice of Genet in a woman, speaking the purest American—the American we write to our friends: utterly informal, tough, a rap—a voice I have heard in my own head for years, come across occasionally in private correspondence, but never seen published. Maryse's is the most authentic voice, in sheer language, that I have heard off a page since the new consciousness hit women.

Ah, but that was the tragedy. The owner of this voice, the mind behind it—the mind of a highly educated American woman, schooled in literature, experienced even in teaching it, a well-read critic—is also a woman who traveled not once, but twice (Part I and Part II are two separate voyages) in order to meet, pick up, get fucked and fucked over by ever younger Mexican toughs, hoods, gigolos. Slowly and certainly they would erode all that she was, destroy her confidence, her self-esteem, even her self-respect. Until one of them, it seems, finally murdered her. Put out this voice, extinguished this mind.

It's an old story. Women go through this all the time. The example of Maryse Holder's execution exaggerates only to make clear. We have all been conditioned to self-destruct, to explode. To take all we have made of our slender opportunities, our extra effort—and blow it all to hell. Ostensibly because A. doesn't call or B. doesn't care or C. is leaving us. But really because we know we should; the world, our history, our own collective past demands the immolation of what little freedom we have ever laid our hands on.

Staked out, made claim to. Even with rhetoric. Because it was all illegal. Against the rules because finally we know the rules.

She does not know the women, she cannot yet. So, without allies, she faced in the men a force she imagined was sexual, hetero flirtation, amour. She underestimated that force, she failed to appreciate its malice. Imagined she could enter and exit as she wished. She could experiment. Instead it destroyed her. Not in Lawrentian pseudo-archeological blood ritual, but in tough Mexico City ruffians, in contemporary feminine neurosis about her looks, in being stood up a thousand times, in booze, in one-night stands, asinine hand-wringing over broken promises and phone calls. It is so banal how they "got" her. She is so naked at the end, reduced to a teenager waiting for her boyfriend to call, aged, boozed, without resources. Except Edith.

The unsung heroine of this martyrdom; the witness. Edith. Friend. Woman friend. We hardly know anything about her. Except what Maryse can say *to* her. Which is everything. Edith will "understand," advise, agree with, listen to anything. The all-forgiving, utterly sympathetic female alter ego, the woman friend all women dream of, the ear. Into this ear was poured a life. What pity I feel, reading this correspondence, that the confidante could not be a lover, the lovers described being so unworthy of confidence. So without love. More like enemies they are. But Stan, the American boyfriend, is rejected out of hand for the exoticism of Miguel, Luis, Andrés, etc. And women seem impossible to love, that taboo harder to break or at least more intimidating than the soulless neck of Mexican male indifference. And so Edith remains the friend, the one who remains when all others abandon the desperate figure in whose consciousness you live—claustrophobically, mercilessly, powerfully—during these pages. And it is into Edith that the spirit flowed as it went under.

As it was conquered and gave out in battle. Maryse was not so much murdered as assassinated. A threat annihilated. A rebel put to the sword. Silenced. "Despite their gentleness of sex and sensibility, they are murderers. They don't abuse the body but twist and retwist the emotions. Kill your heart, your independence." She still underestimates it all. In the earliest pages an insouciant Maryse can toss off remarks like "Sex with men, how can I say, lacks the personal." Smartass, woman of the world.

But Maryse was even a feminist, had been in the Movement in New York. Consciousness Raising. Enough to give her a taste, a vocabulary for rule-breaking. Not enough to protect her. But enough to create a rage to be free, a dreadful vulnerability of expectation. Toward the world, toward herself. She could march into a place like Oaxaca and dare to do it all. Do her thing. Be what she wished to be. Dance as if her life depended upon it (the dance being her metaphor for living, for living as art, as danger), play the lover, be public, be open. Enjoy all the privileges men do. And get by with it. As if that were permitted there. She could sling the rhetoric too, analyze Mexico with a stringent eye, denounce its chauvinism, the sinister Indian malice toward women lying patiently and dangerously under the layers of Spanish hauteur and contempt. Dangerous as that is, dangerous as macho is—there is another force still more implacable, a patriarchy stronger, perhaps and younger than Europe's. Earlier, less softened by time, newer, more virulent. Closer to the moment when matriarchy fell, the Goddess giving way to the terrible rites of the Incas, a strain of pure hatred toward women, the pure masculine arrogance D.H. Lawrence worshipped in *The Plumed Serpent*.

Like Lawrence's "Woman Who Rode Away," Maryse miscalculated. As if the whole colonial experience of gringo and Mexican could be wiped out, canceled in the freedom appointed for herself by one American woman. Daisy Miller again. Never mind the staggering subjection of Mexican women, that will be transcended by the gringa pioneer. Why should she pay the debts of racism? Why indeed? But LeRoi Jones and many third-world male writers leave her the Dutchman holding the bag of white guilt. Because it's easier on them than confronting Charlie.

Even the oppressed strike out against convenient vulnerability. And the white female, though less guilty in objective fact, is, through her own subject status, open to feelings of guilt, of sympathy, of fellow feeling. In abasing herself to macho Mexican youths, she is "making up" for history. She also thinks she has a chance. Can match their disability and oppression with her own. Not for a moment. She hasn't reckoned with their vanity. They *know* they are her superior by virtue of their sex. Their hierarchy older than racism, older than colonialism, older than capital. "The visceral desire leading up to this sordid interlude was extremely pleasant." She is showing off. Bragging, young, in love with the place and its people, talking it up to those at home.

A beautiful woman, her friends say, but her beauty imperfect because of a slight flaw, the result of mastoiditis and surgery to cure the nerves affected—a flaw that haunted her, as her childhood in France still did, the years running from the Nazis, the trauma of learning English at seven in a new country. But the slight flaw in her face most of all. Others say it was charming, ironic, when she smiled it became an asset. But to the merciless critic herself it is agony, she is pathologically aware of it, made vulnerable, susceptible, her own case a paradigm of the general insecurity of women over their looks, their value before the public, their apology for existence before the eyes of men. And in Mexico Maryse flung herself upon the cruel packaging ethic over and over, like a bird flying against a window pane.

She tries very hard to play the game. Describing one lad's brown eyes as "a cliché on its way to becoming a symbol," she is tough, Yank, current. But the undercurrent of drifting into depression (now that her university instructorship is gone, a disappointment she never recovered from), and then to Mexico and then to booze and despair, is always there. Despite her hopes, her marathon sprees of swimming and dancing, her pick-ups, her one-night stands, her insolvent infatuations. She is always losing because she is always falling in love, and the rule is that the one who cares less is the winner. To love is to lose. It's a game. Like war. As with gambling or business you must be totally invulnerable. She never is. Even boasting of her conquests she's riding for a fall. This is not a game women are permitted to win at; to play at all is illegal. Respectability, the *novia* (bride), the prim, the protected—all that is closed to her. She's regarded as immoral, therefore fair game. She loses caste, becomes prey.

But how well she tells it. One thinks of Jean Rhys—indeed Maryse, conscious and well read as she is, thinks of Rhys herself, but there is a difference, a freshness more of our time, experience conveyed directly to the reader as it rarely is in writing. As it would be to a friend, as it would be in conversation.

We were in the trees. So cool. In this other element like birds at night. But he didn't know I had a clit and my dear he fairly panted with long-sufferingness and generosity all through foreplay. I pursued his indifference to my breasts and he finally sighed "O.K." and nuzzled on one nipple, dryly. He had no contraceptives. I did but lied. Finally I figured fuck it—I'm wet, he's big, it would be some pleasure and got up to get my foam. "Goddamn" he muttered disgustedly at one more delay to getting his rocks off (he didn't know actually what I'd gotten up for). I saw the light. "Goddamn is right!" I said and split.

Maryse always sees the light. This is the great paradox of her writing, of her adventure, of her transitional place in time. That, having perfect consciousness, complete understanding of her situation, she nevertheless pursues her self-destruction. You are watching someone undo herself. With the clearest perception, the most analytical comprehension. Finally that is what one comes to admire. The power to understand. Even when one cannot stop the deterioration. The courage to describe it, know its every cunning trick.

And the lust, the enormous romantic lust for experience. An existential appetite for every crumb of living, every husk of sensation. Sex. The great mountain of desire. "The only contact we make is through sexual desire. What else do we live for but to feel alive in this way?" But she is a sensualist in everything. Liquor, language, hotel rooms, jail cells, food (there is a magnificent essay on the metaphysics of the sweet roll), the sea and sand and Mexican beauty, filth, tedium, drumbeat disco—and always the dance. Fucking and dancing: few women (we, who know so much and say so little) have written as directly and openly of the first, and no one that I've ever read has approached her on the second. Strangely disregarded, this adjunct or prelude to sex, this—like the nude—byproduct art form of sexuality. And for this form, as for the other, Maryse nearly gives her life: "Dancing is a meditation, a masturbation, the self fucking the self." A trance-like ecstasy: "At one point I flew, I actually flew . . . I built up the tempo, I accelerated more and more until I took off. Straight out of Castaneda. I wonder if anyone saw it. There was a sensation of weightlessness and no longer touching the ground—I had pushed myself up through increasing height and rhythmic speed until for one long moment I flew . . ." It is how she wanted to live, that passion, that ardor, that rush. She was thirty-six years old when a blunt instrument was used to bash her head in. We can never hear any more from her.

—KATE MILLETT
November, 1978

[13]

PART ONE

Ω

Dear E.,

Had been going to write you ebullient sex letter intermixed with poetic epistemological reflections on being reborn in the crater of civilization but I actually fucked him this afternoon and it was grubby and banal, as you always knew. It is incredibly shocking, their lack of any need but to plug one conquest after another, and that boring whining *pleeeeeeze* to get you to let them shtoop you. Yet I succumbed. He played angry ploy (he would reject me if I didn't) more strongly than I played my "If you care you'll wait until mañana." Sheez. He had metallic breath and I shit-juice in underwear from Exlax-induced runs. So grubadick. Up in some garbage-strewn hill-land in an abandoned concrete swimming pool. Was curious to see his prick since he was my height about and slighter. Prick nice and fat and the color of zetontec (?)—a purplish red volcanic rock common in Mexico. Ditto his full lips. He said, "I want to eat you," but all he did was bite my chin repeatedly, mock lick my ear, scratch my twat trying to wangle his wong in through a side entrance, remark that I had a mustache, non-kiss me with unopened mouth, la la. You understand that he is sullen, twenty, speaks English and some French, has a nasty snarling mouth, chink cheeks and eyes somewhat and is bitter and bored and no doubt training to be a gig. So I really wanted to contemplate the ensemble a bit—purple mouths always please. Wanted him to check me out and pant with anticipated *nachas*. But so grubadick was he. Sex with men, how can I say, lacks the personal. The visceral desire leading up to this sordid interlude was extremely pleasant. Those feelings as the body becomes animate again, drawstring being pulled through one's guts, the cunt pursing. And the head too—lizards on the wall seeming quintessentially him, or Mexico. Unexpected contractions. Done done done.

Plus I'm sick sick sick. Danced my ass off two nights ago in a really swinging disco here, swam my arms off, burned my bod to a crisp and got three hours sleep and BONGA. Now an invalid bored out of her gourd. In this devastated physical condition, natch, was fucked. Yecch.

Sitting in deck chair under frond umbrella on beach looking at bay and drowsing boats. Sun setteth. Live in charmingly primitive room. Take bath with pails cold water. Do laundry outside in big tilted stone sink in patio, where is also a hammock and a hibiscus trellis from which lush blossoms thud to the ground. Is a large expatriate WASP scene here, full of fashionable and genuine, I'm sure, bored despair. Everyone knows it's too late to make the Gauguin scene, that they're really afraid of competing in the States, and the sexual pickings, except for the Mexican boys, don't seem as unlimited as the coconuts, which, young, are macheted open for their plentiful sweet juice and then discarded.

The food here is abominable. Fish, bananas, papayas, coconuts, etc. but to buy the bloody things is a major investment. Like many resort towns, you're conned into a stay with cheap rooms and then whammoed with expensive food.

Studs here finger their balls a lot, a disgusting habit. Everyone spits and so do I, though only saw one or two young girls do it.

The Mexican girls are heavy into basketball and I'm heavy into watching them. It is the only glimpse I get of them as a culture. Needless to say, they don't make the chic intermingling scene the studs do. They're too sweet to resent the foreign twats. One wonders if they ever feel burning ambition for more distant glamors. The studs are college dropouts, some of them, and do a fabulous bump in the disco. The women do the rhumba in the town square.

I can't write more. See ya soon.

M.

Ω

Dear E.,

My unwilling correspondent—so nice you can't object. You probably won't have received my first letter since I entrusted it to Jorge/Andrés, the would-be gigolo sneak mooch, to mail. Am flattered he pocketed the two pesos, if he did, and chose to decipher the letter at his illiterate ease, the work of years.

What can I tell You? The scene perpetually pendeth. New folks move in in cycles and tell us what it was like last year. Vague rumors about Arthur circulate. Edith, we must come here together and make the instant stuff of legends. I, poor lass, am only in pursuit of health and attractiveness. Only occasionally do I stare down the vulgarios of this pueblo. One thing: it ain't so easy to peddle your ass down the Amazon. To be a woman and stranded (I am only a woman, poor self) is to really have to peddle it. And of course one is meat on the hoof, no matter how rugged one is and how extensive and human previous contact. Earlier, before I was not stranded, I thought seriously of peddling myself to some old American male. Surprised at my utter lack of guilt.

Much later, alas. Suppose you received first letter—was assured by Jorge/Andrés he'd sent it. Ah my dear, the stages of lust are many and the most literary interesting always occur the day before.... So he fucked me and the only recourse was to run off in a huff, trailing mumblings about what a shitty lover he was, which worked. We spent days tormenting each other playing hard to get. Until yesterday I was in that complacent phase of the old faggot who is morally superior to the young trash he lusts after.

J/A is the pits. He's half Spanish, half Indian, and deep brown. The other day we were looking at each other's gringo sunburn—me, Stan, and George, a pleasant Alyosha-like hanger-on from Alaska. J/A was mocking us so I said red was beautiful, that he was the wrong color, yellow, which he suddenly looked in the waning sun. An obvious absurdity meant as coquettry (cocketry?). I started working up a flirt with two little Mexican girls across the alley and J/A snarled, "They are uggg-ly." Two and three years old. It was so vicious and weak and ugly in that male way.

He takes everything, gives nothing. Grubs cigarettes, shots of tequila, towels; struts in with absurd braggadocio and strenuous American slang. Everything is "Hey man, what's happenin'?" He lied about where he works—in public relations in some government office—and comes here to shower. I'm sure he lives in the streets. It's out of Gide or Genet his scene, he must grub for food in garbage cans like the diseased and oddly cowardly Mexican dogs. By choice. So I romanticize. It would be fascinating to tail him some day on his snarling peregrinations. He is above nothing.

It's absurd illusion to think he desires me. He's only interested in ripping Stan off. The one time we were together alone after that afternoon (Stan was sick in bed with dysentery) the sex was, once again, cursory. He had that same metallic taste and again rolled his "muy grande!" joint against my stomach. His slightness humiliates me, but my sense of physical foolishness had been part of that pleasant, ironic helplessness of the person who knows better.

There is so much I could tell you about Mexico if I weren't so

[19]

diseased, literally and figuratively. J/A is a festering tropical sore and I am wasting away from La Gripe.

Last night Stan and George refused for hours to lend J/A a towel so he could be spiffy for the disco. I finally begged him to borrow mine, wanting to be kind, dying to do everything possible too make him beautiful for me, connecting directly with him over the hostility of the men. (It's clear I will always be the one to break first in any affair.) He came out smelling of flowers from some oil he rubs on himself, a fresh, lush scent. God, he's out of Tennessee Williams. I'm sure he has a rose tattoo on his ass.

Last night was so awful I barely resisted throwing myself off a parapet. He dashed off after having spent hours wheedling a towel out of us three stony red gringos, as he often does, to wind his own secret trail and appeared at the bar much later. Misery is his absence. It's so stupid, so complacently stupid! Regaining the breath as it were of life when he walked in I said what took you so long? After dancing with him once I never danced with him again. He next asked a woman to dance who refused and then he asked me and I refused and that was the end of contact for that endless dirge of a night. He seemed taken by a very tall Canadian, all large bones. And incredibly, they looked okay together. I withered. Last Saturday it had been a ball and I the belle, but you can only be new once. One our song after another came on. He even stooped to his own kind and he deeply hates his race. One of the muscles de la playa who runs the disco was nasty about the check. He's nineteen so I told him he looks thirty which, because of bleaching his hair, he does. He told me I looked seventy—doesn't she, he asked a fellow bar goon, who nodded. The strap of my top kept sliding off my shoulder as I danced and my elegantly loose Cinnamon pants hung like gatkes off my Miami roasted flesh. I became more of a schmattah as the evening ground on. And that dark stone Indian mask never turned in my direction.

In a way I willed this. I wanted to want him more than I do—did. Coz now I duz. Sex alone was so boring. It's not masochism but a will to desire. In so far as I controlled it, it meant whipping him up by repeated rejection. That he would reject me harder was unforeseen. But, as Proust knew so exhaustively, so is love born.

Now those two Canadian women will probably be in our circle. Heterosexuality—when one is sexual—is a strain on feminism. In a million ways. So Doris was right. I'd give anything to be in my dyke phase again, but it's too late not to feel about J/A. I stare at his beautiful face gluttonously.

In my next letter I'll describe the scene here.

M.

Ω

Dear E.,

Another "Zi" *(as the chic call it) epistle. Andrés and I are now at the you and David stage. I slip a note under this jolly architect's door inviting him to boogie tonight and A. says Man, you're wasting your time. He's an architect—too good for you. I lie and say I'm a U. prof (which I no longer am, by the way, having been, I swear the English department used this term, "terminated"). Ten minutes earlier he asked how such an unattractive woman like me could refuse him. Plus I've hit him, quelle insulte to a Latin. He's trying to be over but I can't fight the good fight. He refuses to let an old, ugly gringa not let him use her hole when no fresher stuff is two feet away.

Later.

I'm here alone now, trying to avoid a winter of discontent. Stan left three days ago and my life since has been a rather monastic one except for bouts of A.'s vicious tongue during the day (but alas not at night!) and one more encounter with his uncircumcised dick one night. He thrusts it mightily in and mightily out, up on his arms, grinning broadly at his own magnificence. The truculent narss is probably a fag like he says. Forget the tits, the clit, the ass. Even looking at my cunt. His cock turns him on. But very pretty, has veins in his arms, brown and smooth, almost no hair on his face.

The teasing we're into now is the roughest of my life and my sense of reality has gone down the toilet. He brushes my pubic hair and moues disgust, wipes his finger vigorously. He's winning.

Pero, no me importa porque I have also been taken out to a

* Zihuatanejo, the town which Maryse Holder made her home during her stay in Mexico, is located on the west coast, about 125 miles northwest of Acapulco, between Acapulco and Manzanillo. Although the town itself is small—a population of only 2,000—it is in the center of an internationally known resort area.

[21]

hurried but expensive dinner by my potential new husband-figure, Gilberto the architect, who is rich by even American standards and a (secret) Marxist. He buys me dinner in order to explain in earnest helpless English that there is no contradiction. I feel a bit like Solanas, charging for conversation. It's a great gig. Andrés, natch, fucks me for nothing, I an old fat gringa who should be grateful she doesn't have to pay. There is some guilt—I'm all feminist and academic with the Marxist and a vulgar sado-masochist with A. A guttersnipe. Punk, actually.

I'm a cripple now as well. Stepped on a thorn in a coconut grove. Hombre número tres, Isidro, a dropout vet student, he says, poked with a needle for ten minutes, next day a nurse with a hypo. I danced, swam, walked, sunned, and my wound got infected, deeper and deeper into the heel. If I had whites and a cane, O.K., but with British walking shorts and a Minnie Mouse watch, a limp has limited appeal.

I miss my feminism and my upstate scene, nothing else. Staying in Zi strangest scene. E.g. sex with A. There is no way to tell him about my clit, or rather that the clit is *the* female sexual organ. No *context*. So frightening to not be able to maintain one's perspective on one's own. Finally, I lose the belief that the clit *is* the organ. All quite "naturally," painlessly. I was drunk the other night and blurted out the forbidden word at the hip disco to these two Canadian women who blushed and immediately got up to dance. So smoothly does reality disappear. So archetypally female this contradiction between the real (our biology even!) and the male version, but it is precisely this sense of the "real" that evaporates, so that there isn't even a dialectic, as I used to think there was, and which I thought made women more philosophically profound, more genuinely, naturlich, engaged in the quest for the real or true. (I wonder what your consciousness is like, as a woman, at this precise moment—keep the flame burning for me.) I guess that's the most profound deprivation women experience—that they are the invisible sex. When I'd forgotten what our problem was (over dinner with the architect), I desperately tried to remember and God hit me with that flash, for which, believe me, I am eternally grateful. Feminism is a vision. And an impossible one here. It's like I'm fifteen again with Andrés. Meek, charmed. I ALMOST FEIGNED AN ORGASM LAST NIGHT. Do you know what I'm talkin' about, man! Oh girl, girl. I lose myself, all sense of female culture, female definitions of life experience. Enuf.

[22]

There are certain kindnesses to women though. I don't feel ugly in Mexico—men don't seem interested in pointing out my flaw. Of course I'm a gringa and automatically attractive in a sluttish way. I've lost a lot of weight and have a deep tan and though I'm far from being la crème de la crème, my walking shorts are becoming universally coveted by the chic North American women. The Queen of Hip wants to buy them.

I find I'm curiously unable to write you of the scene, which I keep promising to do. Only myself interests. What awful thing can this mean? And just yesterday I ended one stage of a dialectical conversation with myself wherein I decided that autobiography is the curse of women's recent literary output (this after I feared not believing Pat Loud's version of her life, feared boredom, and so didn't borrow it from lending library). Essentially, no one *believes* autobiography, only fiction. Autobiography seems too much a product of a temporary perspective or ideology whereas fiction, because it makes no claim to be mimetic, provides a possible model of reality. Badly put. "Freely theoretical" I should've said. Geez. This is just like talking to you without the interruptions. Poor baby, don't you envy me this luxury.

One element of this sojourn I'm enjoying is "feeling my thoughts" again. I like to be alone at least half the day and connect once or twice with people. Being alone feels so luxurious, so clean and clear, so fresh. So so so. I look at a boy. I write. Such a rhythm! I look. I light up a cigarette. I am aware of an English boy's interest in this letter. There is a slight breeze. I'm in the square, overlooking the crowd of vendors, women, boys. The square overlooks the basketball court which is right next to the beach, then ocean. All hemmed in by the right size mountains. Which reminds me of another pleasure, to be the right size in a country. I'm not short here—oh E, such pleasure. I'm never coming (going?) "home." Home is where the height is. And the looks are so pleasant. Another male item. They didn't cheer at a movie scene of a woman being gang-raped. Machismo almost excludes women, or is it the relative non-hostility of an assured master race? My dear, my finger waneth. Come to Mexico. See you soon.

M.

P.S. Finished Jean Rhys's *Wide Sargasso Sea*. Great! Especially for reading in the tropics. Am now in *The Children of Sanchez*. And new stage of dialectical speculation about the "truth" of documentary.

Ω

Dear E.,

The sordid end of a boring day will probably result in one more eviction from paradise. Andrés shunned the cripple today who had more solitude than she could bear all the dead long day. She drank. He appeared at last, so late so late. Full of ironic memory of her claimed detachment from love to the Canadian whose blondness and virtue are an armor, she sported with passion. She took his hand, even a bath, and said "We'll make real love tonight," imagining his lips in a deep kiss, her breasts, his hand or even his mouth on her clit, her licking him—firm young brown impeccable body—all over. She drank and smoked (though he tried to knock the cigarette out of her hand), saying with irony she hoped transcended the language barrier, "te quiero," then, with such heavy sarcasm its deadly seriousness would've been apparent to even an Indian who didn't speak English, or Spanish, "yo te amo." And slid her finger down his firm young arm. Took a shower, as I said, hoping for the best, and brushed her teeth, expecting, for sure, the least.

You know already what transpired but she was so drunk she felt her irony protected her. He was in and out in forty-five seconds, his teeth clamped shut all the time. She beat him to the shower to rinse her cunt of brown, wanted boys, and spit some water out of her mouth audibly, his habit after he'd been with her. He had the nerve to follow suit more vigorously. Am I dirty, she asked truculently and he had the unimaginable but extraordinarily typical cruelty to use her accusation as an excuse to leave, feigning dumbness and anger.

I pulled a knife and refused to let him go. He was genuinely frightened and when Pedro, the benign proprietor who's had his (undoubtedly partly jealous) fill of Andrés, returned, Andrés, after I taunted him to it, began calling Pedro over. I was stone naked, two drawn switchblades on the bed, two bottles of tequila lurched crazily about the beds and a broken lime on the floor. He called for help and tried pulling the door open when my towel was coming off so I pushed against the door. His hand was in it. This went on for minutes. Afterwards, I mock collapsed in his arms (he didn't have the guts to fight me effectively and leave and finally had withdrawn his hand) and begged him to wait till I put some clothes on. Then I tried to enlist him in a common, affectionate attempt to figure out some innocent cover story. Versions were (noble me): I was drunk.

[24]

We'd had a lovers' quarrel. He said he'd handle it. Ha ha, I thought, still scared of me? Desperate to leave, probably, he promised that if I was kicked out we'd find a room together. Edith, what a dumb shithead I was when I said this country is kind to women. I heard horror stories of machismo last night from the Canadian women. God, the too-strong will collapses with a vengeance. What a joke, my superior sociological detachment.

His wrist was somewhat mangled, there wasn't much we could've said. I got dressed, kicked the redrawn knives under the bed, and toppled out of lunacy to Pedro, mea culping at a distance, with the dumb drunk's belief that two feet between me and the sober would mask the obvious. Pedro just shook his head and evicted Andrés once and for all. With a mixture of pride and genuine contrition, I apologized from the bottom of my cunt to Jorge, who asked me for a bag to cart his three shirts and three pairs of pants home in. He had been semi-living in Pedro's messy back shed all the time. The perfect Eve, I offered to share his fate; and the perfect macha, I offered to help him lug his three outfits. He politely refused. I'll do it alone, Marisa. I walked a quick more or less straight path out of the courtyard, realizing too late that Jorge would tell the truth, that is a lie (would he speak of my humiliation and my offended pride?) and stumbled out into nighttime hoping for the worst and best simultaneously. The finale of this Mexican opera had its sweetness. His letting me get dressed; my chiding him for trying to escape: "Did you really think I'd hurt you?" I said, allowing the libretto to waft me back into his arms. "That was dumb, really dumb," I said rationally, with just your body and head gestures, hoping (since I was you) to endear myself to him. There was, too, a final glimpse of his upper torso, which will have to last me my life. It seared me sober with its beauty. I realized for the first time, of course at the moment of irrevocable loss, just how beautiful he'd been. Tu comprends—he was twenty. Oh Edith. He is out of my life forever. And I am out of this room. Telepathize the perfect cover story so I can at least keep the room. I saw in that burning second that I could never have kept him.

So charming he was, and what a charming novel I might've written about him: "Death in Zihuatanejo." Help me my dear. I need a friend, respectability, beauty, to be desired.

M.

Part II
I have a burning need to explain myself to Pedro. What could I

[25]

say? Only my broken Spanish and meager rent can help me. I'm sobering up in a ghastly way, bereft and confronted by misconceived stupid irony. What asshole lack of control. I'm angry at Pedro. The schmuck. How could he not know I was in love with Andrés. Everyone knew. Did he think sixty-year-old benevolence and good advice and his mild flirtation would keep me from fire. "Indio," I used to call Jorge. He claimed that a Mexican girlfriend was the reason he couldn't walk with me in the street. You think I'm old and ugly, I said. He pretends to leave at this: That's your problem. What do you like about me, I ask. What is it you want. Everything, he innocently protests. How could I not have known?

Last night I said is it my eyes, my hair, my mouth. He looked blank until I mentioned my shoulders, about which I'm quite confident. "Of course," he said kindly, meaning it, being tender and sane. Of course my shoulders. We had been developing a language, of passion or machismo, I'm not sure which. The exciting thing was this language, shared only by us, with its pared-down richness. "You need me," he says leaning forward. He's telling me he knows me and, in so doing, that he loves me. A mistake to read Oscar Lewis: one has the illusion that indifference is really disguised pride. "I like you, I don't need you, there's a difference," I respond, all tightly wound up in a chic French West Indies head scarf and turquoise corduroy shirt pulled to by an Indian belt of brilliant blue beads. My face is showing: strong, marred, brown, intelligent, stern, worth a hundred degrees of desire. We wind up in the hammock where Andrés demonstrates sex position #123, to my endearingly child-like amusement (one has to constantly remind oneself of one's own charm with an Andrés). I love his silliness. In walks Sheila, the blond boutique owner from Toronto. "We were just trying out fucking positions in hammocks," I say all blithely tanked and sophisticated and wanting to put her at ease, *include* her, quickly. Shocked, he springs up. "Do you have a girlfriend for me?" he asks. "This woman isn't good enough." Sheila, to my mortification, is outraged on my behalf. How dare he be rude to her friend? Andrés protests. I lie back, too decimated to move, aware only that she considers him beneath her and that I am therefore pathetic to be in love with him. He says to her, "You don't understand, we always talkin like this. I know this woman." And of course he does. He'd been learning me, experimentally, courting me with deprecation. He could call me ugly because I wasn't, was the idea. And because I was and he still wanted me. I felt the same. How explain wit and power playfulness to Canadians. They are a prim lot. He promised, after she'd left and he'd returned, that he'd deprive me of himself for a day, half a day, he amended. (I wouldn't fuck him that night, humiliated into respectability by Sheila's shittiness. Hence his charming threat.)

I think it's over. I'm naive to think much more than a hole was at stake for him. The usual . . . but all those other things. A photograph of me two days ago—no yesterday—though not alone. His letting me, an inferior cunt, take the ones of him and not shithead George. That lazy afternoon serenading me with broken guitar and, after much abuse, writing down the words of a Mexican song I love that is him and this town and this year of my time on earth. A scribbled message on a shoebox cover: something about Señora Mariza, the writer.

So after Sheila left I, strong with cynicism, hit Ringo Mex's chick joint, "The Turtle," where two other Canadian women, whom I like, were hanging out. I amused them no end with my guttersnipe story. But this is a small town. They were inordinately curious about his identity and will soon find out it was reject A. But how amusing I was. If I hadn't felt so ashamed being the only American alone at the flicks tonight, if Andrés had come sooner, if if if. If I hadn't vowed to be triste and passive in my hammock when he finally did come. If tequila . . .

I'm sorry. This is diary, not enlightenment.

M.

Unbelievably, it is the next morning. Failure at work and now at love. My infection is gone. Pedro responded with almost tenderness to my buenos días this morning. Felt like crying. But of course, I sentimentalize, as always. He has merely decided to put a good face on it, having gotten rid of the less lucrative of the sinners. Are Mexicans used to this kind of opera? Macho women? It's hard to look innocent when you're mashing someone's wrist in a door. The whole genius of Catholicism is that it grants absolution.

George is not here—we were supposed to go in a party to the Isla. He was a parasite on Stan and me but now won't permit me to return the favor. The architect seems to have flown the coop and Isidro did not look good at 6:30 yesterday evening. Nor do I understand why a dope dealer would wear a marijuana T-shirt. Dope is dangerous here, or is that one more Mexican illusion meant to raise the price? I feel, however, the need to put myself under someone's protection, write in straight lines and neat letters. To

[27]

type. It's tempting, in this reverie of passivity, to not cross out errors.

North American women are bitter about the men here and say it's their cruelty as lovers that makes women feminists, as if feminism were an avoidable disease. I told Sheila it was for much more general reasons that I was and she didn't believe me. Love is that central in a woman's life.

Andrés was *relieved* last night to be thrown out of his pied à terre. He was really scared for his life.

I shudder to ask about your sex life, knowing the paunch and fag death scene that New York is. I have no idea what I'll do for money when I get back, or whether I'll ever get back into academe. It would be fun to write a series of travel guides for women. I will finally have to break down and schlep over to your remote part of the world and learn to copy edit. I don't look forward to the depression of viewing myself as an economic expendable in a tight money market. Ditto sex. Ditto my awful landlady who misses no opportunity to call me ugly. It is pleasant to escape some of the direct faces of these conditions here.

I had lost much weight—was down to 124.5—but a day without a a shit, without sun and a swim, and I gain a pound. My thin-ness, another illusion.

I hate New York. Must move. Perhaps I'll try and spend more time upstate. You, of course, are free to spend as much time there with me as you want.

Have you been seeing any women friends? Have you seen Selma or Diane? Made any feminist or dyke scenes? I think I will finally sleep with a woman when I get back, it's the only thing left. I haven't thought of Doris once except to think that I haven't thought of her.

If I were still at Lehman, I'd be working on an essay in response to the questionnaire I distributed to female (and some male) faculty about the number of women writers they used, how they felt about women's studies, etc. There were twenty responses, not many, but some were full and typed. How cynical they'll be, those respondents, when yet another women's project comes to nought. I should write them? Tell them I was terminated? My students—fantasies of them picketing on my behalf. Feel this termination as a judgment. Don't don't don't want go back to New York ever ever ever ever ever. Failure at work transmuted itself into sex and failure at sex transmutes into pain at failure at work.

Yesterday, that nightmare, I realized I had been lonely all day, so when Andrés came I was defenseless. But there was no way to know at the time what my motives were. One never knows one's emotional state or what causes it. Three assertive, educated, butchy women came to see Pedro yesterday, previous guests. They said nothing to me though they'd been friendly the first time we met. I sat around conspicuously reading *Sanchez*. No bite. They and Pedro ate the clams they had brought. I sat there. Then I left. Went to eat at this woman's restaurant where Stan, George and I used to go all the time for her cheap comida corrida. I was alone so she didn't heat the molé sauce or even put on the light, seemed actually to resent me. Then the flicks, gangs of chic gregarious Americans all turned out in the latest Soho gear. I "solita." Not a great day. My essential New York self is coming through my wrinkled, peeling turtle skin: hermetic, self-pitying, defenseless, living in letters. AIE! Wonder how you'd handle this scene. Shock all the women, I suppose, which, awful truth—you're absolutely right—is the only way to teach. Not just talk about not leaving a tip for a man but talk and shocking action. Respect! To be cowed by convention is to prove its preferability after all.

Ma chère. I bumble on. Have a weird skin zipper on my left thigh. Write me back. Send to New York. I like writing to you. Is still one of travel's main pleasures.

I'm ausgeburnt and no isla in sight. Will schlep self out to beach and drowse all medicated and hung with ever so slight an infection in hot sun and hope to shed my wrinkled shell.

Horita. Soon.

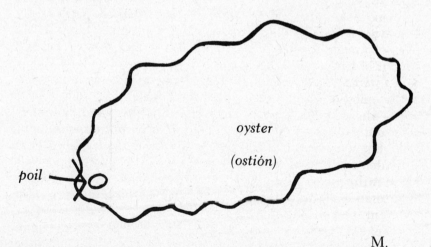

oyster

(ostión)

poil

M.

PPPPPPS. The architect just returned. He is married!

Ω

E.,

No A. today. Didn't mean send second half last letter. Well, speaking of illusions, the biggest one is that I looked good. Thought looked best ever had in life tonight till got stoned. Thought was sylph; more like elph. Took mirror from dark to light and held this way and that. Could lose twenty after all. Plus skin is not that of twenty year old, at least way fits over bod. Hair is lighter (good), lots of reddish, but body of hair falls too low, giving me usual friendly dog look. Looks good pulled back at ear level, gives me a thin, Spaniard look. Face is best though vintage and freckled. Is at least firmest part of bod. Have been eating light, exercising and swimming. Today, resumed health. Insane joy struck me early afternoon after had been kvetching about wretchedness New York. Suddenly realized I wasn't in! But being tanned next to ocean of perfect freshness. Ran in water and let ocean break cold on hot bod. First orgasm of Zi. Needless to say, multiplied.

Discover incontrovertibly tonight am me, as before. Ergo, A. hustling when said "muy bonita" first night saw me. Was beginning of computer program of perfect macho progressions. Wanted free hoo-ah. Love self so much because am diminishing (to be rewarded by real love one day) that wouldn't mind being. My ego, therefore, would seem to be schizophrenically detached from my bod. When someone sees you totally as thing, though, is freeing. Conduces to irony, i.e. self-love.

What I like most about A. is that he's the only one in a crowd who gives me a zing of familiarity. That finally is the effect (if not really at all the cause) of love. Its definition. And intimacy against odds is always great. When Stan left, A. and I manufactured hostility like a John Garfield movie. Our intimacy, our language, in fact. Here I go again, refusing to see his haste and shame. Still, he's the only one who gives me a shock in a crowd. As soon as whatever provisional well of confidence dries up, I will feel like a frightened motherless child. And I will—what? Lessee, I'll beg friends to assure me I'm fascinating, that my soul is complex so I can once more conduce to irony. An abyss opens up.

Someone outside playing guitar. Not Jorge. No more Andrés. My stomach and cheeks suck in with frightened loss. Pain is being a social reject so you can only check out the local Zócalo basketball game. Which has gone co-ed.

Andréslessness!
I am crying of fatigue but consider looking for him at Chololo. You saw *Adèle H.?* She legitimizes every woman's fantasy of limitless pursuit. Pride doesn't conduce to pleasure, nor does health.

(Next day)
But does health lead to pride? Have finally had one perfect Andrésless day. "Perfect" in that not one glimmer. I broke off hastily yesterday because my soft touch architect returned finally from Mexico City with a wife, Elena. Tall, young, studying sociology at the university. Attractive in a semi-plain way with a warm shy radiance that so many Mexican women have. So the three of us went for breakfast and then she and I went to Madera, the groupie beach, and discussed feminism. It was difficult but worthwhile. Bringing her to Madera was like bringing Channel 13 to ABC, though. And this morning she and Gilberto snuck out early. George has gone with La Grupa to Acapulco for several days. I am more and more pared down, isolated. Nights alone are awful. Even pinky, the septuagenarian, shies off from my leprous solitude.
    The Grupa: Terri, the Queen of Hip, living with a cocaine dealer who beats her up.

Six P.M. First and a half A.-less días. Dios! Twilight beginning. Hammock. Tequila. Been gaining weight so shouldn't eat. Hope is antibiotics, not pregnancy or, worse, return of inexorable me-ness. Ichseit. Sat with Chicago couple on beach and brought to Isidro, the last of the possibles. He opened a coconut. When it's young it's all milk. Added some gin. Some j's. Brilliant blue sky. Cows, pigs, chickens, mangy dogs, lost burros, all wander as freely as people. Everytime I have a shit time at Chololo, a lost bull (maleness lost to me), noshes quietly in my alley and flees at my approach. Is somehow benign sign. Met Mr. Muscles, a highly developed Alaskan mystic, on way home after having crashed hotel pool with couple. He said he was busted on Mahogua, beautiful remote beach. Am too loose; must tighten up my cool act. Is not just pretension—is real danger. My foot is not healing evenly. Can't write, can't think. So much easier to pine for lost Andrés. That sumptuous Mexican giggle, almost faggy in its exaggerated head turning away, hand covering mouth. Brown butt. An exotic Tahitian people. Purple gums. He was Chinesey, though his nastiness made him seem sharp-featured. Boy pimp. Good hustle on women. Teases you with how he's going torment you in advance and it still works when it happens. Would I'd never rediscovered men. Can't write about anything else.

Sitting at Elvira's, awful place where the tables are too high. Saw A. He fled. Por qué? Couldn't even taunt him with relative elegance since had to sit at opposite table with head on table. Tried to crack remote Canadian at next table, practiced at Zi. No go. Now what. Boredom rolls in on waves. Carita. That's you. Solita is yo.

I think Pedro told his son Delfo the story of me and A. last night. If he did (even I could pick out few words), is likely Gilberto and Elena heard. Am by now "pendeja" (asshole) of Zi. Can't find new Mexican lover for nada. Sheila's phrase about firm young bodies implanted in mind like cyst.

Dark now. But no magic. Am hitting Chololo tonight. Try not to get more wiped out than am. A day in the sun, some booze and smoke and antibi's and lingering infection and am blotto at six.

Two Mexican women who work in supermarket I think asked me where I was last Saturday, why I wasn't at the dance. (Which?) Is first initiative on part women.

E. You who claim you never knew passion. Surely you jest, cunt. Do ya miss me? Get some money together and let's come back and hit this scene as a team. Bonnie and Clyde.

A.A.A.

Sitting now in a nontourist bar. It says "Ladies Bar" on the outside so I brave it. They seem to want to discourage me from staying. It's too early to hit Chololo and I can't run the Zócalo (square) gauntlet again. This drunken dude wanders over but is stopped by the three people in charge. Not only out of courtesy to me. Women mean trouble. So I write to you, legs spread in tight jeans, hoping to look French and a writer. I'm finding it extraordinarily difficult to be alone here. I haven't developed the knack for attaching myself barnacle-like to others. Finally one has to swill one's booze in one's room so as not to be ridiculously parading one's plague of loneness. You get gorgeous during the day but shit, there's no place to stash it at night. Ladies Bar my ass. It's like they've never seen one before. But I can't brave the Max's Kansas City scene tonight. Gringa money greases the wheels of Mexican goodwill here. It's hard to make a permanent scene here if you're a woman. Gringitas, to come, must go at their allotted times. And the men are not one's class, or they're really not one's class and don't speak English. Anyway, the pool of twenty-year-old English-speaking boys is limited. The older boys (the owners of restaurants) like you to be their customer, or, if you're young and blond, you can be their cashier. Women seem frightened not to spend money though they say it's the easiest thing in the world to ride a man here. Apocryphal stories of canny women who attach themselves to rich Canadians abound but . . . dónde? Canadian men, as you may have guessed, are the world's biggest bores. The loose-floating Americans are not better: they are young, hairy, and wear baggy T-shirts. Whereas the Mex boys are tight and hairless. I think I heard wrong but did a ganglion of them call me over and then call me "vieja"?

This bar is pleasant. Good yodeling Mex music on tape and floor-length curtains shielding me from the eyes of the chic, the attached, the compatriots, Andrés. I can't write his name no more. Shame love is such a kick coz it sure ruins the rest of life: liberty, walking through the streets without shame. Walking now represents a double peril: looking for A., risking being seen alone by him. I want my pride and confidence back. The only way to regain them is to avoid this cursed romantic passivity and hope and commit myself to terminating what only a man would call an affair.

This music is fantastic. It's the first thing in two days not to bore me. Maybe one can make love with only the music when one dances, can bypass the human lover. Or I'm sunk. I need at least dancing. I have acquired some sort of grotesque rep as a good bumper. And this town is small: another difficulty. The ramifications of which, had I not been so gringa arrogant, might've made me hesitate to pull a knife on A. He's a fixture here, he'll badmouth me forever. So I can't even come back. Everyone here tells you everyone else is a bad lot. I've joined the list. Pity. I could see spending some time with a brown smooth body. Straight black hair, Indian features-strangeness. Perhaps I can train myself to dig Puerto Ricans. Actually looking forward to my upstate landlords, who are P.R. This trip has at least expanded the world for me a bit.

Am desultorily wading through *Sanchez* and a Spanish grammar.

Am actually dying for 1. another Rhys; 2. crap.

Next day (twelfth?)

The third day of Andréslessness.

Next day (Friday the thirteenth?)

It would have been fun to describe dancing at the Chololo, which I did Wednesday night, with some L.A. fags, whom, my dear, I must confess I pounced on. My soul is paring down to a bone of insupportable truth. Every day I feel older and less desirable. I am a way station for new tourists on their way to a deeper scene. I am going to have to bypass the human friend as well. Every restorative kindness is penultimate to indifference. I dance with my shadow, and, depending on the angle, and my own indifference, and my ability to dredge up confidence from some ever more remote credentials, I dance well or badly. The fag danced with all the latest double-time and hustle stuff. And I decided—since I almost caught on to his stuff—to dedicate myself to dancing when I got back. I have some control over that at least. Then I come back here in my *real* duds and open up life, perhaps business, as the Queen of Dance.

The tanner I get, the more my ineradicable age and look burn through. It's a high only the first few days, getting a tan. The transformation is so sudden it feels like rebirth. You really do lose yourself. Now only the real self, ever more burnished.

Some hideous waiter tried first to pimp me off to an equally hideous paint salesman with sweaty hands, then bought me two margaritas, chased me home and insisted we fucky-wucky. Sheila, the boutique owner, hasn't responded to my note.

What it is: public reality has completely overwhelmed private experience. It happened first with Andrés, an experience I lived before I understood it. So disillusioning, to feel intimacy sacrificed to an all too common pattern. But by now, that experience is too remote to remember, or even care about. Two days of pain, then yesterday so much new experience that Andrés was cauterized. The world of women began with Carol, in the afternoon was Laverne, and Linda at night. Elena and the three butchy women, whom I grew fond of but never pursued, wove in and out.

Carol is Canadian, tall, has a superb naturally athletic body with the most extraordinary vein above and across her shoulder blades. Long lean muscled thighs, broad shoulders, flat stomach. Thank God she's only twenty-two. Like many Canadian women she has a

[34]

man's absolute freedom, shocking to me. She works just enough to afford travel, hitches everywhere. In a few weeks she's going back to hit the fishing season when she can make two thou in six weeks packing sardines. Hitched, with Linda, with a guy who was making a big score in Mazatlán who took them to the rendezvous in the desert. All these Mex men with sawed-off shotguns, machine guns, six-shooters in back pockets. The story in Zi is you don't go into the hills twenty miles north of here, where the guerrillas who are the pot growers live, for nothing. You don't come back if you do. So I sat there craning forward digging being impressed by her. It was so much more nerve-tingling hearing these experiences come out of a woman's mouth. Vicariousness was possible—that's always. Plus the new, feminist thrill of pride in one's sex. I took her to Madera (I pimp too) and there we met Laverne, a forty-year-old Texan who's "retired." She is inimitable so I won't bother. A bit fat, but firm, standing there with her tits hangin' out, legs astraddle, spinning one travel story after another, playfully falling into a Texas drawl every once in a while, alternating her own reported dialogue of toughness with some past pushy dude with a gentle disclaimer so as not to frighten us, speaking perfect Spanish and English like a lot of women who've been here a while, with sometimes a Spanish accent (peh-sos), spending forty minutes on how the Vera Cruz Carnaval (in two weeks) is the apotheosis of all good times, some story about a meeting she attended in New York for the betterment of Puerto Ricans, some woman she admired a lot for putting herself through school (she herself a Texas oil babe) and her husband, "he was there" . . . she pauses, turns her head to one side, muses, "yes, he was there" to indicate his presence. If I go on nonstop it's because 1. she inimitably did 2. she is Molly Bloom—earthy, sexual, well-lived, vulgar, funny. I suppose nouvelle-riche, certainly at home with the poor. Oh what a mama. Doris would've creamed.

I spent the afternoon being impressed by women telling about the world and their bold movements through it. My dear, reality returneth.

At night, Carol's friend Linda, who looks like an amalgam of all the Beatles and writes songs, recovered briefly from her "Turista" enough to play guitar, talk about the Everglades well. Then she passed out in the street. I thought my god, why can't women be strong, why aren't her songs more sexual, more rhythmic. Felt absolutely repelled by illness, tainted and frightened, hating self for this, scared at abyss. Longing for some thirty-year-old sophisticate.

[35]

Thinking she wanted attention. Fearing being thought dyke holding her up back to room but wanting it same time. Later, Carol told me Linda has leukemia. Hardly had this awful brush with death transpired when Carol was pursued by every stud in town and I realized that her virginal passivity, her seeming lack of awareness of her own attractiveness that afternoon before Mama Laverne was another illusion. She grew before my eyes. Responding to every hello, wondering where the good-looking guy had disappeared to. Walking alone had been such unrespectable hell; walking with her much better-looking guys and approaches which it was the illusion of only minutes to think were more or less equally distributed between us. We went back to their room. Linda was better, drank, smoked, talked. I feeling more and more handicapped by their youth and hip ease. See Linda through romantic filter of leukemia fatality, which is how she plays it, ironic, self-destructive. Funny little haunting stories about her female poodle Cruiser who followed the toke around the room, got lost for days just "trucking," hid under the bed embarrassed after getting a poodle clip. A beautiful lighter, heavy and narrow, silver, with a slightly raised Aztec-deco step motif, a shock of texture and richness every time I raised it to my lips to light yet another cigarette. Linda turning her head ceilingward after a story: "Geez!" Crosslegged Carol splayed out on stomach. Beautiful girls. Had been actually sexually attracted to Linda before the leukemia. Afterwards too though far more morbidly, scavenger bird. Finally kretched out one story of my own-described Terri at last. And left.

Today I need to be alone. It is too palimpsest here. Bits of stories converge like puzzle, interpretations pile up Rashomon-like. Turns out, for instance, that they were the girls supposedly riding that rich Canadian. What actually happened is that he stayed on with them on their lease after his expired and stole their clothes and jewelry, les joies du sexisme. Oh oh oh—one gets lost in other people's definitions following so quickly on each other is the more puzzling thing. Becomes oneself a fractured story, a different style for every different person. Too many movies too soon. I could spend sixteen hours a day at the movies once but I had youth as a back-up, that is, the possibility of romantic enactment. Now, after the stories, I am cast out into my past. I am uncomfortably aware of having become a boring fixture in Zihuatanejo. And I actually eagerly await the arrival of George and La Grupa and the return of artificiality.

[36]

Now, Mahogua, Spanish grammar, a ¡? First some self-respect-enhancing errands. After a last brush through my hair.

Soon, cara, soon.

M.

Ω

E.,

He was always flat and literal when he supplied information about the local men. The only time he didn't lie. I notice lots of things about him now that he's irrevocably gone (and so I have to find his signs in others?). The way he strutted, stuck one hand in his belt and toyed with his rolled-up shirt knot with the other. His coyness and vanity. The way he swayed his body, stretching the hammock voluptuously, twisting his stuff. His voice is harder—it was the first Mexican voice I could distinguish from others, almost the first face.

There is a lack of fullness in my room now. It used to feel completely equipped, almost luxurious; and also a harbinger of potentiality like a movie theater. Now is theater with no movie. He is definitely out of town, though it's hard to believe he actually did meet that Canadian of the letter on the thirteenth (Friday!) to go to the Yucatán. That sting of familiarity gone out of my life, everyone else a boring stranger whom I equally bore. He was the first person I was attracted to in years, quelle accumulation! I now actively search him out, unafraid to look. It's like a strange version of health, feeding the body its specific craving. Besides, he was the healthiest thing in my life here—I liked him, desired him. It was a foolish affair but childlike as well. I felt like a child in it: he was always outraging, obnoxious, adolescent, transparent in his lies. A guttersnipe. And really pretty. Plus he dug me more than others do. He'd elongate my name seductively, whisper for me outside my window. Sometimes look away, mock-distracted, when he spoke to me. And then the thrill of full connection, the glint of metal in the rock. I obviously meant much less to him but my body's hunger bypasses pride so organically that my lust for him seems an abstract physiological thing I'm not the least responsible for. I understand how women tolerate in love what the world sees as humiliation.

One day later. Well, several dozen more fascinating life stories.

[37]

Real psychological overload at this point during the day at least. At night, is my usual vampire act.

Conked out after beer, pot, and a pretentious West coast blond beard last night and woke up in duds freezing in room with light on. Wandered out not knowing what time it was (my watch was stolen) and was picked up at a dance still going on in the square by a gorgeous Mexican twenty-two-year-old ex-Olympic middleweight boxer. Beautiful, beautiful body. Longish dark shag, extraordinary Indian face. Just beautiful. I get hit the first minute with "hermosa" (beautiful), the first hour with "be my novia" (girlfriend), the second hour with marriage. Exhilarating to feel new attraction after post-A. wasteland. We spent an hour by fisherman's bridge in the middle of the night watching them bring in the fish. Lanterns in the boats, silence. Some fat men drinking tequila and chewing the fat. Women carrying huge buckets of fish on their heads to load a truck. And a lush sea odor, as if fish had become flowers. Extraordinary aphrodisiac. Lapping everywhere. Progressive polite intimacy. Back to my alley, nearby, where we leaned against car and had more Mexican opera. Lushness. He called me "mi amor, mi vida." Kissed with his mouth open, his eyes closed. Did a good kissing thing— think sucked on my lip. Little tug that drew me into him. Felt his small hard nipples under his shirt. The dance was beautiful too. All those fresh brown beauties. Turning through open air wonderland of human beauty. Like dream (which waking up at 2 A.M. would induce a sense of). Made a date to meet Joaquín next day at 11. He didn't show. But ran into him at the farthest beach this afternoon and came back to town in boat with him and his friends. Then operatic farewell, he was leaving tonight. One more ploy—he won't leave if he can stay with me in my room! My god they think women are dumb. But if one side is contempt for women, his suave eroticism, unless he's loving himself through me, argues something else as well. His lovemaking was fantastic, though of course it was foreplay before the first time. Once I knew he was leaving I let him know how beautiful I found him. Alas, this American boy was hanging around and it was hard to . . . neck. Joaquín himself seemed reluctant in daylight. Mexican mores. Quién sabe?

I am intensely disliked by the smart male set. The worst night of my stay here, Friday the thirteenth, got into a vicious fight with some local rich meatball shithead in the disco. Shithead Alonso would not give me a light so asked some old dude. Money was still being mentioned, like I'm ugly and have to pay for a match. I say it's worth 15 centavos. Meatball says nasty and comes on like he's from New York, better at New York than I. I give it back. He says "shithead." I say "you're not from the Bronx; that's not what they say there, turkey." The old dude says meatball was teasing but I'm heavy. Meatball says if I'm not gone in three fuckin seconds he'll bash my fuckin face in. The chick stands up for him when I say I'm not talking to meatball but to old dude and her. Says she hasn't been listening and why don't I split. Alonso takes my arm. Three against one. Meatball is hideous, chick is gorgeous. Chick is male, not female. Later, American guy who's been here fifteen years sagely informs me there's no women's lib here. What this means is not clear. Something about letting men shit on you.

There's a gang of maybe twenty Mexican boys who know some English and who mow down all the women. Andrés is not part of this fraternity, not tall or rich enough. The men are awful, cynical and old, even if they're in their twenties. Unfresh. Luckily I am not attractive enough to make their grade. I guess it's hands off the Grupa, however, the semi-permanent rich gringas.

George moved in the dead of afternoon while I was out and left no note. And the Grupa has not extended its generosity to me. Andrés is out of town. I am deserted by every familiar thing. Robbed twice. First time when I went night swimming (that same awful night, Meatball night) with a gorgeous twenty-four-year-old Canadian. Left bag on beach. Next morning, hungover, no sleep, extremely grubby Canadian in bed with dick on the brain, I discover I no longer know the time because my watch is missing, my Russian head scarf, my expensive Bloomie sunglasses. Some money. I finally get rid of Canadian when I flash that I can live without his depression and twenty-four-year-old hippy vacuity and why the hell am I spreading my legs for him to get off. Plus pumping my ass off (exercise!) cause he's strung out on quaaludes. Awful breath. No servicing of me. No clit. Nada nada nada. On and off we sleep the day. He tries once more to prove his manhood on me. Don't I know he has a prick? The prick is the program. "I don't want to fuck," I discover myself saying. He leaves. Pedro rushes over to me and tells me I have to pay more for the room because of double occupancy. My amigo!! Plus I'm definitely sure I've been robbed by this time. Fuckin get out of fuckin Zi immediately! I'm outraged. But then this guy I had a great dancing time with, who's half in, half out of being Mexican but really much more in though he wears violet tinted prescription glasses, making him look darkly bug-eyed and absorbed, kindly, who's the son of a general store owner, gave me this notebook as a gift—I lost the old one—because I was a friend, he said. He's never made a play for me except the first night; is often alone amidst friends. Has a white-on-black Ducati T-shirt so I call him Ducati and tousle his hair when he's sitting alone in Chololo.

A few brief lives:

One of the butchy threesome, from Spain, spoke French so we had a long talk. Her father died when she was fifteen so she sought work in France to support her mother and family. Got a job working as a governess for an Italian princess with whom she stayed for twelve (!) years in Paris and Rome. Then to Mexico where she operates a gallery with the two other women, exporting oil landscapes to Canada. Strange. Exchange of addresses. Hers in lost notebook, along with laboriously written lyrics (Andrés's two years of school) of his and my theme song.

Elena. Gilberto's girlfriend. Is aristocratic. Taught herself English off me in three hours. She and Gilberto not married, just courting for six years. Extraordinary smooching all the time. Begged her address. Am into collecting addresses I shouldn't go home with nada.

What can I tell you? I'm paring down. Losing stuff makes one feel exposed. Literally, of course, as well. There's nothing now between me and the sun. No way to hide grubby hair, tell time. Stripped of everything. And losing weight again. 124 now. Pray it lasts. Do it hard way. Booze, cigarettes, swimming, diet of shit tacos. No protein in days. Lots of sugar is all. Full of phlegm and stigmata but in excellent muscular shape. Feel once again like I'm losing years. Sitting in Pedro's patio, braless with period (!!!grâce à Dieu!!!) in presence of yet another new tourist, which is cramping my style. Good. Just left. Robert, French Canadian, difficult accent, traveling with Marianne, gentle low voice. I spent last night helping them all night, gratis. Have become an Andrés but get no pesos out of it. Pedro gave me the lowdown on A. He's illegitimate, uneducated and makes a poor living hustling tourists—takes them around, gets tipped. I don't.

He hasn't left town after all. I saw him last night when I was with the French Canadian couple. He was standing alone in the square wearing an ugly dark green T-shirt that had a huge stain down the front like a continent. He wouldn't come over so I went to him. He was going to go to Chololo. It was a hundred percent sure these people he'd just met were going to be there, he strangely assured me. He was waiting for a taxi and couldn't promise he'd spend time with me at the disco. It's my last night, Andrés, I said. Come on. He called out where would I be tomorrow to my departing back. He looked mean, sullen, tragically alone (like me) but I missed not him by now but another. Kindness, success, assurance and gaiety, plus superior looks and greater sensuality, are really preferable to neurosis. Miss Joaquín. Though only fact that he was leaving didn't sour that experience, so potentially degrading.

It's become impossible to walk alone down the street. An old man put his hand on my leg today. Boys say hello and then mumble funny Spanish things that make them laugh. I'm trying to establish an image as an athlete but because I can't distinguish one Mexican from another and don't understand the language, or know how the grapevine functions, it's impossible to know if it's taking.

I must stop being a host to new tourists. I am shunned like a leper by everyone. Carlos, friend of Terri, his greeting gets more hurried everyday and I'd thought he was attracted to me. Safer to assume no attraction anywhere and when someone says "bonita" answer "no, fea."

Had tried feministically connecting with women here, helloing every woman and girl in sight, like men do universally. Can no longer. My confidence is shot. Bad experiences have drained my energy and instead of moving on sensibly am awaiting a rite of purification in the place of my downfall. The place that weakened me has to redeem me. I don't completely understand why I haven't been taken up by anyone, connected with some women to rent a house together, for instance, or been invited by Terri. Except that I don't spend much money and there must be enormous money snobbery; also, I am not (so hard to really believe!) attractive and no woman is going to want to take up with someone less attractive than herself. It would be carrying dead weight around when she, if anything, wants to coast on someone else's attractiveness. If, of course, I were legitimately writing an article, I would have all the confidence of my persona as writer and aggress left and right. Protected, as by sunglasses, from full contact.

I am trying to seem as if alone by choice but everyone must see my flaw and know that they reject me. Stan seems more and more a figment of my dream life, though when he was here he bored me to rage. That was when Andrés was flirting around corners. And George, that white slug who's made it, was in tow. From two (or

[41]

three) to nada nada nada. Plus Gilberto, the architect, all warm future invitations, all of which bit the dust after Stan left. A WOMAN TRAVELING ALONE IN MEXICO HAS NO CLASS. She drops out of normal life. To wing it feministically is not possible, like fighting the ocean. There is an ocean of others, of others' views of you, which washes up against you constantly, which, because it's more, knows you more than you know it. One finally wants to escape eyes. It's so potentially dangerous here. Like Daisy Miller, one loses reputation daily, all constructs by which one knows oneself are eroded, all the structures of society which support one are invisibly worn away. No way of knowing it, being a stranger. The town pulls away from one, or washes in suddenly on waves of mockery one doesn't understand. Finally one discovers too late that personality is not inherent in the self but comes from those around us, who have disappeared in my case.

Money. I should have had a stake. There's no way to win without a stake. Hung out at dwarfing Elvira's tables and cultivated my own. No one makes my scene, cheap in-town living. It's bourgeois town living or rugged nearly free camping.

Early every morning I am woken up by roosters, birds in my walls, blaring car horn commercials in the unpaved street, murmurous Mexican lovemaking in adjoining rooms. When the sky is still the grey of old age and death and reminds me of winter New York and all my failures there and I know that despite all my misery here I can't go back. This is good country for failures. The sun bleaches you clean every day. Depression has everything to do with the quality of light. The light here is brilliant; it's like walking through mica and every day it's there. When it hits your face, it makes you a pioneer somehow.

I must start lying, stop telling everyone I'm an unemployed part-time college English teacher. How succinct! And unimpressive. I could've said a temporarily laid-back academic. Or I can lie. I'm a writer. An academic on leave of absence. Or be witty and evasive, like you. Trade only in myths and self-creation. My fantasy now, a drowning woman's, is to drown. To be utterly passive, stern and sad, and dare the world to restore me. I'm too greedy, too self-indulgent, my downfall.

All these Canadians and West Coasters I've met. As I've said before, it is impossible to distinguish individual from group characteristics at this point and my co-linguists are as strange as the Mexicans. (The Mexicans are less strange if anything because my ignorance of Spanish obscures their reality almost totally.) West

[42]

Coasters are insanely, frighteningly artificial. Met two blond beards who are into stoned vocabulary of such universality and banality and eagerness for getting blown by tops, etc etc etc. Did a brilliant linguistic analysis of the difference between East and West coast language to one of the beards and blew him right out of my life (thank god). In New York, would know why. Here, no. This guy looks forty, says he's twenty-nine (like all of us gringas here!) and talks nonstop hippy. Gettin' high. All there is. Managed however to be very expressive. Compelled self to figure out how. Roughly: he has say a vocab of fifty words, I two hundred: I've been taught never to repeat words (wasn't taught Gertrude Stein in college). East Coast language is linear, therefore progressive, perhaps logical. When I want new meaning, seek new word. West Coast language is cumulative, achieves meaning through layering, placing same word in different context, or modifying it. "I got to know her completely right away," Tim says of someone he'd known an hour. Looks at me. "At least a little." The use of stoned vocabulary, the raga-like repetitiveness, produces a mystical tone as well. Spiraling. Layers. Symbols waiting to be exposed. Unclear. Sorry. Paradoxically, too, there is the prestige of activity whereas I'd be more likely to talk about my soul, not what I do on the weekend. The difference between a warm and cold climate, I suppose. Needless to say, felt solaced after this intellectual exercise: 1. wits still functioning. 2. strangeness explained. West Coast style is not one I particularly like, however. It's pretentiously simple, ingenuous.

The Canadians I can't tackle except to be amazed that they exist at all. Met someone who actually majored in Canadian history.

Then there are the female and male distinctions. Because of feminism I actively wish women to flower and fascinate and perhaps because of this I've generally been less impressive with women than men. Still, still. I mentioned one or two good ideas to Lynn, among others. One was a series of travel guides for women. Explained a bit. Is great idea. *I* know this, even I. But she wasn't interested at all but rather launched into her probable future activities. What has been so intensely dismaying is to have been so indifferently treated by women as by men. Of course, if I hadn't been so damn abstract about the relations between the sexes, I would have seen clearly, less cynically—or more—what is meant when three Canadian women looked right through me to flirt with George.

Au revoir. A bientôt. The Quebecois have returned. It's late. The sun calls. Ciao ciao ciao ciao mi amor mi vida. Ha!

M.

[43]

Ω

My shadow on the discoteque wall, on the sand, in the water. I'm trying to hone down to a new language as well. Induced madness. How banal it must strike the gods, my playing la femme maudite. Trying to wring tears for myself in the sun. Sun, take pity!

I'm at this very moment still playing host to the Quebec couple, a couple of adorants, who lack the wit to see the hostess/whore wants a beer. No payment for women. About the curative power of the sun: it's too intense for anything but itself. And it makes you gorgeous. It makes you old and beautiful simultaneously. Burnishes. (But I mustn't repeat a word.)

Passed by La Grupa beach. Saw George. He was like ice. Made no step, no greeting toward me, after sponging off Stan and me for a week. So, I said, what's new. He looked up at the sky through his sunglasses. "It's time for me to get wet," he said. Carlos was there, looking older but still good. Marissa, Marissa, he said, beautiful Mexican mocking bird. Affection, boredom, ridicule, all mixed in together. Carlos, Carlos, I cried. This bit of repartee aroused some sense of obligation in George, who told me he'd seen Jorge. Jorge had asked him if he'd seen me. No, George said he said. Jorge asked him if I'd said anything to him, George. George said no. "What did you do, beat him up?" George asked me with incredible total knowledge of every atom of my absolute non-privacy. I said yes. Really. I must take it back. It will make me seem a heavy woman's libber, weird. Mostly, it will let all Zihuatanejo know my "bad affair with a bad Mexican" was with a ridiculous person only a desperate old ugliness would consider.

I thought you were leaving today, the blond German photographer asks. (How can I be so boring as not to leave the party already?) No, I say. I have new wounds that keep me here, pointing to my knees on which I fell yesterday on the rocks. She laughs at the Jew's familiar persona. I start trundling. Are you off to La Ropa, George asks desultorily. (His cool must now depend on him acting on the recognition that he's advanced in class since being invited by Terri to be a house guest. He will lose it all if he unbends. Worse, I might work into the group and he'd lose his distinction?) "No! Goodbye," I call. The Canadians are temporarily gone. Et tu, brutale! When I thought they bored me worse! But they were sitting unobtrusively under an umbrella. Gently. I fall down on the beach and after minutes will tears. The sun dries them up in advance. Then two people come by in succession to taunt me once more with promises of affection and acceptance. Isidro's friend, who says Isidro is back. "Can I stay there?" I jump up. I said I'd come by in two hours. Then Terri came up to me when I was standing on the shore glaring at the sun. Hi, she beamed, we've been looking for you, she says. You haven't been looking too hard, I say. That's true, she almost laughs. I beg her address off her but (Jeez—someone who looks like Joaquín for a second took my breath away) cut it by saying it was to exploit her, get her to get me a house if I decided to come back. Needless, she does not ask me for mine though she volunteers her San Francisco address as well. La Grupa is finally going to Isla, the beautiful remote island she's been promising us for weeks, all of us. Can I come? Godot is finally arriving, the wait has not been for nothing. No. I'm poor, I say firmly. Tell her I'm going to beachcomb at La Ropa. (Almost tears came when I thought illusion is finally over.) I'm going to my own level if it'll have me. Isidro. My age. Short. Frizzy hair, balding. Very muscular but with effort, a bit stocky, kind. A dealer La Grupa rejects—says he turned someone in. I think it's because he's a Jew, or they think he is. Or he's too eager. Anyway, try the grubby Thoreau scene. His beautiful "palapa"—Tahitian hut he built himself in two weeks, all charm and ingenuity. He climbs the toughest coconut trees in the grove, the straightest and fattest, without a belt, his machete wedged between his bathing suit and his ass. What would his con be? My money, my cunt, both? But one night he was too eager to dance with me, too sweaty, looked out of place at Chololo, bumped me so hard in the groin I had a black and blue mark for a week, and the Grupa was cold to him. (But of course didn't deign a full explanation to me, though I asked.) Terri also promises a party, sort of, tomorrow night at her place—maybe. Am I formally invited? I mock. "Of course," she answers reassuringly, entirely missing my wit, a not uncommon reaction.

Lynn has found herself a cool Friscan. But I seek the intimacy of strangeness. That night with Joaquín. No banality of language could intrude, no true knowledge of me. (A good-looking man who's not ashamed to be seen with me in public is all I want?) Mexican laughter and Mexicans saying "Sí" very slowly, emphatically, comfortingly. Sí-i (two syllables, second goes up).

I need those now. And flash of Joaquín's large brown face, hard

[45]

face, dark silken hair, wide-spaced eyes, lighter than expected. Strong nose, chin, wide mouth, the usual cheekbones slanting up to heaven. Eyes—honey brown, almost yellow in his dark skin. Body like newly inflated tire. But pure solidity under the skin. Intimacy with foreigners. That night can't do it justice. Sitting in hot sun with impatient Canadians at back, torn between Isidro on the left and Terri on the right. (She parted with a magnanimous invitation to her side of the beach.) Mostly, want to mail this fat expensive letter to you which you'll get next month when I'll be back in N.Y., fat and pale. (By the way, up-to-the-minute body news: shit three pounds worth after wrote you 124. So 122, 121. But drank three bottles soda. You'd better compete, kid. And want swim one half mile again, like did last night.

Ciao, pupa. Really ciao.

Stan's Guadalajara letter finally arrived. He missed me already and is even willing to have me call him collect. Some strength from that and how we all do need it.

Your friend, the feminista.

P.S. One more quickie woman on rocks, yesterday, sixty, English, blast furnace supervisor on own. Here for two years. Sardonic. Seule.

Maryse

Curiously comforted by Andrés's presence in town. He was completely displaced by Joaquín. Men are expendable if you're beautiful, whereas the uglier you are, the more romantic.

Hone the fuckin consciousness!

Ω

E.,

I have found my persona at last: the ugly, bitter New York woman. Had some of the usual powerful dope at Isidro's several days ago. Walked home and finally the place jumped with the foreground. It was a mélange of all the old tropics movies, only in the sad deco colors of approaching dusk, everything deepened by the setting sun: maroons, yellows, orange-pinks, the olive of palm trees, the blue gabardine of the sea. It was much sharper than a movie, of course, a chosen moment and I thought why can't this be enough.

Later.

[46]

I loved Andrés. He didn't love me but I loved him. I loved his evil knowledge. The day Stan left he said, "You're going to have a party tonight, huh?"

Back to before the drunken interlude:

I realized that the thing about being old is that you can only be a witness to beauty, you can no longer incarnate it. Every time the world comes alive for me it reminds me of what I can no longer have. And there is such a need to assimilate beauty into the self, to fulfill through one's own vehicle the potential of the landscape, its romantic promise. It was the insight I'd been having since I turned thirty, but in Zihuatanejo, under grass, it almost seemed a commitment to being forever outside whatever beauty would still be vouchsafed to me in the rest of my life, to not expect love (and to therefore find beauty intolerable). God, what were all those movies one lived through in one's youth—only to come together in a supermovie mélange where one couldn't play the heroine.

Joaquín, his sheath of hair.

I look good now, but I won't much longer. Already I can feel when a woman is ten years younger, so surely she can tell I'm ten years older.

Yesterday we went to Isla Grande, the Grupa and I. I caught my first fish, a mackerel. Half an hour after its head had been bashed by the fisherman it momentarily thrashed about. I looked questioningly at him and he said, "Mucha vida, muy bueno"; like me in order to feel life I had to die a painfully unending death as well.

I swam in the nude past Carlos, who was diving for oysters, and flashed my clam at him. Later, with a mask and snorkel, all it takes to make one a complete fish, I followed the fisherman under the water for hours, it felt like. He had a crowbar and was going down for coral. He kept beckoning and I kept following, past blue coral and yellow and blue fish and the undersea mountain ranges, water dark but shafted with light, somehow sleepy. Near the rocks the water buzzes with electricity, it's the only sound you hear, and there is a slight prickliness on the skin.

His hand kept beckoning underwater. Saw his body in front of me, wondering where it would lead, and noticed he had the usual huge, easy Mexican erection. I dug giving it to him, though he didn't attract me. It was a gift and an underwater bond. He'd been married eight days and he was hot to trot. Perhaps it's the weather. I committed myself to expecting nothing in the way of sex, to enjoying the day. Reminding myself other pleasures existed. Ate my

[47]

fish and someone else's, lots of beer and sweet pineapple. Little alive shells walking around, one striated black with a pearl of jade, crabs checking me out on the rocks, tanning nude and grossing out the Mexicans—more Daisy Miller. An easy chat—so hard for me— sunning on the boat deck going back, the sea and rocks sharpening and deepening.

The sea is incredible, it is enough for years of metaphor. This is the first time I've lived intimately with it since my fifteenth summer in a French seaside resort. One day at Mahogua, a remote beach on the open sea, full of confidence that I had mastered the ocean, I tried learning to body surf, kept being knocked down by powerful waves and temporarily drowned. For hours afterwards, as I lay on the beach, as I listened to the surf, I felt a tug every time the wave pulled out, as if I were being sucked out to sea. My stomach tautened and pulled down.

The inside of your body is an ocean. I got my period a few days later and felt even more liquid, a sea of lushness for any fisherman, mujer! (I am so tired of being the derivative species, woman!)

I am boiled down like my piece of coral, to a white skeleton. No, it has actually changed. I had worked down to an efficient non-expectation of love, but now I'm in a new state of feeling nothing new can happen here. More and more people stop and chat, or don't. I almost like the self I've rediscovered and am therefore more of a definer, less mystified, less anguished, more bored. The French Canadian couple—the woman, actually, Marianne, and I are an informal group—so important to have one here you can't imagine. (Why don't I want to write about Marianne?)

I feel rushed. I need grass. I need another block of experience when what I've been having is chips. I can't write.

Spent last night with Gilberto receiving lessons I couldn't fully understand about machismo. He told me one crystalline anecdote however. A macho friend of his is in the habit of going up to a foreign woman on a crowded bus and telling her she's a "pendeja," tells her it means beautiful. The whole bus laughs while she is flattered. Contempt of macho is incredible, as is Gilberto, who purports to be a sweetheart to women, being friends with him. Stan wouldn't. Meanwhile, Gilberto also regales me with which women he finds attractive in our immediate restaurant environs and finally decribes his ideal type: tall, slim, blond and blue-eyed. The formal lesson concerned 1. total contempt men have for women in Mexico 2. the four levels of meaning underlying every Spanish word or

[48]

phrase, three of them sexual. But, as far as I could figure it, this involved nothing more than the seductive intonation one finds everywhere. Gilberto, the renouncer of macho, has a big need to have Mexico and its language win the macho contest. Interesting bit about how ordinary language is multi-intentional and women don't know the other meanings, or do, and therefore can't use even ordinary language, but this turned out to be nada, I think. Plus he tells me the English translation of *Sanchez* tells a completely different story about machismo than the Spanish, which makes no sense. I am fucking lost in anything but ENGLISH. Even French. What the fuck does it mean when an overweight balding architect nine years younger than you tells you how awful Mexican men are and how wonderful is his Elena?

I can't write because I want to hit the town, and if a piece of town hits me, mujer, I wouldn't say no.

I love oysters, pineapple, oranges, tart liquids (like the ocean?). A.'s voice had vinegar. This woman was amazed that I was eating pineapple without salsa picante.

There are lots of passion killings in Mexico. Not for me, though. It's about 5 A.M. now. I'm up because I spent most of yesterday sleeping off a truly burro hangover. Woke up in darkness before the roosters after another dreamless night wondering what I could give myself as consolation for consciousness. Gorged myself on sweet juicy miraculously cold pineapple over my sink.

The rooster crowing sounds like my congested lungs. Last week, swam a half kilometer or more from one beach to another in my suit and tank top after sunset past wondering fishermen. Body can do it fine but lungs racked. Was then at high point of divested self. Of trying to answer question why isn't spectacle of life enough. God, when I was younger (twenty-five in France, for instance) would go on vacation alone, meet no one, would go to see and do. (Don't know if rooster or lungs, that crowing.) How did I manage? Would be marvelous early days full of work and new experience, full of landscape and exaltation. Am now living in Hilton movie, hotel days, like the films of dying directors—clothes, concern and talk about accommodations, landscape blurred through dirty picture window of dulled senses and greedy human need. Fractured days one half this and one half that. Must be age.

Jesus, what generation gaps. Everyone's secret belief that she's a square? Stoned vocabulary, drugs and mysticism are universal to everyone under fifty here. Except me. I guess partly it's a way, among people my age, of establishing commonality when there is none yet. Among the young though it is frighteningly unselfconscious, natural not *learned*.

Had the power of language removed from me by Inés's total glamor. Went to visit her in her house at La Ropa. Thoreau cum charm. Stereo, no running water. Outside bath, with coconut palm in. Outside stove hewn out of boulder side of hill. Mobiles of shells everywhere, and big clay crocks. A loft bed suspended from ceiling, could swing. Beautifully woven hammocks, one over the hill drop. A lemon tree, papaya, banana, plum. Inés herself pulls out her scorpion collection: "Now this little motha fucka hey-ah." A very mellow black style. Whereas Joe, her lover, is cultivated urban Latin. Joe is forty-two, deepest tan ever saw in life, blackest hair and best body. I. has afro, green eyes, and good body too. About forty. Joe went to Brown but speaks pure hip spic. Both are all graciousness, style, and good times. (Just fed the greedy sink a glob of phlegm.) I.'s son Michael (Miguel she called him) was usual hip kid wearing headband and stretched out on bed doodling. My father Irving the tailor flashed on me and I lost my ability to form a complete word. Ah well, it's always the case, when someone's really cooking you're wiped out, right? Women are incredibly good storytellers. Men dispense just facts, or style.

It was more like 3 A.M. Is now 8:30. Pedro's patio, another dreamless few hours. Weeks ago dreamt hadn't lost watch, scarf, sunglasses. Three days ago dreamed some boys blew up one side of their faces—laughed at me and I went up to them and said what are you doing. Better not to dream.

Anyway, ma chère, about developing personae here, you no sooner achieve one (and fail to write it down in time) than an equal and opposite one takes over (and so the first state is unmemorialized forever). I had nothing to do but be hungover yesterday and think despite myself, and it finally occurred to me that I am leading this greedy whore life—drunk and dancing every two days at Chololo, eating men up with my eyes and my body on the beach and in town—because of the life I led in N.Y.; what an unreal existence! No sex, a manless world. So of course here seems like a last chance at love, intensity of feeling. Losing weight, working out, getting tan of course exacerbate my need or what's it all for? And it's true that in N.Y. men are impossible: 1. because they are 2. Stan 3. no more place to meet them 4. discipline of feminism. (In N.Y. I would know that beautiful Joaquín, and the boys playing soccer who aggressed everyone off the beach, were one and the same. Here strangeness and desire protect me) plus 5. I am now hooked on Mexican looks but good. I can't bear anything but dark skin, straight full dark hair and, actually, shortness. Andrés was physically comfortable, like a playmate, much sexier than a god. There are facial features as well—large faces, slanted cheeks, and Mexican speech and laughter, the two warm "Sí's (Sí! and Síi-i!) and the way they work into a laugh, grinning more and more broadly and breaking into a prolonged "aaah" way before the punch line. And the slang, and prosaic expressions, "simón," "ándale," "mande?" * have a totem magic. Stretching out "delicious," like delicious: "Sa-broh-ssoh" when Carlos fed Terri's son oysters. And, of course, I love oysters. Ostiones, they will forever be to me.

Saturday night, two nights ago, went dancing after good day at beach. Marvelous girl from Arizona, Karen, taught me how to do headstand, spun endless stories about hitching alone throughout U.S. Said same thing you did about south, used the word cunt absolutely naturally, really into working out, lived in Indian community in San Andreas (near Puebla) for three years. Then I swam, jogged, ate delicious French Canadian meal prepared on open fire by Marianne and Robert. Had sudden prolonged attack of Turista. Rediscovered my voice in the night. Threw up.

Went home past the "El Gutierrel," site of deco epiphany. Got dressed. Went out hungry for love. Saw Lynn and her entourage at Tortuga, stopped to chat. Saw Andrés looking more beautiful than ever had with two new chicks, actually being hosted by Antonio, one of the chic twenty "muscles de la playa." Hadn't quite realized what a pretty plum he was, mon dieu. And proudly flaunting two new gringas at the chicest restaurant in town. How different from our clandestine sordidness. Even earlier hadn't felt looked good though was wearing outfit had decided was dynamite.

It's always the same story just when I reach the end of a boring task, so much new life happens I'm back into stale recapture—compulsive—of remote past. Am now totally drunk, stoned from an afternoon quite enjoyable, drinking and being bought trinkets by an alcoholic ex-Nazi.

But I should quickly finish off the past.

* "Yes"; "Beat it" or "Get going"; "I'm at your service" or "What can I do for you?", respectively.

After the Tortuga and A. looking fuckin more beautiful than ever before, I went home, drank tequila and went drunk to Chololo. There he was absorbed in it. Must finally have been Candy, who turned out to be short, blond, fat and, tonight I saw, has a pronounced chin. Zi has made me—or has discovered in me—the typical, extremely critical physical appraisal of women. In a word, I am more attractive. But two nights running at Tortuga and tonight I spied her, by accident (looking for the rich, crippled Nazi) sitting in Canaima, quite an expensive restaurant. It is so odd. Everything is figural here. I heard about Omphrey (really "Arnfried," eagle who rescues young doves if you can believe it) my first week here. And this afternoon the legend was fulfilled. I would have said at the beginning that everything was Fire Island Soap Opera because Zi was so small, the third week I would've said it bred instant irony but now I see it is really a perenially self-enacting legend whose end is never in sight. To think I finally saw Candy. And to realize, as I just belatedly did, that his tender and wary absorption in her was that of an angler for a big fish, to think that my ancient insight about money greasing the wheels of sex here would connect up with Andrés! If that's the story, one has absolutely (I am Kraut) a sense of figurality, each thing being a foreshadowing.

How could I predict (though I'd been looking for years) that I'd run into my mother's executioner, that I would like him, that I would whore a sterling silver rose off him (fulfilling that ancient nonfeminist prophecy that "women lay as many traps"—read exploit—on men as men do on women), that the feminista would turn out whore. More bitingly, specifically, that imbibing Arnfried's crippledom all afternoon I would run into a heavy wooden beach chair on my way to drunkenly greet Inés and break my toe and fulfill not only Omphrey's broken present foot but my own recently (just today mending) past one. Is too much, Zi. I am speechless before it. Every day is a new stage, layer, a new cast. It has been, all told, an extraordinarily rich experience. But I sink into the personal. I must 1. finish Chololo 2. dancing 3. women 4. Gilberto 5. the rest 6. the sea 7. my new firsts.

Last first (s). Headstand. Sí. Told you. Yesterday ran over a mile without stop, Marianne and I, who wouldn't have done it alone. Fabulous inspiring competition between women. You wudda been proud, kid. Today swam drunk in the ocean, an extraordinary sensation. Yesterday, too, bought my first dope and saw my first "tops"—yellow blossoms at top of plant, strongest stuff. Two ounces

[52]

for 10 pesos (80¢), not croyable. Flirted with Isidro who had recovered from learning a perfect bump off me and not being able, however, to fuck me though he open-mouth kissed me nice and I called him Mi Amor, Mi Vida. I learn from *Sanchez* how to be macho in sex style. He flirted with Marianne and talked about a rich beautiful French painter who treated him to dinner at Tortuga. Grease. When we were alone, I licked and nipped his neck and he melted in ecstasy and moaned. Mock is still cock in sex. So exciting to make him wet like that, the power and pleasure.

The sea: when your bod is hot and dry and a whole length of wave breaks—hard, wet, cold, shocking—against you. You and the whole ocean—THWACK!

Finally over dis-ease with Inés, adore her but she insists she's a man's woman (she's half Latin-American) and Joe (American Indian) a man's man. Yet another woman with a story of how she rejected some lesbian. Everyone here thinks I am.

Karen, yesterday, on beach. Pure Hepburn, aristocratic girl jock from Arizona who taught me headstand, asks me in water if I'm not bisexual. We pace back and forth across the sand, in the water, back and forth. She adjusts her straw bonnet against the sun while I admire her twenty-two-year-old stomach and strong legs. I wonder if she notices my strong dark thighs, that I do. "Tell me some feminist things," she says, splaying in shallow water. So I talk about women aging, how soiled you feel when you see someone with younger skin. And what I taught. A whole day of finally deciding way I was interesting—my story-spinning ability—came from feminism and it was sink or swim. I had been very guarded, so much sordidness to hide. So I yapped. Gurufied all the women and got hit with the usual sexist banalities which I fielded with all I had and a tact only the sun provided, or a tactlessness only the sun blinded them to. Ah ha! No one is blind. Karen, extraordinary, had just made a threesome the night before. Tara, who's lived here a year, living on favors and doing favors. Céleste (another FC) "pas mal un gang de fun."

"Je t'aime bien, tu sais." Awful flattery. Most dreaded seeing her today, so of course ended up spending early afternoon with her. She had her share of gamine twenty-seven-year-old wisdom. She'd made a play for Brenda, and I wondered if I was her target. All bits of experience coming together or going: part-agreement here (what can it mean if a man doesn't ask you again if you refuse once and you see him immediately with another woman—you're just a cunt), part-disagreement there (no one else seems to be regaled with tales of

[53]

other women when they're being courted). Waves. Discovered that she and I had things to talk about. Always some point in common, some easy slight compromise of style in the service of pleasure.

Body Image: it changes with the light. Daytime, every adiposity shows, every blue tracing, and the crepiness of unyoung bodies. At night, elongated, I contemplate my polished mahogany stomach. I also talk more in the obscurity of night, shy and varicosed in daylight but a scintillating vampire by night. Ah self, what mysteries will remain? Others' bodies undergo the same transformation, and their faces and personalities. No one ever looks the same twice. How could I have thought people stagnated here? It must be having the sea and sun as focus. All the episodicity bounces off it.

The story: Thursday Isidro and I danced. Saturday, drunk, I tried to entice the entire bar so as to look desired in front of A. And to recapture the dance. Got trapped by a gang of bourgeois engineers and architects (gangs of bourgeois invade Zi the weekend from a nearby steel plant) who insisted on intravenous injections of margaritas into me and when I protested that I didn't want any sexual obligations told me I had finally met decent Mexicans. The oldest one, a devil, had a strange way of introducing himself to me, asked me if I spoke Yiddish. (Talk about prefigurations!) Basically, what it is, the place is so small that there's no distraction from coincidence. And the sun, what was it about the sun—oh yes—that in the tropics there is, as it were (AIE!) no corroboration of sorrow in the climate. There must be few suicides here. The high incidence in Sweden (and N.Y.?) becomes perfectly clear.

The dance: the hardest because a "block" experience. Something about at a certain point you switch off consciousness, or transfer control from the brain to the bod, center of intelligence halfway between head and feet; pivot, fulcrum of midriff. Much more precise. Later.

Back to story: Walk to Chololo that night and hear "Save me, save me" by Silver Convention wafting out to sea and me. Night of seeing Andrés finally with Candy in Tortuga. Men are so expendable—it is all so expendable, so quickly unremembered—except Joaquín, disappeared. Fell in love with Mexican Peter Falk lookalike engineer who eyed me all night, made no overt play, rebuffed my drunken advances (when I found out he was thirty-three, my age, and attracted me and I wasn't therefore over the hill plus my sexual desires could approach normal I said "Yo te adoro" and swooped into his chest) by telling me he was a loyal husband. So ironic and

[54]

attractive. And drove me home out of the goodness of his corazón. I was very drunk and I suppose I roused their mettle by playing macho to their machismo, utter gringa cynic. They could not bear I should take the Sanchez family for them.

All so episodic. I am good for a quick mot on the beach or in the disco, but lost in repeating daily relations. I miss Stan though god knows I would've met no one with him. Nor would I have retained my sanity through this without him in the background. And this notebook. When I lost the old one I felt a sense of waste with this new one, fearing I would have it all left over when I left. So I ended up staying much longer and now it is decently used up. Certainly played a part. Part of the magic of this place. Who would've thought I'd get so high off an Ex-Gestapo. But, too, it's very terrific grass. Tops is tops, Mujer! Zee wha ta neh hoh.

The fuckin' figurality of life is too much. Just when the second fuckin' left foot disaster starts healing up, I break my fuckin' left toe. Lynn and Herb will passingly wonder why I didn't show up at the Rincón, Céleste and Debbie why I didn't at Chololo. Isidro, whom I asked Inés on her way home to tell I'd be at Chololo tonight, and whom I ran into hours later when he said he never got message, will no doubt show up. I will be stood up by at least two more pairs of people. Ernesto and his brother-in-law Alonso the doctor who are supposed to bring me some Darvon and the two hippies who are supposed to give me a lift to Acapulco tomorrow. No one will know my toe was broken. (The maybe brother-in-law who is maybe a doctor says it isn't broken just traumatized). And I won't really know why, or expect to be stood up: will be just one or two or more Mexican mysteries. It is amazing how not knowing a language makes life seem far more a miraculously fitting puzzle. Someone please come and rescue me. Ernesto won't because he thinks it's slutty. I should ask if I can drink on Darvon and dance on a foot I can't walk on. Besides, my room is full of sand and detritus. I can't write more.

M.

Ω

Why can't I be the one to stand someone up first? Shit. What else?

[55]

Céleste asking how many men I'd had in Zi. Discovering the company of adult women—good sex talk. So afraid gross out (as do in N.Y.) that was far more reticent than usual. Discovering the company of women again (femin, put an end to that). Women are so sexually frank.

ACAPULCO. Here. Last day and night in Zi fabulous. Spent early part of day with Céleste and reading up on Acap. All that hotel business polluted Zi and made me reluctant to leave. Aft. with Arnfried and Lenore whose address I should get. Inés came along the beach. Then stumbled home. Ernesto did return at 9:30 P.M. Sans Darvon, alas. Put a rather strange make on me that on my dope and booze got me horribly anxious—denouncing machismo. He's different, likes to talk (stares suspiciously at me to see if I'm staring at him).

CHOLOLO. Last night. Oh, before. After Inés, went to say goodbye to Terri and she told me Carlos was her husband's valet/ spy. We had a bet on that I could/couldn't get him off her hands. Tried and lost. But stroked her clean-shaven knee. She's quite rich, and the coolness, that elegant casualness, experience without feeling must be what requires constant dope. Her Indian face and wasted stomach.

At Chololo, Vicente, in whites and pukka beads with his violet-tinted glasses and thick mustache. Lithe, the perfect medium smallish size. Beautiful Vicente ("Ducati"). A white electric eel. Sexually, Mexico has been framed moments of exquisite pleasure. Andrés serenading me when I was convalescing in the hammock, Joaquín in the middle of the night—"White Nights." And Joaquín's body in profile at Las Gatas.

Vicente dances well but misses a beat every minute or so, giving him total control. It was lovely to finally, quite late in the evening after working into a sterile drunk, be paired with a man as exquisite as myself, though I couldn't do my best dancing with him, did Joe Cocker spastic before with blond partner. Do Tina Turner to Tina Turner, and Mick to Eagles, Silver Convention. And Phoebe Snow. Stevie Wonder. How I love that music, that place. Darling, I like it, I can't deny it. Some slow, maybe Snow, came on and V. and I finally came together, his thigh a hard slender cylinder under his white pants. Did an exquisite slow discreet grind. God he made me moist. So gentle and unhurried, the touch so light. So relaxed,

[56]

assured of future mutual pleasure. The pleasure of finally having found a rhythm that suited both of us.

Earlier, Terri and George had told me some incredible story about how Carlos when he was told I was making a play for him had shown exaggerated interest. "¡Simón!" (Yes!!), asked where I lived, had gone into town to meet me at the Rincón restaurant, blah blah. They wanted me to go back with them—take him off their hands, do myself a favor. He never knew, he was just a shy Indian, blah blah. I felt I could not displease the queen, who had earlier told me to cool my act and to whom I had to atone. It was a nifty net of doing it for her. Vicente was saying we'd go to Acapulco but the route seemed to pass through my room. He was forgetting the dance, strain and contempt were creeping into his voice. And so it was that I gave up someone I'd desired for a month to go back with La Grupa to bed down with Carlos Stone Face who has the biggest cock in Zihuatanejo and kept a Berkeley girl down there (not here!) for six weeks.

I had to rouse Carlos from sullen slumber. He lit a cigarette and sat up. The scowl left his face and he became calmly efficient. We ended up in Lynn's bed in an alcove behind mosquito netting. He speaks no English and Terri says he's shy and dour because he can't read or write. All this depressed me. I felt I was sleeping with an animal. I understood everything he said and told him so. Sí, he answered, unsurprised. It's because you say obvious things, I explained. (He acts ticklish and then slowly tells me the word.) I tried rousing him from his impeccable indifference and rouse myself sexually by reviving that day at Isla Grande. Yes, he'd noticed me swimming nude, around the bend with the fishermen. I wanted it to be you, I said. And he'd noticed me "sin ropa" (so polite!) on the beach. "Para tí," I said, and then thought, cool your act, "y el sol," I added. Self-doubt seemed to occupy Carlos' face. "Para tí," I amended. "Para tí!"

Carlos is probably the most beautiful man in Zi, at least Stan thought so. But he lacks exciting Mexican carnality, is impassive. I told him I'd desired him since I heard him say "sa-bro-sso" about the ostiones to T.'s son. Carlos nods understandingly at everything I say; volunteers no desire data about me, however. Sex is getting impossible. So easy and so unwanted. So we smoke Isidro's grass and it takes. I ruffle his hair, his face cracks and becomes illuminated with the personal. His smile maybe means he likes me being there. We do aesthetic, moderately active foreplay. Very Chinese. No smut, lots of time, generous receptivity to my moves. I put a tit in his mouth anxiously, he licks. I am all gratitude and since I'm there on top of him and he's hard, I impale myself upon him. Quite large, but not arrogant about it. Just his organ. I feel pain only once but it is certainly not his intention. His face is hard now, all concentrated focus on me. He does not take over, it is I who stupidly pull him on top of me because my body looks best that way and he comes.

Yesterday, when I left Zi, I felt a repeat of contraction, that physical memory of pleasure that is also desire. First time in so long and only then did I realize it was half decent sex. But that night, it was all so strange, like Ishmael sleeping with Queequeg the dark Indian, like my first night with Ying, so impersonal, exotic, strange. I began to cry, wondering why I rejected (ha ha) men who made me wet from recognition to end up with this passive Indian tenderness. Because Vicente, who speaks English, and has style (all black or all white) and loves to dance and is the perfect size and looks (not beautiful) whom I know, who gave me a notebook when I was down because I was his friend, would feel complete contempt for me after sex. Because I sentimentalize absurdly. It must've been in bed with Carlos that I realized Terri was right. It was all good times, whenever you could grab them, and not much more. That I will lose in almost any competition with a woman. That Carlos was her parting gift to me as well as mine to her (she was then free to fuck George or some absurdity like that).

Well, Carlos did not know from the clit either and so I was left in a condition of absolute desire. Took a shower, brushed my teeth and thought now we will have *my* kind of sex. Stroked him for a while, he was sweet about it. Hoped for endless night of dark love but, Chinese, once was enough. Tried to subtly manipulate myself into his being physically tender to me, an arm cradling my head. This too was not an absolute success. Stupidly felt my crying had wounded his vanity and aroused his interest but in the morning he was gone. Gone. Can you believe it????? What can that last Mexican mystery have meant?? I pray not the obvious but what else? I can't believe that man ever desired me. Though he is so much more passive than Mexican men that it's being one more case of pleased vanity seems dubious. Who cares? I don't remember him much. I thought one magnificent tragic sentence in the middle of the night which made all the suffering of life worthwhile it was so

[58]

lucid and profound and I knew I'd never forget that. And now it's gone, too. When Ernesto took me to eat tacos for the last time (that last night) and I found myself saying, "I love it here," it was a crystallization. Women telling you they like you enormously when sometimes you like, is pleasant as a discipline. It was finally so humanizing to be human.

Hilton movies: a thesis on it some groggy night. Landscape obscured by people. The protagonist always killed. Details of hotels, sightseeing tours, clothes. The death that's mourned is really that of landscape, viewed always from a hotel window, or human eyes, but not alone. Gone. All gone.

Gilberto the architect pleasant my last morning, despite my sexual rejection.

The circle somehow completed with sleeping with Carlos. Out of Murdoch. Machinations. Circular because least expected, therefore most mysterious, pregnant. Now of course all Zi will know but what it took forever to realize was all Zi likes to tell about itself, is endless puzzle fitting itself together tragi-merrily. Last night at Chololo also saw Andrés with Candy, and Terri, saw her paying. So *that* was confirmed. A. suavely said hello to me to boast off but I ignored him to lean animatedly in the Queen of Hip's direction. What a social plum you rejected, shithead. Eat your heart out! He looked sullen when I saw him later, but I let him see me looking at him when he left because I did after all want to see what he looked like. Couldn't really. Had lost most of my sense of him. Very dark, very pretty, with a swaying, faggy walk. Mexican.

Gilberto practically cried when I rejected him. He was a failure as a macho, was important when there was no love, he said. Oh God. The morning I leave his face is friendly, tender and he informs me he's on his way to eat breakfast. Some invitation?

The two American boys from Georgia did show up. My karma—there is no other word for it—had changed. Off we went. They told me Karen was a hooker (!!!), great Karen, that Isidro had stolen their friends' luggage. More puzzle completing. We get to Acapulco and meet these friends and finally a story evolves from third to first hand, traced to origin, in a freak meeting.

We go to a free posh hotel cocktail party. Back to a parking lot. I win a lot of money at poker from these boys (playing an improbable hand once, pure guts in a game called Chicken), turn them all on by finally daring style, instead of compulsive content, mainly by being Inés completely (Hoh! nee). Everyone turns me on. This whole trip is instant sexual transference. Indecisive. Sleep. Some petting in the dead of night with one of the Georgia boys, the moderately attractive one with the odious personality who doesn't like me. Here I sit, ending this monumental oeuvre by a fucking highway. Acap. stinks from this vantage. Had wanted perfect 10 dollar . . .

Ω

Dear Edith,

Four distinct stages have happened in Acapulco. The first involved my rereading my last letter to you and being appalled at how difficult it was to render justice to the richness of life in words. Zi was like a fairy tale of endless meaning and suspense. Particularly the bit about Carlos lacked surprise though in life imagine how it did! How awful that everyone has rich life and can't speak it. How long it took me to learn to give my best and take the consequences: rejection after love. Fuck it.

After the first awful day in Acap. I passed a perfect one when I got settled in a hotel that a man in Zi had recommended at the beginning of my stay despite my insistence that I wouldn't get to it this trip. Spent a day at a small theaterlike beach and an afternoon swimming in someone's pool after having declared myself gorgeous in my room's full-length mirror. I gave up the room and the mirror, alas, and the one I have now is small, dark, and streaked. In it I looked scarred, Indian, and old. But I weigh(ed) 123 pounds today.

The second I can barely bare launching into. I had wanted in Acapulco a kind of dead space between Zi and New York, a pleasant, sexless time of, however, chic and discoteques. Wanted to stop life so I could never have loved or felt anything as much as Zi, wanted to savor it, have wanted nothing but to return there, to have found it the perfect place with perfect people. But I met someone better and I suppose only as painful as Andrés though it feels like more.

Writing is like dancing. It takes a while to lose self-consciousness, settle into a rhythm, accept one's style. A meditation on the difficulty of writing was interrupted in Acapulco by Lucio Salvador.

Don't know where to begin. I talked it all out last night to some

[60]

Canadian hippy. Besides, it's remote, a whole two days ago and much cynicism later. O.K. Short, quite dark, an Indian (mostly) from Oaxaca, hair slightly bleached by sun and salt water. Teaches scuba diving.

I'm in front of a silver shop that's closed looking in for Lynn's fabulous earrings. He says, "It's closed!" I say thanks, I hadn't noticed. He looks slick, a little hoody. Smart ass. But he speaks English and I want to wise ass it up, why not, so I ask for directions to a restaurant. He says to wait till he speaks to the emerging proprietor and he'll accompany me. He reminds me extraordinarily of Andrés, down to the insolence with which he tells me, as I approach him and this man: "I'm speaking to this man." We leave the man and the immediate false personal Mexican name ploy enacts itself. We tool around leisurely. I stop into another open silver shop and spend too long. He has by this time spoken perfect English. I say, "You must've heard this a million times, but where did you learn your fabulous English?" "It has cost me," he says, after he laughs, pleased at my flattery. "It has cost me." I am appalled with pleasure at his turns of phrase. He doesn't like to waste his time, he informs me and shows me a French grammar that is his present project. He learned his English by taking private lessons five hours a week for six years. And he teaches scuba diving; a cut above my usual grade, he is one of the beach boys. No wonder I am anxious that he's bored in the silver shop. I try on a pair of close-to-Lynn's earrings and in a new full-length mirror observe that I look ten pounds fatter than I am but that my head color is lovely: dark skin, rosy cheeks, hair brilliant medium brown bleached here and there by the sun and looking lighter than my skin, sort of tan. The earring looks perfect, glinty chunk of light against matte skin. Perhaps there is hope. Perhaps its perfect deco tastefulness will protect me, I will become unrejectably in perfect taste. I try on the large pair. These are too big, I say. "No," he falters, "they are well, too ... they suit you," he corrects himself. He is all patient, polite attendance, not translating until I ask and doing it with courtesy. This story-telling thing won't capture him.

We go to eat, he kneads my arm skin (... AH! I see my third mistake: He asks me what I plan to do tonight, I say I don't know i.e. I am available to you, lack program, plans, friends, discipline.) Says it's too dry, you should stay out of the sun, the Andrés program. He guesses my age at thirty-two; he is twenty-four, the most exciting conceivable age. He looks twenty, has that nice dressed-up Sunday look that is daily here in Mexico—a pale yellow body shirt tucked into dark pants, a wide white belt and white shoes. The yellow shirt picks up the blond in his hair, giving him a look of cheap gold.

I picked him up because he didn't attract me initially, he seemed too Italian, poolroom hustler, with his broken nose and brassy manner. Therefore he was safe. In both restaurants we were in he positioned me at a table and for horrible moments I wondered if it was to hide me but both times it was near the sidewalk. Such a relief after Andrés. Gratitude heaped upon gratitude that a young flashy Mexican boy was not ashamed to be seen in public with me and admiration upon admiration for his increasing intelligence and discipline.

It is the middle of the night. Woke up with mosquito bites all over my body. I'm waiting it out. No sleep in this town.

Lucio Salvador. Looks like just another Mexican name, but could there be more than one intellectual scuba diver who will only learn the best English from England, speak it so carefully all the vowels are long making him sound Italian, "Maiii I?" large eyes (or small) almost crossed, starry, looking into the near distance as at the word his mouth is forming roundly like a smoke ring? But his name doesn't suit him, it is Italian, not Mexican. But then he is Italian.

He tries to call some guy Barry in Oakland with whom he maybe plans to open a scuba diving school in Zihuatanejo but can't from the restaurant. We walk to the square, see the cathedral, he has difficulty understanding I am deaf on the left side, looks sullen having to sit on the inside. Outside in the square he tells me about his amours: a forty-eight-year-old Swiss woman who looked thirty-one, five feet tall, short hair, a fine complexion; his head up, chin jutting out, lips pursed in thought he moves his head meditatively to one side, at an angle, his eyes blink, he strokes his jutted-out chin and says: "almost no chin," and laughs with me at the literalness, fairness and anticlimax. Tells me all about it, how he didn't know at the beginning whether she wanted him as a son or lover. One night they were sitting on the grass of the tennis court of her hotel, he put his arm around her, took her breast, she gave it to him (he is still all this time looking ahead of him, speaking at a steady literal pace, quite gently) so he sucked it, and then he knew. But they didn't sleep together every day, she didn't like to be out in public often, didn't trust the Mexicans, didn't trust him yet. Now they write to each other; sometimes she sends him money (ah ha! I think with dismay). Just recently $100. He doesn't ask for it and she's made quite clear it isn't a sexual payment.

Then he tells me he will never fall in love with a gringa—they always leave. Four years ago there was a beautiful seventeen-year-old girl from New York, a virgin, they never slept together. They wrote each other passionate love letters for six months until she said it was breaking her up, there was no point, and stopped. A black woman from Philadelphia he stood up to go to his English class (with his private guru he worships). She just wrote him and he was going to go to the post office and answer her until he met me.

I say nothing all this time. There is more sex talk, this time about one of his Mexican girlfriends, how shy they were with each other at the beginning. She was sixteen, he was nineteen. She was a virgin, the church, but gradually they trusted each other more and experimented, did oral sex.

Am sitting now in main square in the middle of a carnival dance from the vantage of a café, vainly hoping new life doesn't overtake me before I can assimilate the old. And trying not to let it work into Lucio, but it is so beautiful to see and it will be over all too soon. Shit, this new pen is too gross. I have also stood up a Mexican merchant marine who reminded me, charmingly, of Carlos and Doris and who was thirty-three.

Anyway, I barely talked; there was no blandness to bounce off of and he was fascinating with his carefully chosen English, his wit, his nostalgia d'antan. At one point he asked me if I'd washed today. Why, I demurely asked. Just wondering. Fox! The Mexican setup. He not only thought I was older (I am twenty-nine here) but fatter, because of my "big hips, broad shoulders and strong legs." You see the mixture of sadism and seduction? We walked through strange streets, a fluorescent lemon yellow house, past a bit of sidewalk hanging right over a tin roof, strange streets, my first time in town, moving too quickly, to see the high diver at La Quebrada. He walked several yards ahead of me without looking back, in that Mexican fashion. I stopped and left to leave, giving myself a Mexican tailor shop as an excuse. I heard him call Maritza! Maritza! Anxious and imperious both. But it was play on my part, I was helplessly towed uphill by desire.

Earlier, in the restaurant, he'd blown my smoke out of his face with offended Mexican cleanliness—they neither drink nor smoke. He had stopped smoking grass two years ago because it messed up his nerves; and sex two months ago because he wanted to become more spiritual. Who remembers the exact moment? It was perhaps his discipline. I had many reasons for calling him sadistic. Irony is always lost on anyone but oneself.

The scene of the high diving: high, labyrinthine path leading down to various platforms, steps carved out of the cliff, the cliffs opposite lit up. The best one is at 11:15 he tells me. There is some handholding and some letting go. Some man behind us says, "I like big strong women." "Do you?" he says loudly, mock ingenuous. Takes me off to a corner, despite the fact that all the good close places are going fast, are gone. Don't worry. I have two rooms, he says, his second mistake in English. Time draws close, the surf is pounding the cliff and crashing. He pushes past some huge pink Americans and says something hostile, embarrassing. "Do you like my country, folks?" Something like that, very loud. He pushes them out of the way verbally and hurtles over the stone fence for sure over the cliff. "This is my girlfriend," he screams back at the folks as he takes my hand to help me onto discovered rocks. There is now no barrier between us and the drop. I am almost too excited to retain consciousness, ready to plunge into the abyss with him, Tristan und Isolde. Only some Mexican boys are out there on the rocks, a privileged untourist place.

The diver and his companion come down the stairway in white trunks. The companion in the water in case of trouble. The diver climbs a 130-foot cliff face in one minute, prays at the altar on top, lights torches on his feet and arches for minutes on the summit, an Aztec sacrificial victim.

He dives, but the impact on water was obscured by some boys. I feel oddly let down and tell him. "No, it was great," he said, "give him a kiss."

God, I'm forgetting huge, important chunks. When I asked him why he was hostile to the Americans he said they were arrogant, thought Mexicans were stupid, were racist. He was too strong, had too great an advantage over me, so I said Mexico was racist, too, considered Indians inferior. It weakened him considerably; he faltered and lost all comprehension of English. And when he said confidingly that he liked being at Quebrada, that it reminded him of beautiful moments in the past, though those were not his words.

There was some more talk of sex as we walked and I wasted more irony by telling him to stop or I would dissolve into a puddle on the sidewalk. We walked in my direction and were suddenly on

[64]

the beachwalk. I was following completely. We were in front of a boat, "El Mundo Silencioso," "The Silent World," his friend's boat that he'd told me about. Tugging ropes to pull in this huge, light boat. He jumped on, abandoning me. I understood nothing. He directed me to pull the left rope. Then to jump across a widening gap. No! Finally I did, thinking, "Now I'm trapped," but unbelievably excited because I'd taken a new physical risk. I search out men who force me to take new risks with my body. He was physical and intellectual, irresistible.

Some soul music was wafting on; we wandered up to the source. His friend was asleep. He dives 98 feet, he told me generously. He spread some pillows on the floor of the lower deck after the narrow seating platform was too narrow, completely without haste. There was never any point at which I could say no, it was so unpressured, so correspondent. We must've initially kissed. It was outdoors, balmy, dark, strange. I was completely sober and in a dream. I had teased him that if I liked his body, I'd consider it. He said it's dark, just like my face, and skinny. Soon he was at my right breast. The bra was off, he was expertly rolling my nipple. I couldn't believe the pleasure. He spent a long time. (I had told him about one of my amours, lousy-at-love Andrés). I don't know—he kissed my neck past my hair. His shirt was off, as was my blouse. We were kneeling facing each other naked from the waist up. My pants were off, his. He parted my cunt thoroughly and I swear it seemed as if he took a breath. It felt like a small wet snake, very cool. I knew I tasted good and he had raved about my pussy, which he called "pushy." He liked that it was full and hairy. Hair excited him terribly. He had none anywhere except on his head and a bit near his prick. Earlier he had raved about the full mound of one of his seventeen-year-old pupils whom he was hoping to lure away from under the eyes of her parents. He likes bourgeois young girls, well-chaperoned. She too was hairy, she has to shave, he says, meaning near her cunt. Her only fault was that her breasts were small. "But the body is beautiful," he says. That incredibly exciting fine line he treads between vulgarity and aestheticism. He told me my breasts were beautiful, white.

Back to my cunt. I was too grateful to be genuinely aroused. We got into the usual position; his cock was the usual huge Indian one and he moved it around inside me well. I thought, fuck it, one perfect night of dark love at least and I fingered myself modestly, with the wrong finger. It was simultaneous if isolated. I waited to be dismissed but wasn't, he wanted me to spend the night. I didn't. He asked to stay a while. Went and got a pail of ocean water for me to wash in. The water was full of light, as of trapped watery glow worms. The rag shook with light. It was the oxygen in the water, he said. He offered me his sock to wash with, the top part was clean. He told me to put on only my underpants, bright apple green that glowed against my dark skin, dark night. Sexy, he said. He was in his underwear too.

Apologized for it not having been longer, or better. I said first times are always clumsy. He mulled the word over. I had liked my body, but I dissolved under his hard impact; nothing moved in any direction on him, a totally willed body. He looks much slighter than I but weighs only two pounds less. It isn't muscle that he has but something far more concentrated. I don't remember—hélas!—the entr'acte talk. Why do I have to leave, that sort of thing. I stay on and on, begin to feel drowsy, comfortable, as if he really needs me to stay. At some point he says, "Do you want to make love to me?" "Yes," I say. So do, he says. His mouth is too small, his only flaw, and when we kissed mine swallowed his up. I remember that like Joaquín he tugged at my lips. Now it is my turn to equal him and rival the Polish woman who taught him sex doggy fashion.

I sucked his nipples (he liked that mine erected so readily, laughed about it), moved down his body. His skin was like sharkskin, real sharkskin. Never felt anything so smooth and tight and finely woven. He was the same shade of deep brown everywhere, no mars except for a small scar on his nose. Which, when I asked him about it, as with everything else, like so many Mexicans, he simply answered, without exertion, so unlike American men who seek always to impress or to impose. I spent some time on his double-layered navel, like yours, and then gave him the most superb blow job of all time. It was his extraordinary beauty and youth—a treat, really, for the aging gringa—curiosity, his generosity, Céleste having said she made love to a man once because she wanted to. I too wanted to make the love myself and be good at it. Earlier I'd asked him what men meant when they said a woman was good in bed.

He never thrust himself up at me or moaned outrageously (he finally did moan with remembered pleasure when he came later). I suppose it was a sort of payment too, not money, or looks, or youth but this. I was kneeling with my legs apart and he was fingering me, the first Mexican who knew where it was. Unbelievably, I finally came from an outside agency, in someone else's presence. Relaxing to give someone a blow job. It was a lot of fun, actually. He was superbly clean, sweet, and courteous. After I came I pulled him on top of me. He wanted to do it from behind but I said no because I wanted to see his face when he came. That must've done it because he came almost immediately, trying to lower his head out of my sight. Xist. I am going to come just from writing about it.

After the second time he seemed totally willing for me to leave; he'd gotten his gringa tithe, I suppose. Put on his clothes down to his belt after telling me he was too lazy to walk me home (but I later realized he must have intended to leave the boat himself). I jumped onto shore and didn't look back. His gift to me was to ask me where I was going tomorrow and when I told him he gave me the name of a boatman friend of his, to say I was a friend of Lucio Salvador and I'd get a free ride to some island. He repeated all the necessary names several times and told me he'd probably see me there with his friend, who'd probably turn me on to some grass. Couldn't see me at night because was going to a civil servant ball because had to buy some land. He had the name of my hotel and I figured my superb b. j. was a hostage to the future.

That night I thought I'd die from remembering it. The next day I located his friend who told me that Lucio used to be a high cliff diver himself, diving 95 feet. I thought I'd die all over again from his total boy-of-the-sea-ness, courage, and modesty in not telling me himself.

I got lost on the island, found myself at some tiny deserted beach where I got full of tar. On the way back found a small tower on a height which I climbed terrified nearly to the top, inspired by male accomplishment. Almost no thought of him except in my total body. The program was to overcome sloth and fatigue and recapture solitary exertion and explorativeness of yore, so sure was I I'd see him again. Back at tiny shady restaurant beach, lost, lied to, paddled out on surfboard by coral seller, me and giant bag full of last letter to you, new risk, to the main island beach which *did* exist. Bored. Hop ride on launch, back to Caleta beach. Strung out on sand finally realizing my total sluggishness is really depression over nonfuturity of—what's his name—Lucio.

Mario, the model from Acapulco I'd met in Zi, comes down beach with friends. I scream hello simultaneous with his sleepy recognition. He returns alone. We chat. I want to swim again. Am so dismally dependent on small acts of attraction or kindness or even recognition to restore me to even physical activity. I decide to make the big pool-crashing Acapulco scene; Mario demurs. Brave lass goes on alone—what's the worst? Mario has given me an up-to-date good disco list and a tentative O.K. on one this evening. Hit the Caleta pool and notice a snorkel; a dark face winks through it, vaguely, wetly, slowly familiar. Yes. It is Lucio, not at the Hyatt Regency Hotel where he said he'd be working that day and where if I went to the beach I might (if I was lucky, no wonder I was depressed) see him. He is giving a lesson to some bland white shiksa with a Sears Roebuck bathing suit but strong legs.

The weird creep had asked me what color my suit was and whether my thing showed through it. He wanted it to be light. He moderately approved of yellow and that my pud came through. All this weirdness and love had prompted me to wonder what color his suit was. I thought, in my trembling state: It must be white. And Lo! It was. There he was in correct whites, with a T-shirt to boot. So incredibly correct, aristocratic. I plunged in and lapped for all I was worth, hoping my splendid shoulders would be visible through his mask. Plus my serious unending swimming—I am an athlete working out. Plus my indifference to him. Every once in a while, after he'd outlasted me and I was drying off on a lounge chair, he'd flash me a thumbs-up, or an it's-in-the-bag finger circle. Twice, to be exact. Small time, but remember he'd screamed, to my undiminishing gratefulness, "This is my girlfriend," been with me in public, held hands, and here he was recognizing me again and perhaps impressed by my presence at the moderately luxe Caleta Hotel.

I had some awful moments over the shiksa, but near the end of the lesson I glommed that that other guy was her boyfriend.

He went and showered and dallied—no words exchanged. I split. Happy. Mario in the wings. Whom I wasn't attracted to but who was good-looking, had a scene, and would be dancing escort where I would be the toast of the disco.

Went out into street. Mario there. Asked about Caleta. Told. Vaguely followed me through my dutiful errands, weighing my most endearing. Mario amused. Also knowing how in Mexico people always turn up and HE HAS THE NAME OF MY HOTEL. The scale reads 56.5 kilos—124, not 123. I turn around upset into beautiful Lucio's amused face. "That's good," he says, not having believed I was the same weight as he. I complain to Mario that I am all wet and holding a pound of gum in my mouth.

I leave them both to search for a taco, which sends me far afield from both of them. Nothing like two attractive men to make one not turn back to inform them of one's change of direction. Ten minutes later they are both there. I feign agitated tacolessness and buy awful stuffless enchiladas; only Lucio follows me, and dumps some pesos into my hand (he had after all at some early pre-sex point the previous evening invited me to dinner).

And payment. That second time. Ah yes! How could I have forgotten—it was his logo for me so long, when he was stretched out all hard he said, considering his cock "what a beeeyoutifull," all elongated Italian "piece of meat." Man, he was superb. No doubt. The wittiest, brightest, best-looking. After the job he said, "But you are a professional," and when he apologized for his very brief stay in my cunt he said, "You sucked me so beautifully, I couldn't wait." He had wanted to come in my mouth, he told me, and seemed a bit dismayed and confused that it hadn't worked out that way.

I offered him a depressing enchilada. He declined, saying he never ate stuff like that. Yes, after the high diver, there was another stint in a restaurant where once again he placed me, once again seemed on the verge of making me pay for him, seemed to have some mocking understanding with the people who worked there. Ordered a bowl of soup for himself and another spoon for me, another glass for himself so he could share my soda. But I made him take the bottle. The girls at the end of the table—one fat and sweet, fifteen—kept smiling at me. I loved her, loved the restaurant, wanted to memorize where it was.

Don't know when talk of money came up that night, told him had none so he offered to set me up as a dope seller but quoted an outrageous price I'd be selling it at: $35 an ounce. Always the Mexican setup. Ironic at being with gringa in a greasy spoon was his mocking glint?

Back to the enchilada stand. He asks me who the "little fellow" is who's trailing after me. Quaint English. Plus Mario is twice his size. He commandeers me away from my direction, is glad he's run into me because he's wanted to tell me something. Doesn't tell me what it is until after he's said, "You're in love with me, aren't you?" Ironically, I tell him yes. The something is a business or the business deal. I don't want business, just friendship, I say. So many dumb moves in a row it's not believable. We are moving ever further in a direction he assures me is shorter to my hotel. I sneak a look at him. He looks like a well-bred school boy, clean and wet in his whites, his hair just beginning to assume its slight wave, like the boy in

Murmur of the Heart, only completely dark and santanic. Are you in love with him yet? Asks me so what am I doing tonight, going dancing with this guy? With anyone in particular? Not necessarily, I coy. "Well, if that's the way you want to be," he says. "No," I protest. "Do you want to go with me?" he asks. Jesus Jesus Jesus Jesus Jesus. Of course I'm at fever pitch and I say yes. It was all he needed to know. Meet him at the central square, he actually translates it as, at 10 P.M. O.K. He turns off, living surprisingly near me, around the corner with his two cartons of orange juice, the proper son. I head on home, pass the place where a woman I met lives (with whom I spent a wild but unpleasurable first night here with two rich Mexican Jews) and assault her with fabulous tales of great lay scubadivers who speak witty perfect English and hanging-around Mario. Two gorgeous men. Three times more beautiful than I, she mutters hollow, envious greats. I'd had a great time with her before the men, but she thinks I'm a dyke lush: I did somewhat proposition her that night. I tell her ah, I think I'll skip it, he probably won't show.

I managed with much procrastination to be early.

He never came. I told these French Canadian men and their Mexican friend Angel, who were hanging out in the Zócalo, my misery. The pretty Canadian fled me, the ugly shy incomprehensible one was overtaken by such confidence that he talked at me in patois for half an hour straight, feeding me endless stories about how Mexicans never show. I ask Angel why this is (*he* shows) and tell him I had planned to go dancing at either Foco Rojo or the Zodiaco and he tells me they're whorehouses in the red light district, bad, bad. I wonder why Lucio at least kept this from me or if Angel is very super uptight. The French Canadians seem to be going to go with me. Half an hour later I find out they're not. Perish me if I go alone. No respectable woman, blah, blah. Angel actually goes to beg 5 pesos off someone to give me and it's at this point I realize he's *not* going in that general direction and splitting a cab with me.

Mexican mysteries, public humiliation, rejection on all fronts—all too much and I begin to cry. I am ready to sob with confusion and being ugly and pathetic but manage to achieve merely huskiness and lurch off in the direction of La Quebrada to there re-enact my desire-laden past like Lucio had done. My sacred place just as Andrés was sacred song. I try to get a cab to go there, torn every which way between the convent urge and the Grushenka pleasure and self-destruction urge. Cabs get more and more expensive the slightly farther away it gets and the far more desperate I get. I try to walk home but the streets have switched on me, I have to head back to the Zócalo. A tremor of hope. Cabs will be cheaper from there; at any rate I will still be able to decide to go. A solitary hippy boy is meandering down La Quebrada dark casbah street alone and I ask him for the Zona Rosa, planning to lure him into pedestrian accompaniment. Works.

We end up in a fabulous red light district—the streets unpaved, every bar blaring, millions of hookers, all young, thousands of cheap and delicious food stands, everything open and lively. Impossible to feel angry, just gay. The Foco Rojo is a large and rustic hall with a mirrored hall, a d. j. Painted columns, a raised dance floor, high ceilings, marvelous. All of this was spoiled by our being taken for respectable tourists and ushered despite my illiterate protests to a table, away from molestation at the hands of young and beautiful Mexican dudes. So I'm stuck with this idiot bearded twenty-two-year-old Canadian gringo who dances free style—you know what I mean. Meanwhile, these Mexican cats are doing The Line. The best dancing I've seen here yet. It was an extraordinary turn-on. The men were all young, beautiful, clean, and in those incredible clothes that attempt and actually achieve having as their purpose to make their wearers attractive to women, a concept disgustingly foreign to Anglos. The dudes are thin and clean for starters. And they're wearing their whites, or white shirt and pink pants, or body shirts and French jeans. Belts match shoes, often white. Pink pants! White shirts! Dark skin! or yellow and maroon. Black and white. Light, bright colors, a play for dramatic contrast, economy of means, color, chiaroscuro.

I bullshit through Crowell's thesaurus because I failed to observe the thing itself closely enough. I had a sense of separate distinct beauties moving to a single rhythm. The whores were beautiful, young, good dancers. The dancing itself was somewhat staid, though excellent, just like the Zi town dances. It is only gringas who fuck on the dance floor. There was a sense too of red light, of light and dark bouncing in a dim glow. I don't know how to put it—like that night I met Joaquín—a feeling of being surrounded by sexual beauty and potentiality. The awful gringo drank beer beer beer. I got fat and undrunk and only one solitary overweight Mexican asked me to dance. Meanwhile, when a man found a woman attractive, they would discuss price, leave to a nearby room,

[71]

and return. No one got drunk. Strange country Mexico. I did begin to get a sense of the tragedy of women's lives here. For instance the women—sixteen, seventeen, to, say, twenty-two, on the average—were all dancing in place to the music while waiting to be asked to dance. It seemed like if a girl dug even just dancing, she had to become a whore to indulge it. Of course it's poverty, etc., but they were so young, so fresh for the most part—very little make-up, sexy conservative clothes—a bunch of teenage girls into moving their bodies. The sexual repression here is something whose depths I'm just beginning to plumb. Lucio (back to that boreass) told me it was due to the church and that women dug machismo. Having read most of *Sanchez* (I am unwilling to finish it because it incarnates Zi. I read it through the filter of Zi, to finish it here would be to destroy Zi.) I knew from the first-hand accounts of the two women that they were confused and hurt by a machismo that was finally translated into concrete components, something Mexican men shy away from doing—being beaten, abandoned, humiliated, cheated on, locked up, kept from having a good time. Told this to L., said no one likes to suffer (only I do, to write).

The next morning, having spent the night rereading the letter. Writing is hard, there are so many approaches. And you never capture the surprise of life, the way things build up on each other, meaning upon meaning. Flaubert did it well in *L'Education*, Tolstoi in *War and Peace*, Márquez in *One Hundred Years of Solitude* (you must read it), Woolf in *A Room of One's Own*.

"Some of the boys call it 'papaya'," he said of cunt. Some of the boys. Love leads to suffering leads to intelligence.

In a strange way I was happy Sunday afternoon, two days after Lucio. I was high on fatigue, I guess. Crystallizations popped in my head. I had an intense sense of place and adventure. Thought Hegelian thoughts about writing and life—finally the mind was up to experience. The essence of the novel flashed in my head, then the novel I would write, and in turn how it would be female and transcendent both. So perfect. The title, too. What was valuable in my experience, how fiction differed from life. All of it came and left. Cashing a traveler's check at the Caleta, an acute appreciation of everyone. A woman passed who was strange and attractive both. I understood immediately why. Had an excited sense of how it might not be so bad to fail at love if one could only put it well. And then, happy to rediscover my feminism, to want also to analyze why love is so important for women, exactly what psychic changes happen.

[72]

Much later in the day (thematic or chronological order in this letter?) I fleshed out the idea of the woman's guide to Mexico: elaborate description of the men, machismo, etiquette, the condition of women, shopping, where to dance, plus (?) the usual stuff. Wondered if shouldn't write literary memoir instead.

Have finally announced myself a writer when people ask me what I do. Marguerite, a beautiful twenty-three-year-old gal I met taught me something when we were drunk, can't remember quite. I just opened myself up to her being younger and different, to her metaphors and therefore I think I had a sense (she was talking explicity about accepting whatever happened to her, if her lover came to pick her up in Mexico or not) of life evolving, of its ever-approaching newness which I would not reject. On Sunday, meanings floated to the top, ready to be written and (later) filmed. Sights and insights were simultaneously interchangeable, life became image and metaphor, all I had wanted from this trip, besides the body that is. And lust. (The title?) "Getting a winter tan"?

Went to a bullfight. It was dull until I changed angles. Discovered excitement for me is in angles and the perfect angle is this:

X ` ` ﹅

Can't do on paper. Down and across but also stuff at same height as me across a space and a three-dimensional diagonal cut down. I think I dream in that angle. Dream angles are unreproduceable.

A single-file parade of brilliantly bedecked tourists trooped in sunlight around one of the rings of the arena while I was in the shade. They were sharp in the distance and the noise was from around me. Impossible. For film.

The first fight made me cry because I had lived in intimacy with animals in Zi (and had remembered Inés's truth when I asked her about scorpions being dangerous: "Nothing attacks.") The bull kept jumping over the fence. He wanted so much to live. The first fight was on horseback. A supple and pretty young man came out on three or four different horses of different colors and plunged banderillas into the bull. The caballero was as elegant as his mounts, and enjoyed his own beauty and agility, a playful knife to the bull's increasing pain and bewilderment. The bull kept going to him as to help. Death as a flirt. Finally, full of pricks, daggers, spears, not believing what was happening to him, the bull collapsed on his knees. I thought surely now they will let him live—he's fought so long, tried so often to jump the fence, which I thought meant bravery (the crowd liked him)—but that was when he was dealt the final blow. In my state of rediscovered pain it was easy to identify with the victim and to read the corrida as an instance of men's relations with women. After the bull was dead, the crowd was still alive and conscious, strange from the bull's (my) perspective.

The second fight, a standard matador affair, was much more clearly allegorical. The torero was not the graceful and gay young man on horseback but an exaggerated version of the stud. His small prick was bulging out down one leg. His game was to attract the bull sexually, give it pleasure. He would thrust his prick in its face and give his head a wicked "come on!" shake, challenging the animal to risk the greatest pleasure it would ever have in its life. God, it's difficult to remember the precise stages. One can't let a single moment elapse or it's gone.

He danced beautifully with the bull. They had a single rhythm, like the beautiful gay boys doing The Line at the Zodiaco (that turn in the middle so liquid)! He was pretty for the bull, the bull was his only partner. Would march up to it seductively, execute perfect passes and then march rigidly away, back turned to the bull, hands on hips with a toss of the head to the crowd's anticipated applause while the bull stood in the center, panting for more. For the last series of passes (God! associations are so quick when you're in a state of feeling. Just realized I killed my own bull in that merchant marine whose name I can't remember and whom I suddenly long to see again because he trusted me and didn't. And said my name with such manifest pleasure and I can't even remember his and so he is lost to me as a moment of Mexico. You won't come, he said. Sí, I said. "La palabra de Mariisssa," he said and smiled. Sí, I said.)

For the last series of passes the torero hid a stiletto behind the blood red capa and winked at us. He and we knew its preordained fate, the same always (Lucio, rescue me with the personal in this strange square where no one knows my name and I am writing about cruelty). Always seductive but this time concealing the knife. ("I want to destroy you," Lucio had said. "I want to strangle you.") What else? What else was there?!?? Oh yes. Would act indifferent sometimes; he made the bull chase its fate. All this time there was that strange mixture of kindness and sadism, Mexican seduction. At the last moment all the seductive light left his face and it became hard and stony. He pulls out the stiletto, and arches it at the bull's

[74]

neck. The bull stands there panting, there is no way it can leave, it must know the end. One superb insertion, blood gushes out of the bull's mouth and it topples over dead. The crowd is wild—the torero struts past it cockily holding out the bull's two ears. So I finally understood the man's world, how men ride horses, are brave, kill bulls and women. A set game with ancient rules.

(Boys of Mexico, sea boys, Carlos with his ostiones, Lucio most completely, and the sailor. To choose only one metaphor is literature.) Arouse, kill, strut. So their beauty is really for themselves, not for women.

Rather wiped out and ultimately bored with bulls being killed, having lost women's perspective in a male world, though at the whorehouse I did wonder how that hard-faced woman had such a young stomach. Why wasn't she discarded rather than given a body lift, shades of *Pimp*. Answered with my/her perspective. *I* want a stomach lift, my life is important to me, I have consciousness, blah blah. And sitting in bull ring seeing women through male eyes, yes women are beautiful, and realizing instantly that women are so much larger than being beautiful. That *they* see. The usual insight, how incredible though that it has to be perpetually renewed; so easy to see women from the outside.

Well, anyway, wiped out, headed into town in my man's shirt, sick of sex and trying to live for mind in a country, especially a city, of exceptionally young and beautiful men. Sick of what's universally known as the Mexican Setup. Am picked up by a fifty-four-year-old French restaurateur who instructs mé in Mexican (and French) machismo. If a man doesn't proposition you the first night there's a chance he'll love you. Women are more spiritual about love, for men it's just a physical need. I agree and say men are automatóns, machines, animals. Not one of these words irritates him; rather they soothe him, and I realize there is much linguistic work to be done by women. Says men always think it will be better elsewhere (I think of Stan's nonstraying from me though he met an interesting woman recently—was too much "trouble," and there was no after-glow of desire) even though it's the same. Says Mexico is repressed; he offered to fix three young men up with whores and they refused. There are only three or four out of twenty thousand hotels here that are for sex, and this explains the country, surely. I explain that if the men were young and good-looking they would be offended at paying for sex. All these young men full of lust, though? He tells me about bordellos in France and here where dissatisfied married women go; they choose the men through one-way mirrors and down a long gallery at the end, waits the woman who chose him.

Like a million other men (I am fast learning the ploy) he bemoans machismo and is totally honest about what a bastard he used to be. It is too depressing. He convinces me—feelings change so quickly here, I no longer feel this now—but then I was convinced that it was all over with Lucio, with men. But men do sometimes feel desire and I ask him when is it they do, for what sort of woman do they feel respect, for what sort contempt. A question he and others were unwilling to answer.

So, with all this information, I vowed I would set up a Mexican dude exactly as I'd been.

The Frenchman paid for my dinner; every night a different man, different payments, but I only fuck the stingy. He was disappointed that I wouldn't and made no further rendezvous. Just as well. I've been going around telling men I'm ugly so as to protect myself against flattery, another of my projects. (He agreed that without the left side of my face I would have had "une belle petite tête.") And also show them women have intelligent consciousness.

I walked home alone past the "Mundo Silencioso" wanting to write about Lucio and so I walked down to the boat to recapture as much as I could. "Sharkskin" came there when I tried to conjure up his image, willing him to materialize on the deck. One thing connected with another. I realized (I went back three times) that "Mundo Silencioso" stood for men's feelings about women, nonexistent, their concealed contempt for us and how silent their world is to us. How it is only for themselves, Lucio and his friend on that boat, all the men involved in the bullfight spectacle, how it is a womanless world, closed up tight. My spirits sank and I thought, Film: blow up the Silent World. Satisfied at one more exciting project I walked home and suddenly the streets were full of sound.

A cop car sidled up to me and hsssted me over: where was I going, in the personal pronoun address. To my hotel. And you? Formal address. "Fucky-wucky?" one asked, fulfilling the Frenchman's question/prophecy about wasn't I ever sexually hassled by the cops when I walked alone. Dozens more cars and men stopped dead in their tracks, honked, called, whistled; even the trees hissed. The Silent World squealed and I was finally being punished for having fucked Lucio, for desiring men, for dancing wildly, for seeking, like them, adventures in the night. How men hate the sexual in women. How incredibly oppressed women are, for surely they all want exactly what I want, and men want, and they are crucified for it. I was afraid Acapulco would stone me to death for waking it up. It was awful, all those explosions of sound and my soiled visibility.

The next day, working Monday, I enacted my plan to hurt a Mexicano—the merchant marine, not only the future stand-up but present sadistic remarks: pointing out his Indianness, noticing his yellow neck wrinkles, telling him he was stupid like a Mexican when he said Norfox instead of Norfolk. "Two months there and you still can't spell it, how Mexican," I said. The light died in his eyes and moved to his invisible heart. I saw it. Told him I was a writer. He wrote poems, he said, and recited the names of all the ports he'd been moored in, very slowly, so I would understand and also because the sounds were pretty. He repeated my name slowly. He was nice but his hair was too short, his clothes not upper class (maroon rayon shirt and pants, black shoes, socks), and his tan ended at his short sleeves. I looked over and saw a woman about my attractiveness with a dazzling, thin, long-shagged boy in whites and I couldn't, like at the Foco Rojo, when a blond girl danced more strictly and better than I. It wouldn't have mattered what he was like though I suppose he had to be less attractive for it to work. It was exhilarating to reject someone though it has cost me. I'm not really cruel, am the victim, not the executioner and he was nice, of Doris and Carlos, and he said my name and one does so need to be known in a strange tropical land. I even declined a beer, what a set-up for his loving me, eh? I refuse to exploit him *and* I am respectable. I think I remember now: it was when the bull looked rejected and the torero was sure of its desire, then that he killed him.

Anyway, that night I wore a skirt, stood this guy up (anything to see him and 1. further the ploy: "I didn't finish my letter," "I got stuck on a bus," etc; or, 2. "Sorry, sorry, sorry, let me kiss and make it better"). Spent evening mainly writing to you in respectable café, took last bus home instead of walking, got home twelve fifteen instead of three. The proprietor was up and beamed his pleasure at me. A totally disciplined day, of total sexual repression and no hsssts, very polite invitations to have a beer at an adjoining table from an unattractive gringo. The writer wearing a skirt repressed at

[77]

work and the world beams beams beams beams beams. It must partly have been to curb my natural sluttishness that I became a feminist.

Oh lord, if Zi was like a developing photograph, Acap. is like one fast fading. Lucio is gone, no one from the past is around. A marvelous middle-aged woman beggar singing fado in street, to whom the prim Frenchman gave nothing, though he raged against the poverty of Mexico. Only when there are children, he said. But Lucio saw me give that long past night; I watched to see if he would, he saw me, laughed, made to drop it in but was too far. Saw me still looking and finally dropped a peso in her cup. So much more life, play, accommodation. He knew that importance of never speaking badly of women, of physical danger, of adapting to a woman.

Must write when experience is fresh, choose one theme or metaphor, be wary of private associations. Prune.

Mail this if can. Save these please.

Love, M.

Ω

E.,

There is always a further page—as I was correcting the letter to you a teenage boy approached, talked, flirted, friendly and human though physically aggressive. No more than seventeen. First shock: "Do you want to make love with me tonight?" After friendly talk about school and how I used to be teacher and we do a good soul song translation together. He's bothering me but I am gracious and really pleasant. Second shock: I am beautiful, he says. No, I say, and he quickly agrees. Somewhat, he amends. But the third was the killer: this little asshole wanted me to take him back with me to the States. I guess he'll perfect the Mexican setup when he gets older. And he was less attractive than I! The fucking arrogance. I said it'll cost you. I say $200, he ups it to $250 here and a year of his wages in the States. After half hour of taking up my time and pretending friendship. It's too disgusting here. Once more I realize the Frenchman is right about men, and that I am ugly (the hardest thing to

[78]

accept) and seen as exploitable by men. This turn deserves another American setup. I'm going to score as many fucked-over men as all of them together score on women.

$$\Omega$$

E.E.,

And one further. The American schmuck my age who rudely pushed past me this morning—it's clear with one's own. That prophetic moment fulfilled. And the Frenchman with his don't you feel like a thing in the street when they call after you. And that Canadian woman from long ago's saying it's how shitty men are in love that makes women feminists. Finally that little aperçu comes due.

Illusions destroyed. All strong now and undistracted by desire but suddenly Spanish doesn't sound so seductive. The one good (?) thing is I for the first time notice the women. Ah Xist. Ah fucking Xist. There's not even writing without sex. The Frenchman's real prediction was that I lived in the clouds, made a whole novel out of a banal sexual encounter. Lord. E. E. E. E. E.

Why didn't I talk about the gang of Indian women who sat in a circle around me on the beach. I bought an onyx elephant from one and passed out cigarettes and they came from all corners of the beach, totally female society like the elephants. Told me their names. One was about fifteen, Lita. Lee-ta. She had that same emphatic way of speaking and used the same musical words and sounds. Said "Sí" the same two ways, as the men. She, too, spoke some English. She was just as clever, just as charming, just as beautiful, just as sexy really as the boys but no American tourists had cutely adopted *her* so that her English would improve and she'd get smarter and more witty. Only the dykes. It was only because she was Indian in Indian dress, really Indian, that she was working the public entrepreneuse route at all.

I tell this stupid acned Mexican boy that I collect Mexican names and I cite only men's. (He too betrayed me after an exchange of wit.) It is all awful, awful.

My lungs are dead from this letter and lack of sleep. I hope to hope for nothing but then I won't have any desire to write.

Poor E. I pity you these letters. Don't read any more. I doubt there'll be more.

M.

Ω

E.,

Can't stop lusting. Would settle for sexless companionship at this point. Don't know whether yesterday's virtue day should be read as a lesson in discipline or repression. Am presently miserable in Acapulco. Destroyed my health to write that last letter and for what? Depressed because not art. Plus no vida idda. Adore Lucio because of two additional things: 1. taught me word for cunt, which A. had and Gilberto couldn't come up with: "cocho." Great!? 2. He said my ring looked like me which I knew all along subliminally. Man, when someone recognizes you, jump! Don't know whether be grateful or angry. Sat in Zócalo tonight digging very evident firm brown thighs of Mexican chiquitas. Of course, he would dig, not, speaking of the sacred animal, my elephant knees.

Had feminist fantasy of opening up school of hustling for Indian girls: teach them English, etc. Tipped these two little girls a peso for escorting me to a notebook vendor in the market today, but it ruined my day. I couldn't do more for them and the vendor lacked the right notebook.

My lungs are shit, painful hot air furnace. Plus what for? I can't write and I can't attract though my color sense is fab. and my blond-tipped hair is purty. I wish you'd answer me. I insist you do from N.Y., cocho. Should be cocha.

I am down, down, down. That asshole Frenchman, one of those schmucks who tells you when you're being treated like shit. One of his big (banal) lessons was that if you show interest in a man, it's all over. Xist. And I passed up the sailor, who was a navigator and a poet. Dreamed of Doris last night. I came back to N.Y. dark and thin and she fell newly in love with me but I was friendly and attracted to some man and she skulked off into the shadows and stopped loving me.

I just can't describe Mexico well. I can't, can't, can't. There is too much to say. A guide is an excellent project. Shall we come here together? It's time we got off our asses wouldn't you say?

I could commit suicide in a second. It's always the same. One is stupid on arriving at a new place and feels new and desirable. Great times first day or two. Then NADA, ever more nada. The town is getting to know me so I have to cool my pick-up act. This cool woman gets on bus last so won't be rubbed against. Only I dig sordid Mexican pick-ups. In districts other than the tourist men don't look at me unless they're old. Ergo, the youngies are out for $ as well.

Mario says there's a gay beach. Shall I go or try and find Lucio Beach Boy from Oaxaca? I lack discipline so no respectable amour will happen. I shouldn't drink, I get vulgar and lose people. I can't bear men my own age, they are so ugly!

Bitterwoman writes on. I am too disgusted with Acapulco filth to concentrate. Zi was utter cleanliness compared to Acap. Or perhaps only an illusion, and Acap. is the sordid underside. Have spent two nights which together form an incomparable education I wish I hadn't had. The pieces of this puzzle together form the certainty that Lucio is forever gone out of my life, plus much more awfulness.

Spent last night being literally abandoned by three men in a row, the last of whom, an eighteen-year-old Mexican—I've lost all sense of reality—danced close with me in yet another disco. I thought he was getting off on me as I was on him. I was melted by him. But he got angry around 3:30 A.M. for no apparent reason, said he wanted to leave. I said "so leave" and he bolted. The illusion was so sweet—when we first danced he was stiff and trembling, like Vicente that last night in Zi, as if Mexican men (boys!) weren't used to holding women close and it was insupportably taboo and exciting to them. The rigidity seemed to speak of courtesy, too. They were treating you the respectful way they would treat their own. We (Felipe and I) dissolved sufficiently to do that subtle, glancing grind. His body, too, pure iron. I suppose he was pissed at nonimminence of either $ or pussy. Desire was enough for me. But there was none on his part; has been none on anyone's I see now. I should've known—looked at myself in the full-length mirror of a posh hotel bathroom, in clinical fluorescent light. My flesh hung from me like melting yellow wax; there were wrinkles and sags and pockets. My skin simply doesn't fit well and there was a tremendous blue river tracing of varicose vein in my right leg. Again, perhaps because it is the part I look at most and therefore the most domesticated to my eyes, my face (that horror!) looked the best. In a word, I fully look my age. It prompted me, this awful view, to meditate on getting a total body lift. Fuck, I only have one life, why not live it as a beauty? I want one more crack at love.

I am almost beyond unhappiness at this point, and into horror at existence as a whole, not only for me.

Everyone on this rich beach I was at early in the day had a much better body than I, though I wouldn't have known it before the El Presidente mirror. My shape is comely but there is no way, after one and a half months of exercise, to tell I am muscle underneath. And now that I am pure disillusion, there is no further motivation to continue, but rather to relax into flab. To resume exercise would be to spur myself into desire and illusion once again and I should heed the Frenchman who said I live in the clouds. I write about desire well, but that can't be my theme because what I perceive (my romantic description of Lucio, et al) is false. So no more theme. No more raison d'écrire. But here I am writing, ergo I don't really believe my fate; I am still hoping to be desired. The view in the mirror was so bad I felt grateful for Stan and amazed I had him. He has lied to me all these years about my attractiveness relative to other women. I've been 60 pounds overweight for most of my life and it has taken its irreversible toll and I am now condemned to a living death because of it. What can Stan want from me? Babe, I am down.

Spent the later afternoon with a gang of beach boys. Was taken sailing (another first) by one with rotting teeth, common here, such an apt symbol, and later set up a date with a still somewhat shy twenty-one-year-old I intended to break. They hope at the very least for quick sex, at the very most for transport to the States. And they think cunts are dumb, as they are.

Only love could wash off the dirt of existence.

Where have I heard that before? Seems my theme song. After Felipe. left, I went back to the motel where he worked and spent a fitful night dreaming of him in his bed. He never did return, one more Mex myth, mist. The other boys were unsurprised at my appearance and totally hung I took a bus "home" in the morning. Spent most of the day in bed; woke up for one horrid instant as from the tomb thinking "I want love" and "I don't want to die." When consciousness returned, the about-which-beach-to-go-to decisions distracted me once more from the shock of being finite. Speaking of a hundred years of solitude—my life—you never do know your own life. Had blinding flash that solitude was the most comprehensive theme of my stay here, my novel, seen from the outside as someone else would see my life.

Truth is, I do lack discipline to wait, like a lady, in a lair. Or submit to boredom and pale skin. Am at point now where even thinking of Mex boys generically makes my womb drop.

The filth alluded to was last night and forms the second part of the insight. Hard to get back to in this bath of sunlight. The Zócalo scene. Sat with two Fr Can boys, Pierre and Marcel, in the square long enough to see as much seaminess as I need for a year. Didn't want to see, didn't. First, we are surrounded by an ever-growing gang of boys who speak some English and mime the rest. They mime ass-fucking to indicate that P. and M. are fags, ask for cigarettes, bug me to go smoke dope with them, a fifteen-year-old in particular. Pierre and Marcel are undercover narcs in Montreal and tell me it's common here to sucker tourists into a Federale trap to make a couple of pesos. I don't want to know I'm a mark, and they are narcs. Marcel retires to watch the pincer action from behind. Mario is sitting nearby with his friend whose eyes are rolling, I belatedly realize, from heroin, not weed. Pierre tells me they and their friends are male whores. Mario, therefore, isn't a model, like he said.

Second, we escape the increasing menace of the boys who taunt and the one sticky fifteen-year-old who won't leave me in peace but prods at what he still thinks is a dumb cunt. We go into respectable cafe where I sit as in a refreshing spring, *Suddenly Last Summer* washing off. Awful little Mex piranhas off off. An ugly, wall-eyed middle-aged woman I'd met the night before in the cafe joins us and makes a heavy play for Marcel, says she's thirty-four. She has scars, her mouth is puckered and one eye rolls blindly around under her cheap sunglasses. Her hair is thin and she is overweight. My heart drops to my knees, I'm so frightened for her, and me. Pierre tells her she looks younger than thirty-four and I can't beat it. She and M. set up a rendezvous, I have no idea why he complies. I am trying simultaneously to protect her and to not be identified with her. I feel acutely my own ugliness with her. After she leaves Marcel says he really has no desire to sleep with her; he'd rather be with someone nineteen than a woman of thirty-five. He cites her fat stomach, her mouth puckers, that she has had three children. I tell him to shut up, I don't want to hear anymore, and also that he has a bit of a gut himself. He raises his shirt and pushes his flesh at me to protest and it is disgusting. I can't bear his flesh or anyone's.

Third, the awful seventeen-year-old who wanted to be trans-

[83]

ported across the border shows up. I had told Pierre about it and he said he could arrange it. Owns a gardening firm, too, and could use another exploitable worker. I hit the kid with the proposition, too aware that I am a dispensable intermediary. The kid walks too close to me; he looks like Sal Mineo, all head and ugly melting huge eyes, acne on his face, a sparse line of hair growing out of a scar on his tiny chin. Do you love me, he asks, willing his disgusting eyes to liquefy. This is business kid, I say, pushing him away, amazed he still thinks I'm dumb and ugly. I go back to Pierre who says he wants to check him out. But I'll miss out on my commission, I say. No, no, Pierre will send me the $100 if it goes through. They meet and the kid immediately cuts me out. More than ever my visceral fantasy of sinking a knife into his gut blinds me. Pierre says the kid is a whore and a bandit, that he has no money and that he's only setting us up—the famous ploy of offering money to get money (he had requested fare to Mexico City in order to pick up his money). The kid can't understand when Pierre speaks Spanish and actually looks appealingly in my direction, touches me disgustingly on the arm, for help. It is all too much. What the fuck am *I* considered, too, sitting in this cesspool square?

Walk home mulling over Marcel's reaction in the woman's presence and his remarks later and realize one Mexican mystery has been solved—I've been to the other side of one particular mountain. Felipe viewed me (and how many others?) the way Marcel viewed that woman. It looks dull on paper, perhaps because I still lack conviction that I'm obviously old, unattractive. This morning my body felt like iron itself. Who knows what one really looks like? It's in the light, and in self-delusion. Anyway, I was so disgusted by the stink of the scene that absolutely no one bothered me on my solitary walk home. Do they smell objectivity? Or was it my man's shirt and man's wool pullover?

M.

Ω

Sweetheart,

You don't know what pain is until you've gotten a boil on your ass and the only man who was ever dumb enough to ignore your ugliness is having an affair. I was just flirting with pain before; on some level thinking: you dumb schmuck, you may think I'm shit

[84]

but what do you know? A tall thin Ph.D. five years younger than me is waiting for me in the States, in fact dumb enough to foot my bills here. Not only that, chérie, but I cut my hair after laboriously, finally, acquiring some whites. I looked super fabulous but thought I'd look even greater so popped, drunk, into a middle-aged beauty parlor and got razor-shorn down to thick dyke dutch boy that totally exposes my revealed ugliness of face. (She puts a brave face on an ugly one, you once thought; remember?)

I am beyond ugliness now and walk as with a bleeding wound through the streets, like having a period on one's face. What an embarrassment, finally, my puss. The reason this letter is so blithely miserable is I persist, as ever, in illusion, and refuse to believe Stan is actually shacking up with Anne. How he loves Annes! There was one in Ithaca too. Oh god, and I thought I had nothing more to say, was beyond new pain. More and more I think I'll become a hooker. Am worth no more than $35, but that's a lot here. Only how to solve these problems: 1. Be sure of payment; 2. Get action; 3. Avoid being known as prostitute by an all-seeing city???

Finally ran into Lucio the day I really stopped believing I'd run into him. I was eating cheap on the street as usual and there he was. My hair was hideous from the ocean and he kept being on my bad side. Offered no explanation for not showing up, oh honey, ain't it always so! Ran off with his sunglasses after he invited me, so as not to be alone, to go to the bullfights (!) with him. Will you pay for me, I asked. He knew a free way (oh Lucio Lucio Lucio) jumping over some wall. Oh baby baby baby. But I said no, had been last week. Next I was weighing myself, seriously considering making off with his inadvertent payment of glasses. Weighed less than before, turned around, bad side first and there he was saying, "You're losing weight, dahrrling!" Ma chère, do you know what love is?? A pure grinning imp. The guttersnipe as achieved aristocrat.

I made sure to record him visually this time: nigger dark, with an old monkey face from the sun, though boyish. His T-shirt said "Divers de Mexico, Acapulco" and he's going to Zi this week to see about opening up a diving school there. He was pissed when I said he looked twenty-eight, not twenty-four, because of his sun wrinkles. Retrieved his sunglasses, really scared, and gave me an extraordinarily firm physical adieu—on shoulder? "A beautiful chiquita," he said when I said scuba diving looked like fun when he was giving the lesson last week. Yes, was, because was holding a beautiful chiquita. This time he asked me, in his worked-out English, how many more men I had destroyed (he knows when he's being witty—he works to be intelligent and witty in a foreign tongue) since him. One, but you were the best. And then some hyperbole which he finally perceived as irony. Ma chère, tout fini.

But that was on Sunday, when I still had my hair. More, much more than Stan, I endlessly keen over my lost glory. I replay the time I had my hair over and over and over and over again. It is a grotesque cut, re-butchered by me. I worked for days to assemble whites and lucked out on a used (!) pair of white "New Digs" jeans that only needed washing, a button, and shortening; actually, I also let out seams. Bought a slightly low-necked tight white T, some huaraches in the mercado from two sisters whom I adored. Held out for days on the haircut, so as to connect up with the FC narcs who knew where good cuts were but they'd forgotten. Said wait one more day, would ask their friend. Came Monday, the whites were all fixed, intended to go to cheap spaghetti dinner at big hotel. Still debating whether or not get cut, should maybe let Gisella, strange Mexican woman who lives in hotel, do? She comes into rooms, takes up time making weird monkey faces over some fight she had with her brother Manolo. I try on whites just to show her. It is by now late. I look fabulous. Even wet my hair is painted with blond light, hangs shaggy and French in face. Glowing. But must be better, better, better. Rush off, some tequila in me and can't even wait to hit young downtown salon but pop into local middle-aged establishment. Her price is cheap. I look so fabulous how could I look but better? I can't can't can't believe I did it. She took it all off. I said cut this more, and this. Because it was all gone and thought might as well go for chic French boy cut. Hideous butchery look. Had been full aureole of buoyant chiaroscuro. The FC had touched it wonderingly and said it's all blond from the sun, as gently as would touch gossamer, afraid to disturb. That's what it was like. Is hideous hideous now. Where before head was lovely and body just support, now body better. Effect is of good though slightly over-ripe bod topped by hard ugly head. And of course nothing hides my face, or softens it, or frames it. Nothing moves when I dance, the light is gone. When I went swimming in it, it sprouted wings. Nothing can illustrate its ugliness.

So I cut more off and now it is grotesque, no longer even a cut. Like a middle-aged woman my hair is too short. And because I'm ugly (and is the action from men ever nonexistent now!) Mexico is no longer sabroso para mí; its light has died too. I suppose I feel chastened, shorn of all illusion, *my* sun wrinkles stand out now. I'd looked so good for weeks I had planned to get an overpriced picture taken of myself. Christ. I don't have enough time left in my life to look shitty for a year at thirty-five-thirty-six. And there will never be the same conjunction of beauty factors: months of sun and sea, thin-ness, being thirty-five. I CAN NEVER LOOK AS GOOD AGAIN. (Lucio—my god, what fun it would've been to be with that firm, mocking young man at the bullfights—he would have grabbed me hard every once in a while and made me stop breathing with desire from yet another perfect conjunction of factors. Asshole, when it's over forget pride and grab at moments of pleasure.)

Why do all middle-aged women wear their hair too short? I debuted into middle-age with this hair. There has been no action since. The only solution for me at this point is to stay down here for another year, somehow managing a trip to Vidal Sassoon, the only place that can make me look good one out of two times, then coming back. Even with this, my hair and skin now are abominably dry. I am turning into ugly old leather.

I bought five dollars worth of scarf material, and swathe myself in turbans at night. The look is sophisticated but much older and I have no freedom when I dance. I used to dance with my flying hair; now, must learn tauter discipline. Discipline: I had thought to earn Lucio by matching his discipline, spending hours and hours at the market to assemble clothes, bleach, thread, borrowing scissors, bargaining, washing, sewing, with many tryings-on for perfect fit. And I blew it on impulse.

Chastened. What an old word. What a dull letter. I am dull now, the world doesn't feel me, and I, therefore, can't feel it. And I am banking my feelings for the future. No, just even trying not to dream about them. What I have to go back to in New York is worse than nada. I finally called Stan after not being able to call him all one night (and right after he'd called you). He had been seeing this Anne since he met her months ago, was outraged I hadn't written him, found he was lonely in my absence but didn't miss me, he didn't think we could go on, he certainly didn't intend stopping the thing with Anne. And of course my neat financial arrangement will cease too. More than that, I'll go insane without him. There was only the pleasure of returning beautiful to New York, and shocking Stan (and you all) with my thinness and wearing all my beautiful size ten clothes. Now, no career, no money, no Stan. I can't go back. Go back to: an ugly town; no work in the broadest sense—that is, no purposeful, enlarging or prestigious pursuit; to no men, since 1. am feminist in my own town—how not be? 2. men are awful 3. they think I'm too old and ugly.

I can't write can't can't but must. Must continue doing minimal morning exercises and some writing, though all I want to do is drink and eat and lie in my bed. I've even almost stopped masturbating. There is so little potentiality left in my life. There is no action from men anymore when before it was an ongoing poem. I'd started to compile a list of their color combinations, but now that I'm ugly for them how can they attract me? Bobbing beauty—that was how they struck me at that dance in Zi, and in the Foco Rojo.

Just ran into Lucio near the Zócalo. Some boy came towards me in trunks, a T and sneakers, with his arms open. Lucio, I breathed, all warm, adult, amused pleasure. Put his arm around me, I put mine around his waist, but it was an on-off affair. Dragged me with him to buy himself a sweet roll and price a new pair of sunglasses. Couldn't beg for love, so begged for English pupils. He promised me two sisters if I go tomorrow to the Caleta pool between ten and twelve. Told me he'd seen me crossing the street the other day with a blond girl—who was she? Do you want her, I asked. Yes, he did. And me, too? Of course. I should bring her tomorrow to the pool and he'd give her a scuba lesson. And me too, of course. Jesus, he saw me without my turban. He'd just come back from Zi where he'd gotten his hair cut, hadn't I noticed? (!!!) Me too, I clamored, but god, he has eyes all over his body to look at himself with. When pressed, he said it looked better, I'd looked, he grimaced, like a hippy before. And I was dressing better. He points to my white jeans and the same orange cotton top I was wearing when he met me. I pull out my white head schmattah hoping, praying, he'll stick around long enough to see the distinct improvement when I wear it, but we are, malheureusement, in front of my café where I tell him I'm going to write a novel about him. I ask him how the bullfight was. He didn't go. I say I'd like to know how to get in free, he actually proffers an invitation for this Sunday. Asks me how many men I've killed since he last saw me. None and I mumble on about the last bullish guy, how he destroyed me inside and I'm taking a rest from brutal Mexican love. He looks lost. He doesn't seem able or willing to understand English when it's spoken *to* him.

I ask him if he has a Mexican girlfriend. Has, but she won't sleep with him, doesn't trust him, thinks if she sleeps with him he'll forsake her. So you pick up gullible Americans, I ask, doubting he understands "gullible." I tell him his English is antiquated, which makes him laugh, I reword the remark so he finally must understand and he presses me anxiously for the contemporary word for "forsaken." Also makes me promise to go to the Caleta tomorrow, or he'll punish me again on his friend's boat. Is that a promise or a threat, I ask. What is a "threat," he asks me.

Feh. It's finally a bore, this Lucio crap. I do actually like him; he may not cross the street to see me but when he walks into me head-on does manage to kretch out some polite formula about how much pleasure he's getting from this encounter, and there is some friendly physicality. Oh, if only I were still (somewhat) beautiful!

Much else has happened. (At least he hasn't fucked anyone since me, so he says. Quel gamin!)

Got royally, horribly laid by a kitchen helper, plugged me with his monstrous prick three times, the last nearly rape. Boasted about his sexual sophistication, which consisted of knowing fifteen different positions from which to plunge his phallus into my hole. Three times in a row, much come each time, huge ass. Awful. The next night his jism was still working its way downstream. I am certainly pregnant now and will give birth to three bulge-ass kitchen assistants who will no sooner have left my bod than they will turn around and plug me in some endless Chinese fuck progression. Next morning, there he was again, so I said you really dig rape, don't you, and managed to get my legs in between us to push him successfully off. Totally hung, I notice he looks different, he *is* different! Who are you, I ask; why, Ricardo, he answers sheepishly. It was the asshole's friend! I put on my horribly soiled digs and plunge out into brilliant, dirty, working-class Acapulco. God knows how I survived the day, though the memory of the sheepish would-be rapist managed to buoy me down the hill with ironic amusement. Of course, I still had long hair and Stan then, and skid row was a fantasy, nada más. Now $30 left, and my respectability is a tattered old dress only basted together.

Monday night, newly shorn, I went for a cheap spaghetti and live music evening at a local big hotel and picked up a captain of waiters, Alfredo, all in whites with a silver lamé belt. Short, dark, thin, with a kind face. Hair on his chest and a bald spot on his head, moderately camouflaged (from a motorcycle accident, so O.K., even glamorous). I sat in the shadows saying I felt triste because I'd just cut my hair. He was thirty and had his own frailties so must've understood. We went dancing afterwards to Charlie's Chilis, one of the places you see jet set beauty. Asked him if he could dance, said

[89]

barely. Turned out to be fabulous dancer who knew hustle and otherwise danced in that closely reined-in Mexican way, like guarding the space immediately in front of him, dicing it with controlled, understated sexuality. Lovely. I was desperately humiliated, especially to view my sweating whites, immensely broad swimmer's and push-up shoulders, topped by ugly bullet head looming above and beyond him. My T was getting trucker all the time. Acapulco has destroyed dancing for me. What can I tell you? Chastened by a more beautiful chic scene.

Even though he'd only had three years of school, I only had to summon him dancing to be attracted, concealed baldness and all. He put his head on my shoulder, had chic accoutrements: a small clutch bag, a cricket lighter in a leather case, numerous packs of international cigarettes, hotel souvenirs, and bought me two drinks and told me where I could learn the hustle.

We took a cab to my hotel and though the night clerk, who has his own monumental bald spot and therefore nurses (nursed, actually, when I was Samson unshorn) a discreet and hopeless passion for me, allowed me to bring Alfredo up I realized it would fast terminate my rep, so A. and I smooched for an hour in the lobby, set up a firm date for the next day, which, natch, he didn't show for. What the fuck—an ugly, poor gringa who won't put out! But a pleasant evening para mí. So Lucio had already been partly replaced by a man who titularly accepted me in my real ugliness.

So much for el sexo.

Then there have been the fascinating women and the middle-aged crowd. More later, cara, cara, cara.

Sitting in discoteca "Le Dôme" faking writing up this joint so as to avoid paying outrageous cover charge. Le Dôme—one of few respectable discos where allow they non-couples. So were blond gringas waiting for Mexican men, who'd brought their girlfriends. Pam and I ran out on bill. My writer ploy elicited nothing but slick cordiality from maître d'. I went to a hotel bar where for a mere $2 you get a styrofoam cup of ice and a rich Mexican architect who speaks near perfect English and invites you to "Boccaccio," a rich disco, to meet two of his friends. Was swinging last night. All of them modestly denied ability to dance and danced marvelously, especially Emilio.

[90]

Too tired to continue. Am sitting in . . .
Blackout!

Next day. Depressed, depressed and bloated. Might be period. Depression beyond the personal; depressed about the shit behind the illusion of beauty. Spent day with "friends," always a mistake. With some slope-backed (?) tall blond blue-eyed Canadian of kraut origin (who else would find nigger me attractive?) and a fifty-(?) year-old Mexican cocktail pianist who lives in my hotel, a garbagy Sunday day. Day began well enough. The pianist, Manolo, the brother of weird Gisella, has a car so the day was full of speed and I moved from a centrifugal to a centripetal view of Acapulco, which nestles on the southern side in an exciting play of precipitous jagged mountains evoking majestic ancient Indian culture. Peaks dotted with shacks. Unusable space used. A fabric of mountains. Then into the "Savannah Chica." The word savannah traced to its origin. Pourtant, Manolo had said at an earlier point that I found Mexico exciting only because I didn't know it—all places were the same. So the day was a strange paradox of feeling this and because of this truism feeling the intelligence of Mexico, and being stimulated by discovered complexity. For the first time Mexico seemed exotic like France, because I understood it only a little. Manolo's Spanish also a joy, until his diminutivizing of words began to reveal itself as a shtick. He does like a joke, though, and has a rich vocabulary. I learn an immediately forgettable Spanish listening to a fascinating stream of information about the best places in Mexico, what is an outdated resort, what the fauna of Vera Cruz is like, where he's worked, what words mean, how he's bored, and more slang, of which I understand one fourth, often incorrectly. His car radio played European muzak, and oddly, it worked, like previous night in café when Mexico suddenly became Italy and I saw life out in the square through a miasma of gloom and fatigue, as from the tomb. (Then a blackout!)
Then the ocean, yet another version, this one a sea of small tough currents chasing each other and colliding in ever new patterns, like the combination of European schmaltz music with jagged, dry Mexico, and African savannahs and intelligent boredom. An ocean of unpredictable shocks against the body. If it hadn't been for human distraction, I would have felt once more inspired to write. Nature is indispensable, such a fresh source of metaphor, and

it impinges in a way social life can't perhaps because language for nature is so less readily available, whereas human life has been thoroughly glossed.

But then, toward late afternoon, my energy drained from me. I was with two men I didn't find sufficiently attractive, had eaten too much, drunk too much, smoked too much, done nothing physical; my period, perhaps, made even the most expensive hotel in Acapulco seem void, filled with badly-dressed fat midwesterners. Desire absent, I bloated, Acapulco schizoid different—not my cozy decadent haven anymore, everything looked bored. It was like being completely dead, awful. Periods do give women a philosophical depth of despair (having nothing to do with aborted fetuses, Didion!) that men can never attain. Deep downer.

Friday, however, was fun. Running into Lucio. Later, spent evening with Pam, an Australian blond who lies on the beach like a giant shrimp pulling in big fish who buy her lobster dinners. Doesn't fuck them and is shocked because I do (sans lobsters). Awful female respectability competition. Each thinks the other a slut. She'd been raped by a Mexican lanchero out at sea and banged around so hated all Mexicans who, she says, consider women just above burros. She's had an extraordinary life—on the road, on and off for five years, in this tightly disciplined way. Lives on under two dollars a day and gets dinners from men. If not, eats fruit (I too !!!). Lived in Greece, adores Greek men. Got deported for working illegally to Turkey, where the police managed to sneak her back into Greece. Always on the edge of poverty. Lived in Hong Kong, South Africa (one of her "lucky" countries). Born in England, now in Australia where works in the tropics, where it's hard to endure, for high high wages. She was somewhat excited over the guide idea but felt it should be directed at women who travel alone, with even a friend is cheating.

Rather puritanical about my having laid five men in two months. Said American women spoiled walking down the street for her! I said men did; gave her whole rap—she was intensely curious about my sexuality—how she was me, no different. American women worked from desire, just like her; even if had mechanical male sexuality, so what? Were women not permitted to want what they as women wanted, or (though they didn't) to want what men wanted? Told her when first heard about her rape felt no outrage— and if she wanted to compete for class, she'd been conventionally raped, therefore more sluttish than I—until she began talking about how she fought and he slapped her all over the deck and gave her a black eye. Realized: of course she would have been outraged at such a direct contravention of her will and terrified and humiliated and physically hurt as well. But this country, as I explained to her, has made me view women through men's eyes. . . .

Another fabulous night in Acap. closing down the Zócalo with the hard-core lonely, losing more and more of my abominable face. In fact, spending the dregs of the evening with Carolina, the ugly chicana I mentioned earlier whom all the Canadian and American geezers think is a whore. Woe is me! This attractive thirty-eight-year-old Swiss (?) blond ambles around trying, I flatter my ugly face, to meet me, but, alas, oh timid one, fails twice in a row. I, desperate not to seem as hard up as I am, attach myself to various geezer groups. Awful old Canadians who are always off like mad hatters to the red light district, afraid to pause for fear you'll exploit a cigarette off them, looking backwards at you with a snicker. And Carolina, much more desperate and aggressive than I. Is too awful. No wonder I was fled by Pam and Marguerite, two younger blonds. I lose more and more in Acapulco. In Zi wasn't possible to lose myself because was such a slow scene in comparison, and no way, too, to escape judgment of a fixed crowd. Here, one can lose oneself. And, there, despite myself made a few abortive friends. Respectability has to be forced on me (like on you, car hoo-ah). I loathe those dreary Canadians, ungenerous to a fault. So wary and dull and stolidly vulgar and totally invulnerable. And Mexicans adore them, prefer them to us! Fifteen Canadians to one American here, they say. Qué lástima! All I wanted to do tonight was write but I thought it's been too long since I danced. To hear Tina or Barry or Stevie or Silver Convention. And I finally learned the hustle. Alas alas oy vay. Called Stan tonight—out out out. Can't take it. Want to destroy him and evil cunt who doesn't want to meet me. She was a lesbian for four years but gave it up, thought it was "abnormal" and she's set her foul cap on el sweeto passivo feministo my caro hombre who's used to weird lesbo dames. I broke him in good for her and I'll never see my commission.

How did I spend the night you ask? Too sordid. Went out with twenty-four-year-old Mexican who shows up in filthy pants, shirt, and nails to escort me to a dinner I pay for plus provide him with cigs all night. Pounding my thrice impoverished thigh all night produces no pesos but a promise from him he'll hunt out a friend and borrow gelt. Shows up seven hours later in Zócalo kibbitzing

[93]

with guess who—the sale gamin who wanted transport across the border. Cara cara cara. Is it possible?

I hear my name, wending my increasingly broken way home and pray even it is him! So lonely, so terrified am I that my essence is dribbling away, my dignity tarnished from being always alone. But, wasn't my name. But, he could speak Spanish, was a giant lesson. Chalk another one up. I hate it here but don't want to leave. The promise of excitement. Saw the woman who used to take the bus rather than walk few blocks home at night alone—the one who took pains with dignity—proudly flaunting herself and a young, well-dressed Mexican novio in Zócalo tonight. Earlier, she was up on the lifeguard's platform at Caleta beach I realize now. Thought she was lifeguard, so pleased, but was only girlfriend, who didn't smile though she did when she was solitary tourist, one and the same I now realize. Strong, attractive blond French Canadian in late thirties. I can't hack this alone. Need female partner cara cara cara. No Stan.

Earlier, fat blond Canadian (Eng.) invited me for boat ride. Thought O.K., will exercise discipline of boredom in exchange for thrill of excursion and peace of dignity. But, flirted with dirty Mexican and awful blond Canadian of Sunday. So, fat boy invited me up to his room after buying me one drink. And my heavy dinner hints! And my impressive credentials! And my opening my intimate little Stan tsuris to him. Weird! Asks me if I'm married. Say no. Say Stan story. Propositions. Awful. Again, a good beginning and ever so dreary and dirty an end, starting at 4:30 P.M., a bad time for everyone?

Weird. Yesterday so bored and broken thought, fuck it, fuck fucking, will *feel* self-respect and behold, suddenly hard-core scuba divers who ignored me as gringa dregs before turn all way around in car seats. I am dressed as tailored dyke and heavy action, simply from an invisible act of self-definition. Life is too mysterious. So mysterious it bores me finally. There's not only no pleasure there's no insight either.

So that when I first hit Mexico, I thought what can those gringas be doing going around without bras, bouncing all that meat in front of the Mexes. No wonder they think we're putas. And being harsh on women's looks. Blah blah. I give Pam a long, long explanation of todo and how I, in particular, was celibate for three years, even of necessity, being a feminist. And psychosis of looking

[94]

at ourselves with suspicion. And how I was on vacation from feminism and how I dug Mexican men.

A boy among three stops and wants a picture taken with us. I jump up all charm (though I refuse once I know it's with us) and later tell her, how *him* I found attractive and she finally makes some minuscule connection—yes, she drooled over Greeks generically. Now she sees, though later I find out from Pablo, the cynical middle-ager who lives in my hotel and who introduced me to her, that she betrayed me after that night in Boccaccio, thinks I "play around," doesn't understand, blah blah. But it was *she* who took me to drink in a hotel bar so we could be picked up. And before at Le Dôme, where lonely gringas in gangs come to ogle sadly the Mex men with their novias and even an extra woman, when we were so bored and skipped out on the bill (after I pulled my writer ploy unsuccessfully on the maître d')—then I was still her pal. Do women prefer to be bored? Or is it simply that my eagerness for pleasure revealed itself too aggressively, like Carolina's. To be safe and bored, assured of respectability with a companion who will not betray one's inner need, or her own inferior attractiveness? Though it was me the architect talked to more, kept telling me I was intelligent and I certainly did step lively after that—it was a stimulus from an inferior Mex. Inconceivable she was jealous! No, she wasn't. She knew she was more attractive, but she also thought I was brighter. Is intelligence no credential among women as well? (I always thought I could violate every taboo because of it. Like you. How awful to have to play by somebody else's rules! But you have to, is no way to fight the ocean, no way. And that's a living metaphor for me, honey!)

I don't want it any more: I don't want the old men, I don't want Carolina, I don't want the diseased Mexican youths. I want something sane and normal and healthy ... I want someone who digs seeing me in my green underpants. I want company that doesn't shit on each other, like the old, callous American men, something genial and my own class. Alas, takes discipline.

The old American men: this man close to sixty from Utica going out with a twenty-eight-year-old Mexican woman; a seventy-five-year-old who only pays 75 pesos for a half hour with a young girl. Tells me about how told this plain woman from Staten Island, elderly (around forty-five!), who was looking to have her expenses taken care of, to get out of Acapulco fast. Who needed her when there were women half her age or less who were cheaper. And she

[95]

wasn't attractive, so naturally no one would pay her any attention (here I am in Zóc listening to this, oh god, thinking oh god, is me). Frankly, etc, this is no city (or was it country) for a woman, blah blah, but for men there was no such thing as old. At this point they cite the ages of their women. Utica man says can say hello and get big smile here whereas back home will be thought dirty old man by . . . he struggles for objective outrage and universally understood description . . . some piggy-looking little girl. "But she would be younger than you," I point out. He crumbles first. Says, yes, he feels he's old. The eighty-year-old, believe me he defines geezer, says it's not how you look, how young you feel. He has three hours more to live, so I don't point out to him he was married for his dough (by a thirty-three-year-old, who looks eighty no doubt). I press home with Utica: these women know how old you are—it's in the face, in the body, in the skin. Accomplished, I add, as graceful grace note, that I dig men ten years younger but I'd be kidding myself to think they don't know I'm ten years older (and in Mexico, mujer, do they know! I say I'm forty-two and nobody blinks a lid. They guess at thirty-two, thirty-three). Utica had blithely informed me the Mex women were poor. I needn't press that—the old point brings that one home as well.

A seventy-five-year-old man telling you what he pays for a beautiful whore, proud of his bargain, repellent.

Anyway, the cynicism of these men about that Staten Island woman (and me?) that let's-face-facts-sister tone, so depleting. They can dish it out but they can't take it. What a surprise—I'd forgotten the White Horse episode. When it comes to defining men, lessons need to be repeated over and over because it's never been charted. What a surprise. The Utica stayed on like a baited fish, squirming in pain, thinking with one huge breath of energy he might jump clear, but ever more tired, punctured, losing life. Because of illusion.

The seventy-five-year-old spins out a dull tale and is vexed when I'm distracted by the more energetic eighty-year-old (who, his wife thinks, is younger than he is!!! Yessir). Do I want to hear the end? No, it's boring I tell him. He ups and crabs off. Utica says, or is it eighty? "He's a pain in the ass, always feeling sorry for himself because his wife died two years ago, always moaning how he misses her." It is the eighty-year-old, flapping his lips in imitation of the other man's grieving. I can't believe it. Utica, the youngest and therefore the closest to normal (!) feeling says it is traumatic. He wants, too, that I should approve of him. I tell him to lose weight, he'll feel better. Ask him to fix me up with younger man but he couldn't with old ugly Staten Island so how with me. I'm off to burden myself onto boring blond Canadian Harold of Sunday. Then Carolina. Then home. So soiled, so old and ugly from those men that to write about twenty-four and twenty-five-year-olds has become, through my own blithe lesson to the elderly, a bitter impossibility. I am as old as they to Lucio et al. As ugly. Oh Lucio! Oh twenty-four and twenty-five year-olds! Gone from me forever?

Next morning: night before dreamed about spies, was almost killed. Last night, about girls' basketball. The girls were wearing voluminous lace panties (under skirts) which to fill out they wore overinflated lifesaving rafts (is that what they're called?) And high heels. They looked grotesque and I told them it was a male ploy to destroy their bodies, their speed, their grace.

I wake up angry; I think of fat boy and how instead of meekly declining his filthy proposition, the way women are used to doing, and getting depressed, I should have bawled the cheap filthy bastard out. Are you kidding, schmuck! For one lousy drink! Or asked what happened to boat ride. From boat ride to mere drink, qué pasa? With delicate ironie, of course. Why have I left my weapons home? And my standards. (Because I refuse to treat Mexico like the real world.)

Second, I am furious at awful Canadians. I find reasons to find all the Canadians I met before dull. And it must be partly because I am using them as a scapegoat for Mexico which I can't bear to hate. It is unbelievable how bad, how dirty and humiliating a time I'm having here. Tell everyone I'm poor. Doesn't endear me to Mexicans either who feel contempt for someone like themselves, worse even, since had the luck to be born in paradise of wealth but too dumb to profit. Or else they think I'm lying. (Andrés used to say you're nothing man, you're just like a Negro. You eat bananas like a monkey.) Tell everyone I have fabulous expensive apt. in N.Y. and country place.

Alas, soon no more. Stan did not sound angry that I was staying on till the first. Three more weeks (from call) of weekends in my country apt. with his shiksa, no doubt. He's out all the time now. This affair will last for years—Xist, it's never the woman who throws in the sponge and he certainly won't, gentle, horny schmuck that he is.

I am furious at him, third. The dumb shithead wipes his hands

[97]

pretty cavalierly of any responsibility in my direction. Sends me a grudging check and letter saying he won't be able to cash it; if any problem, call him Monday. Didn't get letter till yesterday, Tuesday. He knows Mexican mail service is atrocious, took eight days for 600 miles *in* Mexico, airmail. Gives me fourth day deadline from time mailed in N.Y. Was going to write: "You stupid shithead . . . blah . . . blah . . . we're through."

Had written him tender letter after receiving check in relatively nonvicious letter. How had fantasy Anne would be ausgespielt when I returned; even he would want fuck my hot little body; how met man who looked like him (only danced fabulously) and madly attracted (not quite madly, but yes). Witty, affectionate letter. Then he's out. So will send previous unmailed nasty. Realize now utter absurdity of fantasy—I will be with a man who will always be thinking of another woman, always hungering for her company, her body, her mouth, her cunt, her cries of pleasure. Who will be new with her and only dutiful, guilty and bored with me. *That* will be the reality. I remember how it was with Tom. Wish it were possible to revive Tom but it isn't and he's pale and hairy anyway. What will I do?????????

Fuck that bastard. I can't write about Mexico any more.

Am sitting in room listening to a shrill-voiced Mexican imitate a woman. I don't want to know the truth. Calling it machismo makes a charming joke out of it. I am torn after the accumulation of Mexican events to 1. become reclusive and dignified writer and wait for an introduction to Manolo's friend the language teacher. Yawn. He won't be able to dance. But M. makes no move and yesterday he or his sister Gisella, who thinks I'm a whore, shut their door when I came past it. 2. Take the initiative and approach men I find attractive. Become you—witty, provocative, bold. This half and half shit is wipeout.

I have actually been approached by an attractive young Mexican girl who lives in hotel to go into business with her. We will streetwalk and I will translate "Voulez-vous coucher avec moi?" to strolling Americans! Not the most discreet way. She seemed surprised I wasn't a pro; the desk clerk (of monumental baldness) had thought I was. I snub him now. Told her probably not but would consider it since down to $20. Her price is good (500 pesos, $40), but according to geezers, could get gorgeous young girl for 60 pesos. We were—are—supposed to go dancing with her boyfriend (??) who won't fuck me—she mimes the act in imitation of me, who de-

[98]

scribed most Mexican lovers as in and outers. Just like the men, she's curious about how Americans are in bed. Was pleasure to talk about sex to a woman, and clue her in, generalize about men, chart it. Estela. Told her, alas, a bit too much of my scene—being picked up in hotel; having telephone number of architect and pals (they came by and left it, first Mexes not to fuck up but you'll see later why. Another (?) Mex called also but didn't leave name. Alfredo? Lucio? Awful Roberto? Ah yes, awful Zi guy who bought me drink in La Huerta, whorehouse????) She knew this already from the desk. 1. You don't go out alone. 2. hit the Zóc 3. go out with lots of different men here. Staying stuck with one boreass guarantees respectability. Too much. E. is desperate go States. Will help her if can. Like her now, she's ambitious.

How lost out with fat boy. Was bored, so he interested, until he mentioned he was staying at the moderately luxe Caleta and invited me for boat ride. I think having been bored, and being intelligent, absolve me from this universal truth. I remember my tinge of boredom when Alfredo set up a date too soon, too sincerely in "Charlie's Chilis," so of course I forgave Lucio. O.K., buster, you I don't fuck, says the woman, and the man the opposite. Cabrón! I must cultivate patience. Or else sit alone in Zóc, the aggressor. I knew in advance I'd somehow fuck up fat boy.

To recap a bit. Friday night, after Le Dôme and the hotel bar, Pam and I ended up at Boccaccio. Alberto, the architect, was fat, but hard and bumped well. Alfonso, hers, was short, darker than Alberto, thin, and danced better so coveted him but maintained discipline to not molest, as had with Marguerite. Ended up dancing mostly with Emilio—tall, pale, light-eyed, even a mustache, quite Stan. He danced marvelously—not really dicing up space, I realize, but weaving tautly into it with shoulders that seemed pulled by strings from above. Must write in when I see it. Strings pull whole side of body upwards I think. Slight shake of head, as if wonderingly, in double sense. Often, Mexicans of both sexes (every gesture I find charming in the men is present in the women) walk that way with their heads in the street, a kind of loose pivot, bobbing, dancing in the street ever so slightly. Danced danced danced. Place was packed, young, jet set, beautiful. Played flamenco music and one couple at time got into middle of circle, then traded partners. Bullfight music—out came tablecloth and horns, same thing. Beautiful dancing. Such fun. Then, late, Emilio propo'd me, Pam went home in cab alone after I decided I had to go back to

Boccaccio, found all three attractive. Much booze but not drunk, some control, and they were young, rich, from Mexico City so not fuck-ups as much, and of course, like their class, spoke English. Pam must've been dismayed and shocked, god knows why, but that was the last I saw of her after all our talks.

Went back with them and fulfilled her sordid expectations though thank god Alberto's girlfriend from Minnesota was miraculously there, and friendly. He was the least attractive. Begged food. Got offered two pieces of white bread. One slice ham, one of American cheese. Asked for four ham slices. Didn't get. Threw sandwich across room. (Not that sober, guess.) Outraged them but were stiff rather than violent. Long explanation of how when person asks for four, wants four.

Ended up fucking two, simultaneously, once discovered Emilio's prick was three inches long. Had wanted to before anyway. Alfonso, how well I was treated that night, had retired discreetly but we called him back. Emilio all anguish over his prick, I all pity and frustration, fantasizing how can add on? Was fucked by Alfonso while jerked Emilio off, or kissed him passionately. Earlier, evil little prick, he'd tried to force my head down onto his cockito, not that well-treated. Called out Emilio's name, generously, while fucked by Alfonso's adequate tool. Tried giving myself some pleasure in there but too stoned. Oh Emilio! Oh Alfonso! Want only sober sex from now on.

Afterwards, Alfonso discreetly retired again. Em. was cold. I got up and put on my clothes, found Alfonso and got him to 1. take me to cab 2. pay for it and 3. so as not to seem exploitive (!!), come with me, generous to a fault. He mumbles some next day rendezvous; drunk and uncomprehending and intending never to be fooled again, I assent. Next day when I come home after a drained, dull Zócalo night with the blond Canadian, there is a message from them in my box (where else?): their number, call them. But don't want repeat performance and am so leery of being seen in sober daylight and so despairing of being treated well. Frightened of my own class, really step above, richer; owned, three of them, this expensive little Acapulco retreat. Scared they should discover my classlessness. If could call and ask to borrow money. Alberto comes to N.Y. often. I left my address for them on a napkin that ended up folded, ready for disposal? How did they view the evening? Swinging New Yorker or whore? Did like Alberto who said felt inferior because hadn't made his money but inherited it.

[100]

Lucio. Went next day, Saturday, to Caleta pool.

Today augured well from outset. Got both checks. The bank must've had my father's for over a week. By accident was it found and though his bank was an obscure Washington one, latent tears, wiping of sweat off brow and several anguished "Christs," *plus* somehow manager realizing check *had* been sent to their bank, got it cashed. I'm in the money. Entonces, paid for nada today, save writing essentials and some tips to God via beggars and a bus. Went to Woolworth's for pen and pad and was opened door for by bald little gallant whom fell in love with and pursued for one microsecond. Next ran into Utica—Pascal, Patrick—and he laid cheese and ham and a cucumber and coffee on me. Told him he was in my novel, kept him on his best behavior.

Canadians really are shits. Is objective judgment.

Next, lonely on Langosta (Lobster!) beach while gang of fishermen having big fish feed. Ugly muchacho with denticulated teeth propositions me after friendly chat. Says, like he's gifting me, would like spend night with me in my hotel where am sola. Say, you'll have to pay 500 p's, since you think I'm a puta. I shake my head at no one in incredulity after he leaves and figure, fuck it, let's be aggressive and figure I'll ask to buy a coconut off the fishermen. Offer me as gift, plus shell cocktail, ostiones and queen clam. Mujer! Plus tequila and two of them spoke English.

Later: My shoulders are incredibly broad, real swimmer's, look a bit grotesque with my tiny head and stature but I love them and don't want to donate them to the Salvation Army. Tonight, an experience I don't want to repeat. Went sola to the Ritz bar and was picked up by a rich cocky fat pretty young Frenchman whom dragged to a disco where I was confronted with my own hideousness in mirror and outclassed, outaged, outdanced by every woman and boy there. He danced terribly and was sadistic to an attractive Mexican who put the make on him. Patronizing cunt complimented my dancing but my schmattah was falling off my head and my whites were bagging from sweat and my dumpy soul. Estela was there and she dug this asshole too. He owned fifteen factories, seven restaurants; France, Italy, blah blah. The kind who can get anything he wants and ends up with ugly me. Feh on him and on me.

Acapulco has destroyed my dancing, as has my haircut. Forced me to new discipline. Learned hustle and am going again tomorrow to perfect. Trying to master the 1,2, double time on third go round Mexican style.

Way they walk in street—finally figured it out cause mimicked it perfectly: head is pendulum contemplatively beating time to inner beat. Too beautiful. Wish *I* were more than anything and wish could dance like best dancer ever saw in Mexico or life: tall Mexican chick with big tits who hung loose, improvised, swept floor, did castanets in rotation but with such effortless understatement— khakis rolled up, boots, tight and short gamine hair. Just bobbed and clicked and—inimitable verbally, natch, or could do it physically. Just wanted to learn learn learn from her but Frenchie was trying to be devoured by Mex chiquitas and since he'd paid (though squawked [!!!] at) 40 pesos to get in and one drink each felt owed him my ugliness.

Cara, dónde confidence, dónde hair? Took off schmattah thinking let me do ugly to hilt, make it a style.

Come home to domesticated mirror. Look O.K. but shoulders span the world. Ms. Atlas. Never again. Ritz, too, full of gigolos and aging but remarkably preserved women. Think was considered such by maître d', who tried to get some Mexes (successfully) to sit closer to me. Everyone was twenty-nine tonight so was a bit rougher on me than usual.

Went home in cab by self, 10 pesos. Drink, 25 pesos. Dinner, 20 pesos. 55 pesos!! Over $4.00!!! No more.

Afternoon: One fat scuba diver, cómo se llama? Ramón, sí, who spent five and a half years in States, met Rona Barrett; controlled drunk at fish feed, got $20 a day for all those years because had saved some richo's daughter from drowning. Was supposed meet me at Continentale free booze soirée tonight but didn't show. Probably couldn't get in as Mex. No call either. (Some other guy called—with Acapulco accent, desk clerk said—not Lucio, Alfredo? Awful Zi guy?) *Knew Lucio,* whose real name is Lucca. Said didn't want speak ill of friends but I managed to elicit: 1. L. goes out with muchas gringas 2. gives himself over to giving you pleasure (Xist!!!) but when wants you, needs you then, imperiously, or world collapses about him. (Ramón was intelligent and interestingly, got my first *nongeneric* view of a Mexican. L. didn't fit under machismo rubric but individual one.)

Ciao. This asshole letter bores me shitless. My tits sag.

Lucio: That is Lucca: Saturday (if it's possible to write about the past), went to pool as had promised. There he was, in hideous orange T and hideous huge sunglasses with emphatic chrome frames and white shorts and blue sneakers, looking like a badly put together monkey. The photographer potential student hadn't showed. He takes my hand and drags me down to some rocks. I am hung from the freebee and sweating yellow bullets in the pallid overhot sun. He wants to fuck, it seems. I am withdrawn but sweet and touch his leg and tell him nothing moves. "This moves," he says, pointing to his penis, which, unlike his usual style, had actually shown itself as a beginning bulge through his controlled scuba instructor shorts. But you, he says, your skin is flacando (or something like that). Loose, he says, but it's O.K., its because of your age. No, I protest, I was very fat once. And all those beautiful blue veins, he adds, laughing. I am unutterably angry and bored. Finally, my sense of justice is outraged. My legs are fairly good, I'm really moderately attractive (notice, he never picks on my face; projects it onto my bod, like me with Mexico/Canada). Such a fucking bore, him and his overwrought English and nonstudents and utter stupidity when it comes to understanding the language (Ramón agrees. Adore Ramón. Enormously fat, kind Indian whom drunken fishermen cry against.) and wilful ugliness of orange nylon T-shirt and dwarfing glasses and disappearing chin and shorn head. I suppose he's punishing me for my own ugliness. No. For being even moderately attracted to an older, unattractive woman.

I tell him, about the veins, that our skins are different. Mine is naturally fair and shows veins—I point to my corded forearms, which cannot but impress him though he'd earlier remarked on my elephant elbows.

"You're an Indian," I say, alluding to his skin fiber. "Yes, I'm an Indian," he sadly assents.

I leave. He swears he'll contact students and call me at five. After fingering my ring once more, wants it as souvenir of me, will give me 100 pesos for it. Tells me about his trip to Zi, which I drink hungrily.

I leave.

He never calls.

Tuesday, having had day of willed self-respect and utterly fed up with men who don't dig me, see him on bus. Well, hello, I say and move off because he's ugly as usual and I'd sworn to reject him. Come sit. I don't. We get off bus at same stop and I flee on down to beach. Meet boy and poor buck-toothed Mex and there's Harold the Canadian. Encircled by a trio of nonbeauts but the Mex gives me words to "Una Carta," my Andrés theme song and fat boy offers boat trip. Trip on down beach. There's L. walking purposefully

[103]

toward me—SOUGHT ME OUT AT LAST—(but misterioso phone call was Mon. night; this is Tues. aft.). I am wading in water, kibbitzing with Schmendrick sweethearts, urban yids of advanced early middle age, my own. He stands on sand and says: "Marissa, come here!" "If you want to talk to me, come here," I say. "I don't want to get my shoes wet." "Take them off, the water's good for you." He waits a full minute, my back is toward him—flabby? my back thighs—muscled. I hardly suck in my stom, thinking this is me, not so bad, a used body but one that wills itself into shape, that other men desire (so secure was I then!). He stalks off. I look around, later, periodically, but he's gone.

I will sting him to death, like a million jellyfish, "malaguas." He must be in love now. I finally found it absurd how he undervalued me—a university teacher, someone he'd been marvelous to (más o menos) for a night, someone he liked, who liked him according to her own strict standards. And really, eleven years (he thinks eight) is not such a mishegas. Enough already. How nice, I thought, that both of us knew each other when we were beautiful so that our ugliness now doesn't alter that original definition. I changed my mind about this later. Was bored on Sunday to point where couldn't understand why had cried for him. "Oh Lucio, oh Lucio," I bawled, when I was being studded by Roberto the kitchen aide. Had cried for intelligence and the personal element. Lucio, finally someone with sufficient spirit for me—he shudda been proud pass mah test.

Enough. Though am staying on for him, what else?

Stan supposed call back tonight but I didn't wait around. Hope haven't been evicted from N.Y. apartment. Last of triumvirate evils can befall me.

Ciao, cara. Boy, am I ausgespielt.

Want, want, want write encyclopedia of Mexican gestures and verbal habits. Sí.

$$\Omega$$

E.,

What a day of terrible wonders yesterday was. It began rather marvelously with my usual early beach-day boredom, wishing I hadn't rejected the merchant marine who looked like Doris, wishing

I knew his name. I swim, emerge, and there he is. Ola! Ola! I scream out. He had shown up, of course. I lied and said I had too. His name is Arturo, so serious. He said, "Bien, adiós, yo regreso," irrevocable goodbye and false promise all in one. I chased him later where he said he'd be, but nada. Nothing fantastic but his body was acceptable, his face Doris's sad puss, and he was no runaround. A sweet, shy thirty-three-year old. Pleasant. How attractive his offended pride and incomprehension. He left me flat, no more me after that. How sweet his pain. I must chase him down at the naval base. Arturo, listen, I was hurt by a scuba diver, blah, blah, promise I'll be good to you from now on, blah blah.

Then! Smiled at woman who took pains with her dignity and she came over and sat on my towel—was the very attractive *Mexican* mother of the world champion ten-meter dive. In good shape herself, had been professional nightclub dancer for twenty-five years, now lived a bohemian life here, there, everywhere.

Then Lucio once again, and I blew it by an overeager friendliness. Cold worked—he never used to walk on the beach. Wanted him see me with Acapulco's Queen of Hip, a possible lesbian. He said he'd come back later, too. But Manuela invited me for a smoke, I demurred but she said only half an hour, wanted me to see her apartment. I felt vastly less interesting than her but forced myself to have dangerous experience.

She rolled an enormous, tight joint of the densest, most floral grass I've ever seen and then began a wipeout of such terrifying strangeness and brilliance I couldn't ever bear to repeat it.

It began with an amyl nitrite pass-out dizziness and her voice, unperturbed, talking at me as we sat close together on the floor. I was out of my mind with weirds and she utterly prosaic. I couldn't place her anywhere on the planet. She reverted to being French Canadian, then Mexican—but what kind of Mexican? None of the gestures I'd learned were present: even familiar colloquialisms emerged softer, almost confiding. Once she looked like a spic, another, black. My eyes couldn't focus. Was she a dyke? What was my interest for *her?* Intimacy with a totally unrecognizable stranger. Brrr! Her attractiveness terrified me. I felt like a fat New York cockroach with my unease and little kerchief. She told me something of her chic life: a doctor in Tijuana who had given her a big American car, an apartment, money.

She asks me if I want to see some photographs. I want to pass out; even the wish for sanity requires too much effort but, timid and polite forever, what else can I say, after all, I say yes. Already she has shown brilliance. For want of anything else to say, either socially or linguistically, and because as a Yid I need to know what she pays for her apartment, I chat on about it. She describes it a bit, pauses and sings just the refrain from some current great soul song: "I like it."

The showing of the photographs was a magnificent performance tottering on the edge of my wipeout. Miraculously, without understanding a word of Spanish, I understood everything she said, as if some primordial, unconscious bank of universal comprehension was being tapped. She did juxtapositions of extraordinary unexpectedness and discovered rightness. Everything was like that; I remember almost none, too many happened. One: she's showing me her photograph and title in a directory of Mexican show-biz performers. She is listed, among other things, as a "maestra de ceremonias." She looks at me to see if I understand, planes her hand through the air and says, "The Mother." Another, less remembered, she points to a picture of the doctor; whenever he sees her, she makes a hello sign with her hand, it's—she claps her hands.

She went over every picture, sometimes came back but never repeated a comment, and passed through categories of comment, from age to relationship, to beauty, to strangeness. Without ever repeating a word, with the same measured all-the-time-in-the-world pace, she saw to it I understood what she'd said before. I kept trying to memorize her Rimbaud connections, the brilliant, effortless ellipses, but it was too many too fast. Also, all critical detachment was absent; not so much that I was anticipating her comments as that I was having her experiences without benefit of intermediary consciousness, her words were in me simultaneous with her utterance of them.

She seemed interested in showing me how different she looked in various photographs, and there were some of her in seedy-looking nightclubs, or corny costumes, or with ugly, outmoded, teased hair. I was repelled by a memory of unrelieved nightclub sleaziness, much more awful than I can describe in words and coming from god knows what source and I thought: death is ugly associations. How the mad must suffer! I couldn't connect her with this milieu, couldn't valuate her in any way. Had she been a hooker? But, somehow, to her, it would've seemed under the eye of a totally judgmentless sky.

[106]

First, then, was the pure performance, in me as from her, no analysis.

Then she brought in her clean wash from outside. While I was waiting I thought my first idea, which restored me somewhat to sanity and ego: how genius in women is terrifying because it is unassimilable into the self. You can fuck a man and destroy his genius that way, or make its purpose you, or somehow touch it. Along about this time, however, I thought of how frightening a lesbian's genius must be for her lover, actually, since she would be fully exposed to it in love and know better than anyone else how it would always only reside in the other and not the other's gender; there would be no protection.

She brought in her shorts and tops and bathing suits and smiled at me. Folded each garment very slowly. I remember her yellow orlon shorts, a synthetic bikini in orange and black which I found ugly before rapidly seeing how it was forties deco tropical and was quintessentially perfect for her age, her dark skin, her golden hair. The same as with the photographs, a new aspect was revealed always. The last was a cotton tank top with blue and white stripes. How perfect, I felt, then she turned it around and I saw a big white star enclosed in a square. Like an unending firework. Every color, every fabric. I had a sense of the world revealed as limitless combinations, this garment against that. Unrecapturable vision of a bountiful, impassive god whose true gift was this. Thousands of worlds exploded in concert and of course I knew there was life on other planets. My own genius exploded into a thousand worlds. Banal. Banal. But who could've written at a time like that? Thinking was inordinately quick at this point.

She got out of the suit she'd been wearing—(Oh yes, another Rimbaud: one photograph of her with long shapely legs. Is beautiful, no? she asks me. I nod. "I like it," she sings, connecting up with before, which itself had been a connection.)—to show me her breasts, then the bottom, patted her firm stomach, yes, then walked lightly, satisfied, into the next room as if to playfully prove to me that forty-two-year-old women can be beautiful. I felt this was her motive, that my perception of her motives and her acts were inextricable. She put on the dark bikini—see?! Then a perfect top, and shorts, then an old stiff straw hat in front of the mirror which she pushed this way and that for minutes, finally breaking it to make it fit. My head exploded—it was the most shocking thing.

[107]

"Breaks it to make it fit" thundered in my mind, the key to her, to genius, to poetry, to the universe.

First came a sense of "breaking it to make it fit" not being a metaphor, a sense, more precisely, of experience and metaphor being finally one and the same, gapless. Physical and metaphysical reality one and the same. Meaning not added on to experience, every experience its own Platonic, metaphysical essence. Felt I saw god's reality, what can I tell you, what life was really.

Then, a long rumination on the courage, whatever, it took to break the hat. One could only do that if one didn't care about possessions; to possess nothing, associations would always be fresh then, there being nothing old in the way, no cherished attitudes. What fearsome courage this required, to possess absolutely no ideas, no relationships, no things, nothing ever to fall back on, poetry was this, poets must suffer horrible pain of comfortlessness and sci-fi strangeness all the time.

We walked out. She greeted every kid, everyone she knew or didn't with some witticism that elicited, faultlessly, the same surprised pleasure. I had never seen language wielded so adaptively, so that perfect prediction of response was assured. All of this was of course untranslatable. I thought of her, of Lucio, of a third Mexican and how they had this gift too, though less than she did, and I finally felt I owed her some proof of my gratitude and my own intelligence, so I said "the Mexican genius is tone." She looked uncomprehending and sure enough, she had understood "nada, ni madre!" (!!) Her first slip. Before, this tone insight had revolved around the Mexican ability to never offend verbally (Andrés must've been the third—he could tell me I was ugly and make me think he desired me), yet to have an extraordinary range. Gone. Gone.

We parted at the beach, me cursing my Spanishlessness and pedantry—she's a poet, I a critic—but longing to be away from her, away from the sun, away from my own intolerably rich consciousness. Conked out, sleepless, on beach, allowing myself a few more insights, one about how even the sounds of Spanish show a desire to—and here a word from a previous notebook floated off its page and dropped into the middle of my sentence—"agradar," please; Carlos saying "sabroso" so slowly, sah-brroh-sssoh; Arturo reciting ports of call. I thought of ugly, aggressive German, by comparison; of the Spanish proclivity to diminunitivize words, to render the universe charming, to love it through language. I thought, too, of

[108]

how "agradar" came to me and thought this awkward key to the pot experience: "Everything aids unbidden." How suddenly every word one has ever written in a notebook combines, without our consciously willing it, with every other in thousands of revealing new combinations, everything, everything, simultaneously links up.

Then, exhausted and longing for boredom, I plunged into the ocean, went hunting Arturo, finding, to my dismay, that I preferred simple human love to genius. Found not him, but practiced her openness to strangers, her friendly evident will adapting itself patiently to circumstances and was disappointed only once. Met a few men who wanted sex, cheerfully understood this but declined without guilt, anger without offending. Only once did this not work. Briefly moved through life hiding my trembling guts and facing the wind square on, slowly.

Fuck it.

So, best dancer, a woman. And the most brilliant, another. Ditto her dope. Jesus, Acapulco, Jesus, life. Jesus this country that I love with all my heart. Everyone's fucking genius, even the gringo geezers.

Mildly stoned on a joint from Manolo today. We laughed wildly at four old folk on television, who had forgotten where they lived and were waiting to be rescued by the viewing audience. And once a long time ago at a sports commentator whose mouth worked like a fish. But Manolo is forty-five or fifty.

Not stoned enough to forego yet another stab at Silver Convention and desire. Never will be.

After that afternoon, dressed sharp and hit the Zoke. Called Stan to justify my sleazy presence and behind me in line was herself.

(Another vignette of her: each witty comment uttered dryly, without stopping, after which, fait accompli, she strode smartly on without looking back, having dropped one more egg in the world's basket.)

With her was Barbara very short young girl, cynical and wry, braless in short cotton knit top. Manuela was stunning in a long black halter dress and high silver sandals. They invited me to a nightclub where we were to be someone's guests. Empty place, tropical band; semistripper dancers of middle age; one fabulous singer; Manuela's friend the worn-out dancer, singing, doing some Elvis Presley grinds and telling jokes, in black pants and a chintzy, transparent black nylon lace shirt. We were at the artistes' table with all these hookery women, bravely bumping through the night. My dear, along with Manolo, I felt I'd totally penetrated the world of show biz, how flattering for an ex-academic.

chavos maleantes = ZOCALO
claro!
Every woman hates pigs.

This ghastly aside comes from writing in the fucking square where prickface eighteen-year-olds ask you to fuck them and then insult you if you don't. Unshakeable. Awful old men only slightly less direct. Enough.

Manuela, thank God, didn't talk to me but spoke incomprehensible Spanish to everyone else. Barbara grubbed money off me, and did witty things with her hands and voice. Manuela, of course, so understated: a raised eyebrow and an up and down hand movement for a mediocre sandwich. Barbara using her finger as a pointer in sit down dancing. Pretty young men in whites rejected by all women at table and finally, my turn, by me, though one was a taller, more robust Andrés, beautiful. I stay on for him after they leave, get not a single invitation to dance and split after one last, hopeful cigarette—how many of these I give myself. Get handed a BILL for all our drinks, theirs too! Is too awful, another Mex setup??? Manage get out of it. Yet another fabulous Acapulco night.

Now, in square, being a stoned genius writer, having learned Manuela's buddhist wisdom prevents no schmuck from inflicting his contempt for my face, my will, my mind on me and treating me like pure shit. This country that shits.

Two more. See how long it takes them to broach the fuckywucky.

Hate this asshole country.

Ω

Dear Edith,

Have put on my green head rag to write to you. Need a jab of quick beauty I am so grizzly and bitter. Another busto Acapulcunt night. I can hack days fine, but no action, ever, at night. Not one date since got here, only one-night stands for the old uglies. and of course lack the guts to repeat my solo red light escapades, or go to Sottano Bier to schmuck whom know from Zi should see me alone once again, like in Zi. This town, this country is ripping me apart—I get farther and farther from music. I must learn discipline fast, failing money, guts and new-gringa-in-town-allowances. Must barnacle myself onto a woman and play by her rules. Must beg to have someone let me attach myself to her.

After being uglified by numerous town teens who abused me in Spanish for being unable to fuck them (Mexico has its incredibly ugly side; these boys are more vicious than ours, particularly toward Americans whom they consider free penis boxes, high then low), was picked up by bespectacled high-school boy who turns out to be a twenty-one-year-old beach chair salesman from Mexico City. We go on bus to "El Presidente" hotel. Its bar is dark and empty, but we could've stayed and dug the music. But no, onwards. To walk to Boccaccio. But the niño diggeth not to dance, just to walk my feet off and gab. A well-bred boy, actually, who'd visited the States and studied American English at some institute in Mex City, so didn't quite treat me as thing. Veered, but I said *Beware*. Had given him my chavos maleantes spiel and he wore respectable glasses, so he did. Was impressed I was writing a book on Mexico. We take a cab, I forget to bargain, pass up the Sottano Bier, then the red light district, then I say my hotel, I'm tired, then I decide fuck it, go to "Jazz Bar" in my nabe so feel safe. Cab charges *more than double*. Turns out to be one of many who'd given me cheapy five peso rides; had called him "maestro" tonight which from any gringa (I now see) he would find patronizing from any *woman*. Said overcharged because had undercharged before, *maestra*. "Jazz Bar" is empty and five bucks apiece minimum. Walk back to hotel. Another fab Acap. noche. I'm ready to leave; this is absurd. Discos are seven miles from here, three bucks to get in, two bucks a drink, who needs it? Cab back. Kid sets up date for tomorrow but I see in mirror after he leaves I'm ugly. HAVE HAD IT. Ceaseless pursuit of ultimate entertainment-O. Kid is sweet, Chinese-looking, tall, thin, thick straight black hair. Clean clothes. What more could I want? Small feet, thought, small prick? Sober, I find him sexually resistible, has Andrés's bad breath. God, what innocence in Andrés days! Came as such shock some man—some boy!—found me sexually attractive (he didn't; must've thought to score another rich gringa, back-up to his

[111]

Candy). I forgot what I looked like and felt thin, young-looking, attractive. Actually thought my face was invisible. Miss Zi, yes yes yes.

Thought Swiss-y guy would come roaming tonight and finally meet him. Carolina was there, alone, lonely, unattractive, waiting, Xist.

Depression in a reassuringly familiar form, after exploding galaxies, is a relief.

Mañana, the ex-belle of Acap., other women, Pablo, and soul—eventless. Ciao.

Next Day:
I am exactly like Giulietta Massina in *Nights of Cabiria*, with the hopefulness of the eternal reject.

The days have been generally good but it's at night I want action and company.

Yesterday had long talk with the ex-belle of Acapulco, a social genius out of Proust. French, in fact, just turned fifty. Married an American Jew after WW II and has been playing around for years. She's five seven, slender and attractive, and said that twenty years ago she and four other women divided the best men among them. Knows absolutely everyone here, the big restaurateurs and party hostesses who began small. Said *the* dueña of Acapulco started out as a salesgirl at I. Magnin; now in her fifties she keeps herself in fantastic shape with water skiing and twenty-year-old beach boys. Adèle, the French woman, has had love affairs lasting decades with various rich and beautiful men in Acapulco and Mexico City. Her husband prefers Las Vegas. She caught him in one affair which she smartly ended because she didn't want to lose his money, though she inherited $125,000 thirty years ago which through her Mexican doctor lover she invested to advantage in Mexican bonds. Charming, shrewd, pleasure-loving, mercenary woman with a daughter named Jacqueline whom, untypically, she dotes on, obviously preferring a female child to carry on her rich female tradition. Great to hear her escapades of yore, and still today, and her accounts of gourmet meals at the local expensive French restaurant. She offered to buy me a beer, as Donna, another woman in her fifties, offered a snack. None of the asshole old men is so generous.

So the afternoons are full of marvelous chat but the nights, nada.

Pam is still in town but evidently evading me. Discovered,

through talking with one old and one middle-aged German woman, that Pam is puritanical. Her, not my, problem.

The women who are at my hotel were speaking with sympathy of a friend of theirs in her fifties who dug Mexican boys under twenty (I said I only dug them ten years younger). The old woman, in her seventies or eighties, was serving as a guard, she said, for the younger one. They told me I needed one too. I said I did but didn't want one. They laughed and were otherwise open and friendly til I alluded to my tequila-full self.

Talked to a twenty-one-year-old Canadian girl on beach today and found out her social experience has not been vastly different from mine, so am reassured and hitting Boccaccio, probably alone, tonight. The Mex of last night won't show. He hasn't called. I always feel sinkingly the hour at which they haven't and never will.

Hunted Arturo today at naval base. No luck.

My dear: must write to you if only because there is no longer water or food in my room and because desire taps a dying beat in me. Perhaps my hair reveals my age; perhaps it is only the first few days in any place that are any good but I'm living a nightmare of rejection here, not the real world. The sweet boy of yesterday called, as he said he would and confirmed tonight's, Saturday's date.

No. 1: Didn't show and there I was in the square.

No. 2: Decided to crash cruise ship for third time. Was publicly chased off by renowned bastard Mex guard after having been allowed by ship's officers. Explanations from friends and foes: I'm so dark look like Mexican stowaway; I'm so hippy (how with short hair?) I look like thief. Mine: I'm a woman unbeautiful alone and if I weren't so deluded by the potentiality of sex, I would've noticed a long time ago that *women always pay* here as well.

Adèle and I get approached by beach waiter to buy drinks, middle-aged men don't. They are allowed the beach for free. They also get right on ship.

No.3: The most humiliating—Edith, I'm furious. I couldn't get into Boccaccio alone. Got all kinds of excuses, there was no room, reservations were required; meanwhile, as I stood there, everyone else went in, including single men. My writer ploy is a threadbare schmattah (and no one appreciates my true chic). Please kill with me. I hate Acapulco, as you might.

So, go to Dôme, where, guess what? They remember me and charge me $7.50 for last week's bill, which, thank god, a conventioneering Norwegian marine biologist pays. Then it's friends again and I'm as bored there as I was last time listening to him and to their disco muzak. He tells me likes my shape—verdad it's O.K.— broad in shoulders and chest and flat hips, deeply tanned, but no golden hair hides my threadbare evil face. Such an evil town it begs description. I must leave.

Do you know that while I was waiting in the square for Santiago of the beach chairs I saw Lucio making a long distance call? He saw me too and fled. Can you imagine the pits of rejection I've been dumped in? Can you ever imagine it? My face and soul are skeletal by now. You can't ever have experienced anything like it.

I think you and I might be able to hack this place but a woman alone, unattractive (such incentive for you to team up with me! I might be ugly but I'm occasionally attractive) and poor, fares ill. It's an awful place, awful. Some canny gringo said Mexes sometimes don't show because lack the dinero and I did say I was going to B's . . .

As I did, ready to pay but I didn't arrive in a cab, was probably seen going off to beach beforehand with two grungy townies. Dazzled by twenty-one-year-old Canadian girl's tales of waiters absolving her and sis of 30 pesos each cover. But, una mujer sola no se puede.

I try simultaneously to be and not be turned on by Mex men. No point in living if I'm not; slightly less if am. They are beautiful. Some, many, tall enough for you (I like them short, though) and tight tight pants, clean brights, long chic hair, all matadors and dance, they all dance, they all understand that one stays alive and sexual by learning the latest steps, which they perform with liquid, economic grace. They are brown with black hair and tight. Do come back with me, I beg you.

"Desire Frustrated": an account of a woman traveling alone in Mexico.

THEY ARE PUNISHING ME FOR DESIRING THEM!!!

I sing to myself in my room, caring less and less and more and more what people think of me. I get four hours sleep at night. At seven or eight, like the cocks that they are, the Mexes crow to each other. At nine, having woken me up, they disperse. They steal small things off clotheslines: a Gauguin bathing suit top, a pair of brilliant red underpants.

[114]

I'm tired all the time and I can't breathe. There is a distance of four inches air can travel into me. Of course, my solitary holidays have never been different from this. The average woman has 19 out of 20 sordid experiences; I have 1,019. Pam has utterly rejected me and Pablo regularly refers to my loneliness, says I'm pushing too hard, though I've told him nada. How does one push too hard?? BY *DESIRING*. It is outrageous. I can't get into a good disco alone even if I spend the money, so must be accompanied by some dullard who can't dance and talks to me all night so that I can't even *look* at beauty. Beauty, beauty everywhere and not a drop to drink.

Last night we did a slow number, the lights were dim and I kept my eyes wide open and for the first time looked at it. Wanted to stroke its back, its hair, kiss its mouth. Strong brown arms in shiny black shirts wrapped around their women, prolonged kisses as slow as the music.

Boccaccio—I'm going to throw a rock with "gringa" painted on it. How I groveled before the manager. I'm either a piece of shit or a Grrrringa!

Of course it's my face and age. I need long hair to obscure these. So that I can get *into* discoteques at least. I have no freedom as a woman. I'm not allowed to be alone in public, to seek pleasure alone, that is, to seek pleasure. Not allowed to select among men.

The reason their clothes fit so tight-ass is everyone goes to tailors here. Irving! Dónde es?? Having a pair of pants made up for $5. The cloth, a heavy cotton in pewter gray, was $2.50. Wish could have shirt in same color but cloth too heavy and lack p's. As it is, I will have to ask furioso papa for more, más. Mama. Can't break it to make it fit. Break my face to make it fit? Thousands of dólares. Dolores. What kind of time would she have had? Would her quaint gentility have persisted here?

Hate Mexico like a disillusioned convert. The tailor upped the price of the pants 10 p's by lying about original price. The least of it. It's sex, of course. I'm played out and dried out by these unbelievable nights of pure sadism, exploitation, loneliness, lack of respectability.

The women don't help. Yet another Canadian gave me the same rap on how it's women spoil it for women in Mexico. She saw this fat blond, who fairly suffocated this poor guy with her enormous boobs (incredible, no??!!), being amused by a fucking gesture he made with his hand. I hit her with three args:

1. She doesn't dig vulgarity (wrote vulvarity), boys saying "fucky-wucky." I don't. Most women don't. Is, therefore, universal female judgment, in fact, soul.

2. If 90 or 99% of women don't, men must know that 90% of time (at least!) doesn't work. (But of course ten or even one out of hundred makes it worth a try? This arg is bad.) So do it from other motives. Historical evolution. Learned vulgarest words thirty years ago from some gringo because was *his* approach, *his* contempt. Certainly women didn't teach them to turn them on with fuckees. As if women could tell men what they wanted from them sexually, or influence them in anything.

3. Stressed importance of identification. What could have been the blond's experience? (And what did the Canadian actually hear and see, exactly, of the exchange?) (Yesterday, after our beach talk, the same thing happened to me in the mercado and saw that one reaction would be to try and *humanize* a crude if he was attractive.)

She asked why it was that women abandoned their hometown mores when they traveled, an impossibly naive question. At some idiot point, I mimicked a woman's higher voice, because it's there to be done, I suppose. Like her and tits. (Tits are bad. Age is bad. Dark is bad. Smoking is bad.)

She censured her friend for flirting with every Mexican, for wanting sex. It is impossible how repressed and harsh we are.

Anyway, being inundated with gringa consciousness (and no longer by the sea and by a sense of my oceanic attractiveness) has repressed me. New physical discoveries: looking for individual one or two stiff black hairs on face in sunlight, notice for first time that my down is a glowing gossamer blond beard, each of thousands of hairs slenderly at attention. But my upper chest is smooth, unlined, deep coffee shoulders and ribs above breasts. In Tara's room (the Canadian) I see I am really too dark. I do look native; my flesh pouches, my bathing suit bottom is too high, I look my age. Too many hours of seeing my age in harsh sunlight.

These feminist talks restore my New York self too much, remind me of what men are really like and of the flavor, the tone of my New York self, no other way to put it. Plus my unattractiveness. The price of honesty with myself (and clarity about men) is loss of desire, loss of, rapidly, creativity. If I'm not beautiful, they're not beautiful, if the world's not beautiful, there's no desire to celebrate

[116]

it. Of course feminism is more than that; sooner or later attitudes and linguistics would have filtered through to me when the country became ordinary.

More and more of the charm of the women filters through to me—a beautiful (there *I* go!) light black Mexican girl flirting with language: "enchilada ... enchiladita ..." Bright, amused, bony diminutive grace, leaning professionally against a food stand counter. An Indian vendor on Caleta beach who wants me to teach her English (!). A ten-year-old girl who came up to me in the market to sell me watermelon. I said no—how could I? She said she recognized me from Caleta (recognition! we are friends, "country" women). Her voice had that peculiar huskiness some of the women have and she said "Sí" in yet another seductive way. We chatted about how hard her work is but it makes her strong, no? "Siii"—how did she say it?

Women, girls, carry huge buckets of sliced fruit on their heads at the beaches. On buses, no one offers them seats. They can be pregnant or five thousand years old (these also load every part of their body with stuff to schlep) or beautiful. No one gets a seat. There is a matter-of-factness about other people's hard times and one's own.

Am dying (was dying) to read another *Sanchez*-like account of Mexico. So touching, especially the women.

Sought out Pam last night and tried to match her Mex cynicism. Overdid it. Feel so ugly only caustic intelligence is left. Formidable but universally unattractive, at least, alas, in women. She is writing a book too, a memoir, about riding elephants in the circus at sixteen and the rest of her remarkable life. I like her but my is she a taker, like Pablo says.

Pablo says: "Señorita, por favor, you're cynical, you're predatory." How? I beg. "You *look* predatory." How? Also tough, uninnocent. He won't be specific so I am: ugly, dark, breasts. "No!" he moans (shithead), "it's the way you sit with your elbow slung over the balcony," (i.e. I'm not keeping my legs closed) "the way you smoke. You stare at people objectively." Some such crap. He tries to turn me against Pam by a false report of what she said about our first evening together. Like Danny's friend—name?—did with you and me. Tries, too, to fix me up with a sixty-five-year-old rich dull Canadian. Quelle blague. I am wornout leather. I believe Pam when she says women are not above donkeys here, mere breeding animals. But Francisco, the desk clerk, has two daughters. One,

[117]

sixteen, he's grooming for university, to become a teacher. He wants no more children. Who believes him? Men do dote on daughters more here and it results in great liveliness in the women; mothers have a gentle sadness when a female child is sitting on their laps, a disturbing boastfulness when a male child is. Or is it too soon to tell?

I don't know. It was a performance that finally convinced me, my anti-Mex rap to Pam. Lord, lord, to have only brilliant feminism . . .

Suddenly it doesn't seem so bad, actually. Writing a good book full of subtle distinctions and profound original insights would be a high. But what would one use the money for? To finance yet another middle-aged sojourn to the tropics?

Read an odious piece of trash in which old age (forty) in women is described as ugly, cynical, cheap, and in men, pleasantly worn faces, wryness, wisdom. By a woman this drek. My dear, I save the dreadful book it is so clear an illustration of blindness, and the dullness thereof.

I miss Stan in that Stan wants me to write, could help me write and that is all that's left. And the country. Fondly fantasized dinner parties are out because I haven't learned, nor want to, how to cope with men of my own class. How to assert women without giving offense. Want to flirt but also dominate. Shit. I can't even write. Well, this is only letter; the real thing is mind-breaking work; is not life but a cogent and pleasing arrangement of words on a page. In fiction, of possible ideas about the universe. Meaning intrudes as a demand: "universe" is too sci-fi; but "world" too banal, "earth" too physical. You see the hardness of writing. Bah.

Stupidly asked men in my life to send me more gelt here when could've sent to Oaxaca. I really hate Acapulco and need to leave. When I think I could be in Zi, with real ocean, animals, dancing (but bad to good music. Here is great to shit music.)

Acapulco, an ocean of cars. This morning, as always, the radio schmuck passed by my door, ajar to let in non-air, and turned up volume when he got right in front of it. At 7. I screamed at him in English. He smiled sheepishly and contentedly; didn't turn it down immediately, waited til I was completely awake on the usual four hours of sleep. I . . .

Ciao,
M.

Ω

Dear Edith,

When even the sand bears stretch marks, it's time to leave. Acap. has beaten me. I've stopped exercising, swimming, have lost my pick-up nerve, particularly with new gringas, and the last boy I hunted today, Paco, twenty, didn't blink when I said I was forty-two and made no move when I got up to leave. Pity. He has legs like fish, that shape and somewhat translucent, so that the network of corded veins pulse through. Long, slithy legs, slim, supple strong arms, like a shy French écolier and he was at Sotano Bier last night where I almost dragged my latest gringa, Lily, who, though a veggie, hustled drinks in whore bars for two years in the Canaries. We went to Foco Rojo in the red light district and couldn't wangle even a drink, barely a dance. An expensive dull night—nine bucks of fat Mexes not dancing right after I raved to her. It was Thursday, Acapulco ever cheaper and more abusive, I so old nature sags for me. My liveliness impaired, my desire to forge new words evaporated with my desire to forge new flesh. Haven't fucked in two long weeks. Series of exploitive fat men, one of whom I wangled shrimps out of and then necked for payment. Married of course but lied.

This morning decimated Pablo in presence of madre día. Remembered Greer destroyed by Tom Snyder, of all pendejos, every woman saw it and grieved. Played to the women out there—what to lose? The more I gain in hideousness, the more I gain in reckless intellectual strength. He respects women so much he won't read a book by one. Hit him with my women are dropped or pushed out of history spiel. He hit me with: is beauty related to sex? Of course, said I. See! he crowed, only men can see duality. Duality is an invention, not a given, I said. He called me sick but I'd already drunk his booze, leaving him to a notion of a "pure" beauty it was a proof of his superior intelligence to not define.

My god they're assholes. I can win every time but it costs me, as Lucio would say. It puts stretch marks in my appeal for men. Only they are allowed a blithe contempt while flirting. I must choose between sexuality and—what to call it—integrity? Dignity? "Self-constitutiveness, alas, a Kantian (?) term, is the only right word.

"Dassein," warum nicht? Shades of irrevocably lost academe where my mind was trained to see depths absent in Acapulco.

Don't understand Paco's rejection—that I stood him up once—but he understood that and asked me out again. I didn't want Pedro along. That I refused to tell him where I lived? (because you're corrupt Pedro's student, I said). He was hung over. What I wouldn't have given, give, to be in his strong arms last night at Sotano. And unlike all these recent male flops, he likes to dance. Sotano tonight and then Splitsville. Oaxaca? Taxco? Back to Zi? Shorn with no lover, no invitations in tow? I amaze myself by writing this. How dispirited I am no one can know in a godless world. Some guy teased his girlfriend and called her "sport" on the beach and I wanted Stan. Wanted that phony, proprietary affection couples dish out to each other. If we belong to each other, let's make it look good to the world.

Lucio. I writeth on about nada of him. Hideous from sagging belly and dry skin and cutesy hair on top middle-aged bod, I tried to avoid him in street but he chased me around a kiosk, cutely. Everywhere I turned, there he was. (I write this last sentence to show you I was loved.) So I threw the last of my almond drink on him and fled, then decided to board Caleta, our, bus. After a time he came to sit near me and flirted me back to a losing position, why go into details when I finally perceive larger patterns? That the details were never signs.

Kicked me lightly with his foot when I got off. My, he had spirit—he would've been a good match for me. The perfect age too. I am not perceived as a match, only a titty whore. Being pregnant—WHICH I AM!—does nothing to evaporate me in the direction of pure beauty. I am sure I'm pregnant from the ceaseless flow kitchen aide with the big ass. Whoever said it is right—Mailer?—you know when you've been knocked up that night. Remember? I wrote it to you.

Is this cast of characters alive for you? Then remember Hermelinda, that's her name, the little gravelly-voiced watermelon girl. Love her, love her, love her. Want her to be my own.

How dull I've let repression in women make me, and contempt in men. And, of course, my own aging flesh. But tequila restoreth me. Now drink in morning as well. E. I'm lost here. Still, we must do it (for me) one more time but together. Fuck it, mujer, one life, nada más.

[120]

Xist, will I be able to talk to you after these letters. Nah. As usual. How's Danny? You'll soon be able to tell me. I'll be back by the ninth. With mammoth bills and a registered letter from the feds two months uncollected waiting for me. They love their little sucker, fucking world. I got to learn to take, man. Felt like writing Diane, my great teacher in that, also to tell her to quit that evasive dyke life she's living. The world is so much bigger than Barrow Street women who work at being shapeless. Doris's lean flab and sour puss are another thing altogether, the real thing, I like it. But fabricated lesbianism, please. Ah! A Selma echo. Another dead trip, as any number of California Zi transients would say. I speak with borrowed tongues. Not the last time. Can you detect—

Another blackout! Upstairs to Manolo, triste imminent adiós in dying light.

He gives me ride to Mayita. Now that leaving, know how eat cheap. A fifteen-peso meal of many small full good-tasting plates. But writing to you restores my will to slimness so I throw up after setting the place laughing by asking for toilet paper. The food looks and smells delicious in the toilet bowl and I can barely keep myself from scraping it off the porcelain: Spanish rice, tortillas, and, shit, my protein—chicken in green mole sauce. Some beans.

Outside, the street smells of vomit. I need an excuse to be in the square and curse the lot of women, and in this case even men, that prevents me from tippling my anisette comfortably watching people stroll. So I walk over to the phones, needing to needle no one for more dinero but knowing en route that I have this look of a person not on her way to meet anyone. On the phone line, a fat Mex in front of me wears a T-shirt: "Blackbeards of Acapulco, Natural Insemination Team." There is nothing this town doesn't see. A moment later, a thinner one with "Acapulco Playboy." A boy snickers "perra" at me: dog here too! Having established my "raison de Zócalo" after five minutes, acting the anxious impatient, I leave to go to my café, where, as always after I throw up, I fill up on sweet café con leche and pastry. Cheap and skinny I didn't eat today. Here:

Eight oz. brandy and Seven-Up (Pablo) and an orange for breakfast. Negligible cost.

A plate of cunt and crackers: a cold fish cocktail "scviche" of "lapa," our own organ if ever I saw. 12 pesos.

A fruit salad cup from a vendor. This one pineapple, served, as always, with lime, salt and chili powder (or sometime sauce). There was also papaya, cuke, orange. Sometimes mango. Bargained him down to two pesos.

Two aguas de horchata. A sweet drink made from almonds, sugar, and the tan milky color of it from milk? Always at the bottom some dark fresh nut dregs, forever spoiling the immaculate French almond syrup, like scum, for me. Two pesos, one each.

A lemonade. One p. and a one-half glass refill free when I was at a low point after Paco fled past me as I was bargaining the fruit salad vendor down.

A coco frío. Fresh milk of young coconut only this one was old (therefore juiceless) so waiter filled hoary thing with water. Decided to get my 5 p's worth eating one half the coconut. Tall margarita at home.

Fifteen peso comida.

Tall glass hot milk with nescafé; one pastry.

Total: Forty-four pesos. There'll be booze at bar, and 12 pesos for my flask of anís.

My dear, nearly four bucks so far. Money. Food. All that's left. Have never dropped below 121 here and am probably over 123 by now. Am certainly pregnant. Ate nada in Zi and worked out all the time. Should go back but can't after all those postponements and tacky adieus and public sexual failures. Aquí también. Never coming back to Acap. without money and/or a female pal. And there's only one I have in mind. Think you'll dig Mex men. Saw this moderately tall one wearing well-fitting brown pants over tight round butt and beige print shirt with sleeves rolled up and underneath weave was brown too. Long straight black shiny hair, beautiful smile he was bestowing on his chiquita. Definitely you'd dig. No?

I look like Gina Lollobrigida—all non-hips in these pants—unless it's that my shoulders and barrel chest are so overwhelming, and this corporation on top. It's mostly natural and increased large rib cage but tell that to the natives.

I have nada to write. Is pleasant after those ordeals of streaking out driven letters to you full of events I felt compelled to consign to eternity. One morning, drank coffee here and smoked. No sleep, racked lungs, the sun dying out in the square, boys like flies and no surface to write on, rereading, editing, What for?

Have lost confidence. New York asserts itself from outside as well. Read Howar's trashy book and have my usual Gloria Steinem pangs of why-her-and-not-me-and-let's-get-it-on-before-I-reach-my-forties. Then Lily showed me Patty Hearst lost case in *Time* mag. P.H. bored me then and now. This morning Pablo lectures me on how Rockefeller was involved in Kennedy assassination. More boredom. Anxiety from returning scene, however. As Mexico's charm wanes, thoughts of old book ideas return and Haskell floats into mind when I think of my film book and how I'm dilettanting away every possibility by remaining here, not even learning any more Spanish because I learned enough to see that Mexican men didn't love me any more than any others ever have.

But life, as we know, querida, is fueled by fantasy and the current one is to hole up in the country and lose weight, stop smoking, work out, acquire social life, write great book on something or other, get gorgeous and then *return to Mexico!* Get it!? The exact reverse of the old program *for Mexico*. Mexico, because it has hurt me, is now the one I must show! And I now must use the States as a health retreat. Xist. That pattern at least I recognize from my past (no longer) life.

All this stale life and verbiage. No new thoughts. One new sensation today: Hot and dusty all day on beach—the fancy one with rough sea, so didn't go in. Walked along water's edge covered in sand and salt from quick dip. No coconut oil. Dry dry covered with film of salt. Every once in a while, from below, a shock of cold wet when the sea would reach my feet. Perfect.

Nobody ever tries to pick me up in this café. You must know its name—unbearable my letters should be dim shadows of my experience here—"La Flor de Acapulco." Can wring no ironic significance from its name but I'm sure as soon as I emerge from its safe confines into the square, one will drop on my head like a wad of bird shit.

Nah. Those days of portents is gone. Your literal ugly self is your literal ugly self. Grotesque that if I didn't have this flabby outer skin I'd be in superb shape from what I've worked out. Below high bathing suit bottom hip bones stick out and is curve of hard lower stomach. Middle stomach is flabby so that total strangers help me out by suggesting sit-ups which I used to do sixty or seventy a day of, plus swim and leg lifts, very good for stum. Will wear sign on stum saying I never had a child, my cunt is not stretched, I am not hideously old, I just used to be fat once. I am a girl, not a mother.

One of the gang of nice middle-aged men just came in, the kind who don't go to La Huerta, or at least are embarrassed about it. Who recognize their age. He is with a nice young sunburned North

American couple (but he is Italian), not with me. I am shunned as an unclear but nevertheless unclean quantity.

Am being kicked out at last. I hate to impose my lack of revenue on some nice waitress. Will leave her one and a half p. tip. I like sitting here too much to queer it.

No t. p. in toilet. More public appeals but this not a ribald establishment. Out in the square. Select a spitless spot and lack discipline to such an extent I mix Chiclet flavors. Chew three small packages at a time, add one or two when the flavor runs out. Go back to N.Y. (never! never!) with holes in my teeth but my belly filled. Oh my god. I think Mexican geezers are moving in on me. Need a toke of anís. My midriff bulges; it's uncomfortable leaning over to write on my lap.

Just lit a cigarette. Got it!! Smoking is not respectable for a woman! So long to get.

Cased out one more male color combo before left the Flor— deep brown (with lots of yellow in it) cotton knit shirt over pale lime sherbert pants of synthetic gabardine. Usual long full straight black hair. (Will any country ever be as dark and silky and hairless and color-coordinated as this?)

The problem with brown is it's indescribable by comparison with either the natural or artificial world. It only resembles shit. I always thought "café au lait" as a precise description of a certain color of black skin banal and vague. Here, I often put my arm against other people's (to compare tans) and there's always always a difference in color that frustrates me by its descriptionlessness. I've learned to see the different shades of dark hair but again, black is as hard as brown. There's a lot of dark brown hair too, actually. All these differences in a "homogeneous" group. Then there's beach hair, streaked actually blond by the sun, a sign of beauty and corruption.

Lucio's dark face. Took off his glasses (because I'd called them ugly once, no doubt), exposing a darker ridge, some ancient hard knock, above his left brow. A corrugated, subtly multicolored face, brown witty map of (he thinks) complete worldliness.

"You never give up," I said in the bus when he moved to sit across the aisle from me (here goes illusion—some guy across the square is finding me attractive, so I launch into details boring the world with a long story, believing in omens again). "What?" he queried in agony. You don't understand English, only speak it like a tape recorder, I answered, as fast as I normally speak and at regular volume. He understood this somehow and said I was a teacher, he wasn't as intelligent as I. My god! What a thrill coursed through me as I felt:

1. the usual pleasure of superiority
2. that I was hurting him effectively
3. that, Christ, he had finally recognized my value or had known it from the beginning. The most thrilling of all with its element of recognition, especially delayed recognition (either mine of his ancient knowledge of me or his recent one). And no longer actable—on either, adding tragic dimension. To be recognized. A connection was established.

Intelligence is my only vanity.

There's Manuela's friend Barbara walking arm around a mammoth blond middle-aged gringo. She must be a hooker. Manuela was supposed to meet me in Zoke last night to go with a group to La Huerta but it was a hastily proffered invitation and I admonished her that she'd have to pay her way. Natch, no Manuela and no one else either, not blond Harold who calls me "Marisco" (seafood) so that when I see "marisco" signs I feel another stab of sweet, painful self-love. I could almost weep when I see it. But Harold is more loyal to his buddies than to me and refused to crash the buffet at the Continental two nights ago after the free booze. I walked out in a huff, into the open car of one of my fat Mexes who actually did come back for me but not because he'd gone to Cornell summer school but because he hadn't collected on his drinks. I had looked good enough to be asked to dance by a thirty-nine-year-old Chicagoan in tight shape, an ironic bigot who introduced me to his skyscraper fourteen-year-old son and invited me to join them at their table for the buffet dinner. I misconstrued this as an invitation to a 190-peso spread but they pulled out tickets and when I didn't, it was an embarrassing parting, as he barely escaped the clutches of an impostor and hustler.

Time for more gum.

Tonight. Please, please let me find the courage to leave a dozen unsatisfactory men and rejecting discoteques and an unhealthy city and a diseased stalk. ("Sick! Sick!" yipped Pablo.)

Pick-up interlude with another chavo maleante de Acapulco—a waiter from the Foco Rojo—who knows a creep who abused me two weeks ago. Mario in Square knows another. Stab of intense pain. Waiter is now flirting with other woman who is with one of the chavos. Not deterred by other man—I solita once again. Just as well.

[125]

The most flattering thing he could think to say to me was that I was as attractive as tall blond Lily because of my frankness.

A small luminescent gray lizard in the square? After the multitudes of rats. Zócalo de las Ratas. Zócalo de la Pesta Manuela calls it. Vermin square. Mario loves it.

Rejected by asshole waiter. Too awful. Glued to this stone bench in mortification and depression. Can't leave, though must. Suddenly my resolve to go to Sotano Bier alone evaporates. Flimsy flimsy tissue of self-deception about my attractiveness and worth.

God. The style of this letter passes from that of Charlotte Perkins Gilman's *The Yellow Wallpaper* to anguished, unsuccessful Jean Rhys. How escape intact??? The middle-aged Canadian penis-bearers are in their accustomed corner but I can't regale them with self-deprecation any longer and they BORE me.

They find her more attractive than me. I can't think or write. The waiter cranes forth eagerly. They are teaching her to read a Spanish magazine for lowbrows. 1. They are *giving* her 2. Something respectable. 3. She's not even a writer. I kill self and serve self up as ceviche de gringa. Gringa cocktail. Doesn't translate—aha! Can now say that one thing only in Spanish.

Pain is wearing off. Amused superiority returns (illusion), a cycle that will forever repeat itself as yet another man fails to recognize the superiority of superiority, shocking me once more. They are spending time with her, not rushing her into fucky-wucky. Lord, continuing pain. Third guy was just called over by waiter, to supply further instruction no doubt. Three on her match, I go unsmoked. She has been given a cigarette as well! She's laughing, sticks out her bottom jaw when she exhales, quite the conscious smoker. The third has disappeared. The two are now earnestly instructing each other on some point for her benefit. They are giving her seriousness!!! Back to *Acapulco Enquirer*. Nobody notices me noticing their every move. Her original swain is standing up in front of her—she has been leaning in the direction of my waiter. Now he leans back—secure, the prick. Numero uno has left! She looks after him dutifully, to show she had no intention of choosing my waiter. He just crossed his legs. She's leaning now, still bent on deciphering her idiot mag. Using it, rather, as a way of maintaining respectable vocation, distance. He's blowing smoke up in a happy relaxed stream at heaven. Pain pushes my pen once again. Xist, I'm smiling ironically at myself, the two of us perfect companions for each other. She is slightly eager now though her cigarette is nonchalantly,

[126]

dangerously close to the rag. He is the attentive, casually tender, respectful husband, probably already dreaming of a mistress. Not I!! Aha! She has just noticed me! He has betrayed my frankness, of course. I must learn to play better. Unless it's that my pen has at last caught up with the speed of life and my mistress remark was written exactly when it happened and she checked to see who was around. He just turned around too! I avoided his eye.

First guy returned and bore her off. My rejected waiter has—is— ambling off, combing his hair publicly, a universal macho privilege now that they've destroyed our freedom to put on lipstick in public. Yes, he's gone. Gone. Gone. Gone. Gone. Gone. Gone. Alone at last. Alone alone alone alone. Dread freezing into something much stiller than despair: self-knowledge, the death of every effort.

I, alone, am emptying out the square! Freedoms of last nights, last rites, my shame never completely a source of indifference. Hardly any point in fantasizing a pick-up on the way to Sotano— dare I go?—since the waiter's object lesson.

My face, which I so blithely jutted forward in those early Zi days, thinking the sun's burning and the strangeness of Mexico had made invisible. Imprecise.

Flowers blow along the ground, the "Flor" echoes after all. It is that hour when that happens. The breeze of early morning, of tomorrow, of too late for pleasure tonight blows through here.

I have replaced Carolina! And set up real, no longer imaginary, residence in a Tennessee Williams play. Alma in *Summer and Smoke*, last scene. And of course, the metaphor suggested itself because of the Yellow Wall Paper. Everything does get used when you're sober too, only not as simultaneously.

In Oaxaca there are magic mushrooms. I'm afraid to take them, if I go, but must because the clearest envy Stan showed was when (this part dulls me somehow, to write) I mentioned the drug scene in Mexico. His new g. f. is an old hand and he doesn't want to be surpassed by castoff old comfortable zapata me. My dear, I'm embarrassing even the stones. It is time to go. The stones will hurl themselves at me when I do, or shield me within a safe high wall.

In the square chess continues, one long gang of aging boys, one of whom asked me for a light in perfect formal English before. I did not look up and he left politely, practically walking backwards and clicking his heels. So sure was he such a parade of polite form would enable him to bring my bloody carcass back to his lair. Two men; one, white shirt and red-orange pants, has noticed me noticing and

[127]

sits down. His pink-shirted, maroon-pantsed friend stands over him. Two school boys trade shrill anecdotes. Aha! One real seedy-looking pale and uncolorful guy slouches low on his bench with a cigarette, unlit (?), dangling from his lip. A distant short dark man of indeterminate age in day-glow shiny pink/magenta shirt, lilac pants, sitting near a hedge in the shadows. Pink and dark shiny plaid shirt, didn't quite catch the pants, had somewhere to go—strode through, neither left nor right. Two short chunky girls, promising to telephone. Distant group of older men. Minor bureaucrat in pale blue boxy shirt, navy pants runs past me, then subsides into a hip-swaying walk, too fat to be a fag, just self-conscious and pleased with himself. Two more men, white and red and mustache, mid-thirties, aha—open pink short-sleeved square shirt over white pants, two sets of square benches—enclosing trees over. An old North American geezer goes back to his hotel. A God-fearing short fat Mexican father hurries home. Chess, magenta, young men group, farther group, persist. Blockbuster built low, scratches chest past me, all in navy blue gym clothes. Girl goes to phone. Two more teenage girls. Chunky schoolgirls back. New dull man, Puerto Rican looking—go back where you belong. Two more schoolboys in white. Pink plaid—dark green pants, caught it—returns. Stops to chat with open pink over white. Boy on bike, never saw my fish before—I'm making history.

This interest in design patterns—Ch. P. Gilman. Everything serves. Bright yellow shirt, shiny, white pants. Can't can't can't can't. Have dutifully cramped my fingers and ass to bone but still lack courage to unglue myself from this scene and plunge into more dangerous one. Have a horror of going dancing alone because of Acapulco. Dark moss green shirt tucked into white pants. White for a dirty town. The waiter was red shirt over white pants. I, by the way, am wearing a burnt orange short-sleeved French T-shirt over pewter grey cotton pants. And a discreet amount of silver. Will it bring out the glow of the gray? My hair is not the tawny mass of yesterweeks but it is growing out, horizontally, alas, like the rats scurrying across the avenue out of the bushes. They frighten me but the men in low cars that honk discreetly can't touch me on my last night. I've stopped off, en route to dance, at a Mexican soft-ice cream restaurant to finish this letter because my bag will be stolen tonight and I must mail this. This fucking table wobbles. Now sitting in brilliant light on top of main drag so all of Acapulco will see I'm not only streetwalker but writer. Pen runneth out of its own color in service of so many others. My pud grins up at me under my orange tits. A dark man all in Charlotte's bright dirty yellow walks by. I never want to stop writing. As long as I write, I justify myself and escape pain but there is no more ink in this cheap pen. This one is better. For how long? Lord help me I am still praying for a respectable pick-up. Now I remember what I knew I'd forgotten to tell you. The reason I'm wending my way so reluctantly to Sotano is that the guy at the door is one of the Tortuga's owners and danced with me once at Chololo after which he contemptuously dismissed me. He makes p's in Acap. too and every time I see him, there's a repulsion (the nigger to dismiss me who didn't find him attractive!) and a fear that he will report on my hungry failure to Zi. Horrid, horrid. He will of course and everyone will know and shun me in the future. Bah. As Marty, who kicked me out after one unfruitful night, would say: People only care about their own problems. Correcto, as Harold would say. All gone gone.

I wish I spoke Spanish so I could really have become friends with Manuela, the closest thing to you in Mexico.

Ciao,
M.

Ω

Dear E.,
It is now 5:30 A.M. You wouldn't believe to what typical and unusual depths I've sunk tonight. Typical: let guy buy me one drink and I a. stick to him all evening b. buy him a drink c. share my anisette with him. Sum total: Exactly pay him back but not my freedom. Unusual and disgusting: am escorted, after begging, to cab by Marxist architecture student of the shared anisette who is a beefier version of Tom (the bore—no—never) and allow the twenty-year-old cabdriver to jerk off on my ass *in order not to pay the fare.* Don't even know till I get home, was so quick; feel wet spot. Pray Francisco the night clerk didn't notice. Nothing more to say. Is all too disgusting. Testing pens. Goes. Stays? Goes. Stays? Goes. Stays? Stays. Stays. Nigrah. Me me me mc—delgadita, como Alfredo in the good old days of discipline and neo-self-contempt, still theoretical. Alfredo, my waiter captain who treated me good, where are you? Oh Lucio, with whom I had a perfect balance of teacher and

taught, where are you? Twenty-four-year-old maestro and inimical friend? And beautiful phrases, Mexican slow dancing a foot apart. I like it, I said to hippy Mex—"charged distance"—where are you? I've sacrificed all on my last night and no phone messages from no one. It was all a mirage: Lucio, Alfredo, the twofer one. Lily, Pam.

I had two ecstatic pisses on beach—more than that can one ask? Also, I was best dancer on floor tonight. Did hustle by self and remembered how to move, even stone sober tho remembered that drunkenness did lead to takeover by rhythm center. Noted more songs tonight: "Get down tonight," "Baby Face," (Acap.), "Love to Love You, Baby" (ethereal carnality, interstellar sex as told Arturo, the second, the Marxist, tonight), "That's the way I like it," "Extra, Extra, Read All About It." "There is Always Another Girl." Good good music at Sótano, unlike more respectable Dôme. Danced moderately well and if weren't last night and if creep I was with wasn't so cheap, so ultimately sexually dull that had to beg him to rape me on beach, and if weren't so low in self-esteem . . . what? Plumb forgotten terminus this sentence. Wouldn't have allowed cabby to finally collectively collect. You think you saw it all in Harlem? Live a little in Acapulco. Scum everywhere. Pimples of discontent on face, legs, cunt. Itch there. A crab perhaps. An ass rash. DISEASE. Must leave but won't. Will fuck Paco first. My last Acap. lay. A la.

Several days later:
Still in Acapulco. The most astounding juxtaposition: on what was to be my last day here before Taxco run into Arturo who takes me later into the world of *The Children of Sanchez*! Too rich to describe effectively. Phrases, themes, all I can manage at usual 5:30 (?) A.M. Spending hours speaking or listening to Spanish when don't understand the language is sensory overload. Ar.: 1. his decimation of me 2. sexual description 3. the long evening penetrating into the barrio. ("Colonia" here, is equivalent to barrio?) 4. his friends (I am to be a little girl's godmother on Wednesday—is too incredible if all this insanity comes off), smoking, drinking brandy, intense sexuality of lower-class Spanish 5. Sex with Arturo 6. My and his bad taste. 7. My profesor del caló. An evening of slang, his chingas su madre and chingóns and chingadas and chingadazas reminiscent of Manolo (physically too) but more elaborated. Is navigator on destroyer, is no accident he resembles Doris.

I smell my burnt orange top for pit odor and instead smell

[130]

cigarettes, his mild sweat: the smell of an evening with friends. Sex with him may not be good but I feel alive in my body for the first time since Zi, in a different way. I think I may penetrate him (is that why I found myself humping my mattress an hour ago?) Evanescent feeling—can no longer smell my T distinctly since am smoking—feel humanized, life-giving force of human contact, continuity, prosaic acts. No. Anyway, he will stand me up tomorrow for dinner at six in the shack of Rosita and Imaculato. Smell of T reminded me of Tom, familiar odor. Familiarity—family—is in the offing. Uncontrollable fantasies of him moving in here; he is supposed to buy me a dress (por respeto para sus amigos) for the baptism. Wish you could've been there to hear his rich slangy language. Soul is playing on radio, we're sitting drinking good brandy—San Marco?—he's flirting with Alicia, the little girl, who is bouncing from one person to another delightedly receiving love. Imaculato's niece and nephew come in. A discussion of why the niece isn't in school, which escapes me. I ask her directly. She is eager to tell me to my delight, a direct contact which I can't make use of, understanding almost nothing. Delicious roasted chicken from a store, Rosita's own fresh chili sauce in a rough stone mortar. We dip the bird into the sauce and eat without forks or napkins, I lick my fingers clean and then rub what's left into my skin and pick up Alicia—I am her "madrina" so must establish physical contact and she has to give me a kiss on the cheek too—and am no longer afraid of her clean dry sweat, a film of potential sweat; everything is oddly clean, though I can't piss in the communal dump outside once I feel soft wads underfoot and smell shit. They spend hours insisting I go but I don't, thinking too that my finesse is a mark of class that can't but make Arturo love me. His beautiful maroon clothes.

Don't know where to start.

Then there's the twenty-year-old's glasses—cold, transparent, like water—and his dry smooth skin. Again the thrilling counterpoint of dusty body and wet feet of the beach the other day. The evening at Le Dôme, Lily, our boys, "ciclos de deseo," two potential macho fights over nada so I finally believe *Sanchez* (*Sanchez* is coming alive). Before that Sotano. Dancing—what it's like in Mexico and the U. S. In Zi and Acap. as well. Felt so good from dancing, and well, at Sotano Friday night, and at Le Dôme Saturday night. At Sotano, because did well and with three boys, and because felt desirable for first time in weeks. Dancing gets me into exercise again.

[131]

Andrés: his essence crept back unbidden, Proust-like, Saturday on beach. Remembered—felt it anew—my passion for him, quite unlike Lucio thing. Wholeness that can never be repeated. I know too many Mexicans now but then he was the first I met in a strange and beautiful country and he was the country. Everything referred itself to him. He was my sole symbol. Now, experience is fractured, and I must strain after metaphors, when before everything was him in a premetaphoric state. I remember him as pirouetting, and one image repeated itself again and again: him swirling past me in a half-round while giggling, past my clutches, at the door of my room in Zi. He had a fag's shivery femaleness. Then another of him beaming tenderness at me in the night, illuminated from the left by the light from the shower at the back. Then, less specific, how he'd bounce into the courtyard and thrill me with his presence. Life had acid when he was around.

My surrogate parents here: Donna and Al whose love sky-rocketed when they let me discover they weren't Jewish but Italian. (?!!?) It is too much. I can't. I flag.

Guttersnipe appeal: polite men of my own class are unacidic. Perhaps not my own class. Young, I was upwardly mobile, dug Harvard boys. Bores me now. In Mexico, even before at Lehman, where dug brilliant black Jacky Richards, one of my students, who wrote marvelous accounts of 'his childhood in South Carolina. Absolutely incorrect but I thought of him as a black Dostoevsky (perhaps because of D's *White Nights?*) and had been dancing "off" him and Tina Turner til hit Acapulco, where my act fell apart to be reconstructed into an almost natural Mexican style. Got a lot of confidence working off nostalgic memory of American blacks in Zi, knowing Mexicans would think I'd imported hip. Danced way imagined Jacky would, and way Tina did. The sexual fantasy was Jacky, the imitation was Tina. Men and women.

"Volleys of spit." Spitting in Mexico. Love the guttural sounds, each with different function.

Next day: Lily says he'll show but not with my luck. He's hard to masturbate to, but I force myself, part of my masturbation disci-pline, exercise like others, force myself to stay hot. Part of the difficulty is he did a superb description of how he makes love, also thereby providing me with body vocabulary, straight and slang. First he abused me.

I ran into him, he into me, at Caleta and forced him to stay;

[132]

told him truth, he still bitter, how can I prove my sincerity, I said, that I'm cured of vengeance? Some remark about my "pussy." I stared in bitter disbelief but continued to try and soften him up. I mooched hundreds of his cigs, fearing he'd split if I went to get mine and getting three-minute stalls with each one as well. Finally, invites me for a beer and begins a long peroration on how he hasn't the slightest desire for me. Looks down at my belly and says one, two, then looks above ass, three rolls, only one is permitted. Flips my underarm flab—just a relaxed arm, is all; says I should row. What about my legs, I ask, standing up. The same, he says. Your only attractive features are your breasts and what lies between your legs. It's big, he says, do you stuff it with paper? Something about a horse, laughing all the time. I am sitting over a beer he's just bought me in shocked disbelief that I'm still sitting there. Pinned by the unutterably awful. Do you want me to lie, he asks, like other Mexicans. La Verdad Mexicana, I say bitterly. No, my truth, he insists. I have no reason to lie, don't have the slightest interest in you. Is this your idea of vengeance, I ask. He denies this and I ask why if he finds me so unbeautiful and undesirable he approached me in the first place. My intelligence! he answers, he seeks friend- ship is all and evidently intelligence is visible in those incapable of language. Do you want me to tell you you're beautiful, he asks. You're not. But you are intelligent. Anyway, he goes on, he's getting married to a twenty-nine-year-old university teacher of literature. Pulls out a photograph of her which is on her school I.D. which says "Normale Superiore." University? I wonder aloud what she sees in a sailor and don't understand his answer. Conversation modulates into sex. He doesn't with her, she's a virgin, but does with married women. I ask him what he does, figuring fuck it, might as well get sex out of this since won't get love and he gives a lengthy descrip- tion of an act he says takes one hour at least.

It is now six. He isn't coming. I'm too tired to continue.

7:30.

Cycles of desire, cycles of vengeance, motorcycles of despair. Of course I will chronicle the whole thing but first I must say, how fitting that he should have completed the vendetta by standing me up. . . . I like it!

Back to him. About his girl: she's ugly, he said, but not to me. Una morena, through she looked lighter than he. I expressed shock at twenty-nine-year-old virginity, sealing my own doom. How he must have hated me, and I thought he was so lonely, thirty-three,

Doris. Probably not hate. Probably just standard Mex treatment of cunts. The beach boy with rotten teeth who rents inner tubes who's been giving me friendly smiles for a month and who today waggled his thick long whitish tongue in the direction of my cunt forever should've told me what it did: that I am a thing for them, that I am never humanized through friendliness, intelligence, hours of athletics, daily contact, whatever. But they love their own women—this is not such a racist country.

His sex act: he starts by kissing the mouth, then the cheeks (I will have to omit a lot through forgetting), spends a great deal of time on the shoulders (a word that sounds like hombre) and then the shoulder bones. He goes down to one breast until the nipple (boleta?) is hard, then to the other. Shows me how is only gentle licks with tongue at this point. Then to ombilico—asks me English word: one of our/his pacts, remembered from old first meeting, is that he is to be my professor of slang, and new addition, I his English professor, for which he will pay me whatever I want—circles one direction, then other. Down one leg, stopping at back of knee, all way down to toes, up other. He stops the account. Nu? I ask, breathless. The cunt: he parts it? Gives the cleetorís picatitas—quick small darts of tongue. I'm getting unbearably hot writing it. Hearing it, was suspended in agony of desire to be getting wet from man who found me oh so excitingly repulsive. Slow slow narrative—I in state of suspended animation, not believing this as I didn't believe the earlier abuse (and let me not forget to go into my tit-for-tat response—later, más tarde). (Why are you saying these things to me I asked, on the point of tears, willing them, that's when he said do you want me to tell you you're beautiful.)

Sex: think he circles in one direction, then another, on clit too. ("Quién no mama, no ama," he was later to say: who doesn't suck doesn't love.) Then harder, tongue more extended, long laps from underneath. I am staring at his Aztec face using his tongue so privately it is like listening to whispered conversation, straining to understand every word, which, as with Manuela, I do. My cunt rather than my head is the intelligent agent. I can't believe I'm hearing this superb recital of superb sex. When he feels her heaving and her eyes roll back into her head—and here I nearly pass out—he kisses her eyes! Then, good things ending never, he is inhaling (?) into her air. A small clarification period at this point, no clarification however. Tongues the ears, usual. Now spends time on cheek bones. When do you enter (penetrate, my theme word for Arturo) I

[134]

ask. What pleasure do you get. Assures me his pleasure is giving pleasure: feeling a woman que se mueve. His leg and mine are no longer touching companionably as they were sitting at the water's edge earlier, or before the abuse sitting in a sort of impressionist beer garden area of Caleta. Dumb cunt to the end, nth, I machinate how to restore sex or create it de ovo, never scenting an ancient ploy.

(Am presently sitting in a brightly lit restaurant pouring out my anís in a furtive public way into the empty glass I requested of the waitress. I stink of anisette but am almost free because of fatigue and anger.) What's the point? I spent a superb day penetrating Mexico in a state of sexual desire. I must learn not to want more. But I do. The closer it got to six, the more my juices flowed—though I was hard to come—when I thought of him and oh what pleasure, moving him into my room, standing proud madrina next to his padrino at Alicia's baptism in the church. Shopping for clothes he was going to buy me—such a turn-on, being bought clothes by a man you desire. Remembering his matching cablestitch short-sleeved maroon sweater with buttons, over his square-elegant loose, exactly matching maroon pants. Big Indian feet, his palms almost as dark as his skin, his hair that I ate, short but spiky, clean and fine though it looked coarse. Tu eres guapo, I murmured, but all he said was mamacita. He was in bed with a thing; I was trying to enact my desire for him. Explaining my standing him up to Lily I said the man had to be attractive to me and understood for first time discipline so tight was able to deny desire, rise above it, female macha like male macho. CONTROL. My dear, I lost, lost, lost, lost.

Well, after ears and if she still wasn't hot, a repeat on clit, he enters and first his movement is despacito, circles in one direction, then other, pulls out tantalizingly, plunges in. Repeat. Refrain. Pain.

When we made love, though didn't either of us consummate, he stared hard at me to see me when he/I came. Xist. Xist. Xist. Xist. He said he was arriba—not full contact. At some point in the narrative—here I flagged for want of interest (I'd come already) her legs over his shoulders. More or less end.

My abuse: his stuckout ears, elephant ears, he laughingly obliged, wrinkles in the soft skin below his neck, his yellow and red eyes, filled with almost veins. So unsmooth were they I later saw. Borracho eyes, I said. Here they're marijuana eyes, he said. His skin,

[135]

yellow as well, and his teeth a bit. Hair on part of his legs. A nose that turned up a bit when it shouldn't have at all. His shapeless delgado than should've been, somewhat boxlike. His hair too short, his clothes (at the beach) cheap-looking (a bad safari chambray shirt, beach togs). Of course he was delighted to hear this; I (who have absolute taste I informed him) should teach him how to dress as well. He's on the point of ordering more beer but I say no. We sway off down beach and I introduce him to Donna, after asking him if he wants to be presented to her. "Hello, Señorita Donna," he drunkenly, lower-classly responds, embarrasing me beyond help. Have you eaten, he asks. No. On to my hotel, "Vacaciones" (!!). En route maps out evening: I will change, he will change at a friend's in town, we will go to eat in the mercado (NO!) and then visit a friend who has the best café Mexicano in the country; every week a new shipment with buds. I wonder at this special trip for coffee but I HAVE FOUND HIM AGAIN and am his wherever he goes.

I change. He's still there. Hope he digs my ass in tight Stan jeans, my size now, though for how long?

(I can't believe he's gone—what pleasure we would have given each other. I must call the hotel. He can't have stood me up.)

Back home, no message. Francisco asks me what's up, something about la buena vida. I give him a third finger salute and say, "Chinga a la buena vida," which I hope means fuck the good life and doesn't take personally but he turns an offended back to me. What the fuck do I care? I can't believe this country's brutalization of me.

How is it possible to go on—*Memories of Desire* my novel— describing a beautiful past full of future happiness when I feel the usual outrage and humiliation. How to cure myself of illusion alguna and at what enormous cost in sparking fantasy. I should've known by the certifiable elaboration of my own fantasy that A. would not show. And something more concrete: the way he actually did make love, calling me mamacita and not Marisa, rushing through his repertoire mechanically, taking not one, not one moment of delight in my body or me, not thrilled to be in bed with the me as I was with the him. Telling the assembled company outside I had a lot of pubic hair. Asking was it sí or was it no for a hotel with him and sounding like the final judgment. Not noticing when I called him guapo. Asking me to go down on him. Almost pulling my head down. Shit, clues are clues; only I try to charm and nag indifference into affection, try to prove indifference exists to the

[136]

indifferent, so they will love me for my insight? What insight??? A schmuck sailor I stood up asked me to marry him and I said I didn't believe him! Who else would bother?! Edith: A PERFECT REC-ORD, do you realize? of being fucked-over. This one the most elaborate setup yet unless it comes with natural elegance to these people to lie. One exploitative asshole after another asks me to be his English professor, just name my price and I believe. I believe every lie, every flattery, every program for the future.

Tonight, on my way home, the cops tried to stop me again. "Hey, Lady, mira," so I crossed the street and saw another cop car pull alongside the first, after which it U-turned, so I crossed again, the first having gone ahead. No problems. They knew I knew they weren't kosher, so they left me alone. Like the geezers in the square knew that to be a godparent was not an honor but a way for Mexicans to collect. But Donna said it was an honor for them to have a gringa godparent. Men know how evil they are and they talk about us being exploitative. What an asshole I must've looked last night nodding to soul music on brandy, understanding not a word of their talk, the perfect exploitable dunce. Of course when I jumped at asshole's suggestion that he buy me proper church attire, the gig was up. Even planning, I, to buy the little chinga girl a present—some diminutive gold earrings. I would've been a generous compadre in my own flattered, cheap way. A little girl after all (though Hermelinda was my choice). Xist, what corruption poverty breeds. And males. How naturally corrupt they are. If women but knew they'd be infinitely more powerful and sad unto death. I must keep reminding myself that a few young attractive women score. Oh Xist. One of the thrills of losing weight in the Big Apple was to have men find me attractive so I could then reject them in perfect good faith. Repugnante, disgusting.

Should I resume my chronicle See. I still believe in love to do so. Sí. Mira mira.

I have never been so exploited by a country in my life, so abused and lied to. Hear me, great judge in the sky and render justice!

For all this, I love this country like no other. I love its landscape, its beautiful people, its language, its misterioso. About its sexual slang, Lily asked, it was hard to remember on the spot: When I wouldn't piss on shit slope, Arturo said she digs being gone down on but won't shit outside. He proudly informs me Imaculato was his oral sex teacher. Imaculato, sitting, is fed a piece of chicken by Rosita, standing, so the meat is at the same level as hers. He stares up at her wantonly and blows the chicken while he's eating it. Reaches hand under her dress to feel her pussy. A million chingas change mouths. Everything referred to sex. The niece and nephew are present while all four of us are smooching. Xist, Arturo him I loved. I was bastante pendeja to tell him "Yo te amo," like the song.

I mustn't ever leave here or I won't get back, or I'll be old when I do. How to hack it? I'm willing to sacrifice my life to pursue Mexican illusions. It's a fever this country. I am hopelessly in love with Arturo. The same precondition of time existed with him as with Andrés, only he is not a twenty-year-old Andrés.

Did like his body. Absolutely smooth where was no hair and hair only on outer thighs. Hard diminutive butt, strong legs, puzzled Aztec face in bed, that hair, purple mouth not as full as mine or as I like but full enough. Brown, large eyes in dirty whites. The pupils reflecting light so they looked white like in *Omega Man*, though they were dark. Like pieces of glass in his eyes. The perfect height— two inches taller, maybe six, ten pounds heavier. We were a boxy, companionable pair of matching playmates. Oh A. A. A. A. A. A. A. A. E.—do you believe me? Could anyone? I adored him. Followed him like an intelligent charmed dumb one—in both senses—into the exotic lower life of Mexico.

He had a sister who is a lawyer but is washing dishes in Houston. I believed. At fourteen he was a waiter in "Quinta Raquel," one of the three top whorehouses; at fifteen, a barman. I believed. Adopted by an American evangelist, won first prize of "oratorio" (?), some religious category—but was discovered to be parented, so unadopted after four months in States. Believed. All this after, at beergarden, French, French, he had ASKED ME TO MARRY HIM! Why, I ask, to live in the States? No—he knows the States— sister, evangelists, is shit. Why if getting married in June and find me sexually unattractive? Because with my background—intellectual, American—I'm worth far more in Mexico. We could open up a negocio together (CLUE!!). Why, if you don't care about dinero? To buy me all the asshole things women always want. You perceive he pulled a circular argument on me and didn't think I'd notice? I did and didn't. I believed he wanted me for my class and that my class made me infinitely sexually attractive. Xistos. (My whore value is 500 pesos after all, by the way, he said.) They know how our desire for love overwhelms our intelligence, they know it all over the world.

Penetration, Alice in Mexicoland, into *Sanchez*: Taxi to where he rents a place to change into civvies. I spurn its toilet (newspaper for t. p.). A poodle and her two pups, a parrot in a cage. Chickens and turkeys, plants in rusty oversize cans. Pink houses. Him him him. I in tight jeans, light-haired by comparison, spangling clean and beautiful, in love, while he asks me to wait on corner while he goes into grocery store (to be with a cansada, I out of the way?). No, have watch fixed. He explains five enormous tourist buses are part of current president's entourage. He's staying at "Plaza International" Hotel, lessons, understanding, evening before dusk, neat floral streets. The señora a pleasure. He pleasures her somehow, and before, on the way, a hose pissing on sidewalk in front of us, arrested by some witty remark of his. Manuela.

He emerges in best clothes. I am helpless. Even before, in pink, mangoed streets had thought: I'm in love. Cab. To a poorer place than before. In the hills. A "colonia," at last. I can't can't do justice. Concrete floor, TV, gas stove, good radio. Double bed. Cots. Few clothes in open closet. Laughing young light-skinned black Mexican woman, pregnant. Fortyish man with melted eyes and tender filthy endearments matched by her. "Chingón viejo," I think, once, understood because of one of innumerable lessons of Arturo: old lady, old man for one's lovers. No, wasn't chingoń viejo. Mexican coffee turns out to be pot which, flatteringly, A. assumed I'd remember as a lesson he gave me our first meeting.

I am in a state of blessed exhaustion—four hours sleep from Sotano Friday night, three hours from Le Dôme, Saturday. So don't inhale the smoke and space the brandy and so laid back don't mind not listening, appearing out of place and stupid. Want only to savor the unbelievably hip adventure of being in Sanchezland, living in the book! and digging good music and that A. has friends who dig good music. Sing some words along, so will appear superhip importation and intelligent though dumb-seeming.

The first "she walks, she talks, she thinks" epiphany occurs. Mac. remembers me from market. Oh oh, I think, one of the innumerable filthies I was pissed at. Some story. Takes me minutes. Finally I remember: he sold plastic cloth. "And you said 12 pesos," I said. "Aha! What a memory," he said. She walks, she talks. Rosita meanwhile is preparing, serving, cleaning, fetching, sending out to fetch. I'm too tired to be uncomfortable and glom onto the sociology only eventually: R. is one of I's unmarried wives. Alicia is their child.

[139]

They are physically and psychologically extremely affectionate with each other and with their child and Arturo with Alicia is unbearably tender and sexual. I am melting from a thousand reasons in a thousand regions of my brain and body. A single hanging bulb. We put out our cigarettes on the floor. Arturo in his maroon pants that don't show his prick. Oh lord. Good brandy, another lesson. Arturo faultlessly (almost tremulously) telling anecdotes, heavily sexually spiced. I NEEDING TO UNDERSTAND NOTHING MORE THAN WHAT I DO—entiendes? Experience full enough so I don't need language—language might even be distraction from tone. Oh Xist. Imaculato's drunken eyes ringed by laugh lines, Rosita's sprightly light black tenderness and pulled-back wavy hair. Fat Alicia beaming up at others while Arturo is being her slang professor and physicalizing her, Imaculato reaching under Rosita's dress. The lilt of her retorts and acceptance. Always Arturo's maroonness illuminated by the single warm yellow bulb. The ease of cigarettes on the floor, brandy in cup, chicken in fingers, all effortlessly available whenever they are because I'm too tired to want, or for schedules. Such an easy pace therefore. Every once in a while some discussion directed to or about me which shows me that though I'm laid-back I exist; there is connection (unlike with Manuela). How? That I am a physical, specific presence in the room. I accept this and am comfortingly reassured of reality, and perhaps affection, of being included. No, I can't. That I am as real for them as I am for myself. (Close enough.) Reassuring.

I want mostly to just dig the music and brandy and glamor of the experience. Arturo asks me whether I want more chicken. No. Grass. No. Tongue. Sí, I say, forgetting the absence of Mexican comprehension of gringa irony. I add, hastily, I'm savoring the experience but I must say this incomprehensibly for he asks me about splitting to an otro lado. I dig foursome smooches, chaperoned sex, the first time around, even always, so I must somehow indicate this, not resist begging any longer. So physically remote was he to me throughout our stay there previously. Foursome smooch begins. I am unaware of this but our scene must seem realer than theirs because they split. Xist. We kiss a while. Then he removes my lower garments and I tremble fearing he will only remove his lower ones when what I want is his chest: that is, a proof of totalness, of estheticism, and an experience of his beautiful upper torso. Wordy. He removes his shirt first. Xist. Relief, desire flood me. I remove mine. I don't want animal sex. He leans his length down upon me.

[140]

Must stop—out of cigs. Drunk—will be hung over mañana and will miraculously have to postpone leaving in order to pursue Arturo.

All I want is some man to take delight in me.

5:30? 6:30 A.M. as usual, no cigs. Better a maudlin drunk than a sterile one. My pimples are more like small boils; I have the plague. My lip is split. My tits are swollen and I can't ever sleep. I now breathe with my heart, which skips rope.

Back to sex?

First: utter clarity of all omens telling me what would happen and was happening with Arturo this morning in dawn light while birds chatter. Guts snake into chest. Illusion cleared like mist. Talked about how massage would cure my face, I think, for a minute. Lily said sailors are the same as beach boys. Gilberto said the Mexican man flatters women (always, always promises to see her in the future). Arturo telling me how I looked to him, that he was getting married, then hitting me with an absurd proposal. Those keen questions disguised as casual comments: and of course we can't go to your hotel, he says. Of course not, I aver. So, has to fork out for hotel to cheap godmother. What's in it?

Those eyes in certain bright Mexicans of lower or bohemian class that suddenly go blind. Stare ahead reflecting light, not hearing you or seeing you; or doing so in pain? A little vacation from consciousness in the middle of a conversation.

Sex: horribly anxious because of his description. Tried making myself come, which disturbed him, which disturbed me but even without, couldn't've. I didn't let him come because I feared he would forsake me if I did.

Outside, he discusses me and I protest. Also kept telling him during sex that I don't like to be called mamacita. He said it was an endearment (una carillena. Also: "mujeriego"—womanizer; grosera and its vulgar verb. Oh yes: longeza, longaleza—a stretched-out form of "length"). But I want to be Marisía. Ma-ri-sía, he says. You like la longeza, huh? "Sí," I answer, "sa-bro-so." He actually tries to repeat this sequence to a bored Rosita and Imaculato, so charmed is he, so less could they care about the antics of a gringa. Arturo says I will teach Rosita English but she says she can neither read nor write, she is a real ranchera.

Tennessee Williams stalks me so. He has an actual rose tattoo on his chest. "I have a rose, you have a rose, what is dee problem?" he says.

[141]

Wry blind eyes, bored blind eyes, pained blind eyes. Eyes cocked at angle, diagonally upwards—Manolo, Arturo (?) Straight ahead—Lucio. Don't remember Andrés's—think laterally diagonal.

Well, back to Camino Real. Neighbor adolescent boys sitting on step. Us on small chairs. Tied-up turkey. The niece and nephew in and out of our charmed circle. I say mamacita would like if he comes to N. Y. and he's Mexican, and everyone will call him Paco I lie, remembering a Lily story. But I'm not Paco, I'm Arturo, he says, pained. And I'm not mamacita! He beams that: she walks, she talks, look folks, she's my girlfriend. Second and last of such epiphanies.

He teaches me a four-part handshake. 1. ordinary, meaning ordinary. 2. with thumbs—comrades. 3. with tips fingers pull—"macitos" (?) Potheads? 4. Up with delicately fisted arm as if sounding crystal air, an elegant little jerk, or knock, "Mokos." Also potheads? Or good luck with getting laid. I master this to everyone's amusement. What filtho thing has he taught me?

Tells me story how he tells gringas their ass is big in Spanish and they don't understand. Everyone laughs but me, who says it's cheating, which I can't say in Spanish. So say cheap and explain. Clues everywhere, only I blind like the gringas, I don't see when I'm being laughed at. I teach him some Harlem shake which elicits a volley of spits from the adolescents, which I assume is an indication of delight. I say I'll teach him how to dance to "musica moderna" but though the niece brings out a radio, this comes not off.

So. It has been arranged that we shall meet Monday night at six for dinner, and Wednesday will be the baptism. Also his day off and we will buy me clothes. But not so quick: I have also offended everyone by offering the six-year-old niece a toke of brandy, so stoned am I that I must test to see if this is the real world, ready to swoon in delight if she accepts at the sheer dreaminess of it all. She scurries off offended. It was only a joke, I say. De mal gusto, he says. Like your remarks about my pubic hair, I add. I am shocked at everyone's shock, and at how they protect children but not women.

I feel suddenly cheap and bereft. "Sí o no, Marisía," he says into my ear, my good one (I had problems getting him to walk on my good side when this meant I was alongside the street—and he's no macho!). O. K. I finally say, fatigued into despair that all this rich texture should resolve itself into something so banal and uncaring. In the cab I insist he stop off and buy contraceptives and then I say, if I go with you tonight, you won't see me tomorrow or Wednesday, so choose. He chooses the Vacaciones! I'm in love! I watch for signs of anger but his arm is still around my shoulder, though just hanging there. I squeeze his thigh through loose synthetic pants. Again that blindness, that sign of discontent. Finally he kisses me. (Xist—how many cabdrivers have seen me kiss how many men—why he never came? My sex life running the cab circuit.) I like the way he kisses at least and know I'll like sex if only he'll provide the personal element. Complained he didn't all night. Assholes are born, not made. Not borne, made. And I want him all sober, like with Lucio, want to really get into him.

He makes the cab go on a bit before my hotel. Por qué? I get out and look anxiously back. "Mañana a las seis," he reassures me. It is a little after eleven, and Francisco asks me what's up. Maybe something good! I answer and bound upstairs and fall asleep with the light on. (The light in their room; against the wall so that it was behind him and to the left when he sat in front of me charming their daughter. Soft light.)

How is it possible after all those invitations and the godmother thing that he should stand me up??? Taking me to his friends. My, how Rosita worked her ass off while Imaculato sat around. *She* didn't drink, or smoke, or toke. Clues.

I'm exhausted and miserable. Forlorn. Hopeless. It could've been so good with him. But even he thought he was too good for me. Just feel the loss of repeating that good night in the future. So rich, so rich. But he was just a Mexican version of male, incapable of love. And I incapable of anything else. "You were laughing at me after you stood me up," he said. No, crying, I said (like when you hurt something you like in order to induce self-pity; locked up a kitten in a basement when I was fourteen). He was my kitten, how I loved him, how I loved redeeming him. I should've known he'd want to laugh at me. Vengeance comes full circle again to me, where pain belongs. All I feel is the loss, he was thirty-three so it would've been possible to have a marvelous ten days. Now nada nada nada nada. And though I can't believe he won't, he won't suffer. The godmother proposal—just to test if I'd accept, take flattery or ridicule or acceptance of them to an extreme? Had spoken not three words to Rosita when she asked.

Incredible story, no?

Were they shocked when they walked in and saw us nude? After all their carrying on? Did the gringa unwittingly violate the usual dozens of taboos—who knows what goes here? Only I, apparently, can be violated.

I can't write about dancing or Le Dôme. Love's loss obsesses me. How sweet it is. . . . I like it. Men are missing something.

Oh well. Think the old boy was showing off a gringa and a professor yet to his chums in the ghetto. I the chump. Dig this asshole style yet. Dig how I can't say asshole and live in this country. Shit. Shit Holder bombs again. Xist . . .

Hsst. Pssst. How they call you. Walk past you and if they dig what they see, spit. Shit, "Chumino." Other cunt word, very vulgar. Were mine, too? How in bad taste I must've seemed, an illiterate blithely mouthing vulgarities with a heavy foreign accent. Imagine some bozo from Sweden who doesn't speak English beaming foolishly as he shows off his "pussy" and "prick."

Ciao, pussy.

Oh yes—I said "a volley of spits" out loud and Arturo wanted to know what I said. Couldn't translate of course and that's when I knew I could never live in Mexico permanently. Knew it even before when Rosita called Imaculato—that was it! a "pinche viejo"—she could curse but it would always seem cutesy and vulgar if I did. I could never never speak "naturally." I would always be an imitation, an embarrassment even. A cloddish Kraut.

("Volley of spits" is difficult. God knows I can usually paraphrase, good lexicographic training speaking to foreigners—Ying—or being one yourself. 1. Not sure I have specific enough grip on "volley." 2. (perhaps because of 1.) is connotation rather than denotation that characterizes the expression.)

Ausgespielt at last. Restored to sanity by little linguistic push-up.

Nearly went insane a few hours ago trying to sleep. Suddenly all the strangeness of Mexico fell away and I had no protection any more. Perhaps it was because like my T, which smelled not only of Tom but of all my lovers before him, this rejection felt to every sense like every rejection. There was a muddle of sense memories which resolved itself into being back at Cornell. I kept staring at my blue towel wishing myself back in Mexico but the turquoise walls weren't Mexican, they were just turquoise walls. Perhaps it was being out in the street at seven? in grubby clothes, braless, with a hideous haircut, no beautiful hair to delude me, just like after an all-night grind writing papers. I was overcharged for cigarettes which made me feel un-in the place, and saw

[144]

men going off to work, dozens of them not noticing me, as in serious life.

I tried to read myself to sleep when I got back, a cheap Gothic, and suddenly some complex insight about tone seemed to brew below the surface of consciousness. I didn't—couldn't?—pursue it. What I let assail me was disdain for my previous self-congratulation over an idiot's linguistic understanding. And I remembered how I used to do real work, have genuinely accomplished insights at Cornell and in C.U.N.Y. and how I'd either lost some intelligence or, and, had let myself run down, had opted for ease and stupidity. Must've been brooding all the time I was writing over my insouciant imprecision. The illusion of my intelligence destroyed, the fabric of my personality shredded, I closed my eyes and had a vision of my father helping two other men toil a jeep filled with heavy articles up a short flight of stairs in a completely dark place except for a source of light on the right. His heart was pounding, his lungs, actually, and I thought why hasn't he been told that what he's doing is physically dangerous and could lead to death. The thought of his dying off in the northwest before we got to know each other filled me with panic. Almost I could describe *why* it was profoundly awful, thinking Howar, no one has done justice to the experience in literature.

Probably it was that I'd been so close to a source of love and hadn't been able to touch it, to the concept of family. The false metaphor of hearth suggests itself: Arturo and Alicia bathed in the bulb's glow on the far side, myself just beyond its warmth. But this is cheap writing. Insanity's virtue is that it restores dignity so one doesn't stoop to cheap, untrue verbal descriptions. Somehow it must not have been a Mexican adventure but a real need for me. I must've wanted like anything to be loved, have felt I could be, by him. But again, before I went out for cigarettes this morning, I saw my real face in the mirror and knew I was ugly here like I was ugly there. Life was real for him only I was . . . I can't find the correct way to say it. In rapid succession, then, I must have felt I'd lost not only love but my beauty, my intelligence and my health. My lungs are unusually sacrificed when I write to you and then if I produce inferiority . . .

No good. I've lost the experience. What is clear this late morning is that, before it totally wears off (and writing's function is to make the self persist in its vanities), I am in a state of feeling that I am no longer escaping reality, that I am up against my own

[145]

despairing realities. Cheap. Meeting my problems and my digusting self and my inability to be loved. There, that's prosaic but it. How I could've woven a metaphoric tapestry revolving around blindness, sources of light, hearths, emblems! It's too late for that though. My face is ugly. I have no family. I have sacrificed intellectual ability and possible fame. I'm not good enough to be retained as an academic hack at a coolie's wages (this last I refuse to believe), I am smoking myself to death, I am desperately in need of love. And, I am a latent schizophrenic (some price attends this statement). And I don't write as well . . . here I *won't* finish.

There you're just one of thousands of English professors but here you'd be on top, he'd said. Oh I'm on top there too, I said. I'm the best. What did he make of me, how translate me? Understand when I said I was out of work? Resolve the contradiction in my favor? DIDN'T BOTHER doing any of the above. A cunt is a cunt is a cunt. No. An ugly woman.

One more thing I remember now from my bout of being crazy—image of myself striding alongside two or three enormous lesbians down a New York street and here I was filled with a very clearly-known anguish. I don't want to return to a town of tall women. I can't bear it. Can't bear being physically inferior that way too. Here I fit. How can my proud memory of fitting in Mexico ever telepath-ize itself to those arrogant cunts who think they're better than me because they're taller. How can Doris and Paula stand life, I wondered. I felt an almost-image of hunting them out again and holing up with them and never going out into the streets.

I certainly don't want to go back but it would be cheap to return to escapism, though it's all I want. If psychosis didn't bring on my period, it certainly brought on myself, that famous confron-tation all travelers are supposed to seek, or at least experience. Shit, who seeks it?? Only love brings on one's period.

Ciao, bambina,
M.

Ω

E.,
My room looks like a hospital now! Tile floors, a dropped rectangle housing vents over the bed I sleep in. Another bed, sheets,

[146]

no spreads and a large awful near-wall of plastic, diagonally inserted slats. A wall of light. This wears off as I flutteringly think to hunt down Imaculato in the market and through him Arturo. I have learned nothing. The need for love has always struck me as theoretical—I don't perceive it directly, only through what results when I don't get it. It is foolish to stay in Acapulco. But there is no longer any motive to seek out Oaxaca's friendly Indians and beautiful wares, or Zi's health and strength-giving properties.

I did finally ask Claudio, the other desk clerk, if anyone came for me. Afterwards I sat in the lobby letting myself look depressed, not knowing I needed human company. Charming typical Mexicans walked by and bored me. The world has shrunk, after having expanded so much. I realize that Lily's own often vacant eyes and rude coldness are her nervous breakdown. How depressed she is too. And how patronizingly she assured me that Arturo would come. I long to tell her he didn't. I cannot come to a decision. I want to be surprised by human affection. All these authors write about the restorative effects of human love, or the stuff of "human love." I've always found it Platonic and sentimental, being an orphan and an existentialist. *L'Education sentimentale* is the only novel I respect, though there are others I love. That I therefore should bank so much on sexual love . . . But surely that is different from "human love," which assumes a maternal god somewhere behind human manifestations, assumes constancy of feeling. Donna and Al did not exchange addresses with me, after all.

My chest is now in advanced pain, so I write on. What to do? It is two o'clock and I've been sleeping and writing and drinking and smoking in three-hour cycles. There is some mescal left. Drink.

From a night filled with the golden glow of human affection—now do you see what garbage that is? How anthropomorphically absurd "glow of human affection"? Unpinnable down in the physical world. Admittedly. Admittedly (she lectures on), it's a corny sentence, but doesn't matter. Too, any compassion for one's characters, as in Eliot's *Middlemarch*, argues an all-seeing, all-loving, all-pitying god when none exists. Desire is real though. And oh my my, I did. When he said something in English correctly and I laughed because he had and he got (amusedly) paranoid and accused me of laughing at his errors. Meanwhile, he laughs inside at my absolute taste, preferring his own and finding mine seedy. My dirty royal blue Danish school bag is always remarkable here, Imaculato mentioned it. You have a pretty waist, Arturo said, the first unsolicited compliment, why don't you show it off. Waiting for him last night I did, bright apple green tank top tucked into tight pewter gray pants girded by brilliant blue Indian beaded belt. How I longed to be elegant for him. He remembered me sufficiently from past to notice minute changes. I'd shaved my legs, my skin was darker, my eyelashes more golden. Solicited compliments included: my eyes, large, intelligent (again, absurd, unphysical, unanalytical). My chin, an awful word in Spanish that sounds like beard, and how many infinite numbers of women wouldn't envy its cleft. He would spend ten minutes on that, he assured me. And my underarm hair, five minutes each pit. At least an hour and a half on me, he laughed and then he rushed!

Booze. It makes me happy. I am happy. I am mad, mad, mad (the false note of vanity in that. The dialectic is between self-love and truth). Surely, E, you're not above a great deal of vanity though you flatter yourself you are. I suppose *that's* your vanity. If I swallow the red worm at the bottom of the bottle will it bring me good luck as they say? How close I was once again to suicide. How close I should still be. No. My room looking like a hospital, I can't support it. I will go insane. Pain, death, insanity is unrepellable ugly associations. Better illusion. Swallowed the worm! A beautiful Mexican chiquita walked past my open door. Why does no one perceive my beauty? Sometimes I seem strong-faced, with lively (absurd) eyes. I like my smoking visually. Reduced to masturbation once again, only the figurative kind from now on perhaps. What else was he, Arturo, before I lay him to rest? His penis, slimmer than the average Indian cock, having that look of outer liquid covering that Paco's thigh did. A stir in cunt. The fish still living three hours out of water. God, Flaubert, only he saw through metaphors! It is a brilliant book; I was its most brilliant perceiver, though Victor Brombert was frighteningly excellent. That I know. And that I used to have a gift for movies. That you knew as well. Should I add "as well"? Destroys rhythm but is truer. Now, anything left? All my empty tiny bottles, those of a self-deluding alcoholic. Well, no surprise of human affection yet. Pablo is through with me since I won't flatter his masculine superiority and Manolo because I won't fuck him, I suppose. Mexican men are somewhat interested in telling me I'm intelligent and Arturo delivered stern advice to Imaculato's niece about how I was a college teacher, and all American women had professions, and she should follow my example. But she said yes when I asked her if she wanted to go to school!

[148]

They are canny. They figure they can't flatter my appearance so flatter whatever's left, evidently intelligence. Only Andrés, bless him—absurd, my continuing vanity of "bless him"—called me stupid. It was all-out drag-out with him so I must've wounded him. Not one Mexican who's made a sexual or financial play for me has ever mentioned my deformity. Everything else in loving specificity. But it, what else, has brought me such bad luck in love. Stan was the last man. God only knows his motives (oh the chatty, self-loving tone of this—absurd). But was it him staying with an ugly woman that incurred your contempt for him as a weak man? I delight myself with my insight—would I similarly charm the Mexes if I spoke their language? I didn't in France; only my contempt for Mexicans makes me think it will be different here.

My hair. My hair is the source of my problems.

I put my scarf on after drunken unfinished sex and A. said I looked like a real Acapulqueña.

Lily, who's physically harsh, doesn't disagree when I run through my faults, as she's just finished running through hers, though I did disagree. She too likes dark, hairless people. A tall blond who finds Swedes repellent, with characterless faces. Odd midwestern reticence.

A.—anything else. Can't think. Long to talk to Lily at Caleta beach.

New pen. With durable nylon point. Crap. Spent perfect day of no sun, no sea, no exercise, eating everything I wanted. Had seven aguas de horchata, sandia. One malt in the mercado, where went to hunt Imaculato. Window-shopped for little girl earrings hoping this would insure that I would be the child's godmother tomorrow. Spent some time at mercado and another, craft, market teaching girls and women English. Promised them ten words but ended up more. The first gang wanted a lot of sex: give me a kiss, you're good looking, divorced, wife, mi vida, papacito! Took my address, blah blah. The second gang was more into words like silver, reasonable prices, ring, how's your work going? (to marry rich gringo?) though there were some requests for cariñosa (?), bonito, etc. Both gangs and the Indian man who practically gave me the malt wanted me to return tomorrow. To the boys who speak street-slick English I'm rude. One said I was bonita and I said no I'm fea, why don't you tell the truth. All these Mexican lies. Mexicans are good they said. No, they're shit, I said, actually shocking them.

I look like shit. Arturo digs monochromatic outfits. So do I.

[149]

Imaculato wasn't at the mercado, left early to attend to arranging Alicia's baptism (christening?). Am sitting in Sanborn's buying overpriced weak drink, having promised self would if managed to steal from next door Woolworth's Dial's *The Conquest of New Spain*, a contemporary account of Cortez's conquest of Mexico, and particularly his capture of Montezuma. Dying to read Octavio Paz's *Labyrinth of Solitude* and anything else. Tired of shit. Why? Why? When I am beyond beauty, schmattah head, flabby arms and pregnant belly full of shit.

Arturo hadn't heard of *One Hundred Years of Solitude*; didn't know the name of the Aztec goddess of life and death, Coatlique, which he insisted I mispronounced though I learned it laboriously from a tape-recorded museum commentary. Spent eight hours each for three days at the Museo de Antropologia in Mexico City. Got turned on to point wanting do trip of visiting every Mexican ruin. Good old pre-sex days. Still had hair then too. Xist. Sanborn's bar is a fag hangout. Guy at bar eyeing my bad side. My puny White Russian has run out.

The lesson at Le Dôme: that any woman I'm with is more attractive than I. How could I have felt I had a good time? 1. Was asked to dance first. (Seating) 2. Found his friend more attractive. Turned to Lily and said was turn-on being turned on by attractive unavailable man dancing to shit music in overpriced disco. He was dancing with someone else: wearing small dark round shades, tallish, built. It was his air of being a displaced Dostoevsky character. In whites. With a ski-nose—ah yes, looked like Fernando Lamas, whom I loathe. Jerked his head spastically to one side then to other, 180 degree angle apart, when danced. Reminded me of Jerry Lewis too. And Elvis Presley. Loved to lindy. Was about thirty. Intellectual who danced idiosyncratically, with an abandon aristocratically oblivious to others. And slim rather than built. *Was* turn-on. He asks me to dance. We do. I don't look particularly good that night but we dance a set and of course I lindy like a French monkey. He pulls hard, which I love in a lindy. Do feel antique but ... Other boy I'd pointed out to Lily as attractive (love this female pastime, love, love) asks me! Is taller, slimmer, twenty, and wearing clear round rimless glasses. Dark-skinned, Chinese features. Indio. Straight black hair. Lights dim—it is the slow set and one mystery resolves itself, for I am now one of the group of Mexican gringas who are swaying and kissing in the dark. That quick. His mouth, thank god, is as large as mine and he envelops it with his, all soft lips and warm young tongue, rhythmically spaced entries, soft, lush.

[150]

There is a shock of cold glass as he crushes his face down, a period to the more leisurely commas. His skin is warm dry stone, twenty. I pull away eventually because want ski-nose Bernardo, Bernie, and can't have him thinking I'm a tramp. Nor this overweening boy. Dance proper Mex way. Is pleasant to pull away from him as he's pulling back; I bend all the way backwards as he reaches to kiss me. I'm wryly disappointed this stranger scene was the beautiful intimacy of yore and want to indicate that I'm not old and ugly enough to publicly announce my sexual desperation. Ultimately, I go back to the table. He's mumbling some invitation to the Princess Hotel, horses, introduce me to his friends. I sit down next to Bernie, saying I am with him and unbelievably, the slim young water ski instructor or scuba diver at the best hotel in town (he says) argues. His voice is tense and he won't leave! I've never seen anything like it in the States. I dance with a stone stranger for ten minutes and he's ready, well-bred slimness, to kill a man he saw me dancing with before. I am cast in the usual female role of mediator, flattered out of my gourd. Bernie and I dance some more. The lights are bright, the floor nearly empty, the music shitty as usual, and I wonder if I've made the right choice. Suddenly, boredom assails me and my body drags through the remaining steps. Back at the table, Bernie still on my wrong side. So I make him change places. He's now sitting on my good side and next to Lily, my hand on his capable knee, his hand on mine. Slowly, by degrees, his contact ceases. I hover my hand above his knee like a neurotic bird but his leg doesn't notice— he is switching all attention to Lily, who doesn't dance but does speak Spanish. That was that. I am stuck with his unavoidably shorter, twenty-two-year-old friend, Manuel, the pleasant boy who first asked me to dance, who is dressed in crisp gray cotton, with a kind face, widely-spaced eyes, dimples? Good-looking but not my type, black rather than Indian. We go out for coffee. I've forgotten my serape. Manuel and I run back, find it; outside a guy asks me about Lily. I say she's with another guy and it's rude to ask one woman about another. He wants to speak to her. Manuel says sure. I say are you out of your mind?! She's with your friend, the evening's over. No, it's O.K., blah, blah. Later, I find out all this was to avoid a fight (for my sake, of course). Machismo.

Anyway, I'm terribly relaxed in "Denny's," the McDonald's of Mexico, ugly side to Bernie. He's in love with Lily, I say to Manuel. He is atento, Manuel concurs. We take cab. It is past 7. I think I've had a good time.

Not one, not one, Mexican man has found me attractive.

Manuel is short, Lily is five feet eight inches and was wearing three-inch heels. Two architecture students from Mexico City, working their way through school. A cursory invitation to go to the Continentale with them where they're being put up by their jobs—actually, to me. (The Frenchman said if a man doesn't proposition you the first time he meets you, you stand a chance he'll love you.) Howzaboutdat.

Sunday I was nonetheless energized, decent night with girlfriend played its part. Walked to Caleta after doing my exes. Swam. Sat at water's edge. Arturo. You know the rest.

Am now drinking pretty steadily. It is Wednesday morning, the day of Alicia's baptism. Last night I bought a bottle of "San Marcos," thrilled to hear from some American Mensa type that it was the best thing in Mexico. Arturo, then, was the master of perfect taste. It is delicious stuff though I just swig it now and it no longer reminds me of him.

(Him and Alicia in the light. Quieres bailar? he asks her. Romantico? he asks her again. "Romantico," in such a gentle matter-of-fact way. I'm sitting on Rosita's bed beating down my hand not to snake out to him.)

Arturo. Ahrrtoorro. No defenses against him, he was thirty-three. It is impossible to believe this has happened—that he would give me up, that he felt nothing, when we were such a strongly-built pair roughly the same size walking shyly hand-in-hand from Caleta beach. As with Andrés, there was time before sex. But I said mañana for sex and Mexicans interpret that in their own jaundiced, yellow-brown way. But that wasn't it. And I doubt it was revenge—how? I made it clear I dug him, no? I wasn't worth it. Worth nada. The most elaborate set-up yet. *And I can't leave Acapulco.*

I can't remember the title of the Truffaut film about Hugo's daughter but I too am a pursuer, like how many millions of others, Owens for one. And I want to hound him. Make him love me or kill him. (Did I ever tell you why I pulled a knife on Andrés? That night, I took a shower and came out naked to him, showing my body for the first time in three years, very timidly of course but felt equivocally proud of it. I asked him to dry me off. He did. Then, forty-five seconds, etc.) God, no one knew my affairs in Zi. Here, I tell all. Most women are much slower to kindle than I. Less starved, I suppose, used to being rejecters. You too. Well, Arturo will be my last. I . . . I . . . I . . . what? I turn no one on. They all fall away, only A. and A. stay with me. Arturo's charm and guts.

[152]

Money, a Mexican motif: all those Mexicans who told me don't care about it and then rip or seek to rip me off in small ways: Manuela, Arturo, even Isidro (a parting gift of grass that cost me ten p's—cheap, natch. But . . . a gift?).

Should return to Zi to lick wounds. But there'll be no further relationship with Terri, now that George has gone. I'm so drunk now feel sure there could be, so bold and interesting am I. My dear, I'm a lush, prefigured by my own fears and Lowry's awful Mexican novel. I fulfill all prophecies. Must write Terri. The Queen of Hip of Zi. She had the effrontery to tell me she cultivated me in order to meet George. See how increasingly in the past I live? Thank god it's overcast and I don't have to feel compelled to hit beach.

Next day. Usual four hours sleep. Got back around 4 A.M. after drinking all day. My heart skips rope all the time from smoking and I've stopped exercising. One benefit is I let my old skin hang out, I relax. Nothing can hurt me. Yesterday I went up to the inner-tube renter and said, "Your tongue is as ugly as your teeth" three times. The first reaction: he heard "tongue" and waggled it at me again; the second: he smiled; the third: he looked puzzled and said, "Por qué, amiga?" Being a woman, I was touched. Can you believe how dumb cunts are? Not even clean revenge, just like with Arturo whom I pursued to lick his wounds.

Last night this asshole asked me to fuck him after buying me one beer after I: 1. made it clear I was fleeing a gang of three chavos maleantes one of whom a. asked me to fuck him b. asked me for a cigarette c. asked for some of my beer and then d. actually tried to dip his hand into my bag when I wasn't looking. 2. told him I didn't like to be asked the question (would you prefer force? was his one, gringa, alternative). 3. Told him to go to the Zona if he wanted sex (said if that's what he wanted he'd be there, but he wanted to dance, have a few beers, is todo. So? I said, that's what you're having. He looks puzzled at my intelligence but not for long). 4. Told him I'd been celibate for three years. 5. Because feminist; thought all men were maleantes. (No, he's not like other Mexes.) 6. Had no contraceptives. 7. My Lord, required affection. 8. Said no firmly a dozen times. Still asking at cab door. Doesn't pay for cab. I get to go back for my usual 5 p's, the driver takes forever and invites me to go dancing that night. There is really nothing left. I stuck with the asshole in Sotano because 1. alone at bar I was hideously hassled, a public piece of shit, like Zócalo. 2. Bought me a $1 beer. 3. He smoked like Andrés, in two directions: puffed in one, blew out in another, but kept his eyes straight ahead as twisted his neck and mouth. Sí? Quién se recuerda? Quién cares?

Dancing. Woman did beautifully. Little hop-kick from waist, very subtle, whole length of leg absorbs the most discreet shift of balance and beat, reduces angle. Just sways her whole length around the room. My style is shorter, more horizontal. What I do best is black ass (which I however lack); liquid pelvic rotation. Still trying to dance like fabulous chick (met her on Caleta) at Botella. Asshole wearing stretched T ("Blackbeard's natural insemination team"), fattish, Spanish rather than Indian. Big ass—has nerve to look at himself in mirror *the whole time*. Can't dance 1. after I tell him and he stops 2. the women 3. my lungs can't breathe.

I am an inventive dancer but that's not what I want to be: I want a solid underbase of automatic repetitive rhythmic steps; on top, O.K., anything. Was able to dance inspiringly off Jacky because still fantasized myself as Lehman professor (and his) *(was,* until Feb. 1). Contact with Bronx, blacks, status. And also fantasized Jacky's attraction to me.

Am smoking and not doing exes, third day in row. I am so beyond happiness in love. Work must be enough, but of course, nasty syllogism still holds: no desire, no work.

Exhausted. Am hung from days and days.

Spent pleasant . . .

Am on Condesa Beach today. Lying on beach formulated it clearly: for Mexicans I am just a thing to plug. Was then bought soda by middle-aged lifeguard who insisted on reading boring revolutionary flyer I took out to show him I'm an intellectual. Suddenly, one minute after a modulation from politics to sex he asks me to fuck him. There is no kindness.

Then there are the vendors. "Lady! Hey Lady!" They wake you up, come up to you when you're writing, talking, ignoring them. Come to Acapulco and feel the complete thing.

I am perching on a beach chair trying to avoid a rough ocean that pounds up this entire narrow beach, wondering whether to pursue Arturo further, and how. It is April 1 and I have missed seeing Lily, so am free to be the compleat fool.

The only talk you hear on any of the beaches here is money. I felt physically revolted yesterday.

This morning I tried to do sit-ups but was overcome by cramps; my pain is now dignified by psychosomatic symptoms. Or, likely, I am pregnant. Don't relish having to bother about and fork out for abortion of a kitchen aide's fetus when I return.

Imagined rich Japs talking over impoverished New York and how we'd hate them, exploit them, and view them generically as things. That's what Americans are here. But I am me, not Paco!

Pablo says they hate Americans, no matter how charming they seem. He saw a nice blond American boy (his estimation, not mine) who'd been detained for questioning with his girlfriend in a cab, make a run for it. The cop pulled out a forty-five and fired. The guy put his hands up and the cop came behind him and hit him as hard as he could on the back of the head. The guy drops. Minutes later, blood coming out of his head, he struggles groggily up. The cop has meanwhile been joined by cronies and they all kick the guy in the back as hard as they can. A crowd of Mexicans is standing laughing at the spectacle of an American being beaten the shit out of.

Arturo asked me if the States had ever been invaded. I couldn't think of when they had. Pancho Villa was the only one who ever succeeded he crowed triumphantly.

Plus we stole their land. Streets in Mexico City are named "heroic sons" for schoolboys who jumped to their death rather than be captured by our brutal troops in some nineteenth-century civil war.

Then there are the prison stories: (these men are shaking hands, only two-part—I rue Arturo's four-part; some mention of Zihuatanejo took me off the page and some joke I actually understood elicited that broad, brash drawnout laugh I'd forgotten I loved).

The prison stories told to me by Charles, who lives on the Island, wants to see me in N.Y., a forty-five-year-old bald Mensa type to whom I told my Arturo story (and to Louise and Pablo). His sympathy did not prevent him from propositioning the wrecked prisoner of sex. He said Arturo would never be back, that it had been a thrill to show me off around town and to his friend and that he had no further use for me. And Lily agrees that we need them much more than they need us. A woman Charles knew, thirty, married an attractive Mexican her own age, supported him for two years while he ran around to the Zona, and then divorced him. One hears stories of Mexicans beating up their gringa women while living off them. Everywhere sexual horrors.

Prison:

1. Friend of Charles's found with grass. Prison five months. Beaten. Five thousand bucks paid for his food, clothing, a bed, but

they still kept him, suspected he had more. Five thousand more to get out. No trial.

2. Far more awful, a whore friend of his sitting with him and friends is dragged away from their table in the Zona, accused of stealing. They spend the night firing pistols alongside her ear and stringing her up naked to apply electric prods to her tits, pussy, and everywhere else. She is released after signing a confession and forking over a lot of dinero; black and blue all over, blood coming out of her nose, *permanently* deaf in one ear. God knows whether her clit was burned off, her nipples. Charles says she was with him the night she was supposed to have committed the crime, so she wasn't even guilty.

3. Lily has a Spain story: a girlfriend of hers framed by an ex-boyfriend who said she had sold him dope: three years. But Lily thinks Mexico is worse. Cop cars everywhere, and soldiers and federales travel in open trucks with drawn guns, machine guns. Never been in a dictatorship before. Terrifying country.

Mexican cops rob tourists freely. Incredible country. Built on the violence of the conquistadors, L. explains. Indians are supposed to be gentle. Lord love the oppressed. Like mujeres.

Lily also has an interesting theory of why Mexes believe us when we tell them we're much older than we are. She says they don't know from strangely tall women and extend this ignorance to all other gringa characteristics. Besides, there's a myth we're supposed to keep better than tropical women.

A sex story, Pablo's, I like it best. He has had a Mexican girlfriend for six years. She is forty, he forty-five, is divorced—no, must be widowed—and has two daughters in their early twenties. He used to live in her upstairs rooms for two years, six or seven months at a time but then the neighbors started to talk, said they were sleeping together. Well, weren't you, I said. Apparently they weren't! She is holding out for a ring. The story amazes me not only for the woman's part in it—I hadn't thought sexual repression went so far—but also for Pablo's part. He stands for this. He respects this, digs it. (And why shouldn't he, it is man's program.) Says she tempts him with sexy caresses, etc. Quite Mexican—salty puritanism. I ask him to introduce me to the daughters who speak English. But señorita, he protests, they're innocent! A universal sickness.

It is 4:05. Arturo gets off at five and may head to his rented closet. I could surprise him there if I can find the place again or hunt out Imaculato.

[156]

April first, baby!

What have I ever learned?

4:30? I am not at La Base. Stay with me as I retrace this mystery. I cannot be alone on this trip.

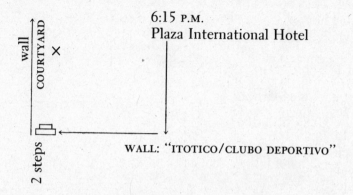

Retraced path successfully. Found out his full name from Señora who takes care of thirty sailors: Arturo Alvarez Rivera, she thinks. A man I took to be her son sees me in the street and we say hola and chat. He is another sailor, about twenty-seven. Taller, slimmer, with dark skin and pure Indian features. Indian crow's feet laugh lines. Kind face. Wants to know if A. is a "familiar friend." Helps me with my mystery—to locate him. He stops several fellow sailors who might know what ship he's on. A., according to the señora, left for Mex. City two days ago. Is impossible—today is Friday, the baptism Weds. Is possible he left afterwards, or stayed with Rosita and Imaculato. (They had pulled out cots for us and I think I was invited to spend the night.)

His name is Juan Fernando (Francisco?) Velez. He says his full name as a sign of respect but doesn't correct my incorrect memory of it later. Is a radio operator, a sergeant. Thinks navigators lack rank. Very different in style from Arturo. Eager to inform me about Mexico, addresses me as Usted. He looks pure Indian, though tall, but comes from Mexico City and used to be an "artisan"—a cabinetmaker. Clues me in on Mexico: minimum wages, agricultural products of various regions. Admires American organization. Would like to see New York. Asks what hotel I'm at. I give him general area. Maybe this is why after several broad hints from me later he does not accept my invitation to spend the evening with me. Feel Arturo-anguish melting into Juan-anguish. And feel a taste

[157]

for short-haired, clean, thin, Indian-Mexican sailors with shyly
stooped backs entrenching itself in me. I have also said I seek to
evade tourist spots because they're filled with corrupt Mexicans. He
may be afraid to be one. Who knows? I barely speak the language. I
think he asked me if I had anything to do later that night and I said
no. (But was it "irme"? and does that mean "go with me"?) He said
I spoke some Spanish and most tourists spoke none. He was lovely,
really lovely. I was playing the sad reserved one to the hilt and
flirted only once. Was somewhat impatient with his good manners
and encyclopedia notion of conversation. I prefer to get directly to
the filth. Though the only reason I now have to miss A. is the
picture of him in his loosely elegant maroon pants and shirt, legs
splayed, sitting in Rosita's hut. My dear. What a life. I will start
haunting La Base Señora's. A respectful artisan/radio operator.
Really! Too much for my sagging flesh. Xist. I wanted to beg him to
spend time with me, I felt so cut-up over A. but mostly over the
whole corrupt Acapulco scene and loneliness. And no Lily.

What we did was this: we interrogated sailors. I hung back
humiliated. I invited him to have a refresco but he'd just had one
and paid for mine. This was to hang out where I could have a good
view of sailors leaving the base. About forty minutes of this. Had
asked me if I was on my way to the Centro. Said sí. Said O.K. he'd
accompany me? Said sí. But stalled with refresco bit.

I am a rejectable mess. And drunk again on San Marcos.

We get on bus, his leg grazing mine. He has paid for bus as well.
I feel ambivalent about leg. Want to fuck his giant Indian cock and
shyness. Omit to tell him my two big selling points: born in France,
academic or writer. He will return to base at 7 or 8—habit going to
bed early. Where will I get off? Say hotel a little farther than
Centro, to change, blah blah. The blah blah is I think he said
cambiarse and want to make sure. And he adds bagnarse and one
other I laughingly agree to but don't understand. Pass movie
theater. *Tom Jones.* He loves films. Say I've never been in A. Say
why. Say dying to. He's leaving for Mexico City tomorrow morning.
I for Taxco. Asked me how long would be here but is standard
question. Is no point. Was better looking than what's-his-name and
was dying bring him home to mother, Francisco. Please spare me
further chavos maleantes.

Am still drinking, puta!

Can't think fast when sober. Should've left address purportedly
for A. with Juan. Do you believe this whore? All I need is to be

rejected by an Indian and I'm in love! How I do dig Indios. Mujer, who wouldn't. They is dark, hairless, has hair, black and thick, and is sweetness itself. Or filth itself—but absolutely, except for lancheros—elegant filth. Or elegant kindness.

Lily says all Latins are cruel when I tell her the prison story. Dónde estás, amiga?

He actually knew that the Feds were helping N.Y. City. Xist. A fucking intellectual turn-on here. I add some bore stuff about how is joke this aid, blah blah. HOW DO I RETAIN CONTACT WITH THESE PENDEJOS?

He gets off bus before me, to call long distance. Sober I'm worth nothing. Drunk I'm all shrewdly maneuvering desire.

Well, if he knows where you're staying in Acapulco there's no problem about contacting *him* he says of Arturo. Xist. La Base laughingstock.

That's It Folks!

Later in Flor, unable to vomit up completely the fifteen tortillas and chicken in mole rojo I had. Vomiting my metaphor. Only one can't vomit up age. Ate all day: Octopus, ostiones, chicken in chocolate sauce, tortillas, beer, brandy, café con leche. Saw Carolina few minutes ago. Treated her to coffee the other night and asked her to treat me tonight. Sure! she said but seconds later she started falling back and looked in agony. Et tu, Carolina? And sodas. Sodas.

Saw Harold, too, who calls me Marisco and who charmed me, bored me, bored me (the tall blond Canadian, remember), stood me up to go dancing at La Huerta with a group (along with Manuela, and everyone else) and finally therefore turned me on, faute de mieux, but also because I might've failed to mention this, except for a swayback, he is conventionally good-looking and wears rimless glasses, not because he has to but because he was once a pilot and had to see clearly for two thousand feet, which he retained as a taste for seeing far distance sharply. (As I have acquired—I never lost it—a taste for innocent men.)

The interrupted "pleasant" of a few pages back referred to drinking beers with him and Charles and their friend Pete at a cantina, finalmente, talking about sex and gringo/native marriages and Zona stories. Harold was bitter because sixteen-year-old Florita from the taco stand had married a pinche gringo. Was vague about bitterness—lack of respect for Mexicans? But drunkenly eloquent about, sure, the beauty, beautiful, everywhere. A desire streak in

[159]

him. They asked me what I was looking for and I said love and embarrassed the drunken crew into a compliment on my being franker than most. Xist. Told them Indian cocks were huge and some Mexes went down. Etc. Left them—they wanted to get laid in the Zona anyway—to a crashingly dull night at Sotano.

Tonight came up behind Harold in square and put my hands over his eyes. Said I'm leaving, Harold. No one's sending me off. Buy a beer in the Zona would be terrific. So write me. Does he have my address, he asks my ghost. I dunno, I say, just send it to Marisco, New York. So you'll write your book and publish it and I'll buy a copy. Yeah, I said. So bye.

Historia de mi vida. Who would spend money?

Mañana, Taxco.

Also said good-bye to an indifferent Manolo, after he offered to fucking *drive* me the 150 kilometers there.

Fantasies of slimming down and resuming exercise and CON-SUMING consume me. Silver, silver, silver. Before that a pair of Acapulco gold earrings for 170 pesos. Ha! Will never find the mercado viejo. Will never find the earrings and *never* get them for 170 p's. Beautiful. Women here wear them. They will make my hair grow. All's left: gardening in Modena. I've even lost the discipline of hitting the sun, deluding myself it's to let my skin rest, as not exercising is to let my body rest.

Juan so touched me that all the longhaired tight-pantsed boys who comb their hair in the street and speak English repelled me.

Pablo at least gave me his address.

My dear, I suck.

James Brown is coming to Acap. tomorrow night. To have heard him with Lucio or Arturo!

Juan: one of the things about love is memory and memory requires length of time. So I'll forget everyone but Andrés, Arturo, Lucio, perhaps, and perhaps Gilberto.

Write to Arturo and send him my address. Tell him to write.

Idiot fantasy. Tell him the cycle of revenge is completed. I am not a puta. I am beautiful and brilliant and chockful of status. That I forgive him. That my hair will grow back and I will row boats to have better arms. Beg him to beg me to come back to Mexico. (He and I and Imaculato and I arm-wrestled and they marveled at my strength which they both overcame. They wanted to know if I was a lesbian.) Tell him I love bright guttersnipes. And do tell him about his maroon pants. Be sure to include that.

[160]

And take me dancing tonight. And . . . yes, tell him I'll wear dangling gold earrings for him and write brilliant books and be famous and he can then really be proud of me.

Carissima. How can you stand staying in New York?

Burned my tongue on my second c. c. l.

No man I am attracted to will ever find me attractive. And I don't want to weigh 162 again. And watch TV all my life. But short of going to discoteques every night, full of big, blond fags—pyuch. . . .

Saw a couple of American heavies on the bus tonight. So feo! That will to ugliness, to capitalize on their natural mammoth size by building themselves into beef, to differentiate themselves ever more from women and show how the last thing they want is to be found wanting to be physically attractive to them. Ponytails, beards, torn loose denim and trucker T's. I can't. Don't you see?

Indian men have tiny hard brown nipples.

Lime on everything—on roasted peanuts!!! Chili in everything—on the octopus with chopped onion, tomatoes, and salsa picante.

Shall I return to work here? Will have to curb lust. Fuck, repress sexuality completely. And swallow disgust at their Francophilia. But will I delight? Poor record.

Have nada, thank god, to write más.

5 A.M.?

Airless, wake up.

I know what I wanted to tell you. That more moments of Mexico's ordinary-lifeness occurred: once on a bus, people looked merely dark, merely on their way to market or coming home from work, dropping fares into the busdriver's outstretched hand like so many tokens in a turnstile. So that N. Y. is already here, the despair of real life. And in a way how absurd (said she, sounding like Delia) that I, a figment of my own imagination, should have expected to be embraced as real.

I don't know if I'll return to Mexico so soon. Already, visions of a cool French mountain vacation loom, and of the blond Swisslike young man who gave Stan and me a lift and told us how you could make a tour of the lower Alps that surround Annecy Lake in the mountains themselves, in three weeks, a commentary I understood. France is my country—why abandon a language and a culture I have partially acquired? And intellectual heritage.

(Because it was a source of pain that I'd done it incompletely.)

More and more I feel the tawdriness of this vacation, of the

[161]

country and myself, of my letters, so without discipline, and my mind, so cheap. So I had my "Death in Mexico," an inferior imitation of a masterpiece. But God it was a heady indulgence at times!

To be in a country nearly three months and not learn its language! (And to feel always that its language is not worth learning, that its intellectual heritage would benefit me no way in the world intellectual community. But of course it was from the failure of incomplete mastery of intellectual content I was running and I thought I could trade intellectualism for tawdry "Life" and have it come out equal. Of course I projected this cheapness on Mexico myself, somewhat. My boredom with any Mexican intellectualism— it seemed derivative but also, it forced me to confront what I was evading.)

A cock crows in the distance. So, if can scrape together body and energy, will leave for Taxco later today, boozed-out and smoked-up.

I hate to escape and wish it could be like it was before. I am terrified of returning to N. Y., of having missed three more months of work and being up-to-date. I don't know how to catch up. There'll be enormous debts of all kinds. Money is the only one it's tolerable to think of: at least a thou. Then there'll be a changed Stan, who doesn't really want a garden again, or to pay for upstate by himself, or to make such a commitment to me, though he needs that place as much as I do. And, Xist, graduate school: wringing a thesis out of Flaubert and years of academe from stale nerves, years out of date. Meeting Cassie, who's busily in academic mainstream, and all those other women, and trying to get into one more school? Childish indecision and sloth half a lifetime before death. And writing: all that competition, mostly Molly Haskell, whom I wish dead. And a host of smaller problems: being evicted every month, living with my hideous storm windows, belaboring my apartment, belaboring my lesbian act, belaboring my lousy friends (Doris, especially). Is *that* real life? Feeling every energy die, watching TV all day and doing nothing creative with it, occasionally full of bright ideas that keep me alive with their promise of being actualized. But also too many, too many choices. Wouldn't it be simpler to chuck it all and live in Mexico for a year? And Europe, too, why not? I am lost. The ultimate criterion is I don't want whatever I do to produce cheap thinking, cheap writing. I want to wring a masterpiece out of my life. But on what subject? In what form? Lord, I need another vacation.

[162]

I wonder if any of this strikes a chord in you, whether my experience is universal or merely personal and neurotic.

Ordinary dreams have returned, though I still forget them.

The drawnout Mexican laugh, badly described earlier: it is a kind of exhaled huff.

Trim off sloppy threads of perception. (Selma and her perfect metaphors—but her I can't go back to. She is exactly like Pablo, of whom Lily said, with unnerving penetration, "I've never met anyone so full of concepts." Her mother, being from Indiana, was a country girl; I, a cynical Big-Towner). But these are details that pull off the main flow. Boy, is that a hideous sentence!

It comes to this: I can't go back. But I can't stay either. Sex is some reason to but there is none. It just looks too bad in Mexico to be a starved vampire. And it feels bad. Arturo would've been a nice escape.

It is getting light. Soon the birds will pitch in their various chimes over the artificial landscape of Acapulco swimming pools, condominiums, and traffic.

My letters to you have been in some regard a way of being accompanied by a fellow traveler, unshared perception so unbearable, but I know that what I write is not what I see. There is no way you can see Acapulco, or ever feel it the way I do. "Swimming pools" etc. makes it sound like Miami; it isn't. It's uniquely Acapulco. (Get thee behind me, unbidden evocation of the States. Too soon! Too soon!)

I long for strangeness. Only sameness is insanity.

Spent my last hour in Acapulco teaching Estela whore pick-up English. Now ain't that cool. Will be unbearable to be in the presence of anyone who hasn't lived in Mexico for a while. Then that will wear off. And that will be a source of pain. Less than one week. I can't bear it. Suddenly I feel grateful for Stan's having been with me. He'll know some of it, and I'll be able to tell him the rest— and, joy, he's dying to know. But he won't help me with my life, evidently that's a purely female trip. Oh good! I chose "trip" instead of "function." Zi's Californians restore Mexico to me. Xist, will there even be a Stan? I've been so fantasy-land willing to sacrifice him to take up imagined new lives with illiterate sailors. (I can't. I'm going mad again. It is early morning booze, I think. It is early morning. Early, early morning.) He, however, has a real thing going. Good, that sentence is banal enough, sounds enough like the tone of my Mexican output to exorcise unassimilable newness.

[163]

Early Cornell mornings: times when genius and madness coincide, but genius, because there is a highly specific task at hand, wins.

I *am* a vampire. I've always hated dawn, going from dark to light.

What is it? Again it eludes me (and am I glad!).

Unassimilable newness. But it's sameness too. Sameness in new setting? Sure, that would lead to madness, the clash and then the disturbing mess of associations. Approximately O.K. for that one, but what was it about seeing the light come??

I'm signing off, praying for sleep. And an ordinary pleasure in Taxco.

Dawn evokes every previous life. Is that it? And so reminds us of all the lives we have lost?

Lord, I reread this letter and it is not impregnated with Acapulco tone. It is filtered through New York or Miami. You will not read it as I wrote it. The words no longer stand for the thing but will be read through the wrong filter. I cannot even express it. It's making me mad, in both senses, with grief. The tone, the feeling of this place is gone—only an abstract, universal version remains. I want only Acapulco tone and it's gone! I'm in Allentown, Pennsylvania and in Miami. Of course, I'm nine and in Miami, where my Allentown relatives are staying. No—worse—I'm nine in Allentown and it reminds me of Miami. Xist, I'm going mad. There is no more Acapulco! Is that all it came to? Not even that is reality.

Perhaps only the men come across unchanged. But no, your own associations will take over. Mine. Some sick new filter. I am going mad.

Men are right: their perfect affectlessness makes their accounts fixed. (Vendors saying Hey, Lady! The informational relatively fixed in associativeness.)

On way to Taxco with Lily. Bought $14 gold fishwoman earrings. Look ugly so will hang self in jewels.

M.

Ω

Dear E.,

There is as usual too much to write—Lily has finally left so I have the freedom to write. We went to Taxco together on Friday. Today is Sunday in Taxco. My one solid relationship in Mexico turns out to be with a woman whom I find myself suppressing a jump in my heart over after she's left, thinking about her extraordinarily generous and aristocratic way of never lording it over me with her perfect Spanish.

My last few hours in Acapulco: Lily calls at 8:45 to ask if I'm going to Taxco after all. We meet. I buy fabulous fish vendor gold earrings—manage to locate them and buy at price she did. Send letter to you. Buy new notebook. Last errand: hit Imaculato at market. He looks dull and respectable and makes believe he hasn't caught sight of me. I confer with Lily about soundness of this pursuit, basically afraid she'll disapprove of my lack of dignity. But Lily, as I am to discover more and more, is totally human. We approach him; he looks ill at ease. What happened? I ask. He looks ruffled and says that Arturo never showed. I believe this provisionally since it fits in with my image of Mexicans but have Lily tell him I had wanted to be Alicia's madrina, so he should disculpate (?) me. Customers are milling around his plastic tablecloth stand and I think that's why he's distracted. He repeats that he doesn't know what happened to A. I say O.K., bye, and he smiles tightly and practically collapses in relief when we move off. I have at least shown him that I have a friend, that she is tall, blond, attractive, even aristocratic-looking, eminently respectable, and SPEAKS PERFECT SPANISH. This means that I'm no fool, through her I can penetrate Mexico, and also, I'm serious about speaking Spanish. Plus I've taken the godmother bit seriously enough to bring a U.N. interpreter in tow to get serious answers. Even without her, that I respect myself enough to crap about a broken promise.

L. and I discuss it and agree that he was lying. Otherwise, L. says, all the curiosity and eagerness would have been on his side. She figures A. said I was worthless though of course it could easily have been Imaculato and Rosita who were appalled at my being found naked in their bed with A., and the brandy bit, etc. Now Imaculato has to answer to me having presumed A. had dismissed me. L.'s rundown has me depressed as a potential sexual superiority ploy on her part but she says this neutrally, like a computer. I'm somewhat reassured it's the product of having had similar experiences. A mystery more or less solved, and some revenge in making I. squirm and showing him I was not dismissable, through Arturo.

We spend an hour knocking off the chavos maleantes in the craft market; I am thrilled to discover L. is into power and revenge and strategy. We use several ploys: 1. confuse them when they call "Lady!" and speak to us in English, by looking at each other in amusement and responding in French. L. speaks good French and we speak it even out of earshot to get into the role. 2. We laugh at them and their physical flaws; one vulgar boy with a wretched mouth full of silver teeth catches on even though he doesn't understand French. We are also amused at their antics to each other. 3. I invent a variation on L.'s "Paco" story: we reverse their assumption that all gringas are sluts and potheads; I pick up an onyx pipe and ask if it is for grass. Sí, the chavo answers. Do you like pot, I ask slyly. "Nooo." Síiiiii! I laugh back, all Mexicans smoke pot. One after another collapses.

The language thing was excellent since the strategy of a vendor is that 1. once you look 2. once he addresses you in your language and 3. asks: "what will you give me for it?" you've suddenly signed his contract.

We lose only once: five of them saying things like "sixty-nine!" and laughing uproariously. L. says we can't win because we're not allowed sexual language—will only make ourselves look bad.

Then we hit the women and teach them English. Same group.

We leave.

En route to Taxco she tells me she works in a massage parlor in Miami; I tell her about Andrés. (His combined expression of sultriness, narcissism, and tenderness. All my other men were related to water; he was related to cardboard; when Pedro evicted him from the garden of Eden, I was melodramatically ready to follow him to the next piece of cardboard. The hand in the door. How you can never penetrate Latins, Andrés turned out live on a piece of cardboard in Pedro's junk shed. Layers of Latins. We are laughing uproariously. I tell her a précis of Zi. The scene. Asks me if it was comfortable for me. Say no but grew into it. Everything quick and full simultaneously. Is journey, with Lily, of ever more surprised at her nonshockability and penetration. She used to try to shock the Spaniards but we agree can't in strange country, end up embittered outcaste. I can't do her or the connection justice. She too was born in Europe. Went to Indiana U., studied languages. Is twenty-six. There's nothing I didn't tell her except my age. We talked about class. Later, in Taxco, about men—in Spain she chose, as I would have, of three, the one she was least attracted to, though one stood her up, though she's tall, blond and was younger four years ago. What he meant to her was the Islands, and she had no pleasure in sex. The joy of a shared, deep, analytic female perspective. A natural feminist—when told her why was teaching only women English said 1. men owned shops 2. women wouldn't understand my purpose; I said whatever I said. She partially agreed. Disagreed from common base of interests and logic, goals. Preferred sugar-sons to sugar-daddies. Had same taste in men. Described Stan: tall, thin, hair on chest (she grimaces), losing hair on head, which hurts me more than him since I'm not so hot-looking myself and need to be reflected in someone good-looking. She laughs. No embarrassed social worker disclaimers. No patronage. A joy, niña. A woman interested in the truth. Pam in retrospect remembered as a woman who was always telling you she was loved, preferred over you. Lily not at all. Lily detached somewhat from her own attractiveness, would see it as a given element in a situation, hardly her natural essence. It was like writing letters to you only more succinct, wittier, filling in the spots when was necessary, and the confirmation of her own experience. Frightening in a way, kept wondering when we'd run out of stories and mutuality but we kept having new experiences and she was as interested as I in analyzing them on the spot, and from same perspective.

Taxco: the major theme of men taken up once again. I experienced a total revulsion of men in Taxco. We first hit there Friday night, a cool, quaint mountain town that instantly beatifies. Some guy asks, in formal pronouns, where we're going. Cheap hotel. Politely escorts us to $10/night. No. Other. No. We want Casa Grande. Leaves us. Is he a runner? Perceive glimmerings of rarified nonsexuality but a more disturbing, because more detached, exploitativeness. We go dancing in local disco. Practically paid by boy maître d' to enter. Shit music. Better music (we choose) but on forty-five's! We end up with geology students from Mex. City. Boring college-time conversation of young men who provisionally respect you. I get mine, chosen, to dance. He gyrates each long thigh like an individual cylinder. I warm up. It reminds me of Zi, Acap., is familiar as well as sexy, that good Mexican dancing. He's a good partner too. Looks at me with pleasure and has pleasure in my

[167]

pleasure in him.. It is to give me pleasure that he's dancing. Pleased I'm pleased. His tallness repels me somewhat, since I'd gotten depressed and started eating, I'd begun to revert to tall men as an etiolation of my own horizontal bulk. It represents the need to balance my fatness, leaving my smaller, lither, grounded self. (It will mean this later on in Taxco and Mex. City, from which, by the way, I'm writing this.)

There is no time. I'm leaving tomorrow at eight, loaded down with crap.

I must start in new notebook. . . .

NEW NOTEBOOK

O.K. What I experienced in the last days of Mexico—what I'm feeling still—is nausea, there is no other way to put it. I see Indian faces and I want to vomit. It is like seeing the dark face of the stranger in some disgusting primeval archetypal unconscious.

Taxco:

The Boy walked me home and said did I think all Mexicans were alike (for I'd gotten him off politics and onto sex by the simple method of yawning). I said yes, like he thought all gringas were alike. He sighed. Full of trembling controlled sexual desire; I too. We grazed against each other in the street (my move, actually) to avoid a car. In slow dancing, no closeness. He led me to my door and fled to take a cold shower. That was the next-to-last time I felt any desire. And he was pale and tall (how disgusting tall men are, such a waste of space and flesh, so uncompact). (I am hideous myself now. Discovered in new, M.C., mirror that skin is a jungle of pearly stretch marks all over. Face sags too. Always new awful discoveries. If could only vomit up age like the food I relentlessly wolf.)

Next day L. and I get bought drink by a tall fat European Mexican who tells us Americans taught Mexicans how to . . . I supply "be human beings." And he assents! We taught them nutrition, before which they were mentally retarded. This awful remark, which I consciously mock, lodges in my brain forever and changes the face of Indians. We had gone to the market, a disgustingly charming thing arranged in endless labyrinthine tiers of stairs, like a giant mock-up of an ancient Indian market. There were genuine Indians there—unmixed, untouched by modernity—very short. This had already troubled me, as had the Taxqueños, who

[168]

seem unbored in a dead town. Buying silver was unpleasant, young men who hustled you respectfully for dinero, nada más. Young storekeepers the same, unbudgeable through teasing. I was missing the filthy sultriness of Acapulco. Sex, in a word, seemed totally absent from Taxco and from Indians (to whom we were probably repellent too).

After the European, who bought us a bad, light meal (which I didn't know beforehand he would pay for, which put me in the ghastly position of not knowing whether to be scared or strong, flattered or bitter, which dilemma I solved by ordering a lot of food, vowing to pay the 50 p's if it came to that)—all of which food I threw up. Anyway, after this sentence, L. and I were respectfully let off at our hotel in states of depression and fatigue, I traumatized by the intense repression of sexuality and freedom to be respected incurred (I couldn't even talk about Acapulco corruption). We decide to hit the town. Run into boy knew from Zi, craggy kind type who invites us to his pad to smoke. There are three other conscious ones there in a Spanishy high-ceilinged room, disgustingly un-Mexican. One guy is Spanish himself, although dark—that enormous long waist, the general narrowness. Repellent! Alejandro. He's attractive at first, but I progressively perceive through the terrifying clarity of drug and without benefit of much Spanish, an utter banality in his use of slang. He repeats chinga and pinche and cabrón at fixed, frequent intervals, never varying their form or placement and connecting them up with maybe fifty words. The fucking Dick, the fucking Jane ... It is impossible to relax cozily into a semblance of Arturo's spontaneous earthy richness. Unbelievably, he is more afraid of boring us than we are of boring him. I get one of his sentences clearly: I am unique, you are unique. Another: we have a lot more to learn, cabrón! It is Hesse time in Kindergarten. L. and I peek at each other and it seems—who can tell under pot?—we are feeling the same thing. We make a silent pact to leave in five minutes, and do. Walking strange in street some cab picks us up and deposits us at a dive in name only, "El Rebozo." We walk down ugly stone stairs endlessly plowing down a mountainside and enter a red hell-haven. A guy with slicked-back Elvis hair in a nice-boy maroon satin windbreaker asks me to dance. He is absolutely repulsive up close (I'm overworking repulsive, I know, pinche cabrón), looks like Troy Donahue but completely dark! Sharp white features. A strange, wrong mix. The band is playing Puerto Rican or Cuban music rather than Mexican. There is a black light on. Pink walls? It isn't Mexico. I pray it isn't Puerto Rico and 116th St. and Madison Ave in Taxco, which I already hate, but which is in *Mexico*, no?

A second bozo asks me to dance, this one like the pig-assed kitchen aide. He is all suave, and like a puppet, boneless, an excellent dancer. *BUT*: I can't match him and the more I can't the more narcissistically intricate he gets. And the dancing is too liquid, too uncontrolled. I figure fuck it, I'll do my own thing and curious too to see if my withdrawal of energy from him will result in what I anticipate. Pot miraculous, it does. I look at him two minutes later and he's awkward and perplexed, moving stiffly. (This epiphany is flat sober.) So I look at him again and click! He suddenly turns on like an automatic Jerry Lewis in a forties' Jane Powell-Jose Iturbi movie. He flashes his teeth and he's off. I manage to get off the floor without vomiting, so weird is he, the previous guy, this bar. Go back and tell Lily magic energy transaction and all about monkey. Really?!!? she exclaims. She finally both sees it exactly the same and/or believes me; I the same with her. Fifty to sixty-five percent of pot isolation is overcome and I decide that the miraculous communication we are experiencing comes from, simply, believing another person. Distrust is gone; as in the car with the maniac cabdriver, who Lily thought was going to bring us to his friends where we'd be worked over, and I thought we'd plunge off a cliff (O.K., I thought, I've never done that before), there was, at least on my part, no fear. Rather, a sense of being able to adapt gracefully to any circumstance, actually make it serve my purpose.

But the other pot effect is the uncontrollable explosion of simultaneous, jarring associations.

Dancer #3 approaches, the best-looking stud in the bar. Here too there are awful false notes. For one, he looks—is—Indian. Two, his questions are wrong. In Acap., they were in this order: 1. Where are you from? 2. Are you married?

I forget what he asks me, polite questions about my job or how long I've been in Mexico. *Gott waist*. Awful, dull, questions. A cripple guide (How I love cripples! They are always innocent.) had said Taxco was a highly Catholic town. Thirty-five churches in a town of forty thousand. I can't bear it. Yawn with perfect pot aplomb, caring less if I bore him, bored to point of suicide. I somehow miraculously elicit sex from him but on the dance floor, slow number, there is no tension in his body; he is a gorgeous limp vacuum. Mumbles. I understand nada. L. says he's drunk. I can't find Mexico in Taxco. We flee, L. and I, in cab. Fifteen minutes later comes a soft knock on our door, in the dark. "Corek, it is Mike. Corek. Corek. It is Mike." It is him, droning in a spineless litany. Corek! My name!

Next day L. and I dialecticize, she slightly prefers sexless respect, I prefer sexual contempt.

I can't describe Taxco, only the children had sex. Christ, with women, old people, one likes there is always a sexual element. L. agrees (one of the difficulties of describing women is there are two things involved: a theme and them. With men, only them. Themes—what one talks about, conversation—render badly in literature; like paintings of statues, the double thing doesn't work). L. agrees! Not another small miracle? What time we saved, time for the important.

A people without sex. I felt I was on another planet. Not being able to tease, prod, play, fight.

Mauricio was also, natch, tall.

Lily leaves. I stay on one more night and spend the first night of my life bitten awake all night by bedbugs. It is too much. So I flee Taxco to Cuernavaca. Spend two hours in that indescribably filthy city looking in vain for a cheap cheerful room to write you in. Flee Cuernavaca, a mess of nerves and fatigue.

En route to Mexico City, landscape assails me with strangeness. Africa, India, the Midwest? I've never seen it, but must have. Consciousness or present perception can never refer back to nothingness? Nausea at strange mixes. Feel am going mad. No glamor in it at all. Can't control my perception. Was mistake to tell L. about Arturo in Taxco, to *infect* him with Taxco. But there is no way to encapsulate him in Acapulco. Every new place I'm in will add its disturbing association to the past.

In Mexico City, I will buy *Los Hijos de Sanchez* in Spanish and nauseate myself with that translation. In English it was more tragic, more metaphoric for me: Mexico via English. In Spanish it will seem maudlin; no longer, too, a gift to a tourist but an en-soi, a thing proper to Mexico. Bouts of sexual revulsion, like Turista, return. Of course it must be due partly to pregnancy. Though again, one has no control over the body's control of the mind. It feels psychological; it is psychological. How men made me physically ill this morning. When I walked down the street clutching my stomach, they looked at me with lust. Who needed that? I was in physical and psychological pain. They would murmur at my swollen tits, that they had given me, longing to suck the milk from them. Oh god. Are all pregnant women nauseated by men?

I suddenly feel there is nothing more to say. A blessed relief. There is nothing more to say. Once the sex instinct dies, so dies the need to memorialize it, i.e. life.

No fantasies reign. I'm not depressed; just indifferent. Stayed too long in Mexico. Stayed until the romance wore off. At this point Mexico seems both intensely foreign, en-soi, and intensely banal. I think I've penetrated the male attitude toward sex and there is no way to survive it. The choice is exactly between boredom/dignity and excitement/abuse. And I've always lacked the discipline of boredom. Xist! Mexico—Andrés, Arturo—was for me the intense gratitude of being able to feel again.

Arturo: eyes; long lashes. Heavy, looking past you at angle, furtive, like scared cat. Not letting you see them seeing you see them. Small pendulum nods. Yawns. Time out for Alpha state tristesse. Sad monkey Mexicans.

My spiel to L. about American social advantage: we are white, American, educated. No way. We are cunts. Only in our own country can we forge rules.

I was broken by Arturo. Everything that happened before was the failure of my youth; with A., it was the failure of love. I shouldn't write this—it will destroy his last pulse in my blood—but he said, "Tu tienes una rosa, yo tengo una rosa, what is de problem?" I was wearing my silver rose and he had a rose tattoo on his chest.

The problem is I am drinking San Marcos and it no longer reminds me of him or tastes good.

I cannot write. I suppose it is because I'm living in the future already. Mexico is gone.

Mexico City. Well, nothing much. Nothing I feel passionate to write about any longer.

The last attractive man picked up on bus coming into the city, looked Doris-Arturo bohemian from afar. Close up he had one quarter inch of dirt under each nail, hobbled, and had hair growing out of his nose. His skin could not possibly be shaved it was so pocked. I ended up at a fleabag hotel the first night. He picked me up and we went to the M.C. equivalent of Coney Island, Plaza Garibaldi, where all the lower-class Mexicans go to hear Mariachi. *Everyone* was cleaner and chicer than him. But in the street he hovered a nursing hand over his no doubt hugely budding Mexican erection, dug his unfortunately sweating hand into my side and murmured um huuh. Once he even called me mamacita. I couldn't help it if my cunt responded.

[172]

Now when I masturbate, I invariably give myself cramps. It must be all the heavy female influence I've been under lately. Lily, for all her openness and luridness, is not horny, and I passed up two men in Taxco because of her (and all the others, sans doute). But to be sexless is to be fat and I'd rather be anything than that ever again. God, good ole Zi where the only thing that prevented fucking was that it was a small town and Pedro.

So I've been eating and vomiting and trying to be turned on by Indians again, partially succeeding my last night. But I can't bear straight contempt. With Arturo, it was a resolution between contempt for me as gringa whore and awe of me as college professor. (So why why did it end the same banal and painful way? He was too inferior to reject me.)

I've destroyed the private potency of the rose remark.

With Andrés, as Lily explained, I actually gained caste from having a companion. An unaccompanied woman is the lowest evidently.

I flouted the authority of some asshole who wouldn't let me into the Hotel Hilton Continental bar last night. Big deal. Ended up with two creeps mile away from home. Subway back after fear for my life and my travelers checks. But had to reward my rescuers! I can't ever walk away from a gift.

Some student bought me an orange juice at the University and after hours of surprisingly intricate (because in Spanish) explanation of the American and female Weltanschauung asked me my opinion of love and told me he liked my body—it was that of a "woman." I'll cut one off and say "here!" with a bitter flourish.

Mex. City: the men are taller, lighter. The sex action is lighter than in Acap. but less attractive. Men licking your tits appreciatively with murmurings, longing to be filthy infants. An ugly man decides he'll take me. An old one thinks to conquer me with a direct, compassionate look. The students are formal but mechanically sly underneath. Nowhere a soul in sight. I got rid of two vaguely possibles today. One a Peruvian who slurped Spanish through thick lips, tall. Another, taller, who approached me in street and split fast when I said, "I don't like tall men, man!" A nostalgic chicano, I guess. Is it that I've died or that there is no sex away from the sea?

I pushed two slobs away from me, yelled obscenities at another and gave three fingers.

I'm bored and longing to have a drink at this place I just discovered. Quizás?

[173]

Food nauseates me too. There is nothing I want to eat. Yes. Café con leche and pastry. The smell of pork innards and tortillas, almost any kind of meat, sickens me. I want—no—I don't want clean food. Cheese and radishes disgust me too now. Chinese food (but not now) but only in Mexico. Metaphor.

Mauricio looked Chinese. Oh god. It's all disgusting. But I don't want home either. What will I do with tall Stan who's been seeing Anne for months?

Next time I travel is without him and with whorish female pal. Guess who.

The worst thing of all, of course, what I'm really suffering from, is not being able to recapture the past.

I will not go to this place, the "Rendezvous." I'm exhausted and will get less than five hours sleep. And there will be no way to schlep this crap anywhere, it'll get lost or robbed. I've translated everything into goods when before, in Zi especially, I was ready to receive the news that my apartment had burned down with complete equanimity. God, had rediscovered living. Back into acquiring. And have acquired things with improper associations. I am sick, sick, sick. And no longer vaguely attractive. Lizard skin, cold climate on tan, shebang. Instant old age. Dorian Gray. You will be physically disappointed. The only remote fantasy is getting back into shape. Good luck with no sex.

But not to go to this place is to abdicate sex and with it life. My last night. I should force myself to feel that attraction once again. A Mex band playing American; shades of Acapulco gold.

7:15 A.M.? This expensive pen sucks. Haven't been laid in over a month. How I've wasted Mexico, wasted it to point of not wanting to return. I fear only disgust and boredom. This hotel thinks I'm respectable. To incur that tribute I had to kill my pleasure. A rough country. To be dead if you're a woman.

I'm late. Train. Off. Border town will depress me—won't be my Mexico. Nothing will make me want to return. Everything will disgust and bore me.

M.

PART TWO

Ω

Why did Maryse return to Mexico, to the inferno? Because she essentially had no choice. In America, she was ugly. A disfigured face masked her natural beauty and heightened her self-consciousness to a painful degree, never allowing her to be free of a painful self-image. She found American men unattractive in general, with their lack of sensuality. In America, the macho man (and he is the most attractive man sexually in America) equates sensuality with sissiness or femininity. Thus, for Maryse, what was considered the most sexually attractive man in America was the least sensual and the most consciously cruel to her (because of the facial imperfection). In America her sexual life was proscribed, limited in general to sexually unexciting men.

In Mexico, Maryse could lose this painful self-consciousness. In this hot, sensual land, a land of great beauty and great poverty, "imperfection" is accepted much more as a part of nature (poor people cannot afford the luxury of an aesthetic that demands perfectly straight teeth, a perfectly straight nose, and a perfectly straight morality). In the labyrinthine turnings of Maryse's hot soul in that profuse land, a land that she loved for its rich colors, smells, sights, range of people, she could lose the straitjacket of middle-class morality (especially when playing the role of writer, investigator of life) and slip and slide sensuously, and with rich pleasure, into one amour after another—all with dark, darkly beautiful, lean young men. And Maryse loved, adored, caressed with her soul, the lean, hard, young bodies of men. She loved their dark straight hair, their noses, their cheekbones, their asses, their cocks, their muscled legs—as she worshipped (at times) her own muscled body which she had given herself through the rigor and strict discipline of daily exercise.

In one area, Maryse transcended her painful self-image, and that was on the dance floor. Here she could flirt aggressively and create a world of magic and glamor. She loved to dance, but in New York City, her middle-class identity (which she could not lose there) forbade her from frequenting Latin discos and condemned her to the sexual barrenness of white heterosexual discos (and sexually aggressive women are not rewarded in America by white middle-class heterosexuals, at least not in "proper" settings). In Mexico,

[177]

Maryse on the dance floor was the star she had always yearned to be. Saint, slut, what was the difference? She was being rewarded in the here and now for being a sexually provocative woman. She was consciously politicizing sexuality by transcending the sexually-determined role for the woman on the dance floor. She was boldly aggressive, and in that she was truly beautiful, truly a star.

One might say that her return to Mexico was a dance with death. She knew she was close to death, but she wanted to turn it into a high. In Mexico she was free to act out her inner torment, her inner anguish, and get high off it. She was free to indulge her sensuality, her sexuality, thus gaining her artistic freedom. In going to her death, Maryse wanted to experience it as an artist—consciously and yet with abandon. Maryse was impelled toward her own death, but she wanted to transfrom it into art. And she has. Her soul and her artistic honesty shine through, illuminating what for most would be seen as ugly truths. In transforming her life into a work of art, she lost her life, but she kept her soul.

*   *   *

I edited the second set of letters, which follows, from 1,000 pages Maryse sent to me during her second trip to Mexico (March to September 1977). The letters from the first trip, which took place during the spring and summer of the preceding year, have been published in toto.

And so now, my dear darling Maryse, your tale will be told. May you rest in peace forever and ever.

—EDITH JONES
May, 1978

Ω

Dear Edith,

I haven't written before for three reasons: 1. Stan was here. 2. Fear of not living up to past letters. 3. Different this year.

Came back to Zi hoping as you know to recapture a past intensified by a year of mythic intensification in the States. Zi was initially like a town expunged of ghosts. Some of the same people were here—Andrés, Carlos—but without their ability to mystify me.

No one drinks. Everyone smokes and is spiritual. The women do not get laid. One visited me en passant this afternoon and laughed at my doing women's rights in the midst of imminent world famine. Fucking she described as loose morals but said she didn't disapprove. You know California logic. . . .

I wrote to Miguel whom I neither fucked nor sufficiently attracted to warrant a date. Nevertheless, he made my sap run. More specifically, he loosened menstrual blood frozen for decades.

Miguel digs Hitler but as Idi Amin. When I left in (mock) outrage saying I was a Jew, he instantly sobered up and litanized endlessly "Forgive me, forgive me." I pointed out that as an Indian he would have been gassed a lot sooner than I, which I doubt he understood though he nodded. At any rate, my revelation produced in him a respectful sadistic attraction for the victim I had suddenly become. We stared each other into a pant.

He has scars all over from a motorcycle accident so I suppose my face and deep leg scar are a tender bond.

He was with two others, one hustles gay boys: so his scene is equivocal.

I think he dug my silver frog, not me. Or was he honing his casual charm on one more?

Anyway, fascists and capitalists treat me best.

Miguel. I guess I played the Jew's outrage as a flirtatious escape from my face. A more superficial wound.

Wish I remembered more. Yes. He was very into lexicos. Slang words. Low voice. Danced solito in disco. Pranced like tired but rhythmic horse around the dance floor. Had dark face that shone with yellow light from underneath. The large brown eyes that were eons of substance and knowledge. A cliché on the way to becoming a symbol.

Eyeballed him at Stan's departure. Later that night he appears with buddies. We drink and dance and flirt the night away. I accuse him of stealing an earring. He tries to rape my mouth. Next day I decide so what if he stole my earring, made my period come and was lovely and strange and full of Mexican lexicos. We flirt on beach. Nada más until two days later. He leaves for Mexico City and we exchange addresses, I having spent previous night mourning his absence at Chololo and finally having fucked a passable if not rapturous Mexican.

He says "Cuidado hijita." I write him. His scars appeal. His nickname is Blackie because he digs black power. Alternately, it is Black and White, because when he drinks, he digs blonds. He says he sells leather in Mexico City. He's missing half a tooth diagonally spliced. Wears trinket around neck. Five ft. eight.

I didn't memorize his face.

He is the second to loosen me. . . .

Love
M.

Ω

Dear E.,

"Margaret's ass" is my third worded thought this fresh morning. I think it because I notice for the first time how my ass folds together when I lie on it. It had been my only idea of an ass before I saw and felt Margaret's ample, firm white orbs. With the thought of Margaret's ass comes the memory not only of my pleasure (and dismay) feeling it but of a kind of concupiscent humming leer emanating from Stan—like his eyeballs had become alive, greedy hands that buzzed their lust. I saw them making love. He can't get hard from me except at the very moment I'm touching him and then with difficulty, but his cock stands at the mere thought of Margaret's ass. What can I say? Every once in a while the reality of somebody else's desire shines through our beclouded egoism. Anyway, I was filled with a mixed feeling common to me: utter hopeless dejection at my undesirableness, intense jealousy of Margaret, a feeling of having been stupid, so goddamn self-deceived to think he would end it with her (as he implied repeatedly), a feeling of rage at having been deceived and having Margaret preferred, and an imme-

[180]

diate desire to stop doing my sit-ups, smoke cigarettes, and fuck my cunt out. Finally, it became a kind of self-destructive strength. Fuck the world, fuck Stan, punish him, punish myself and in so doing, have the guts to seek out what I want which is to fuck Mexicans, despite the thinly veiled injunction not to by the American women here who would regard my sexual freedom as a dent in their communal chastity.

Margaret fills Stan. She fills his apartment, my apartment in the country, his days at the lab with phone calls, his nights. She fills him with feeling alive. She is literally inside him. The only contact we ever make is through sexual desire. What else do we live for but to feel alive in this way?

To fuck Mexicans, that is to indulge my need for their beauty.

I tried two nights ago with one Raúl. He gardens and caretakes a *House and Gardens* palace where Lauren Hutton stays when she comes here. We tried to make it in one of the many mosquito-tented sleeping lofts. We were in the trees. So cool. In this other element like birds at night. But he didn't know I had a clit and my dear he fairly panted with long-sufferingness and generosity all through foreplay. I pursued his indifference to my breasts and he finally sighed "O.K." and nuzzled on one nipple, dryly. He had no contraceptives. I did but lied. Finally I figured fuck it—I'm wet, he's big, it would be some pleasure—and got up to get my foam. "Goddamn" he muttered disgustedly at one more delay to getting his rocks off (he didn't know actually what I'd gotten up for). I saw the light. "Goddamn is right!" I said and split.

Love,
M.

Ω

Dear E.,

Miguel's letter, that's as good a place as any to start. He answered my letter two weeks after he received it and two weeks after I knew he'd never answer it. My letter was charming. I addressed him as "little son" since he had called me "little daughter." I asked him if we could meet in Acapulco some weekend.

Lily had come into town so I no longer needed being validated through friendships at home. And, of course, I felt no desire to write. She was an open ear, as close to myself in sensibility so as to seem miraculous at times. We made ourselves smarter and smarter and more and more mystified as we pursued our research on passion in Mexico, an interest I must say she revived for me.

When Lily came, my fragile discipline collapsed. She took me out of my scene, dragged me into hers. No longer was I the solitary writer experiencing a momentary block, timid and gently curious about people's lives here, influenced by Stan's dictum that I could make being alone strong—if I exercised and *really* wrote—so that I could walk in town alone, go to the movies by myself, etc. I became, suddenly, Lily's. I was unhappy she'd come. I wanted her to be my escape and contact in Acapulco. Under the influence of new influences, I'd been smoking a bit of pot and trying to brave the terror of having penetrating insights about what seemed the very origins of language, thought, and just what it was possible, if anything, to communicate to others. Shy, lonely, bored, but trying to develop the strength to lead a rich contemplative life. I knew intellectual life had its excitement. I came very close at times to saying things that had never been said before, to creating—how odd I should have felt this—finally a way of explaining life, as if enough people hadn't been doing this all along. I wasn't going to ignore the past but synthesize it and fill in the gaps. The new synthesis, which could only have been a perfect expression of my own consciousness, would nevertheless have expressed everyone's. I've always felt this, that if one could only express one's own perceptions *exactly*, one would explain everyone's. The past then (I think of Hazlitt's essay on "Going [for] a Walk," a work I found "perfect" in the above sense when I read it) was not enough because it only formed the basis of one's future thought. Everything one has read is only the stuff of further dialectic.

Anyway, that's where I was heading when Lily came. Thinking how pot induces imagistic thinking; how in the very act of mixing up the senses (synesthesia) it permits us to finally distinguish between them and see how one translates into the other. Perfecting a perfect science of perception, and of knowledge of the Other—of other people, of how influence works, of how everyone contains a rich individuality which is nevertheless universal as well. Timing the duration of a wave, almost, with my eyes closed, sensing through some unknown organ when it will crest because of a suspended hush—a kind of vacuum—that comes before it.

[182]

Oh well, I've lost the point again to indulge in Freshman grad school metaphysics.

Lily came and with her the world of sexual feeling and social life. Sociology became my major, an inferior one but nonetheless the stuff of most literature.

I am in, or have worked myself into, an abstract mood, partly, if psychology can win out over other comprehensive explanations, as a defense against the pain of Lily and my universal rejection by men and her beginning to see that it is hard on her to hang out with someone who is older and uglier when that person makes her suffer for it and so beginning to cultivate another woman's friendhsip just in case. . . . Or is it that I *must* have isolation in order to write? That I must get back to that discipline? A sense of self slowly forms, like a human figure fashioned out of clay, inside me, and only because I have been weaned by circumstances from Lily. And had I lost my separate self before and come to rely too exclusively on her judgments of me, and was this a burden on her, and on me, of course, exploding in hate at finally, finally, the opportunity. But how could I have not relied on her judgments when we were pursuing the investigation of sex and she won repeatedly? They like her more. But to have *not* been in that race for real would have been to again be detached and bored. I had to believe I had a chance of course.

I do see why Lily wins, and others. It's not just the looks, it's the lack of need, the patience, the control, a female macho analogous to theirs. I'm putting it positively. I could equally say: passivity, docility. How I am in a bar: drunk gay, asking men to dance, picking them, promiscuous, grinding them on the dance floor: sexual. I talk more. This morning I think: they, like me, prefer remoteness to social directors, hidden depths to aggressive restlessness, bad dancers to intimidatingly good ones, persons who don't flex their biceps, appreciation of wit—gentleness—rather than wit itself.

Enough. I'm in Acapulco after two months in Zi. Miguel sent the identical letter here (to be sure to reach me I suppose). Thinks of me as a Harlem Jew? Maybe he's a bandido, or gigolo, or wants American citizenship. The latter seems possible. Anyway, I've written to, and scattered several more letters for him all over.

Lily and I slutted through Zi and provided a contra-onda (onda = vibe—the slang here is five-year-old American). Plus I became a martyr: evicted from restaurants, attacked left and right. Rather awful and fascinating to become a witch. The scapegoat for their collective rage at Americans (pick on a weak *woman* of course), at gringas who were grinding off or fucking everyone but them, and at a presence they perceived as critical—*mirando*—seeing. L. and I and another woman were sort of a gang gossiping up the chavos. I suppose they know I'm a feminist. And it's economic as well. You buy goodwill in Mexico. Anyway, two months in Zi was a revelation. Acapulco bores me but I suppose I'll wait a few more days for my chavo to show and exploit me.

I haven't slept in days and am all packed, waiting to move to another hotel, to leave Lily here. What a painful separation.

Love,
M.

Ω

Dear E.,

Of course I still want him to show up. Miguel. He didn't. When Lily and I translated Mexicans into Americans, we understood them. There is no mystery; it is just that no one has taken the trouble to do the translation. For instance, May is the equivalent of August in Paris, the end of summer, so it is the same as with us. We take our vacations at the end of summer. It is not therefore because the Mexicans are like swallows who for no apparent reason fly south by instinct. May is not the mystical month of my stay in a hotel on Cinque de Mayo in Mexico City. Or that I should greet a friend's saying that May is a good month for tourism with amazement. It is life here, nada más.

I smoked some grass this morning, shortly after 10, when Miguel was supposed to have shown. I realized that I had misunderstood the reasons for my anxiety, which came more from the quality of the light, that of late afternoon when the fading of the light makes one feel prematurely dead and comes as a revelation after the brilliance of the morning. That dull yellow light feels like a revealed truth: that *it* is what one finally ends up with. It is the later, therefore more authentic, truth.

I had wanted something for nothing with Miguel. Of course he would feel nothing but kindly pranksterism for a woman he'd met a month ago and hadn't pursued at the time.

I've eaten six sweet rolls so far and two huge glasses of con leche.

[184]

It's the pot/funk munchies. There is no point believing I can ever be desired: so says late afternoon.

I am getting old. The quality of my masturbation has changed. It is dry and forced now. Only believing that you are attractive makes you moist.

When I think of Miguel there is a feeling, as of an iron bar bending ever so slightly against its own strength, inside my gut. But this desire cannot be satisfied by sex. I am impotent like eighty-year-old Pepe from Zi who said he'd sacrifice all the muscularity to which he's retraining his body (after a stroke) for one good erection. I shouldn't have sneered at him as being a typical dirty old man. There is real pain in the loss of desire. Impotence is the body's secret knowledge that it is no longer desirable. That no one will ever go down on you first and eagerly. What agony to be in love with twenty and twenty-five-year-olds and know they're doing you a favor, that from now on it is you who must do the tricks and get nothing in return. No one marveling at your beauties. Though your leg is hard it is covered by late skin. No one except a Pepe. To know that ever more you will become like the ugly man at the next table who induces a tortured search in others for a reason for his existence. For how can impenetrable beings walk the same earth? People whom we can't understand why anyone would ever want them, and whom we could never connect with because the only contact is through desire. *That* is what Miguel's rejection means. That I am the man at the next table.

So why did he call? If I translate in American terms he called in a moment of boredom at work, or in a momentary lull in his life; the way, as teenagers, we would call random telephone numbers and tease. Or again, he didn't show because of a different boredom: his request about visiting my room. When I accepted, then he had me and felt the boredom I did when I thought now I won't be able to see anyone else. Two birds in the bush are preferable, always.

It is too late now to wonder if a fat attractive man sitting at a far table finds me attractive. I am full of food.

There were certain kinds of sweet rolls I wanted to eat this morning but ended up eating ones that bored me. I can't even get what I want with food. I almost never eat delicious food when I gorge. I think I eat sweet rolls and coffee because they are such abstract food. It involves no choice and sweet rolls, seeming crude, uncooked, sweet white blandness—what? What is the difference between turtle stew and a roll? Turtle stew commits one to life. It has the *influences*—herbs and other ingredients, way of preparation, which when eaten imply a willingness to participate in the multifariousness of life and include oneself in the stream of time. Better not to want anything when one is weak and one chooses the nullity of rolls. . . .

Oh Miguel, why did you do this to me? The unreality should have told me. My inability to plan our days together. The whole enterprise was a fantastic figment. Why can't I live without being a man-junky?

Oh well.

I ate to insure I believed Miguel wouldn't show. I am so sad. The music at the Flor, as usual, is sad outre-monde muzak which places one squarely out of Mexico. This wrong music fills my emptiness. I am a balloon of international muzak.

Only loss permits depth. When Miguel didn't show and I smoked the grass and saw one of the peripheral bars of the balcony grill flex only then did I understand my physical feeling for him.

But pain subjects one to the rules of reality. One is no different and one therefore understands others. Plus disappointment of the ego means one has to reconstitute reality. Or is it just a contact with reality? No. What is it about pain that makes one search for deeper words?

Cooked food represents the willingness to be influenced, cut up and reconstituted a certain way. In order to accept turtle stew then I must believe in or at least risk change, the ephemeralness of relationships, and in order to do this I must believe that pleasure is in store for me in the future. A roll is a frozen miracle, it has not passed through individuality or time; is unrejectable. It is not specific, but bland and uniformly sweet. Just as there is no more turtle stew for me, no one will seek my individuality out. I am a sweet roll.

If only he had shown I would still be thin. I've eaten ten rolls by now, a fruit cup, two big milk coffees. The fruit cup hurt to buy—I was admitting I was present. Rolls make me invisible. The fruit cup was a return to the time I was being thin for love. It is weak to be thin. Only the fat are not deceived. . . .

I am almost back into that mind-set of the fifties and early sixties—that you are who chooses you. I can't explain it, it's mystical. Anyone who chooses you, you deserve. Feminism—Lily and I choosing a different boy every night—is not the rule of reality. How

[186]

sweet with Lily. Eliseo was eighteen, Tomás twenty-two, Federico twenty-two. I told Federico to keep his teeth bared at all costs and then I tried to force my tongue in, tugged at his lips, twisted my head this way and that to move him. My panting increased—he let me in a bit and kept his arm under my head all night. Eliseo had three different angles when he bobbed a close dance. Head one way, shoulders opposite angle, while knee sliced in diagonally. Above me, Indian but blond and blue-eyed, he was a sun of remote and tender amusement at my surprise and pleasure.

It was fantastic with Lily in Zi. Everyone knew us as a team and for a while, we were into a male set of feeling that all other things being equal, we'd go for a new chavo rather than one we'd had. Except that occasionally I wondered if they didn't feel a tremor of remembered desire in their loins as I did. Rafael the homosexual said they avoided us after because of Catholic guilt. L. and I decided it was boredom, as with us. We understood that if we lived in a world where women could choose, could be old, ugly, be assured of always leaving someone wanting us, everything men have, we could do it too. Be assured of always being attractive.

Whose is the truth? Whom I choose or who chooses me?

This early afternoon a brusque knock on my door made me actually get up filthy and indifferent. It was one of the numerous nameless tribe of desk boys to tell me a Señor N. [Miguel] was calling me from Mexico City.

I was cool. Waited for his moves. He said his car broke down. He'd borrow another. He no longer sold leather goods. Was going to be loaned money by his family to buy a restaurant. What was I doing with my time? Oh, swimming. Did I go out to dance? Yes, last night, Le Dôme. . . . How much longer was I going to stay in Acapulco?

You do see the tone of the conversation? Half yes *I'm* coming, half what are *you* going to do next. It gives me pleasure to hear your voice, he says. I am silent. Somewhere I put in "no te creo; toda esta cosa es una abstracción, una ficción." We met a month ago, you don't remember me, and I too can hardly remember you. "No, me acuerdo," he gently protests. He really wants to see me, and communicar with me, an odd choice of word if I transliterate, a word of commercial transaction. "Why do you want to see me?" I ask. "Tu me caes bien, Marise." He says Marise instead of Marissa or Maritza, which is really intimate.

[187]

All I want to say is, Chilango,* why did you make me suffer like this? Is this a novia test? Do you crucify women to brand them as yours? Oh Chilango, why?

He said he would come tomorrow, giving no time of arrival. He'd be my companion in Acapulco since I was alone and we'd have a good time. How? Dancing. Had I gone . . . and that was the rhythm of the thing. Why the asshole pursues this is anyone's guess. Dinero, probably, which I made it quite clear I wasn't about to supply.

As I crossed the street before, I thought: I daren't understand too much. Especially in Lily's absence. When she was present, the objective realities we discovered through observation and transla-tion—understanding everything until we understood yet another layer—didn't hurt me so much because they applied to her, a more attractive woman, as well. To understand is to bar myself from the other food, the one that makes me thin, delicious fantasy. . . .

Jesus, is this life that I feel in Mexico? Unimaginable despairs at decaying after exquisite glancings off youth. And the dancing. Sometimes when I'm drunk my body moves in new directions and in undiscovered tempos.

Dancing. I must do justice to it before I die, which is soon to judge by the terminal dry hacking that spasms through my body. If the price of health is isolation, boredom and stupidity, it is too high. Yet, of course, an effort at health, like any discipline, will renew my card-carrying membership in the club of life. I will have merited to live. And, who knows, perhaps it will improve my looks, give me another year of attracting tit-and pussy-hung chavos before the money vultures start hovering over my tan but flabby, well-preserved path to the grave. My theme really must be the pain, the processes of getting older, not only as a woman but as a conscious-ness ever more remote from origins and ever wiser about the last stages. I cannot bear to write this. Surely you're weeping too at reading this. How unutterably sad: to be born only in order to decay and depart forever from places one has mastered, that have be-longed to one, or even from a life one hasn't yet had a chance to deserve inheriting because of laziness and fear. I can't put it well, that self of the absurdity of leaving life, of leaving this grubby, lively municipal beach across from the Zócalo where already I am a phantom, unseen by the cavorting teenage girls splashing in the

* Nickname for someone from Mexico City.

[188]

shallow water as the wind carries their thin shrieks of delight, their "ándales!" in currents out to sea, and not to me. . . .

This is the second day I haven't exercised or swum. I was so truly beautiful before, 112, imagine! Such a pronounced waist, flat stomach. Everywhere thinness slanting into shallow curves, shoals. Broad and narrow balances. Broad shoulders, flat stomach; waist sliding into sloping curve of ass in a profile view. Strong thighs thicker than my waist, muscled. Everywhere balance, shape. . . .

Why should I call Chilango back? Is he an exception to the rules that govern the universe, the eternal va et vient of Mexican relations? Will he admire my body's profile in the mirror? Will he grant me, rather than another, deed to life?

If only my pen were up to my experience and my clit could erect spontaneously without my dry and labored intercession. Poor Pepe. Poor me, poor you, poor Lily soon. We were very close in Zi but not here. Acapulco is too big to hit with a contra-onda which was our one real bond—discussing the day's activity in Zi's small life laboratory. What enamored researchers we were and so penetrating, satirical, and hard-living we shocked the town into awareness of its being observed. It was so dense, mystical, ever-enlarging. So interrelating. So conducive to insight and mystification both. The tides, the veritable ondas, of understanding. . . .

It is too late to call Miguel but why else do I risk disapproval by pouring myself some tequila in this brightly lit cheap family-style restaurant where the waitress beams kindly recognition on me from last year? And why is my cunt reminding me of its existence, sending moist signals to my brain, a premature rainy season, at least for the country. "Sí, me acuerdo de tí," he said. You can't imagine the sexist repression of women in Mexico and at the same time, the tenderness of the men towards women.

Call—not call. I can't of course. He called. I was cold and said I don't believe you anymore. Do what you want. To call would be so pussy, would insure his fucking conquest and permanent indifference. If I don't call, I remain forever a tender acuerdo, misted in sentimental what-might-have-been plus the tenderness induced in him by the bad treatment of me. Lily and I agreed on this too: how tenderly we feel toward men we hurt as if, Lily said, it made us equals at the very least, or else was such a rare feeling . . . no, I don't remember. Not only did we share this feeling, but we found it universal. We began, because of our gringa sluttishness, our behaving like men, to feel that women and men share the same psychol ogy. It's a question of circumstances. Like men, if we had power—knowledge, the ability to manipulate—we would experience, as we finally agreed they did, one night of perfect desire, to be followed the next by a search for a different pleasure, a different beauty. Anyway, José said the novia of a twenty-five-year-old is sixteen—always young—because then she'll know passion only with him. Not only his fear of infidelity, but more—a desire to identify himself, his very own self, with the feeling. To become Pan. To steal the knowledge of desire from her. To have a young novia signifies: To domesticate a woman, like an animal, by socially castrating her. They don't castrate women, just remove their desire for other men, or remove the knowledge of the independent nature of their desire. One castrates horses and other animals to make them submissive. It is incredible to imagine that men view us as domestic animals, but I think this is often true, that they see us as a *function*.

It is odd that I should feel objectively more attractive yet get less attention this year than last. They know when you're used; they want only virgin gringas. Somehow the wind carries the facts of your life down to your most ridiculous and speculative desires.

Looking is a crime here, I think, for a woman.

Oh lord, almost 10:30. So very late to call a rejecting Chilango who lives with a female relative. . . .

It is 10:35. What could I use as pretext? Forgive my earlier sullenness. I want to see you. If it's too much hassle for you to come here I'll meet you in Mexico City. You are my Chilango after all, and I will be your gringa novia. . . . I want to insure seeing him. Yet I am clean now, I have survived. I am in my butch look, freshly laundered, and I have won the last round. If I give him up, he will be my sweet might-have-been. If only, however, there were replacements. I will go home and sleep. Miguel was my Calvary. My sign, my test from God: if I can conquer my desire to pursue him, I will come out all right in the end, I will have proved myself macha. *But*—the cost is respectable boredom. If I call him and he rejects me and there is pain and shame, I have an excuse to slut off into the night and replenish desire.

What can I learn of them? Why do they lie so? I ask the barefoot guy crossing the street. Like the Guatemalan, I come to an impasse in understanding I cannot bridge. Desire could leap across it, understanding peers blindly across the abyss. I am being allegorical these days rather than metaphorical. Ah yes. Metaphor is the

[190]

miracle of unsuspected connection: one thing leaping to join another. What is allegory, she asks, tailbone in aching contact with the balcony floor, wondering why she didn't bring the tequila out with her but not worrying too much about getting her khaki pants dirty. Soon, again, they'll be too big for her, if she can only ignore the profound bass, the pits, of her mission on earth. To be crucified for her desire, the ugly woman in aching contact with the stone immovability of others. . . . But oh, the rest of the world is *so* dull, so matter-of-fact, so *homed*, you might say. Only an orphan can be so concerned with perception, so unassuming about everything.

How can I, so young, so eternally young, unformed, naive and intelligent, so willing to be gay, to take risks, to learn, so willing always to pursue the only truth, the truth I merit—beauty, beauty, the word is an incantation, my incantation—how can I so thin and young and brown and strong, how can I be viewed, how can I *be*, old?

Writing, like the dance, something unknown to one, a profound melody takes over and guides our pen away into new risks, new detachments.

I prefer, I need, I need it, I tell you, to be desired by Miguel. There is nothing else I can have. You can't offer me anything else.

Ω

Dear E.,
Latest version of letter to Miguel:
Dear Blackie,
I don't know what your game is but I'd like to fuck you once before I leave Mexico, if you have a cock.

Love,
Maritza

Ω

Dear E.,
Outside the church, a very dark fat matron wedding guest made me realize another reason Mexicans would of course hate us. It was

the third reason so I'll give the other two first. The first, when I passed a silver shop, was that they would hate the ease with which we could purchase our pleasures. The second, which made my feeling of godly understanding explicit, was the requiem: "This is a Catholic country after all." I realized that *they* had been here before us and considered *their* forms original. And of course would resent our patronizing ignorance of their greater claim to being the one true form of life, our regarding them as undeveloped or unevolved, our forms more preeminent in the world, taking over theirs. The third, as result of the dark matron, was that we had completely killed off half—at least—of their *blood* I want to say rather than "ancestry." As if we'd gone into their bodies with saws and pumps and hacked and drained away all the Indian in them. They of course perceive us as savagely racist.

My dear. I am better when I rue my lost sapphire earring, each item a totem object to insure Miguel. What totem magic clothes have for women, this I know.

But yesterday, after all the aridity and nonswimming, I immersed myself in an ocean it seemed Acapulco could produce after all for at least an hour. If wetness couldn't be in me, I could be in it. It was such unmitigated joy to be in water, wet, moving, slicing, weightless, finally in contact with it, turning in different directions, maneuvering my body like a car, transporting myself wherever I wanted. Out to some rocks, over to the hotel, out to sea, to China, back again when a lifeguard blew a warning whistle. To be in the water again was to be joyfully reunited with my mother, my element. Water, water—everywhere. I swam a half-mile. Couldn't keep myself out of it. I loved swimming—not just the hard exercise and then the meditation—but the moving of limbs in the wet, "malleating" it. I walked all told eight miles at least yesterday and danced five or six hours straight. Though in my mood last night it was hard not to feel I had reached my limit and was merely doing a stale parody of myself.

Am I destined to be an expatriate? I've always felt temporary in America, or whatever scene I was in. Is this finally my home? Or is it that Mexico is really permanent temporariness?

Ω

Dearest E. babe,
Mexico City is a *city*, a conservative place, there are filthy Indian chavos on the subway. Life seems lost in a Spaniard-y maze of cars and courtesies, subways and real jobs, apartments, families, dirt, businesses—the stuff of yet another life-support system whose assumptions I haven't yet mastered. Oh laconic Californians who wisely blink when you speak your strange piece and pronounce: "Culture shock!"

I called him twice, the fink who was supposed to meet me at the terminal. . . .

I feel a tremorous foreboding—cars whir outside my window—that I will never hear from him again. Just as I came to the end of the line with the bus and must switch terminals to go south. He will elude me at the heart of the labryinth. . . .

I thought, as I held the bus back with all my strength on curves: what I had was what I got and the journey, the getting there, is all there ever is. Yesterday I felt that everything I'd written you was somehow stained and that I would wash it away as I do the day's dirt from my clothes, with a new letter. Every previous day's perceptions seem soiled. It is only a way of saying that it all changes. The "mediated strangeness" I wrote about was something I felt in my blood. It was a twilight understanding washed away by the morning's bright sexuality. I woke up yesterday feeling tender about all the boys I'd slept with, and I strung together a necklace of all the things I'd done with them that I suddenly remembered again.

So I took Eliseo up to Greta's house. Then began an hour-long series of passionate embraces of recognition, discovery, that I initiated, I think, but that he with passionate gratitude, relief, and personal need reciprocated. You know those hugs where one steps back to see if it is really *the* one at long last. Is it really you? You can't believe it, you don't want to believe it, and when the embrace begins to be ever so slightly boring, ever so slightly anonymous, you pull back to renew the magic of him. Him! I mean he grabbed me, he crushed me to his breast, he ground his mouth down on mine, twisting his head to move his mouth in every direction on and in mine. He showed me proudly the strength in his young arms and in his beautiful back and I did exactly the same and my physical strength turned him on. Chums, passionate friends in Eros. Oh

[193]

Jesus, Jesus Jesus. It is almost 10 A.M. A glassful of cigs, a nervous maid outside, no dimetapps, no Miguel, but a sty and a gray sky and no discipline to do exercises let alone tasks.

The hugging went on interminably. The bamboo loft platform was spacious and the flat sheet-covered foam mattress lay neat and yellow illumined under its tied-overhead pale lavender mosquito net. Everywhere the beauty of natural materials and nothing but two beds far apart and the one candle, everywhere taste—my good taste impressing him—and freedom and action. Privacy, space, coolness, the exactly right light. I felt my body was beautiful and he smiled every time I wanted him to. That too is so Mexican, that charmed passivity. When I think of American men making love it is of them grimly twisting you this way and that, putting a pillow under your ass, etc. Mexican boys are so pleased to learn, such sweet pupils. . . .

And then he was in me, unarrogantly huge and easy and then I was stretched out taut to make myself come and he kept his hand there too. And after I'd come he did this incredible two places at once thing to my cunt with this relaxed and practiced hand, a rhythm as regular and relaxed as his dancing. Moist. I was wet. I should've let him do it forever. Yes, I panted. That whole night Eliseo and I panted. We worked ourselves up to a pant, a heat, a dead heat in a race. Equals. Arm wrestlers. Congratulating each other on our mutual win, our ability to give each other equal pleasure to really belong together. Yes, it *was* discovery.

M. called. No allusion to his promise to meet me at the terminal. We had arranged to meet at 4 and go shopping. My rigor mortis grin of despairing captivation must've distorted the telephone wires. What is your job? I managed to loosen my mouth to ask seductively. He'll tell me when he sees me. Pimp???

Love,
M.

Ω

Dear E.,

It is all too rich—and too soon to be over—to write. Spent from 6 P.M. Tuesday to 11:30 A.M. Thursday with my samurai Miguel, who lives in the Mexican equivalent of Bay Ridge or Canarsie, where I had lunch with his family yesterday. He is twenty-eight and has a

[194]

small potbelly—panza—and is the darkest in his family, pretty close to a pure blood and absolutely such an animated face and incantatory way of speaking and a strange N.Y. Italian life. He looks Italian in the day and Japanese in bed, only dark, a dark that looks yellow at times, gray and dusky at others. Pure black hair which he washes every morning, shakes dry, combs and shapes. . . .

Yesterday, he dragged me everywhere in his new neighborhood and we necked in little groceries. . . .

Does only Don Juan—because he's sexless, goddamit—know that nothing matters. I know this. . . .

He just called: 10:15. I understand them now. Castaneda. It flees quicker than the pen. What? That they use language more figuratively than we do. When he asked me out for a "fiesta," a party, he meant "to party," or the possibility of partying.

Now I need him to explain Indian mysticism. This country tears me evenly between rationality and mysticism. Oh E., do come, it's another, more beautiful, world. Last night under pot I thought: He is all the dark flowers I've ever wanted in the world collapsed into one, and managed to convey this to him. Though what he was telling me, far more important, I couldn't understand. I am absolutely, banally—that is in a way that only a drunk would perceive and unperceive as original—in love with him. Last night, his eyes rolled out of his eyeballs to fall off the face of the earth as he danced like Eliseo with his samurai face. What I told him is true however, if he doesn't show within ten (fifteen) minutes—my time not his goddamnit—I will lurch off into the night to hit cheap Garibaldi square and pick up a better-looker.

What will happen to me without a man, sex? It is my theme. I thought, at the final stage, to define love at last with him as unwitting collaborator. Yes. He knows I want him. Knows he's the best I can get with my face and age. Must've deduced it from my skin or from rummaging in my stuff. Will he wonder why the cards in his case sit differently and attribute it to Indian magic? Oh mystical country, country of my heart, country where my will to not understand triumphs. . . .

Four days later. Am in the café next door having left Miguel sleeping in my bed muttering darkly that he'd had a bad dream.

M. introduced me to nearly all his family of two brothers and six marvelous sisters, assorted nieces and nephews. He is the least bourgeois and last night broke the magic spell I'd been under with him of living an unmediated opera out of Rhys or Owens: shacking up in my high-ceilinged hotel room, drinking and turning on all night, sleeping through the day, never any money, sex at any hour, both of us breaking some sort of record. My wondering whether his face, his eyes, his color, will be an inexhaustible insurance that I will never be bored, and being grateful this morning—Sunday—that for the first time he asked me if I would let him sleep a little longer. . . . My anxiety about his inferior status in his family as a dark and delinquent Indian and the way he unavoidably suffers from this infuriates but finally convinces me will be alleviated by his contempt for me, for old ugliness, *my* source of shame.

Getting high with him initially was one of the greatest pleasures of my life. I never thought grass, or grass with someone else, could be so sheerly pleasurable: that utter relaxation in the midst of a brilliant making sense of life. I feared no ugly revelation with him as I did forever after a bad experience with—; a boredom that had lain coiled up all along suddenly sprang up and I felt a despair so intense it drove me to attempt suicide. This, because Miguel is dark, because of my adoration of his face, could not happen with him. Physical attraction, for me, is an indestructible, because physical, base. I told him this but don't know if he understood. Often a wrong preposition, or tense, or literalism instead of an idiom, destroys an entire fabric of explanation.

Yesterday I thought my, my, at least he never bores me.

He asked me yesterday (after I roiled above him in charming beggary to please take me dancing) to perform an insane task: call up a crippled woman friend of his with some story about his having landed in jail and ask to borrow 150 p's. Oh lord, I thought, he is a *pimp*—that's what it's all about. And when he acted angry that I was angry at the request, I thought more male ploy, one I'm too familiar with, and sprang out of bed vowing that a sacrifice of my very intelligence was too much, *that* was *my* limit. We tortured each other for hours afterwards. He said he'd known last night would be our last, that I would leave him after oh jesus three hours of the most incredible intellectual and physical intimacy, when I called him my soul and he said—oh wondrous Indianness—that the beetle had circled me interminably one stoned night in Zi because it thought I was the sun and I absolutely believed he was correct, that this was a legitimate way of seeing. Called him my love in that rare balance of believing my admission of love would bore neither him nor me, that our perfection of intimacy had been cosmically approved; we were in God's hands. He was my soul, nada más. Desire which completes itself = love.

[196]

So, after this, I found it dismaying to be manipulated into being rejected as if I was too dumb to see who was really rejecting whom. We parlayed for hours after which I worked myself up into an acute sense of loss and managed to screw out a few tears as I struggled, with my newly-washed tan hair flying, to break free of his hold. He dragged me down onto the bed and begged me to hit him. Slapped me gently a few times to incite me. Wicked Chilango with his hoody long black shag and meanly tender slit eyes when he's lying down. . . . And his eyes are an endless movie under his arched eyebrows.

After this incredible scene—an incredible week in every regard—we go to his primary house and sneak exquisite food: a creamy cake, sweet ripe mamey and salpicón, cold marinated shreds of beef with tomato chili, tomato, avocado and who knows what else to make you feel alive. Spent a pleasant boring hour, I watching TV with yet another sister and discussing the hustle with his niece and then we head for another sister's house. On the way he actually presses money on me (I'd finally decided I couldn't afford him) and we go to this other house where he is supposed to be able to negotiate free dwelling for the two of us. . . . I feel I can smoke for the first time, unlike house number one, filled with religious images. Sunday—today—we were supposed to eat goat meat at his brother's restaurant in some resort-y park on the outskirts of the city, and go horseback riding. I must go back to the hotel, a dread pervades me that I really was dismissed half an hour ago.

But for him it is real life, not an unmediated tourist romance. And real life returned last night: *work,* primarily. I returned to the hotel depressed that I had no career and that all the truth of highs and unmediated romances was false.

He is shaving now. The few thoughts I wanted to transcribe scattered by sex and the flood of everything I felt about him in the past. All the ideas. He is the high. It is an intellectual delirium with him. He lacks imaginative grace as a lover but has such kindness. I can't write. It splits apart after physical closeness.

Under pot—knowing I could make no wrong move and that underneath everything in him too lay this quality of peaceful rationality, of a pleasure in thinking that would not take offense at any admission of, for instance, the fleetingness of emotion—believing in my kindness as well and fundamental good intentions. . . .

Are we or aren't we at 2:30 setting out to the country? He'll call

[197]

a friend who'll lend a car, I think he says. But what will actually transpire is an easygoing uncertainty.

I see nothing out of my dirty sunglasses through the dirty train window as I leave Mexico City for Oaxaca and it's true, I understand nothing. Rather, I understand only too well that I've been sent on my way, along with his purple towel and talismanic book and reluctantly proffered little silver bell. This morning, a stripe of warmth from his arm across my chest, the smell of a wet towel draped around his back as he shaved in front of our mirror. The room was ours. And to think that all this only cost me 380 pesos! He had the incredible charm to ask me for money even at the very end: 5 p's, but I bargained him down to 2. His last gesture was to mime that I call him: ¿Sí o no? Sí, sí. . . . After an opera of self-pity and grubbing need you wouldn't believe, begging me not to leave him: no me deja! no me deja! Everyone I've ever wanted has left me. Don't leave me, don't leave me. Why? Why? Why does everyone leave? Marry me, etc. After a performance complete with a quantity of tears, he is gay the next day, telephoning for me to find out when I can leave Mexico, leave him already.

After my night of celibate discipline, touching him never, I cried this morning to see his beauty. How rejection improves looks! Before, when I was winning, even his incredible face looked doggy and his wide hips, his unfortunate bones. His deformed toes. Now, jesus, his hair, his nose, his lips, the pouch formed by the angles in his cheek, the slight lisp though the missing tooth, the eyes—how to describe them? In sex, when closed, they reduce, become small marbles bent on mysterious journeys. Or, before, slits, because dark and reflecting all light, shining as is the way of dark eyes, you never know where they are—they slide off the page and suddenly are focused on you. Chinese slits. Samurai.

No wonder this room in Oaxaca is so cheap. The loudest voice I've ever heard in my life—no, a louder one just followed it—is coming through an amplifier. How they fill their lives with noise. It is a torture this voice, it drives me out of my home—I can't get back into my head—it is an actual physical force, a hand, holding me off from my door.

Here I am surrounded by the same turquoise enamel walls, ready to rush out, tits flying, to scream at him to shut up. I'm almost at that point. I haven't slept in weeks. Did I already tell you

I'm living an exhausted dream, in both senses? Christ. These letters mean nothing to you, to which you never respond, which must frighten if not bore you, which you are no longer excited about since, despite your show of strong autonomy, you were so easily persuaded they were unpublishable. Yet I cling to them. If only to show that I have *passed through*. Pussy New York 77.

What I wanted, what one travels for, are these small differences. What an idiot Miguel was, he wanted to be an "individual" like all my freshman students. "Say Miguel" was the last thing he said to me on the train. "Sí, eres Miguel y yo soy Maryse," I assured him when all I wanted in him was the quintessence of Mexico, of Mexicanness more precisely, since I no longer tour countries, just souls.

I remember thinking once: my god, after all these years, I found a man who loves me. How strange, I felt, in a way I perceived as detached and intellectual. You are too sick to love or be loved, I thought. Not "sick," exactly, just too detached from the world of feeling, from the planet itself. I felt then that I preferred the noncommitting world of one-night stands.

Everything we said to each other was right. Everything about him was about me. One specific thing I remember was that he too was a vampire who lived at night. Though I remember feeling anxious: some lit-up corner of my brain said but the sun is in the day, the sun that makes you beautiful, and how I also love the world of brightness and ocean and exercise. But this folded quickly into our eternal night. It was a night we lived those first few days, with the night's deep secret communion, its unquestioned magic.

Drunken Thursday I successfully translated five pages, those I'd written so far of this letter to you. I could do that then. There was nothing I was afraid to share, it was all so if-fy and strange. I was a bold, drunken, and trusting gambler then. I let him see my errant feelings and he took no offense, had that same dry, wry, warm detachment that I did and which nine hours of separation . . . I had said something about needing time apart in order to regain my ordinary self, to define life in my own terms. We live to lose what we have lived.

We were stoned and boozed a lot and that was our love. It needed that. Oh female vision, when that gringo George said four days of perfect love and no more, that was reality and he was right.

Gringo said: four days. Onto new. Asked self: female truth, too? Answered: yes. Power thing. Their need for power greater, ours for (passive) approval. Don't know, babe. Only felt—god, is this all there is? Four days, nada más?

Miguel vowed eternal protection of me when we parted. Men are so dumb. He said: I will always be at your side, inside you, wherever you go. And never more outside? I wailed. Sí, sí. He learned. Early on, I said cool your tragedy act and perfect your endgame, and yes, I prefer lies to truth, be a hypocrite, why not, where women are concerned. Unbelievably—it made me love him— he learned that quickly.

Gringo said he pulls weakness on fourth day to get chick to reject him. But later, confused by my recital of M.'s very voluminous tears, said, maybe he felt it. Yes. He felt it *at the time.* Oh Mexicans! Oh men. Oh me who believes everyone but me knows the truth, holds a precious treasure in their hands.

So what? I felt. Is this all that life offers? Four days. Yes. Except for accident or will. And my terror that we should separate—that I would never see that Indian icon again—kept him at my side so long, too long.

Tequila, my only friend.... Wish I missed him. I don't. Tequila is my ally, in Don Juan's sense. All there is. I am the bruja of dance, I told him, and quite the literal truth. But that joke wore thin faster than the vampire one. Yet so true. So very true....

So maybe I meant something after all. So what? He's intelligent enough to have experienced intelligence before. But sabes qué? That was one of the miracles—to be loved by and love a man, a boy, whose intelligence I felt equal to. I actually, in my rico-est moments, dug that he was at least as good as I. No, that we were the same. Oh what teasing fun, ripping off a pastry in a store, leaving the cabdriver waiting forever for the rest of his money as we tore off to his house with our own private joke....

I did one last joke. I told him I liked "Gracias a la vida," a song by Violeta Parra, whose second line was "Que me ha dado tanto." Thanks to life, which has given me so much. As we crossed the street to buy booze, he saved me from an oncoming bus. I riposted: "Gracias por *mi vida,* que me ha dado tanto." Thanks for my life (kid) which has given me so much (namely you) and he maybe—who remembers?—squeezed my arm.

If only I could've explained my latest life-theory to him: eternal paradox. Oh, what was his name who ever more I become? Bauldert? *Baudelaire.* Who could salvage from living experience only the dry nuggets of aphorism.

[200]

Did he believe I'd been a college prof? Yes, of course, in that same va and vient, dialectic, of Mexican lies on their way to becoming truth.$ Oh yes, let the accident of crossed-out "s" looking like a dollar sign remain. Oh E. I am lost. Oh Miguel, why did it die?

I could've written to you that this year I went crazy from love as last year I did from being unloved. Is it only, as a gringa I met said, the two-and-a-half-month crazies syndrome after all? And does he know this, as he knows all things, or is he only a blundering ignorance like me?

"One can go crazy from love the same way one can from being unloved." Oh aphorism! But something I didn't want to learn. After all, being rejected is so *easy* to deal with. I am so used to Tennessee Williams's aging female romantics, after all. It is such a comfortable old theme and then this madness, where I had more power that I'd ever dreamed of in my life. The poor dark illiterate one who broke down and sobbed don't ever leave me so that I was ready to take the next flight out to Oaxaca and Lily and the rational ironic world. What absolute terror!

And yet it was a program, meant to scare me. And, at the same time, wasn't, says the gringo, whom I believe as I believe everyone more than my own computer mind. What a transformation, hija! Oh awful life. It was his and my last intellectual investigation: his passing in one night from terrifying need to remote gaiety. Did he understand this? Why did he speak to me in a language I couldn't understand all that long week? I'm insane now. No pleasure, as usual, in it. My insanity insures its overness. Plus that my letter to him speaks of things I don't speak of to you. Is there no one truth, no one depository of one's authentic being?

A million things. At one point, after three days, four? I would've died happy. I've had it all, I thought. What a miracle at thirty-six, to have this gorgeous hood chavo in love with me.

Oaxaca enchants in the day: the colors of houses ... I will do mañana para tí but at night, qué mala onda. Qué non-onda. ...

Cockroaches approach me here. I let them. Beetles are my allies, I let them live but wish they wouldn't worship me at such proximity. ...

Next day. I manage a quick dry rub-off to thoughts of Miguel, not sex but our domestic intimacy.

Sex. So difficult to describe a cosmic cycle of the creation and degeneration of a star. And despite myself I chose to live rather than write. I could've written the magic of his face say up to the fourth night if I'd stepped back, or he'd dismissed me, which is perhaps why I'm better on one-night stands.

Miguel. He got hard easily, but lost it at my portals. I pitied and loved and was flattered by his impotence. He said in midweek that he sometimes didn't come with women. Imagine a man, so are Mexicans, so passive, gentle and adaptive, so sad and cosmically accepting, that he'd not insist on getting his rocks off. Once I let him come in my mouth. His come was thicker and whiter than other men's and had a unique almond sweetness, it was dulce, was a dulce, a sweet, a flan. Toward the end I also figured it was his problem that he wouldn't lick my cunt, whose image as a coral interesting fruit, clean smelling and almond too, floated up and filled my head. My head became this lovely cunt fruit. This was after he'd gotten used to my coming from my clit, after many verbal and physical lessons, and I'd gotten comfortable with him knowing my anatomy, and its normalcy. What a plum you'll be for gringas, I teased him, once I've taught you the clit, the dance, and the English language.

We made it on a chair once. He wanted to fuck me in the ass but I hadn't shit in over a week and was afraid of a deluge of shit in mid-sex. Besides, it was bait for the future. It's a night thing I said, punning on depth, darkness, disease, decadence—death? Once I called his dark looks the inside of a volcano. How pleased he was!

In the cathedral, which he'd never entered before, he asked whether I liked a huge baroque altar table. I didn't know, had no time to get into its onda. All I could remember was that at twenty-five that was what I used to do in France, get mystically historically tranced in front of ancient architectures. I don't know I said, do you? Well, he faltered, he really was so adaptive. Finally I forced myself to perceive the outer sensory world and saw four rich red tones on the altar, the rug, the seats, some sacred cloths. How rich the world is in colors, I said, and he seemed ungrateful for this info, which, however, relieved me. I'd gone through a rapid anxious little dialetic there—rueing the lost acuteness of perception of yesteryear, both sensory and intellectual—the discipline of seeing, and amassing, a huge variegated knowledge of the world both wide and deep. And then had consoled myself with the thought that one can't retain all one's modes, all one's knowledges, that I was pursuing a different knowledge now, a sociological, sexual, even (life) mystical one—knowledge of love, aging, Mexico, translation—but of course I

[202]

must've felt diminished by my loss of acute and independent, intellectual, youth, as one always mourns any loss. And, more subliminally, worrisomely, must have at some level felt a thinness in my present consciousness, if only because of his anxiety about his cultural vacuity, or, more precisely, that he felt he had to round himself out, *increase* himself, no—add culture to himself to make himself richer for me as if what he was, what we were living, wasn't dense enough. So I produced color. It was a jolt, waking up from my rich and wordless dream—our life of consciousness in bed, deep, warm, undifferentiated and cosmic, dark interstellar exploding galaxy—to a world of highly distinct forms, and history.

Sex. Almost the last time we made it, when I'd lost the ability to see his eyes, I was on top of him, stretching my beautiful shape (this I definitely have) tautly tanly back from his waist, anxious as usual about whether his prick would slide out at that tense angle. I'd just taken a bath and my hair was wet golden shaggy. I was getting off on my own beauts, as you see, and he began doing a complicated dance with his mouth. That same slight slipping out of the tongue that he'd regaled me with that night dancing in Zi and which then I'd thought was vulgarity incarnate though it didn't prevent my amusement and desire, and which I had finally understood as a sign of irrepressible delectation, if this sentence is followable. Anyway, that little snake of a tongue slid out and in and to all corners of the world, all the hemispheres, at varying intervals. It was a language, damn it. When his cock touched my walls, it came out or went in—who analyzed conjunctions then?—was a sensory language of desire completing itself. Which is so irreducibly aphoristic for me that I should, alas, forever imprison its private totem magic for me in quotation marks. Desire—delectation—in the mouth and tongue in the very act of lower down achieving itself. *That* is good sex. For me, though, it wasn't happening down below, seeing his mouth opera made me quiver, made me pant esthetically and finally sexually. The perfect trust, too, of his play, of his letting me see it. I am coming. I will lock the door for another, moister, run.

But I return to the page, trying to beat out further perceptions, so that I can transcribe that writing is a come and *that* is what his mouth meant. That other besides genital things were come. But back to trust, that was very sexually exciting. What do I mean?

Trust. I don't know. He let me see him experimenting, taking risks. Let me see him at loosest experimental play, directed at me, and which could have either repelled or bored me. We maintained

[203]

complete eye contact except for when my eyes took in his mouth
only to return with greater knowledge and desire. Let me witness his
privacy, his fantasy, and of course we both so brilliantly perceived
what he was doing and I was witnessing as a language, and a
wordless one. So that all that fear we both experienced in the
cathedral at our noncultural, therefore, traditionally nonintelligent,
life was brilliantly redeemed. . . .

That hot day when I was in widow's existential black, distracted
in my bureaucratic rounds by five interesting people, away, away
from my Chilango lover, experiencing, reveling in, dazzling a
world—the outside world—I excelled in with wit and play and
cynicism. I am researching the world of desire, I told a French
student.

Then there was this extraordinary couple that aroused my
deepest tenderness. I was first introduced to them by a dull Canadian chick's ironic amused disapproval of the woman, who was
creating a scene about some document she shared with a seedy
cowed-looking Mexican, as if he'd robbed or raped her. She was a
blowsy illiterate from Chicago, missing a tooth, married to this guy
who wore black synthetic sharkskin pants with cheap light-colored
gaucho inserts in his pants below the knees. A grubbier pair you
never saw. He'd been an illegal immigrant, they'd married, he'd still
been scared to go for citizenship papers and despite his marriage to
her, a U.S. citizen, he'd been deported. Couldn't find a job in
Mexico, her rich uncle (how could she have one?) had stopped
sending her money. They'd been through the Kafka maze we all
had been through. When their situation explained itself, each
taking gentle, loving, turns, they relaxed into such a gently unfortunate and generous intimacy with us, we were fascinated and sympathetic. I can't. They told me of a cheap hotel, held my number as I
left to tell sweating-in-the-streets Miguel it would only be a "rato"
más. Ran back in. It was a fiesta, verdad. I suppose what appealed
deepest was the tenderness of superior (missing tooth) woman and
inferior (speaking Spanish; getting liked, one of them, to Mexican
bureaucrats) man. That through this all, they'd stuck together.
Both ugly in different ways: she fat but loving him, her anger a
frustrated caress; he Mexican and intelligent, soft and low-spoken,
and tender about her, despite her masculinity and public pillorying.
They'd been through it, would go through more but she had
married an illegal entrant for reasons of her own. Had so dug his
dark Chinese thinness and low voice, low warm looks, and he her

[204]

energy and one must assume, undisputed passion for his dark oppressed gentleness. What can I add? Couple on the equivocal trip of life. . . .

Long interruption of charming thirty-three-year-old maid whom gave a shot of tequila to and who knows I dig straight hair because it moves in the baile, dance. I tell you Oaxaqueñan women know how to smack men around, Juanita says. Incredible woman. . . . That's what I mean about women here: they bond with women. The buddy system that prevails [in Oaxaca] is *female*. Love this city's, state's, women. Dig dancing close, she asks? Depends, I say. My Guerrero friend I'm fixing you up with tomorrow is good for slow dancing, she says, and por aquí también, she adds, slapping the bed. They are marvelous, E., our own. As we are all our own. As it has taken me, us, so long to figure out we are all our own. . . . Sweet docile Indians. What crap. Oaxaca is where the women hang out. She digs güeros, light-skinned men, I morenos. Sure, she says, 'cause you're light. Nothing she doesn't know. She has a cunt and I have a cunt and we want to put them to some use before we die. Miguel. How right. My love for women sometimes competes with my love for men.

Back to Miguel. Well, imagine, after this whole bureaucratic fiesta, after my dim stupidity and then my deeply moved and analogous passion for the gringa-chicano seedy couple, there he is, sweating in his black leather, patiently Indian waiting in the cooking alive city streets, for me. I had missed seeing him on my last foray an hour earlier and had thought, oh well, it was more than even this aging piece of gringa meat expected, this on Friday. And had been less than festive with stewardess and couple, distracted by past needs, unready to move on to present and future pleasures, which, not so oddly, were made possible only by his steady dark sullen presence, as if gaiety were only a proof to him of my desirability, as well as a necessary recreation from his imprisoning simplicity.

One of my earliest and most grateful surprises about him was his almost masochistic way of cleaning up after my errors. I'd spill an ash and he'd wipe it up from the floor. Gracias, I would murmur from my bowels, moved that deep. He'd fold up a pair of my pants. Oh lord.

You're an adult at night, I say one stoned night, and a child, an adolescent, during the day. An adult is one who understands everything, a child nothing, I intone, and to this gibberish defini-

[205]

tion by daylight standards he assents in full recognition. Ah! stoned
mysteries. You are the brujo of the day, I the night bruja, I say. My
frog, which he coveted and which I no longer wore, he spent a half
hour one evening cleaning. When I left Mexico City, Miguel
pointed to my frog—my bruja emblem—and said it goes out shining:
"Se va brillante." Oh my poetic babe. Is this whole letter symbols
looking for a home?

And of course I learned from Augusta too that there are
universal verities. My dear, I thought, love, sex, men are not
enough. I am missing the truth somewhere. The truth is larger than
him. On the seventh or eighth day, I looked out my windows to a
begrimed iron balcony railing and beyond, the concrete facade,
almost gargoyle in aspect, of some dour government edifice, and my
lord, it must've been three-year-old me on our grimy Paris balcony
in the dixième arrondissement and I went loca and thought, one
can go mad from love as one can from unlove. Awful disorientation.
Anyway, I thought, Augusta is right—Miguel cannot contain me
since he excluded the madness of Paris pawn shop balcony views.
The strangeness of the voyage—to plunge into it and emerge with
an intelligible and beautiful translation, this must be the truth.
Though at the time, it was a more specific, more Augusta version of
mysticism; the very idea of God.

Ciao,
M.

Ω

Oh dear E.,

Why is it that when I have just finished destroying my 112
pound beauty with one fruit cup, two flaky pastries filled respectively with pineapple and vanilla custard, one bowl of onion soup
with a thick sponge roll to sop it up with, a plate of rice, a dish of
riñones, (kidneys, a la Mexican, in a sauce), with one more huge roll
and tortilla to combine with whatever sauce is left over, and beans
and flan and café con leche—why when the last bit of roll, the very
crust is sopping up the last wet on the plate, when I have eaten
ravenously, one dish following the other in my hungry gut, why
when that tiny pyramidical crust is staring up at me, a miniature
Indian ruin, do I remember the second, delicious, Miguel memory?

It must've been on stoned Thursday, the "Fiesta" night he almost didn't come except for my imperious command, and came to find me lushed, a volatile Carmen of cynicism, ardor, lost dreams, piercing intelligence, a lion (leónita, little lion, he once called me) and though duly impressed fed me grass to calm me. Stoned, I rolled above his face and twisted away from its impenetrable and unpossessable beauty. I could not look at his face. He looked pantherish himself. To see his face was to want it knowing I never could have it. His eyes were curious black almond slits and his hair lay about him, skeins of ebony silk. Once I told him he had a sharp face, a nose like a hatchet, everything chiseled, as I caressed it in my broken Spanish.

I suppose—oh psychology—I ate because he didn't feed me a letter and because I caught sight of my tan, muscular but flaccidly old arms in a papelería window today. So that Rolando's age guess of thirty or thirty-five made visible sense. You see that was part of the magic, that this was happening to me when it no longer could. When I could only be a sex guru to eighteen-year-olds for one intoxicating night. Hey, the old broad really swings. Hey look at Bessie Smith boogie in the disco. She still gives pleasure.

Something awful just happened to me in the market on my way home after picking up a young dude who escorted me to a switch-blade and then asked for a fuck rendezvous. I was walking down the street past endless Indian women squatting beside piles of inter-minable vegetables, a blur of tomatoes, chilies, limes, onions, po-tatoes. I had passed from the red to the brown, when I thought I saw my hotel across them. There seemed no break in the vegetables and after a moment's hesitation, I jumped across a pile of small potatoes in my red dress. I heard an angry noise and almost simultaneously felt a sharp, unidentifiable blow on my right leg. The Indian woman on my right, in a tattered dirty apple-green rayon dress had struck me. The man on the left and she began angrily asking me what was the big idea. I said I lived across the street; they pointed further down the row of vegetables. I mimed that I hadn't seen a break. They kept on and on and finally I said, excuse me, I didn't know—meaning, I don't know your mores. Faultlessly polite to the last. The man called me a "cochina," a pig. Everyone is listening up and down the street, six rows deep—stores, vendors in front of stores and rows on either side of the gutter—this is Mexico's biggest market day. I was stunned and said you're a cochino. No, you, said the woman. No, you, I addressed her, in the familiar. I rushed back to my hotel and whipped off my bikini bathing suit bottom and smelled it close up. Despite being worn nearly a whole day and a half and the first bout of diarrhea I've had this year, there is absolutely no odor. (I wash after I shit, as pendeja as they are.) I stick my finger up into my cunt, and still nothing. What did I do? I asked after I said "no sabe," I didn't know. That's when the man didn't respond, called me a pig. And, truth told, my moment's hesitation before I nimbly hurdled the potatoes was that my cunt might smell, that they might smell it.

But for them, my cunt exuded a miasma that would waft down and taint the potatoes. As if I would have if I really stank. Oh lord, lord. I have ruined their day's sales. They will blame bad crops on me. Ellen passes in review: all the little boys without underpants but never the little girls, that's why they're a pussy-hung country, she says. A shadow passes over Miguel's face, an unsolicited darkness, and I am filled with black hatred for their hatred, their disgust, their fear, their divine destruction, of my cunt, your cunt, the schmuck who never went down on me properly after I bathed and parted myself. Once I incanted, "sepárame, divísame." Separate me, separate me. But he wouldn't even guide his own prick in but force my head down to his cock, that yes. Once he was on top of me, we were attempting to sixty-nine before my period, and I smelled the rancid sweet odor that lodges behind men's balls because they don't wash properly and swallowed my disgust as well as, later, his almond syrup, his jugo de horchata—more than agua. More than jugo. Even with my period I taught him, after he made some ghastly remark about not being a vampire—sixty-nine was wafting about as usual, as well as ass-fucking—and which he infuriatingly denied, the way he denied every offense, daring me to make my clarity or anger about his viciousness explicit and risk losing him, not to fear blood, even sixty-nine. And he lied to me—you're the first one I've ever gone down on, he says. What he did once (cursorily lick my clit three times with a frightened tongue) he calls a blow job. All those obnoxious times he said he wanted to eat me, or else licked his tongue with gusto but only, always, to thrust my head down onto his deficient organ which I tolerated for his sake. And the complaints about *all* the other women! How he'd wanted to go down on them but they were too tonta, too *idiotic*, imagine, to permit it. I actually launch into an explanation of how Mexico—the world, natch, but his country especially—makes women loathe their organs. Even masturbation is not—and he actually helps me complete the

[208]

sentence—tolerated in women. I felt clean after this explanation, restored to a normal sense of things and liked my cunt more and more. More and more it seemed a fresh delectable fruit. I told him the words I knew for it—biscocho, and papaya, and semilla seed. He taught me "mamey" (an exquisite coral fruit) and "calabaza" (squash).

I suppose after a while I knew he was into me for sexual experiments. Puta gringa pussy whore. Asshole. Fucking asshole prick with that wretched odor in his thatched straight black hair crotch, smell stuck to the thatching. . . .

Behind their Indian sweetness lurks this horror, this hatred, this primitive black stupidity. I want the sweet eighteenth-century coral tint of reason.

Miguel. You've bewitched me, he said, and once we spent part of an afternoon dragging through the streets him telling me all his clothes of yore: ten suits, tailor-made in thin-striped fine cashmere; white on grey or dark blue and a suit of café. Imagine creamy brown on his skin. All in brown, he said he liked to dress, or all in black. He liked me best all in black, that thin tired Friday when I finally got my safe exit letter and I thought he was worshipping the stewardess.

Outside, the streets have been covered over with canopies. It is like walking in an Arab bazaar. There are at least fifty kinds of chilies at every chili stand. It is impossible not to live here, despite my weak will. Two more pastries and a thick ball of crude grainy chocolate.

Come to Oaxaca. It's it. But you'll need a cast iron will to resist the food, the sheer variety.

This city's men attract me incredibly but you do get choosy after a while and select the best pineapple.

The dances were incredible. Some more piña stuff. Three men join two women. The central one, the most Indian, a short, dark, matador in rolled-up white pants and with a blood red apron over his loins, skin-hacks a pineapple and then voluptuously chomps into it. The crowd roars. The women are demure. And then, an extraordinary last dance: a troop of Mexican (as opposed to straight Indian) women in dazzling huipils I think they're called—poncholike deeply embroidered dresses reaching below the knee, beneath which protrude bright cotton flounces—come on. First it was the sheer complexity of each individual dress. I remember only one: a background of white strewn with a deeply colored profusion of abstract purple, maroon, red, blue flowers in the center. Each one a year's work and a signature. In their hair, brilliant grosgrain ribbons flying. It is a spectacle of female as beauty, of the complexity and finesse of genuine (and female) Indian art, of the Mexican delight in color, ever more and always different color.

They have come on with a pineapple too and begin a series of complicated formations and interpenetrations. The lead dancer, relatively güera, with short red hair and maybe our age—I dance again! Lawd be praised—is an energetic Circe, vigorous legs flying as she strews her munificence. (The Latin love of dance, the *respect* for it.) At one extraordinary point she and one other hunker down over the pineapples, now on the ground. They beat a spiral down around them, around our own organ, with unrivaled joy, rhythm, strength. I am rapturous, as is the audience. The women beat the couples!

It is basically a marvelous city, only a hundred-forty thousand, the perfect size. Two universities, extraordinary churches that move me and that I want to explore. A rich cultural life and pleasures thereof. This place wakes my head up. Maybe I only needed a new place to regain my sense of place.

Love,
M.

P.S. The mathematics of perception, my field, I told M.

Ω

E.,

I sit here in the theater. Remembering more to a scratchy sentimental tape in a sleazy environment, he loved the movies. I'm bigger than sentimentality at this point. To will tears, how lovely, the self its own mama and papa and tears will propitiate the mama and papa of the world. I regarded him stonily when he wept on Sunday—the foolish child. The baby. Had he suffered more than anyone else (than I)? Did the world owe him love, to be his mama and papa?

It was about us. Me and Miguel. When Delon's abandoned wife peers whitely out of a sanatorium window, I nearly bit my head off in shame that I'd called and said, "Te amo." He and his lover in bed. The intimacy I'd forgotten. Every morning he'd roll over to me. In the night, sleep against my back. Once, very stoned, I fell

[210]

asleep on his chest, while he was talking. He got up to close the window and put me back in the same position and still I didn't wake up, I think he said the next morning. The first few mornings, I'd try to go back to sleep, facing away from him but unable to deprive myself of the miracle next to me, and his eyes always were open to catch mine. He'd open them just in time as I turned my head, a smile contentedly etched down his cheeks, his eyes peaceful.

The movie told me also somehow that he cared for me. The sending his book business—como quieres—his power riposte. The broken promises, fairly frequent amongst men. If only winning weren't so boring, and being bored so terrifying.

I saw too from that B−/C+ flick that one has to have, to choose, a theme. Christ, which with Miguel? The va and vient of sexual relations. But what I'd forgotten was that I had the real thing ever so briefly.

To my utter embarrassment I thought of marrying him at some point early on; I felt I'd found my soulmate at last. In midweek I proposed a six months in New York, six months in Mexico deal to which he warmly agreed. There was some question of my having important contacts who could land him a job. But I can't abandon career—or can I? Aren't I? Aren't these letters precisely that? No more source of excellence, just kretch out the banal miracle that Maryse Holder was loved for seventeen hours once in her life. . . .

Listen, it's a whole other world out here. I finally discovered it with Eduardo. My world is—was—Europe. His is Latin America. He wants to know not only Mexico but Central and Latin America. Period. That is his world. Impossible to believe but there are other planets right here on earth.

When the woman who directed me to the rodeo on Saturday spoke to me in the market on Monday, Eduardo retired discreetly. They are different here. It is rude to interrupt by even one's mere presence, a private dialogue, or even an act.

Permit me to digress, as a Mexican would graciously put it, but class, class alone, prevents love in my own country. Men are either higher or lower in class to me and I am so classless anyway at this point. That's why when Miguel started acting lower-class in love with upper on Saturday and Sunday, it freaked me out. He woke me up from that literary dream of the classless bed in a foreign milieu that is the earmark locale of Owens and Rhys.

And memories of Miguel. I'll break down and tell you:
"The Miracle of the Snot"

The first morning in my bed together, I woke up first, my nose full of snot. I didn't want to schlep out to the hall bathroom to have a proper honk-out, so cleaned my nose the best I could in the room, never blowing hard so as to not wake Miguel up. Mission accomplished, I lay back down and turned to face him. He looked at me tenderly and before I knew it, had snaked a hand out, and I felt a rubbery tugging out of my nose. He had pulled out this long snot. I was mortified and hid in the pillow, but so tenderized at the same time. No disgust on his part, just like a cat cleaning a kitten. He was amused at my reaction, I think, and I was melted by his. After that, I felt no fear waking up in the morning with him and used to clean the whitish stuff out of his eyes.

That was the charm of domestic intimacy at first, though toward the end, I would have farted—perhaps discreetly did—from very different motives. From boredom, contempt with domestic intimacy, from a core that had dissolved to leave a hole.

We no longer lived through each other but apart, no longer needed to share everything—it was pointless drudge world. Oh lawd. From snot to fart. . . .

M. called in Alfonso's jealous hearing and we had a low, slow, long talk that was like making love. I told him I'd almost finished writing his story, that he'd be famous someday, esperemos—which I said first right, then wrong, to be uncorrected. I guess lovers, or Miguels, don't correct.

Maybe shouldn't've told him his story was finished. Bad omen. Asked me if I was screwing around. No, and I start laughing, thinking he and I were both lying. Why are you laughing, he asks; Oh, you know Oaxaqueños, I say disparagingly, under Alfonso's frowns. These chavitos with their tremulosos, and I tell him about Eduardo . . . that I might meet him in La Ventosa, that he taught me a lot of Spanish. . . .

Yes. Miguel called. The above refers to that. I barely remember what we said, not very much in the way of love reassurances. I remember more how I leaned over the counter girlishly to be more intimate with the phone and his voice, which I could barely hear, so oddly low was it. Alfonso was hanging around jealously. I hold on to Miguel with two phrases he used repeatedly: "sabes qué?" and "ya vistés? which he accented on the second word or second syllable of second word. The second he asked with excitement: did you see it? Now do you believe me? Or, do you *believe* it? And the first he pronounced as if he were offering a secret gift.

Eduardo has made me remember more of M., though once again, much has escaped. I once said to M., as we passed the movie studios, that it would be marvelous if a movie could be, could have been, made of us over the last few days (early ones). The way couples are at the beginning. We lived a movie.

He thought I was tough, a mafiosa. Now Eduardo thinks I'm a francesita, a little French chickie.

Well, anyway, dig it—he called. Parted with I'll always take care of you: "Siempre te cuidaré," which gave me awful shivers of NEVERMORE. I begged to know if he was or wasn't coming to Zi. Assured me he could make it in midweek if necessary.

So, though engineering didn't show (Alfonso gave out phony hotel numbers to him and Eduardo), I was up up up up. The schmuck *called*, maybe it wasn't over. Even if it was, man, he gave me a lot of affection, loyalty, respect, emotional responsibility. He didn't make an ass of me in Oaxaca so that I could never attract anyone else. He didn't leave me bitter, he took care of me in truth.

I had a few more things to write you and finally I was going to be through writing and onto touristing. Off to the Monte Alban ruins.

It was a brilliantly sunny day, full of colors that seemed to vibrate in the excited air. I walked in a leisurely way through new streets in my nifty and cool little red dress with which I don't need a bra and which has deep pockets. My comfortable sandals, my big black canvas Danish school bag with my sunglasses, a guidebook, paper, pen, cigs. I was clean, still tan, shockingly thin from diarrhea, weighed 110 that morning. "Can't keep anything down," I thought with glee. And all the necessities of life in a neat, pared-down way. I buy a ticket and stand on the sidewalk, face tilted to the sun. Four adolescent boys pass and one mutters slyly almost under his breath, "¿Qué onda, Maritza?" Dazed for seconds, I've never seen the little bastard before, I do nothing. But the day is so good I decide to be a hero and chase the truth—no one will laugh at my crooked face today.

I chase around the corner and yell out "¡Oyé!" and crook my finger beckoningly. For a second they stand there smiling, suspended, to quickly disappear through a blue door. My guts, pure playful will, I decide to pursue. On through the door and into a strange patioland: solid perimeter on all sides of both rich and poor dwellings. I pass a poor concrete room and see an old man with an enormous nose fixing a shoe, on my way to a grinning teenage boy.

[213]

Did you just see four chavos come in? I ask. They went that away, he points and I dash off to be confronted by a large pink patio, restaurant-like, and two mammoth Indian women, evidently servants. I ask about the boys but the women deny any knowledge, are stony obdurate guardians at the gates of purgatory. Back to the teenage boy, my day risking sourness. He asks what the servants said and laughs at the lie. Asks why I hunted. I explain. He smiles sympathetically with me at the mystery of life. Alice-in-Wonderland and the four mad hatters. The strangest. God knows who's seen me drunk, hanging out, at the races, or at the whorehouse, or at the disco, or in the market, or in the hotel lobby. My *name*. Comes wafting out to me. I don't know them, but everyone seems to know me, including the small boy who wanted to sell me a serape here at the cafe, smiled recognition when he recognized me, Ah you! Very different onda from Zi. . . .

On the bus. A good-looking young man, with his buddies, boards and smiles warmly, probably a Chilango tourist, a student. I feel twenty, attractive, and indeed—yes—French, in the dress. Miguel helped, showing me off to all his friends, all the merchants, all his family, though one strained and, as usual, exhausted night, when we were at the lively sisters', deep fatigue etched my old face.

But, miraculously, the landscape as we climb up into the mountains is fantastic and draws me out of myself.

There are things bigger than sex, I felt myself flooding with as, on the left, houses dotted the upland, life adapting itself up mountains. Unlike Guerrero, Oaxaca is green. Food grazes and grows in a landscape so clean and fresh it makes poverty sweet-smelling. On my right, the receding valley and the incredible mountains, corrugated, multicolored, everywhere circling protectively around the tiny bus. Mounds of hills in between with a few white still oxen, or black cows. The bus offering constantly changing contours, approaching and receding from domestic life, or from augustness. I thought of Augusta and her mysticism-greater-than-human-relations ethos and I understood finally Eduardo's love of the sierra, the trees and mountains. Never, except maybe at Les Baux, in France, had I ever seen anything so beautiful. I was later to praise Oaxaca to him.

The ruins are on a plateau in the middle of heaven. For hundreds of miles, it feels like, I am embraced by mountains, reflected in the variegated sky. On the bus, I passed a row of five behind each other on one side: in the distance, blue, then mauve,

[214]

buff, gray, green. All my feeling of something bigger than sex, here, at Monte Alban, merges in my loins with Miguel to a splendid gratitude. There are nothing but ruins, gray, in this brilliantly green plateau and all around me, every possible shade of subtler color. Down the sides, sloping hills in every adaptive direction. . . .

If Miguel was style, and Eduardo intelligence, Gabriel was sweet simplicity and naturalness. A threnody: Miguel, Eduardo. Gabriel.

Next aft. Some middle-aged man in a shoe repair shop asked me if I went to high school. Oaxaca is doing strange things to me. Once again the boys look beautiful, I'm on the sex merry-go-round again. Eduardo spent two and a half seconds in my cunt this morning and did nothing for me, but he's paying the tab, so fine. Besides, I'm not terribly physically attracted to him. He's too tall and his hair is "crespo."

Eduardo has an excellent torso and arms, though not as hard as Stan's, and his legs, in pants, are elegant. He drives well, effortlessly reaches out an arm to fiddle with the car's tape deck, legs wide apart, takes a drag of cig, looks ahead. In profile, his face is stunningly chiseled. Some of them have olive drab eyes and wear graying green shirts, an exquisite sense of color.

I am not physically in love with Eduardo; wonder whether passion is more complete than intellectual rapport because literally more of the body feels it. The "love" Eduardo and I share is as cool as dry ice, or slivers of blue glass. Our souls fuck when we smoke, but rarely our bodies.

Tuesday.

I thought for sure I was a goner last night but he went down on me. I am way up then way down. My life terrifies me. I wanted to cry because I couldn't remember how Miguel touched me in the street—where he put his hand, how it felt, how we sat on the buses. The question I asked Eduardo the first? second? night was answered by experience: the new displaces the old. Just as yesterday's experience squashes flat everything that came before it, squats on it. And yet what I felt! How much has been lost because I lacked the discipline to write, in the vividness of the present. What awful new metaphor is this, that life is rolling over art, drowning it? Each day an enormous wave washing away the previous one, itself a moment, waves upon waves, to overwhelm and then dissolve.

I had two moments of exquisite pleasure yesterday, one, protracted gray rainy afternoon at Monte Alban with Gabrielito and that night, tooling around in E.'s broken-down American car in the rain, listening to some black women sing "An Everlasting Love." Eduardo's elegant twenty-two-year-old youth and strange devotion for me, occasioned, I suppose, by my own natural elegant coolness which comes from my lack of physical desire.

I was rather good with Eduardo. After an absence of seven hours, huge holes of silent boredom in the car and in the restaurant later into which I dizzyingly fell, his maniacal need to be stoned, the car breaking down in a totally uninhabited sierra after I thought we were going to some ruins. I'd smoked, was utterly convinced he was going to kill me with a knife he took out of the trunk to explain something about a nonworking telefoto lens he insisted worked, wanted me to sell for him. The car stereo was missing. I was sure the lens was stolen. I haven't seen a single piece of paper with his name on it. Every explanation he gave for everything rang false. Sometimes, though, I understood enough Spanish to discern a truth. Imagine being lied to in a language you don't understand by a twenty-two-year-old who after days of saying he loves you doesn't incline his leg towards yours when you tickle the nape of his neck while he's driving.

He twisted around narrow curves above sheer drops, silent and stony. Christ, Christ, Christ. I bought my life with sex and wondered if you'd think I was "masochistic" (a forever questionable word for *me*) for being with men I find terrifying. Came, through his hand or my own and jerked him off in his handkerchief. I check to see if he has a huge erection to know whether I've gotten one more reprieve. Nothing can convey the fear, the absolute separateness of him from me.

Later, at a disco he insisted on going to, he sat far away, didn't want to drink, looked at another woman while we danced and sat in a high-school prom sort of place. I felt my age fall on my shoulders like a heavy stone. So age tells after all.

The sudden not-being-desired is the ghastliest experience of all. Suddenly, the *world* doesn't look at you. Like a turtle, you withdraw your head into your body and walk through the streets invisible. The sudden shock of privacy, of having nothing to trade with the world, valueless, only your own rueful irony for companion.

He lies in bed now, face covered with the spread, with the faint funky almond of my cunt. I feel such tenderness and pleasure for him because of last night. He did it thoroughly, deeply, endlessly, though I finally had to reach down and rub my clit because he refuses (they all do) to believe in our anatomy. I think too that this is the end, like when José went down endlessly on L. to viciously shun her the next day. I think they go down on you with passion, if they do, to make you love them, to break your will so they can move on.

He looked so good last night, so lean and elegant with one hand in his light blue synthetic pants, his shirt tucked in so his ass showed, and the way the shirt bloused narrowly over his waist, I couldn't bear to leave, couldn't understand why he was so suddenly bored, remote, stricken, it seemed. Or whether the grass had made him paranoid.

Miguel adored my clothes, liked my style. Eduardo wants me to have long braids and wear native embroideries.

When we left, once more he headed for the pitch black, wet mountains. The city a receding jewel one could only attain by hurtling over the edge. Pure terror, as opposed to my previous unimaginable despair, assailed me. Survival surfaced. Get back to hotel, ditch Eduardo. Enough. It's awfully sad. I think I touched his arm with one ghostly finger; I couldn't bear to part after the present, couldn't bear to see the present becoming the past, to live the death of all that sweet illusion and hopefulness about being twenty-eight—my Eduardo age—and being pursued, for his own mysterious reasons, to which I could feel pleasantly superior, by an intense twenty-two-year-old with weird habits.

I got him back into the city and played it this way: it is the death of us, I said. O.K., he said. I looked at him in a disbelief more frustrating than when I caressed his indifferent neck. I'm not going to Salina Cruz with you, I pursued. It's the end, I said, wondering whether I could risk one more grammatical explanation, because you didn't respond when I said it's the end. And you don't correct me anymore. Well, if that's what you feel, what can I do, he said with that infuriatingly stony willful misunderstanding men lay on you that challenges you, at the risk of alienating them, to speak truth at last. I didn't risk proving he didn't love me—to do so would have been the truth and it was intolerable. But to be perceived as stupid, or worse, cowardly, is something I don't forgive men, or women, when I see them doing it. Why our need for them? To sacrifice anger and truth and bravery for them?

My lovely pussy, so warmed, like a tortilla, by his hot and unembarrassed tongue. He had an enormous cock, a joyous thing that erected easily, that filled his light blue synthetic pants, that

[217]

kept me alive. You do see what I mean by waves? I never told you his response this morning. Briefly, I parted through his evasions and false logic, told him he'd never pass the course this way. He is enormously bright, and I've gone from being a whore to being his chingada a el solo. His private fucked-over. From exploitation to being exploited. Fuck, he paid for the hotel, bought me a silver jar pendant, meals, dancing. He paid my thirty-six-year-old tab, that smashing twenty-two-year-old. I was, I suppose, his little mama, his mamacita. Shit, he literally could've been my son. My sun. All the stars and planets around your head for you, he said.

I'm totally smashed now and triste and furious. If he shows, I'll make a satisfying scene.

I hate to say this, but I prefer love to comprehension, after all.

To Eduardo: why do you dig me, I'm older and uglier than you are, I said. They all love my mind—that ugly I am for them? Or speak they strange truth? I think they feel guilty where I'm concerned. I'm so manifestly open, affectionate, paranoid, bright, skeptical. I'm so tired of being loved (liked) for my "mente." Anyway, these assholes—beauties—all claim to be ugly and dumb. God forbid you should say you're the queen of brights, a predictable drunken failing of mine.

Adiós, Eduardo, I should've said. But to be cynical, to *know,* is to never experience renewal and desire. Yes, Lily, how bored they must be. Better to be a pussy than bright?

There comes a point, what can I say, when one stops caring about why they are as they are and just wants to live one's own self. I am: bright, analytical, open, friendly, polymorphously sexual, possessive, blah, blah. I could go on and on speculating, but to what end?

Yet, drunkenly, I think he'll show. The sex was good. No, he won't. Good sex is easy for them. And he *was* afraid of me after all, of my claims to greater intelligence, of my compulsive jotting down notes while we were juntos, of my poverty and exploitation, of my nonfidelity, of my age and ugliness. He did love my mind—who wouldn't—and Mexicans are generous that way.

Just danced with the coolest number in here after a gorgeous thin Indian chicness of young rejected me. I don't dance cool. I dance hot with all my body, but I do unexpected syncopations. I'm almost always on beat—a point of pro dancer's pride with me to not falter, to master my condition. A point of honor, you might say, a respect for the goddess. And I'm sexy and inventive. As an Amer-

[218]

ican chick in New Paltz and I once heartily concurred, dancing is a meditation, a masturbation, the self fucking the self.

I hate him. Eduardo. He teaches me more than I need to know. I won't survive this knowledge that despite their gentleness of sex and sensibility, they are murderers. They don't abuse the body, but twist and retwist the emotions. Kill your heart, your independence. What supreme irony—sure his motif—that the miracle of his reappearance should plunge me into a despair I hadn't yet learned, a need to die, like the kid, to escape my own death.

The mention of my poverty bent his head in private irresponsibility.

Perhaps that translates what I meant about contradiction. The rising and the falling and the pause—like their ¿sí o no?—to give the truth a chance, a test, then a chance to react. They are far more interreacting than we. Genuinely dialectic, intellectually generous. Yes, they do like exchange, love to trade. Have a vision of life that you can be penniless and survive. Your tragedy is your own but you belong to the world, there is an exchange. The pause to incite shared laughter, comprehension, *response*. . . .

And the onda of hatred for Eduardo is past. *That's* what they understand, the constant flux. Oh Eduardo, to wash so completely away Miguel. But I think I don't want him anymore. I won't know what I'll feel in the very next microsecond, however. Oh to be a secure little novia; the lot of an amante is a tough one. That is how the system works, how the sexes equalize power. The men are free, the women are virgins. I know no more at this point. So, I signeth off. Perhaps I'll get to tell the tale someday.

I could have insisted Eduardo spend the night with me, but I remembered that power led to contempt when I forced Miguel to come that night. But also to tenderness and gratitude. Perhaps the tenderness one feels for a wounded animal. What did I feel? I felt a Valkyrie, an immense god, I was brilliantly drunk. I felt free, wise. Obviously narcissistic. What did I feel for him (to resume my school exam subliminal track)? I felt for him: passion, a gratitude, a relief—enormous relief that I'd rescued his beauty from my assured ugliness, could view him once again. My strength of cynical knowledge soared above the basso contento of my relief. It was an operatic night.

Even before Eduardo's return, I didn't know whether I missed Miguel. I looked at the Xeroxes of the pictures. They finally acquired pleasure and "reality" to such a vivid point I thought I should redirect this oeuvre to a study of the process of memory. For weeks they bored me, the photographs. Tonight they became not us, which, frustratingly, I wish them to be, but a—how shall I say—a *language* of us, a sign, an analogue. No. Truest = a pretty play that came out of us. No longer did they have to reveal to me the life we'd lived, or the desire I felt, or his beauty. But a charming abstraction, in exactly the way language is a play on life, a pattern in another mode, a game, a mathematics derived from, but independent of, life. Two parallel worlds. Not a representation, but a product.

Also, they did make me want to see him, and revive my sense of his fun and attractiveness, and our comfortableness together. He was so much easier to be with than Eduardo. I remembered the pleasure I felt when he bounded up and down stairs in his house, and now I remember how he'd turn around to look at me affectionately and teasingly in the kitchen, when he was preparing food for us. To have me catch him catching me catching him off-guard. A pearl of a boy. Eduardo catches me grimacing as I do my exercises, my face contorted in unconscious effort and is suspended/shocked, I think. I adored M.'s face, I can't ever tell you how much. E.'s leaves me cold.

You speak metaphorically and they love it here. There is little intellectual warring between the sexes, that is to say, men don't hate your intelligence. No way it threatens their supremacy, after all. They have their freedom and the women have their chastity belts and domestic corrals. How free and outrageous, poetic, bright, bold, you can be when you don't speak the language or know the rules. Pure abstraction, play.

But comprehension, so dead compared to passion. And why, again today I think, bother with this research, and with learning Spanish, bother checking out whether some sixteen-year-old would try to fuck me when I took my clothes off, why be a student of life if not to merit love one day? Fucking graduate. How can the moment be enough if you know its imminent death? Only because I'm a woman, and an older, less attractive lover of the men I choose or who choose me, can I not tolerate this ephemerality.

Latest theory: Eduardo is working me up, through pain, desire, and poverty, to whore dope for him.

I'll tell the tale yet.

Love,
M.

Ω

Dear E.,

I'm curious about whether or not I'm attracted to his type so when he approaches, I am polite, "liberale" (open, almost trashy—well, depends on your orientation). Despite the sleep, I am divinely exhausted, my face a banished impertinence. I cannot fail to be right, so tired am I, so indifferent, passive, beautiful, and neutrally curious in a relaxed way.

Eduardo. Who cares? Bad breath. Too tall. Hand contact that wasn't there but the universality of the good head of being stoned. We use only eight percent of our intelligence normally, he proffers banally as we sit on some escarpment high above the valley Oaxaca nests in. Thirty-three percent when high, I ask rhetorically. And seventy-five percent in love, I affirm, remembering the rush of every past idea and experience I'd had with Miguel when we made love sometimes. For Eduardo, the hijo, the couple, was a hundred percent. Trust, and the sweetness of feeling.

Te amo, I schmuckily told Miguel. What a joke, no? What desperate simplification.

Love,
M.

Ω

Edith,

In the morning the wounds in my feet ache again, those I get from walking on the thorns that litter this island, from cactus and crabs. Three deep pricks in my right foot. At night when I lie in my hammock my right ear no longer buried in my mattress but open to every nuance, I think I hear pricks objectifying me: "Esta cambrona," says one, "¿Está Marisa?" asks the other, feet away. A long plaint on age begun by the first, the words "chamaco," and "de 17 años," a querulousness about age. The word "face." My hands, clasped between my knees, expand to seventeen times their normal size, they grow like stone cauliflowers with the strain of lying still pretending sleep in order to hear the truth. My knees and arms weigh more and more. At the end, I weigh five thousand pounds and will break through the hammock.

Days later. Paranoia passing but never far away.

Eduardo came. I don't know what to write about. Sex? The candle's dim glow obliterates the night sky. The ocean sounds. He sleeps in a littered Gauguin room off the palapa: beer cartons, boat motors, stiff sandals, empty soda bottles, a plastic water container, and my luggage. The palapa roof is forty feet high, a more intimate, but still impressive sky.

At my scuzziest yet: four days without a sweet water bath, hair an undreadlocked mat of salt and grease, my right foot a spreading fungus and one deep inside my cunt that produces a thick white paste. I was gone down on in a sort of cactus garden on the beach by a diabolically bright and beautiful Mexican Mick Jagger this afternoon as I was half asleep and probably in full view of the silent creeping Indian fisherman community.

My hair is clean now but I walked into the lower verandah roof before. A new scar—it's blood I taste on my hand though I can't see its color.

I love Salina Cruz, the small city near La Ventosa. It is my idea of Vera Cruz, the tropic port of forties movies, full of sailors in white or tired, wrinkled blue. Very gay, very public, lively, seedy. I am Santa Marisa de los Marineros, I told Jagger-Eusebio. "Say marinero," he said, and tried to tell me a charming grosera but failed, called my cunt "cosita" and not papaya or biscocho. There are three kinds of sailors I said: the clean, sweet, decent choirboys, the ones who are charmingly vulgar, and the braggarts. And you're none of these so you're not a sailor, I said. You're a god. When he wanted to make love, I protested that a god was higher than a saint but he said God needed someone by his side to feel—and he hesitated a second—"completo."

His light café eyes looked gray-blue. He wasn't Mexican. His hair was thick, so black and curly it sucked in all the light and gave back none. I'm rica I said when he mentioned money and I understood that his only possible interest in me could be a gigolo's. Puerto Rica, I said, then "puerta rica," rich door, rich port, meaning of course my cunt. Of the numerous miracles he performed, one was to always understand my jokes, and more, to pursue them. I was stoned and merely being poetic, quite surprised that his irony could

[222]

stoop to a lust that seemed always to see what new melody could be yielded. I found his beauty irresistible, though I explained that not all beauties were commodo or convenable. And then there were the kind that reassured you, Miguel of course.

His lovemaking was as terrifyingly expert as his non-Mexican pronunciation of "His Satanic Majesty," the Jagger title he requested. He denied being a rock musician but I was certainly a groupie captive to his serpentine charm.

What didn't he do in that cactus grove? He played 117 tunes on and in my mouth, understood that kissing is an analogue, asked for my lenguita to show me what he'd do to my clit. I wanted only to contemplate the screen of his flat black hair against the screen of the brilliant green cactus against the blue construction-paper sky, but he injected an acupuncture needle of sensation in my nipples, untied my bathing suit bottom, inserted his head into my cunt, parted it, looked at it, sucked out every bit of my juice, stuck his finger into my ass when I was half asleep, gave me a rim job. Afterwards, he was less godlike but even more expert, technically wise and impartial. Nothing would ever surprise or capture him without his knowing that it was the nature of life to be overwhelmed in a three-day love affair. It's one of the best experiences life offers, he said and added in English, after he said it in Spanish, a gift of the gods. As brief and unintelligible as a miracle.

Tonight, Eduardo's spread legs, when they were above my head as he was sucking me, looked like a butterfly. More frighteningly, like a decapitated torso—mere shoulders, though soon after his large hooked prick seemed the wormlike head. Awful image. . . .

In the morning, an oyster opened up in the sky, and a hut like a giant coconut squatted next to Don Chavo's palapa.

I saw the night through. The sky was silent bursts of machine gun fire, flashes of yellow-orange light along the horizon. The sea was silent until a long wave exploded horizontally, catching blaze like a TNT cord. This morning, the waves twist like long tense snots.

And with an indescribable sadness that I understood came from spontaneous, too quick sex. . . . I didn't physically love Eduardo either but now there is a love of gratitude, affection, mutual physical pleasure. I stick my finger in his ass, something I've never done with anyone before (my gift of newness to him) and it emerges smelling like a dark attar of roses. The tremor of remembered pleasure I feel in my cunt he feels in his cock and folds me to him

[223]

after I return from my night's trip. I think a desperate letter to Miguel in the night, after Eduardo's greedy and relieved embrace:

Dear Miguel,
I am writing this in English because I'm in a rush. Save me! Sálvame—I am being stolen from you by the gods.
Maryse

Eduardo has just appeared from nowhere. What were you doing, I ask, feeling somewhat rejected. Thinking of you, he has the nerve to say. I'm horribly pettily downcast and jealous and have a scar on my forehead. I'm off to bathe in the lagoon—fuck everyone.

Last night, the sea smelled like a giant tortilla.

I'm alone during the day, now. Went to look for my fisherboy who yesterday said he'd come by at four to take me fishing for crabs. First he had to eat. And I? I said, no Eduardo in sight and down to $30. Would you like some shrimp, he asked. "Sí!" I greedily concurred; and he emptied out his whole morning's catch for me on the sand. I regarded this gift as a novia dowry, equal to the silver trinkets of the Chilangos, and the hard green stone of the ox-herder. He was too beautiful and I too ugly for me to be self-conscious. Into my fourth matted day, I had become a thing of nature, no longer to be marveled at. Without a cigarette, mirror, barrettes, cleanliness, I asked for shrimp and him, in utter unself-consciousness. Today, there was a stunning boy in the water who wasn't wearing rose shorts but black ones, against which his ass strained in a firm outward force. Was it Enrique? with the perpetually shining hair—short but I now see chic, shagged, willed loveliness in the plenitude of youth. More than anything I wanted to be equal to that beauty, not be told by a middle-aged provincial city slicker from La Ventosa that I had a lovely waist. I long for the young fisherman because he is what I have always liked most: beauty and innocence. A clear palabra. Intelligence, which I seem ever more to attract, frightens me. Alberto was to me as I am to the world: a shock of unexpected grace. I write about him because he was a moment's jewel, easy for me. I was sure he was a homosexual—so beautiful, contemptuous, assured. He tossed his hair and cavorted with me as with the ocean. Tossed this way and that in full pleasure of himself.

Eduardo and I are now engaged in earnest research to discover why he didn't call from Mexico City to let me know he couldn't make it at the scheduled time. His usual tactic is to evade and bring up a red herring. So much for that analysis. I know it, it bores me, I've exposed it to him and still he foolishly persists. You said to me, he repeatedly says, that I went down on you to secure you. But that wasn't the reason. I know, I know, I plead, but that isn't the question. The question: why did you risk losing me forever four times? What is the fascination for you in abandoning a woman? Does it augment your desire or is it to augment hers? He toys with the persona of "loco," "soy un poco loco." But clearly I've hit a lode because once more he's fled into the company of others, abandoning me anew. As if I should care though I do. . . .

Luisa and I spent a fractured day. After hunting for my fisherman all day I settle on watching a dark, thin guy who looked a bit like him fighting the ocean in his ineffective underwear, which he finally took off in the water to wring out and put back on. When the cavorter emerged he had that same face, that same instantaneous effect on me, as Miguel had. Something about the eyes, eyes that instantly *see* you, penetrating and kind both. A thin face, very dark skin that had absorbed and was giving back all the sun's warmth. A jaw that thrust out a bit, thin purple lips, teeth pushing against lips that I love so much. Straight black hair. A bad tooth!! Miguel, totally, down to the figure of a star in turquoise beads he wore around his neck. And a lovely thin muscular body. . . . My size, maybe five inches taller. It was figural love at first, second, third sight. The Miguel figure. I asked him where he was from; he looks down at his darkness and says, can't you tell? Doesn't like his color, etc. Gorgeous you understand. A person I instantly feel attractive with. I fought to stay polite with the Chiapan mescal proferrer but finally just turned to lie on the sand and beam back at the source of light. He works in soldering and also fishes but from a boat. Hates the fishing because it's solitary work. Problems with his family. . . .

To bring the usual long story to its usual brusque conclusion, we ended up necking passionately on the beach in sight of the increasingly incredulous town. My g-string bathing suit, hastily butchered by a seamstress in Acapulco, my solitary cruises down the beach, my thousands of pick-ups, my arm-in-arm with Eduardo, fucking Alberto, etc. I DO NOT CARE, as usual.

His cock was hanging out in the sea, so could my tongue on shore. Eduardo passed by dozens of times and seemed later to have gone into business ferrying short gentle Indians who spoke perfect English from correspondence courses.

[225]

Paquito's eyes were closed and every time we kissed, as with Alberto in the cactus grove, a bird sounded.

Eduardo offers nothing—he isn't hungry. After all my plans to go, him and me, and exploit a little marisco off him later in the day, it is too much. I think of throwing myself over the restaurant balcony in violent frustration. I twist and turn in my spangling dark adorable and "mince thin," Luisa actually called me, cleanliness, and decide that despite Eduardo's infatuation with Luisa's long muscular blond-haired and tendon-articulated thighs, he must prefer me. Had said he did on the path. The nonspecificity of Mexicano love is matched only by my own. As they are a single figure for me, I am for them the liberal gringa, the chick who agarras the onda. I "ando de roll"—loose, adaptive, adventurous, the perfect playmate of the moment. They loved not me but the gringa mentality. It is loathsome to be a figure. Yet to love Mexico through figurality is pure romance.

I fear, my deah, that I will never love again. I want them all and each one is insufficient. Where I acquired this masculine mentality I haven't the vaguest idea. My nose is pleasantly full of medium rubber cement; cleaning snot, I pick happily away. The wilderness offers simpler pleasures.

Everyone in Mexico knows everyone else. Victor, Luisa's novio, whom in my recently acquired mescality I adore, knows everyone in Salina Cruz. All Chilangos know each other. Life is public in Mexico, not only the enormously extended family, with its comadres, compadres, madrinas, padrinos, its phony tías and tíos, but the life in the streets, as Luisa says. Like Luisa. Mexico respects her as a serious student of them. My study is not perceived as quite so academic. How anyone—Luisa—could settle for a single man is beyond me at this point. I suppose it's the law of sexual economics: there are no young available women on this peninsula.

Narcissism knows no bounds. But it makes for secure friendship, no? As we cozily indulge, ironically smile at, and like the confidence of a divulged self-love, the other's ironic self-adoration. Life is a dream, a Lorca Spanish title. I barely dream at night because the day is a dream. I do need affection, but an affection that recognizes the real me, and the not easy wielder of wise and open confession, as I am for Luisa.

Everytime the dogs bark, anytime anything these last twenty-four hours, I think it's Miguel. Miguel has not yet confounded—confused—mixed—mescal'ed—himself into Stan, is still seen as my

[226]

savior—my tona, si tu veux. Why? Physical adoration of his face; reassurance of tragic, bathetic human pain via his ugly body. His wit, charm, warmth, failure. Why do I down-slant? Why, despite my high, is it my underriding truth? I am at heart a nonbeliever. At heart, a heart. That's why more than head, Alberto more than genitals, Eduardo, the heart, the emotions, the simple doglike warmth of conviviality and sweet pain of family rejection appeal to me. And I thought I was all bored head. Yet it is the heart shining through pain in a medium that, bien sûr, is young, dark, beautiful, that melts me.

And of course Miguel's grace on the stairs. If only I can break away. . . .

But light arrives before insight. The vampire's self-deprecating magic terminates to be replaced by the equivalent magic of day's fatigue. Yes, I told Victor's boring pretentious academic poet friend (who wrote good stuff)—poetry and not the novel or the autobiography is finally the form one must adopt, adapt, for transcribing Mexico.

Love,
M.

Ω

Edith,

There is a poetry in illiteracy, I imagine. I shouldn't be as flattered as I used to be when they admired me verbally. I told Eduardo I liked his elegant legs and arms. I'll give you the list in English. Mine: 1. His long elegant legs and arms 2. His smile 3. That he teaches me Spanish and Mexico 4. His skin 5. His body (exquisitely beautiful) 6. ? There were 15. Oh yes, 6. His large cock, the largest I've ever seen, I said, forgetting yesterday's dicks. When he's in me I *feel* him. Real pleasure, though natch no orgasm. 7. His Techuana gramma—did I tell him that? 7. No. So—7. The way he makes love. 8. His color 9. His skin texture—twenty-two-year-old sharkskin, I discovered, before he once more walked out of my life. 10. His belly button. . .

He's the first the sensation of his dick in me stays with me. What can I say? I forget my ugliness except for once again when he left me. I remembered my old skin twice with him. Both times I

[227]

looked down at my crepe and was intensely thrilled and scared to be with a young lover.

The yellow piss of desire—my mescal. So much to say, so little time to say it. There are four things I need to tell you immediately.

1. That I can no longer remember the titles, plots, directors, actors of films. All has melted into a gigantic cream. The Bowie film took an hour to recall its mere name. No longer am I in an intellectual milieu; no longer do I studiously memorize the world, carry a little notebook in my head for each of life's compartments.

2. For me, Depardieu and Mexico are a nameless melting dream, a mystery. For them, a commonplace. So it is that I enchant, if I do—no one knows for sure. The burden of my knowledge is too intense. I need to obliterate it with booze. Almost always I feel I know more than I can write, that I know it all. Sex the only thing I can transcribe, because it is suspended time. All these assholes who ridicule you for simplicity when you say you live for desire. With me it's more complex, they always say, my Freshman 101 students. And I, the maestra, as often as not lack words, when I am in their presence, to elucidate the true complications of the things. So as not to repeat "desire," a mot-clef for me.

3. That one knows what one knows up to the moment. That chacune has sa petite connaissance. You bring to the interpretation of what's happening to you the completion of all your experience. You're always right but never is the puzzle solved, because, especially in Mexico I feel this, never is anything permanent. ¿Quién sabe? after all.

4. This morning, after Luisa expressed firm ganas last night to go to her house in Ixtapec today, neither she nor I wanted to. It's a perfect day for tanning she says, partly because my color had worked its way into her desires. I experienced four stages myself this morning. I got up. I took a toke of mesc, a cig or two. I spent time with the couple. I left. I exercised. After another cig, did the sixty sit-ups (a rule I learned as a rhetorician: stick in a precise detail). I rested. Observed a tree changing intensity of color. A blackbird. A miraculous pair of jeans hanging on the fence. I sunned, I dozed. I did half of the next exercise, the side leg lifts. I dozed. I should do it all in twenty minutes, I rejected that idea. Knew that my perfectly adaptive will—an exquisite balance of necessity and desire—would steer me through. You understand what I'm saying? I got up and left company without rejection or haste when I wanted to, they the

[228]

same. So that "La Educación de la Voluntad" is a very real title in Mexico. The country sucks away at the organized will.

Huge portions of my memory bank are down the tubes. Perhaps that is what the mystical vision is.

A transparent will is evidently an anathema to Mexicanos, they must be the unpremeditated donors. Hence, Eduardo's constant reappearance scant minutes or hours or even a day after I've successfully evicted him from my system.

There are thousands of things I understand about Mexico, but still the mystery of sexual tides eludes me. Is it Pythagoras, I ask Christopher, who is the Greek mathematician who said you can never arrive at the end of a certain distance, but only halve continually? While he sought the answer, I wrote the last five lines. Such is my temp, my style, here. I drink openly, to the delighted comprehension of the man with ugly teeth. Ah! that explains you he thinks. Perhaps I've occupied considerably more space in his consciousness than he in mine, though he leaves to go dining and never buys a beer.

Partly, I'm exhausted. I remember barely nothing which is why I feel compelled to be compulsive. I long for a calendar. On May 24, Miguel and I went, at 3:41 P.M., to eat at his house for the first time. (Compulsion is asking the gods to interpret your life, giving all the evidence, seeing the world as clues. Writing is playing with the available. Playfully constructing a theory.)

Enough. I'm bombed and longing for action and to be beautiful.

The male contempt for loose women is their fear that we find more than one of them attractive. I reassure myself with this unbidden female insight because last night I couldn't avoid feeling like a puta, hanging out with two chavos, one I adored second to Marco, in the street. The waitress's ass strains against my insight and I think: woman's heroism, her lucha, her poor victory—to hold out—to insure heroically her own suppression. What supreme irony! We must all be Don Juanas at heart. What is this love crap? Anyway, for me, I doubt it's possible any longer. Beauty abounds here, and a few more months of illusion that they actually like my liberty, not just that I am a walking free piece of ass, no matter how old, ugly, uncharming.

The waitress coolly offers me what I requested. Once more the ocean rises up against me. Pleasurably roll grains of sand off my

[229]

dark, beautiful skin. It is hot in Salina Cruz, unequivocally summer. How can one not love a land of eternal summer? And of slim dark men with broad shoulders in shirts the color of my café con leche tucked into slim beige pants. Speaking of food, Eduardo ate me well. He didn't exactly hit the correct spot all the time (this is Coca, not Pepsi, country) but I had the feeling with him that I haven't had since I was eighteen that he dug pussy, he relished my marisco.

Ω

Dear Edith,

I wish I could write in a foreign language. I am risking permanent deportation from the only thing I live for: Mexico. I am writing you from the jail in Salina Cruz. You can't force a country to love you, I thought, pacing up and down the courtyard. It is a kind of justice—always poetic—but will there ever be more after Mexico?

I was with a Marco lookalike, who was the Miguel lookalike. We crashed a fiesta, he was sixteen. You transgress, you get punished. We ended up at a segundaria ball and he got busted after breaking up a fight. He was carrying my bag—they weren't interested in me but once I screamed for my bag, that was it. The lovely child. He would've been my third lover. I didn't care that he was sixteen, though he looked it and I looked my age in that high school open-air gym light. I was told, after they searched me, that I'd been arrested for being with a "rata," a ladrón (a thief) and a marijuana smoker. And on my own cuenta, for drinking in the streets—i.e., for being lucidly bombed. All Luisa's warnings about carrying papers, her worry of last night—all came home to roost. A rough port town. Not quite a thousand nights and/or provocative questions later, and barely, I thought, escaping gang rape, I ended up in this women's room. Outside, in the courtyard, two strange things: 1. a party 2. looms. After much difficulty I got to schlep my bag in with me—cigs, paper, and silliest of all my bright color barrettes, afraid they'd be lost. I've done nothing, I demurred from rape and incarceration. I'm a professor and a writer. Three other tacks: 1. Would you like this to happen to your daughter (to the warden). 2. Fígate, I say, I'd been writing un libro de amor sobre Mexico—and now this. A definite zilch. Can't remember 3, sino hundreds: explain this country to me. I need to know, finally. A look through his books, waylaid American paperbacks and Spanish religious books. I invoke God. He says he's a brujo. I say I'm a bruja. He's returned his pistol to its holster. I don't want to lose Mexico. Do you have any gelt, he asks. No, I say. Oh yes, idiot tack number 3, a drunk's, was to inform him that Mexico was doing this to me because it hated the States for among other things, its treatment of Mexicans.

One of these angered him, though not obviously the latter—they take delayed revenge. And my last illusion, that illusion restored by his Vera Cruz dancing at the sweet fifteen-year-old party way up in the hills he dragged me to, all the small boys throwing pebbles of desire and hositlity at me. His dip—the way he dipped his shoulders on the fourth or fifth beat—his beautiful effectiveness that whole night, finding me a place to dance, and then another and then the miracle: after I'd clamored for food for an hour, after he broke up the fight, two plates of corned beef and some delicious cider (the only thing in the world I crave I told Christopher the other day) appeared to exist on our table. I laughed at the incredible joke. It is taking its hideous revenge on me now. You don't laugh at anyone or anything in Mexico.

I slept for fifteen minutes in the hammock, was awakened by voices. And a bright light shining through an open door I thought an exit. A woman walked through it laughing and I knew I couldn't. It was the same door I'd walked in through—only sleep had displaced it.

He sucked at my lips like a guppy while the wind wrapped us in sheets. My light hair danced. Like Miguel, how could I not once again melt from those laughing eyes up so close? I thought a magnificent sentence in English, which I lost then and now forever, for once not quite the biggest tragedy of my life. And my frog, coveted by the warden—and the ring—finally they find their home. And I lose my charm. Sex with him, as with Marco—desire never becoming pleasure.

Oh lord, how do I play this? I am fiercely possessive, superstitious and plain greedy about my few beautiful trinkets. Will I always prefer things to life?

Lowdown on the scene here. Women are mota prisoners. Five years. Pay for food. Allowed to screw with male prisoners (locked up across the alley). Weave and embroider during the day, talk, it passes the time. If I have 500 p's I get out, if not, fifteen days. And dig this, sweetheart—the woman I talked to thought they might've taken me in because *I was walking alone in the streets*. Other places, like Mexico City, she says, you can walk around. Oh Christ, E., I must get out. We must do a revenge. I write in crypt for apparent reasons.

No wonder too Luisa said no you couldn't live in Salina Cruz. I foolishly tried to keep my rep intact by not letting the beautiful kid put his arm around me. I might live here, I thought, I might be a maestra here, it's close to the sea only falta pistes de baile. I ran after the kid and cops when they dragged him off. And really the worst possibility of all. That sixteen, like almost twenty-two, was too young. That I was a quick buck to a beauty that reanimated me. He wanted transport to the States. Either, therefore, I am his or he's my bad vibe. Will either of us ever know? Far more likely, he was the snitch. I, after all, did not drag him anywhere, or even approach him. And Teresa was awfully silent in that about-to-divulge Mexican way when I said they hadn't brought him here as well. I jumped in with both feet and after politely asking rhetorically whether it wasn't strange, answered myself affirmatively yes, very strange.

"Hoy tengo ganas de tí," (oh M.) plays distortedly through the thick wall. If only I hadn't pushed my detective metaphor quite so often with Luisa, down to humming the Pink Panther theme so Victor Mexican would share my joke for once. Oh M.: too this has happened because I didn't choose you soon enough. How I miss him. T. keeps asking me to lie down and sleep. My vigilance, my writing here, is keeping her awake. She made the coffee especially for me. I must concur. Her matter-of-factness about her five years. Así es la vida.

That was the first night, an exhausted vigil. The first day was more ghastly than fun. I'd had no sleep, slept fitfully during the day, was filthy, and vowed I would hunger strike my way out of here. Had a cup of coffee that first night but zilch after, until this morning thirty-six hours later. More coffee, three-quarters of a cup. I am slackly thin and about to lose my tan. I am, as far as I can tell, here for two reasons: being the companion of a beautiful boy and being moderately drunk. Of course, no one can tell me anything. I am basically here because I'm another, and richer, source of income for the corrupt police—1,000 p's to get out (the Mexican price is 500, roughly $25). I don't have the mon so the women, the personnel, the male inmates as well, are eyeing my jewelry and

[232]

proposing various jobs I could do during my mandatory fifteen days here. Laundress is one real possibility, that plus my Minnie Mouse watch. I won't part with the frog or my woman's face ring.

It is, as far as I can tell, a fiesta here. During the day mostly men weave hammocks and make macramé bags. The women cook and clean, mostly we take care of our own room.

The radio goes on at 6 and yesterday afternoon someone with a tape played "Midnight Train to Georgia," "I Shot the Sheriff," etc. *Finally,* the fucking baile. The room across from ours becomes a cantina from 4 P.M. on. The men play cards, watch TV, play music. All the implements and furniture are their personal property, as the beds and stoves and pots and pans in our room are.

Almost everyone here is in for dope, five years *after* sentencing, which can take ¿Quién sabe?—forever. The law has gotten stricter with the change of government, an older inmate explains. I am sometimes allowed to flirt with the men who are locked up. Unlike us, they don't weave. They are mostly young, dark, and alas attractive. There are five at least I find attractive, though one, less Indian than the others, more: he has a deep booming voice. Yesterday afternoon, when I was sleeping on what I didn't know was Amalia's bed, he walked into our room; I stared up at him suddenly awake and alarmed, after ugly dreams. "Duerme! Duerme!" he commanded in a tone that combined annoyance that I should be worried about him, and a certain rough protectiveness. Sleep, get the fatigue and the trauma over with, a soupçon of cuidate with a healthy dose of Mexican take-it-on-the-chin. The deep sexuality of his voice, the care I foolishly imagined underlay its harshness, and his attractiveness, a thing that saved me from total doom, made me sob. I wept and wept. The women came in; occasionally, if you work hard enough, they'll give you a little sympathy, these Mexicans. I told them I was crying because Mexico was the only thing I lived for, that it was being destroyed for me by this nightmare, and that I might in fact be deported forever and that I'd done nothing, nothing at all. In the evening, when Rábano ("Radish," Belita's lover) told me it was fifteen days if I couldn't come up with the scratch, I tried a little madness, and then a second sob-set—quite sincere—when I realized I'd lose all that lovely and necessary dinero waiting for me in Oaxaca. I'd lose my tan and lose fifteen days as well. I'm up shit's creek here. I'm down to 30 p's—enough for two days more of cigs and *no* food.

Belita is doing exercises. She's the youngest and thinnest. Everytime our eyes meet, she smiles. I'm wearing clothes she loaned me while my own dry. I keep my requests down to a minimum; a cup of coffee, a little toothpaste, and offer my scanty, intermittent services. Washing the floor... We come and go but lack TV, radio, tape deck.

Teresa, is twenty-nine and has two grandchildren. She looks nineteen or twenty-five. She had her first kid at thirteen, married to a man twenty-one years older, because her mother had too many kids and needed to get rid of some of them. The third remaining woman is in her late forties or early fifties, and the only one, from what I can gather, who likes grass. The others were transporting? I told at least ten men here why I was but shouldn't be here, but though they lived in the same room, more and more kept asking me. A strange grapevine. They all still thought dope had been found on me.

More later—I'm out.

Love,
M.

Eduardo has returned.

Ω

Dear Edith,

There is always another onda. I came back from prison bored with liberty. There was such *compactness* inside. It was a small medieval village. And I'd begun a convent-like flirtation with my gruff-voiced savior, Gustavo from Guadalajara. I finally bought my way out with a 470 p. loan from an inmate, against the security of Minnie Mouse [watch] and my silver feminist ring. I loved it in there and long to return. I miss prison. But next time, I go with nothing valuable and with money somewhere waiting for me.

Luisa and Victor interrupted this letter. I was waxing interesting on prison life, what I wrote so far on how I missed it. Victor walked off, as he often does when I talk. Luisa says he does this with her. I try to recap the onda but Luisa is distracted and chases after him. Too, for me, it was less interesting to capture only her attention, and not a male's. But, more to the point of this novel, I think I understand why Victor walked away. He was upset that after my desperate letter I should long to go back, that I was as changeable as a Mexican. They demand dull constancy of women, the predictable.

The warden said I carried on like a whore with Mexicans, like a dog, and that I was in prison because I was a "pintado de negro." To insult me they called me India. Jésus said this meant having a police record, painted in black.

Gustavo. All silver teeth of him in his denim cabdriver cap and that rumble of a voice. Well, I couldn't stay there much longer though god knows the reason I was glad to wake up day two was I knew I'd see him again. And would have seen him for years. He could never have fallen out of love, imagine. He could never have stood me up, we would always have remained more or less in a condition of desire, sex being permitted to the deserving only every eight days, except for Belita who fucks the top inmate who sleeps outside of the cell. I began attracting Teresa's guy which is why I think *she* robbed me. Also, when I asked her to lend me 70 p's she lied and said she'd spent all of the 3,000 she sold her bracelet for yesterday and when I offered the belt as security, she snorted contemptuously. The bitch had it already. Still, I gave her a condom so she wouldn't get knocked up again in prison. The older woman, a good witch who was patiently teaching me how to cook, loaned me 5. Her I trusted.

I weep, I moan, I clutch but we women lack pleasurable society. The middle-aged woman in prison, Felisa (a dyke?) tried to lure me with cuisine away from the easy gross rapport, the sexuality, the non-fear of shocking, that I have with men. I could've learned to cook superbly, and to weave hammocks. Oh well. Next trip.

And the loca I wanted to fuck. I met her on the road going to Salina Cruz Saturday. Pé pe pé pepepé pépepé pe Pe she said and said, pointing to wounds inflicted on her by fight. She was dark, slim, my size, mad, free, and I wanted to caress her, fuck her, pump some other syllable into her.

This country sucks away my marrow. How high a price I paid in prison—paranoia forever, and the impossibility of letting go. Women who drink in public, or are drunk in private locales or on public thoroughfares are fed to the police. Men, of course—well . . .

Eduardo turned out to be a homosexual and a bandido. The last sex, I had to drag him away from the nomadic male herd, was awful. Luisa and Victor charged me for the night, after I supplicated money off them to get me out of jail.

Love,
M.

[235]

Ω

Edith,

It's like being a child again, or newly-crippled, and having to learn how to talk and walk all over again, being here. No matter what I do, I can't master the rules, though certain hideous verities seem unprovisional: 1. that in some godlike way I was punished for my strength, that insight I had in Pepe's restaurant about why men created the loose woman.

I've just been served the worst café con leche of my life by a waitress who lied that they had no mineral water here. She didn't want me here, god knows why, and though I wait for a call to be placed to Mexico City, I know that that too is an impossibility. I will never be summoned by the other woman to give my number. Indifferent sailors care less about my café or my call. Young, short-haired, in whites, they chat dutifully with Mexican chicks.

The persona "writer" is of course a perfect cover for a whore. It permits me freedom and a cover of poverty, the two things I need here. A strange man, no stranger than any of them, I guess, who offered me a lift when I was hitching back to Ventosa after prison, congratulated me on my desire never to marry, on my liberty. It's so hard to know what they like, or whether they're all the same.

The paranoia I feel now in Salina Cruz is totally justified in two ways: 1. Yes, the town, the whole town, is laughing at me and 2. I can no longer flaunt my solitary courage in its face.

In another restaurant, they made me touch a live ice box—it was somehow conducting electricity to which the waitresses were immune—and guffawed on and on when the man who'd initiated the second charge held out his hand in a friendly way, saying "trust me," with a brisk kind nod of the head, to have me suffer once again. They are a nation of practical jokers, and unbelievably cruel. And I will never ever talk to Miguel again. And after all, what does it matter since in him I will only see gestures I saw dozens of times before him and thousands of times after him?

Tell me, tell me what happened to you, Eduardo begged when he returned half an hour later after my return from prison. Take me to Salina Cruz and I'll tell you everything, I said. Why did he reject me? Luisa, with her petite-maîtresse philosophy, her incarceration in the domestic couple, says I had hard manners with him. When I

[236]

was writing and he approached me tentatively, I ignored him she said. The Mexican man's unimaginable control over an unimaginable pride is so perfectly seamed that I will never know if his sadism was a response to my coldness, quite intelligible, I thought, and needed a bit of warmth. He rejects me, I am cold, he ignores me and later cavorts on the beach with the ugly black parasite kid who bummed cigs off me without shame or gracias and who stole, who stole Eduardo away . . .

Very stoned earlier, I had far larger issues to write about, far more despairingness, so awesome and terrifying I ran into the ocean to wash away my insights. As wave after wave submerged me I wondered whether I was finally destined to get over my fear of waves. While it was happening I was unafraid, but then once again when I saw the ocean rise up against me, I panicked. I shouted pleasantries across to Jésus and briefly held his finger in mine in the water. I forget what pretext I found or he seemed to want me to find.

Lord, Eduardo and the kid lay in each other's arms in a single hammock, so pleased, and chased around the beach with sticks trying to kill crabs, squealing with delight. At night, all the men were companionable, lounging against each other. I must've been slightly drunk after Memo's treat of fish and booze and accused Eduardo of being a "puta," a whore: I meant he wanted money for sex; generally was a parasite. He chose to insist I'd called him a "puto," a homosexual, either because it was a stronger pretext for rejecting me or I'd hit on a truth.

This afternoon, after that unbelievable pain last night, I waxed poetic wise and brilliant. But it is all consigned to air. Never more will that or any other tale be told by me. I feel it now, the age, the despair, the end of the journey. My age was guessed at thirty in prison. My pouched face bags out. The face is a tired wallet. Men ignore me totally tonight. Is it that this is the equivalent of a private fiesta to which nevertheless outsiders may come to look and where no one but no one asks you to dance—i.e., a public respectable place?

I sit as always in an emptying square, translations littered at my feet, the abstract metaphors of death.

What are old vain ugly women for but what I have? Oh Oaxaca and Miguel, Eduardo and Rolando—how you deceived me with your false reflections. Up until prison, I felt I was getting younger and younger the longer I stayed in Mexico. Oaxaca was like a dry

[237]

fountain of eternal youth. Alfonso will not have a room for me. Why should he? I lost my red dress.

It's raining.

Back to the afternoon, when love was still possible and I was capable of larger despairs. My despair was over Mexico's homosexuality, so keen that, drunk and lying between Eduardo and some other schmuck in my underwear, the cigarettes I'd tucked into my panties having modestly snuck around to rest demurely on my pussy when I fished the pack out to give someone one, I think I cried aloud with ridiculous gratitude that Stan and Margaret were together.

God the kid, the snitch from Vera Cruz, was beautiful. Slow, stoned, seductive, he leaned in close to smile knowledgeably and expectantly both when I told him I'd seen him at a fiesta the night before, and how he danced.

Luisa would infuriatingly offer incomplete analyses and plenty of unsolicited bromides and walk out when you begin to launch into your own version, saying it doesn't interest her. I told her Eduardo was half in love with her and she denied this, with the contempt with which the beautiful stupidly try to shield their superiority over the ugly. Look, I say, you're beautiful but there are attractive things about me, too. I'm personally jealous, because it's Eduardo, but not generally jealous. Yes, Christopher agreed, she has a superb body. I died, of course. I saw Eduardo gazing at her. He confided in her gently he felt he'd found a new mamá, somebody who'd understand him.

My dear, they're well rid of my moodiness, narcissism, and tsuris. And did you have a good time, Victor asked, with us? Oh yeah, I said. La Ventosa, my undoing. Time, my undoing. Well, it's almost time to sleep. No letter from even you, dear cunt, will console me because it can't tell me what happened with Miguel. Either you're bored and adored or in luf and rebuffed.

The warden is right, I lay with dogs, with scum. With beautiful penniless scum. Marco, all these poor penniless young men of Mexico.

Enough. Off tomorrow to friendly Oaxaca. . . .

Dancing is the only thing left, I told Luisa and Christopher. My controlled folly. Desire. Renewal. Imitating a black pimp's swagger. Yech. Suddenly the boredom of that night I spent writing you about dancing assails me. Or a rhythm, it leads you; it's new, but always you retain control. Perhaps Luisa and Victor felt deserted

[238]

and used. I prefer being taken to taking, I told Luisa, it's more common, ergo, comfortable for me. She laughed with rather than at, a grace she extends half the time.

Suffice it to say that professionals of ranks lower than my ex bore me. Scum is infinitely preferable. I *won't* lose caste. I just won't. He was incredibly gorgeous but instantly I felt such a rush of superiority, of boredom, that his corded forearms, green or café eyes, his light dark skin, his full and articulated mouth, his classy bones and thick sculpted slightly-wavy hair with poignant traces of gray on his twenty-two-year-old head ... NO. He was a second-grade teacher. Older men are generous only to younger women. No matter how ridiculous it is, I am now going to be younger by two years than any creep I meet. My last age was twenty-eight. No, twenty-six, unless they're twenty-six. Then twenty-four. Obviously, I can't go much lower. With a twenty-two-year-old, I can't be twenty.

Returned to better spot to be spotted by friends of Eusebio-Jagger who invited me for a refresco. The guys were charming. Sebio was a marinero. He'd pointed me out to them as a chick he met on the beach. So I spilled the frijoles and said I'd laid him spontanteously. They'd precipitated my confession by a generalization about insouciant lay Americanas. So I endeavored to explain the circumstances. That his beauty and genius fascinated me though I hadn't come to Mexico to find Jagger. That I felt also that he was too beautiful for me.

They were curious about why Luisa was with dumpy Victor and I paid for my coke with the remark that beautiful women are narcissistic and prefer their radiance uncontested.

And *money*. Fantasies of black embroidered blouse, *tight* pink cord jeans, handwoven fabric to have dress copied. Belt irreplaceable. Washing my clothes. Writing. A *bed*. Seven days out of two weeks on the ground, I'm full of bruises. The possibility of almost constant cleanliness. Fillings in my teeth. A trinket or two. Room #14 in the Hotel Rivera. Sending out cards to all the young Oaxacan dudes whose addresses I have saying I'm receiving again.

Ah yes, Eduardo. Another pattern: cruel remoteness followed by extraordinary lovemaking followed by unannounced departure.

I analyze a perfect male politics; a perfect politics of any kind but of course my thesis is feminism. There is this older woman who has been screwed; if I touch her, I think she will contaminate me, remove me from male grace, that it happened to her but *wouldn't to me*; when the reality is she holds the truth and rather than harming me, would help me by both telling me the reality and by our being a combined force. How men have separated women from each other! How we fear what could be our salvation. The loose woman thing is what they've used of course, and the bitter woman and the ugly woman and the aggressive woman. It won't happen to you kid if you play your cards right.

As, in jail, on the first awful day, I'd thought in horror, my god I've been kidnapped. They read me as trash and abducted me to serve as a whore for the male prisoners for their own profit. No one will ever know where I am. All letters will be intercepted. They will starve me into submission since after a while my few p's would've run out. I would've incurred a tremendous debt. (I thought I heard a male trustee say it would cost me 15 p's a night to sleep "tranquilo," unmolested. Edith, the horror!)

I then ask someone to dance. Suffice it to say that I found the lost coordination and was magnificent. Extraordinary thing happened—at one point I flew, I actually flew. I'd been dancing on tiptoe as I sometimes do when I want to bounce, and also exercise, and I built up the tempo, I accelerated more and more until I took off. Straight out of Castaneda. I wonder if anyone saw it. There was a sensation of weightlessness and no longer touching the ground—I had pushed myself up through increasing height and rhythmic speed until for one long moment I flew.

The pimp of dance, the dry elegant Dionysus of Los Arcos, joined the dancers. The dance floor is huge and boys often dance alone, hopping all over the place, a strange scene, my dear. Every disco too has its own política. Dión came on and twisted delicate quarter turns on the soles of his feet as his shoulders caught up later. And because it gave me such detached pleasure to watch his slim height, and his tight round butt, a visible curve at last through his ivory sharkskin pants, I turned increasingly to include him; actually, to subtly myself shift, from one to the other, with a slow irony I hoped he found attractive: O.K., you're right, we belong together. My dear, he is far too flawless for me, a real god of elegance. And though I vowed I deserved and deserved what I wanted (sharkskin chic and good dancing), he terrified me.

The number ended. I'd danced a hard sweaty thirty minutes with the first guy. Was tired, sat down. A guy comes over. And a few minutes later so does Mr. Elegance.

Choice: whether to act on lessons or not and learn more.

Ate my way home. Poor E., a culinary tour of my depression. I

[240]

am so increasing-debt tired all the time. Mme Bovary. No way to pay it off. They'll crucify me yet. The more I eat, the hungrier I become.

Where, oh where, is my insouciant arrogance of yesterday? My boredom with passion, my grand insights? Where oh where is a decent pen and a clean style? The bags of despair deepen under my eyes.

How I really read it, and Cecilia, the anthropology student agrees, is that I was being punished for being a free woman, and for having a polymorphous sexuality, a word that actually got effortlessly swallowed by the company. How painful for them, I said, explaining my preincarceration Salina Cruz loose woman insight, that women should find everyone else besides themselves attractive.

Seconds later he asked with his head if I wanted to dance. I nodded. Off we went to boogie tropicál, which he did well, very well, sensually with gyration from waist on down and some taut twistings away from each other as we held hands. Pulling away, you know.

We spoke with our heads and faces mostly. His repertory was there, and, of course, infinite. I could not feel through my senses that I had once had a boyfriend, that he'd said endearments, that his giant cock had been in me, that he'd licked my cunt and made me feel good. Mostly, he spoke stylistically/psychologically with his head. He looked to look appealing, did appeal. I shyly and delightedly obscured my ugly smile in a classical gesture of modesty that was also apparently enactment of classical, emblematic gestures. I played and he knew it. We built up this incredibly embarrassing and charming fugue of head motions. He did the bob, or pendulum, better and more consciously than anyone else yet. He *knew* it as a language. You sway it to the left and you sway it to the right—Mexico! My Mexico, they say, Pronouncing it, a veces, American. It was a language I perfectly understood and he used actual words to tell me that though I came from New York and he from Mexico, what a miracle we were the same, and had known each other through the dance.

It was lovely, my third boyfriend. I looked smashing—tall, sleek, fresh, chic, bobbing hair, in brilliant white denim tight pants and vest—those great muscley shoulders with little sharp bones that the thin have, you know? It was *me*.

When we dance, he asks me for some Chiclets, mouth to mouth

regumitation we perform for my unending loss of rep. I try to indicate to the audience that I'm indulging a harmless drunk. But I am also indulging my own sense of fun, why not?

Today is Wednesday. Despair at ever attracting man in my life again. The brilliance of pot with Eduardo over, the passion with Miguel. They've taken away dance, too, you see. There's nothing to do now but eat, an athlete without a playing field. . . .

Love,
M.

Ω

Dear E.,

What can I do but whirl so fast when I dance that it flies off me, my face. . . .

How painful the transition from sex object to money object. People marveled at my graciousness in rejecting vendors. No longer. I'm taking it out on everyone, on the little girls I just said no to for their Chiclets. I was stern and philosophic with them, spoke to them in English. I don't want to buy anything tonight I said. Yo no te comprendo tampoco, I said. Oh please buy some Chiclets they whined. No, there are times one buys and times one doesn't. Tonight I'm not buying. That's life. Life is hard. You'll see, I said. Uncomprehending and infected with bitterness, they left.

I am as usual drunk. It is 9:45. I'm dying to leave Oaxaca.

But something in me—and this is what disturbs me—was a pocket of alternative, something in me could will him out of the room so I could drink mescal and pack and do something decisive and quickly get out of Oaxaca. Something could say, I exist apart from this littered room and this cunt only temporarily full of gallons of sperm. Too, as always, I did, like they say, feel energized after sex, after human contact in the night though this actually, since it was blind and deaf to my reality, could have been a further source of dissociation.

So what was he—a boy whom I too didn't desire enough because there hadn't been time and desire. But then, too, what was Miguel—a will on my part to have him represent something significant. That there are no real feelings, that every feeling is not only ephemeral but *theoretical*, represents an interpretation such as a

[242]

computer would make over a given state of temporary data. How awful.

And my fatigue and unhappiness are making me insane again. This evening, the trees again looked wrong, as if, despite being painted white on the bottoms of their trunks, they should be called elms. The city that once was beautiful and full of pockets of color had become a flat plain without shelter. The sky, what little of it showed between the cathedral and the massed trees, was choked with bluish atomic clouds. Strange breezes from other times and places blew in. I was frightened; had a vision of the ineradicable ugliness of the human soul, the greed and self-interest at the base of everyone; even lovers were no exception.

Mexico is teaching me lessons I won't understand till later.

Lousy group, hard to dance to, outdoors and chilly in the courtyard, schlepping my bag—where to put?—but for all that, exciting. Packed with fresh youth which I could not fully gaze upon, imprisoned as I was by Antonio's invitation, so could be neither bored nor sluttish but decent and repressed, the normal female condition.

In Jaime's place he said he masturbated daily. Big deal, I said, so do I, wishing of course I hadn't. So, back in my room, he asked to witness this rare phenomenon. I complied since I do it always anyway when I make love to these assholes and since it turned me on that it turned him on and even without it doing anything to him, it's always been a top ten fantasy of mine lo these long hit-parade years of my life. Then his turn, on and on grinding off the walls of my cunt . . . .

I think I dreamed of Miguel last night. Lord what metaphors men are for women.

The guy is your perfect athlete and as with "El Elegante" of Los Arcos, I basically want from him a ringside seat at his event. He is too flawless for me but he gives me incredible pleasure to watch and hear.

I, natch, dig the Miguels, the flawed physically and psychologically, the weak. The ones with gaps in their bellies where the will escapes, as Don Juan would say.

I'm drunk again. Write now I think as an excuse to drink. Love love love to be high.

Miguel? Hair first, eyes second. Eduardo? Intelligence, lean hard body, cock, way he made love. Miguel had the charm, the naturally elegant and sexy and lispy missing-tooth way of talking. The childish excitement and laughter. Eduardo lacked humor and his attempts to satirize me were not only groundless but leaden. I failed to be charmed by this construction, by his attempt to gain affectionate supremacy over me. As if men were gods of definition.

M. thinks all women are cunts. They all do.

Wondering how to mask breath and state to keeper of the gates, another brutal old man. How I loathe old men, men in their prime of dominance, false false, but they have the power and I a simple pussy, man-hung . . .

Eleven A.M., two, three, four days later, Acapulco. Casa Rosita, a casa de huéspedes, guest house, where Lily is staying. I am in the last stages of illness. My infection is very bad and I continue not to fix teeth (perhaps origin of infection), and go on smoking and drinking. Haven't exercised in weeks and am thick around the middle, Lily observed. My skin is taking on the pleasant soft antique leather of soon-to-be a forty-year-old divorcée prowler after dark youth.

I tell Lily mystery stories about Miguel and Eduardo but they are mysteries I know as well as don't: Miguel, quick desire over soon; Eduardo, a construct who loved a construct, the more genuine mystery of the two but to me a bore.

The game that Lily and I played with gusto before: solving Mexican mysteries—what can I say?—she was absent for two months when I underwent my mysterious amours; recollection is always stale for the purpose of solution and I don't care. I have lost so much physical energy, that is the key, that I no longer care. Now I look and feel an undesirable creature. My bruja glow is gone. I am mere conserved flesh, no longer willing not to sag. And my insides are polluted.

Will Miguel ever respond to my calls? Will we sober up together and work out?

My folds of stum obscure my deeper thought. Perhaps it was along the lines of Augusta; does human, i.e., sexual, love, supersede the dull phlegm of cosmic truth?

Dates. You'll notice dates. I told L. that I desperately needed a calendar in order to understand *causality*. (The more private, shameful, reason is that I can only *acquire* the experience if I can name it with a date.) Whatever, it annoys me hideously. It's as if I lived it all in vain—that I can't remember when I or he or she or it

[244]

did what and where and when I arrived and left. Dateless, my life perishes ... But what I really felt, awakened by Lily's curiosity about my negative response, her prodding, was this: 1. political rage that men were stealing crying as they'd stolen clothes, interior decoration, dancing, from women. The whole androgyny business which added to men and subtracted from women (Jaggers, but where were the butches?). And that we'd have one more weapon removed from us—manipulation through tears—when we are already so shorn. More "sensitive" men, yech! How would it benefit us in any way?

Everything on the way to the restaurant, getting lost in Oaxaca's new-angled familiar streets turned fresh and disorienting—from what vantage point were the shops and streets real, fixed? Everything passing in quick review. . . .

Like Helen abducted from known shores but *herself* a hero, an adventurer (why does everyone ignore this, ignore her consciousness in this affair?), she the quester if only after her own mystery, I was kidnapped by forces greater than any my rationality could encompass so that I wrote, too: "Will I ever see M. again?" Something was going to be revealed to me by Eduardo and Ixtepec, my true face in the mirror.

I ask myself why I don't ask the old man of the courtyard, a meek beer lush, what the names of some of these trees are. Is it because I feel I could stay on in Mexico forever and the pressure of time, that instant nostalgifier, is absent? Will I ever feel landscape again? Is it only my own I can respond to? Does one need names before one can smell plants, *be* in their midst? Is smoking, is age, the reason I can only gaze blankly through the window at the tumble of green? What courage it takes to pursue nature and not love as one gets older. Nature, after all, is, at my age, a reminder of mortality; love is an escape from that.

Lily and I are separated at this point. I can't understand her living for love, as I so recently did. All that matters to me is health. Survival. I have neither energy nor hope for passion.

Again, then, there is a perfect boredom. Born, I suppose, of my perfect lack of will. I should go back to Zi and check my mail at least, but shit—four hours in each direction and what to do with my luggage? I should go to a doctor and a dentist. But whom?

Sometimes, when I was very sick and/or very down, a fantasy of perfect passivity would fall upon my shoulders like a heavy cape I

[245]

could barely drag through the streets. I'd long for Stan, to be taken in hand, taken care of. It gets so hard being alone, especially traveling, especially when you're ill, and don't have money.

I described you and our friendship very well to Lily and I think she feels she can't match the intellectual thrills we gave each other, and the deep pash, my dear, I felt for you, that sense that you and I were each other's souls.

And today, that awful fatigue and the hopelessness of calling Miguel . . .

Acapulco stinks, as usual. Last night, at "El Presidente" disco, horror vision of young plump mosquito Aca boys waiting around to suck the blood of older gringa tourist. An acquaintance of Lily's, an "animator," gets free drinks from the disco to ask women who aren't being attended to, to dance. An unattractive older woman fawned over by a hideous pup . . .

"Le Dôme" worse, worst. Lily says it's where the chavos maleantes take women they've picked up on the beach to steal their bags. They seat you in the Dôme, and have contempt for you, and lousy music, and I have a flawless hatred for it, for all of them, for this whole boring city where I have all the liberty I want, the dancing, the late hours. "Black Magic," a cheap direct imitation of "Daddy Cool," plays now from a fiesta blaringly setting itself up near our casa and is a fitting emblem of the music and the scene: parody of desire.

A *Brave New World* pleasure city, with programmed music produced by anonymous groups, programmed mass-produced decors, and abstract, "material disposable" chavos . . .

And I'm gaining weight so fast! Food is almost a healthy desire to grab at something indispensably interesting. The days are so alike! We sweat a lot, I look ugly, Lily says I need a haircut. I'm tired. I hate this town. Oaxaca had intelligent, tortured, gorgeous men; Salina Cruz had brilliant gorgeous men imprisoned in dull fates. Acapulco is full of fat cats, every pleasure stripped of desire.

Lily can't leave, of course. Like Miguel was my manifest destiny, despite Mexico City, A., Le Dôme's doorman, is hers. Must track down a lover, hunt desire in its lair. What I couldn't predict was of course—since I thought—all I wanted to have happened was an *achieved*, a realized short affair. I wanted to have been loved, to have loved, for once, for once, in Mexico, site of my focused dark desire. This happened and I thought, before it did, that I'd be happy with the trophy. I couldn't have predicted that, quite simply,

[246]

there'd be *time* afterwards. That past accomplishment couldn't fill the present forever; that I'd still be "young," still desiring life since after I was still living, no?

That there'd be time to fill. There is no other way to put it. And that the confidence from having won Miguel wouldn't carry me for the rest of my life. What does the world care? I feel so valuelesss now, a valuelessness I extend to everyone, thinking we are all nothing, mere surface—pretty or not—and underneath the same emptiness. This obscures a more personal feeling, my own un-attractiveness.

But lord, remember my boredom? I mean with Miguel? I was sustained then by a sense of my brilliant worthiness. And Jesus, how brilliant I was in those early days, with both of them. So that the word "bruja" could really be used by me and them. We validated a poetic vision—we lived literature. Now of course it would be impossible to describe myself as a bruja to anyone. But then I was a sorceress, an enchanter; it was all so fresh, so mysterious. As ununderstood love always is.

Now I see only the money motif. How could I have been blind to my age and ugliness in those days? And blinded effectively the rest of the world?

I absurdly felt I was going always further back in time, getting younger all the time in Oaxaca. I even got La Ventosa to share in my delusional system, that's how strong it was. I *was* a Don Juan—made others, through sheer force of a magical will, an undeterrable belief in my potency, my attraction—see me as a "gran maestra de hadas," and in my twenties.

Partly, of course, this came about because of my quasi-insane devotion to the bod in Zi, six weeks of exercise—fifteen minutes of hard exercise in the morning, including swinging ten pounds of weight thirty-five times with each arm, a half kilometer or mile of swimming, four hours of solid dancing, and climbing hills and walking miles of sand two or three times, all this *daily*, and eating nearly nothing; You understand this spurs one to delusions of beauty and worth.

Now who cares? I substituted beautiful clothes for a beautiful body in later Oaxaca. And being undesired produces a lazy will.

Now I think only if Miguel could know I was thirty-six would it be possible, love? Nine years, an infinity in Mexico. He's *so* cute, so gamin. Almost my pure desire for him gives me confidence to call him and risk rejection once again. Only if he knew I was thirty-six

[247]

would the whole thing be believable, an inexplicability, a dream. What, finally, a strain, being all these various younger ages for everyone here; thirty for Lily, twenty-eight for Miguel and Eduardo, etc. If I were thirty-six, then the world might truly marvel at how young I looked (at how young thirty-six-year-old women are), and I wouldn't have to hide my experience. What utter relaxation. My charm would be mine and not a will to false youth. It would be *accidentally* thirty-six-year-old Maryse's.

Oddly, Eduardo was the only one I came close to telling.

With this, I, drunk, leave.

Ciao!
M.

One drinks to feel one's power again.

$$\Omega$$

Edith,

In Acapulco, I get drunk, dance, desire and have nothing to say in the morning, am dull and timid the next day, furtive, as if I've been caught out in my true ugliness, something I drink to forget. Fernando, the seventeen-year-old, I fled him before I was drunk— I couldn't image what on earth he saw in me. After I was drunk I pursued him. Neither Lily nor I went, though all day I kept thinking I'd make the mad dash to the other side of town, just to see him again—he got me back into the Zi thing of worship of, gratitude for, perfect young beauty. That would be its own incredible reward, that in bed—affection would be insane to expect and not necessary. An old woman like me getting to be next to that perfection. It was rough on me when we danced. I felt directly competitive with him—seventeen, and what didn't he do well? To be seventeen, beautiful, chic, dance well, be strong, have a career in front of one, be male with all *those* privileges. So, I competed directly with him. There had to be some reason I had lived twice as long.

I had to work out, to test whether my muscles were looser, whether I could go longer, easier, more floatingly. Insane effort on two hours of sleep, *but* a finally heroic despair, an adrenalin sadness,

[248]

so deep, authentic, indifferent to sex and puritanical looking-on women.

I lay on the beach, suddenly hard bony muscular after a Roman end-of-empire gluttony last night, supported emotionally and financially by an ugly fat red-haired homosexual waiter who knew I was at the end of both resources he supplied—endless food and a quick rub through my hair, and the booze, the sun, the exertion, the pain, the realization of his looks, broke some membrane in me and I felt luscious tears. So the fourth time I swam out was to be alone and cry out loud and to answer this question I posed myself strung out shrimplike and practically bare-tit because I was athletic and not sexual, on the shore line: why is beauty dull when we have it? Why didn't I cream constantly over Miguel when I had him? This good question began stirring Hegelian responses in me but I needed space in which to moan and talk to myself.

The answer is available but I was tired and am still. Just imagining the two situations:

1. With and uncreaming
2. Away from him and creaming $\Big\}$ = answer.

Only remains to put it in words, the difference. The situation is universal, so only to articulate the consciousnesses, no? What is it? Here is the premier abord: To be creaming at the time would prevent one from being in the situation, that much intimidation would not be supportable by either party for nine days. Can't, can't, get it. Can't, that's all. But must.

Back to the water, where the answer eluded me but which like tears were my natural element, swimming in my own tears. Hanging off anchor ropes behind boats whimpering, sobbing while doing the side stroke, beating the pain out of my body while pounding it hard; willing it to be as tough and strong and muscular as those of men who hurt me. The water more and more a crystalline mattress; it became more my element than land. Always in its light aqua light, lightness. No longer on shore where a blink of an eye later one more beauty had disappeared, like a briefly seen fish resembling almost every other of its kind so I couldn't, once again, even know which *one* had gotten away, couldn't add him to my list.

The water's gentle rising at Caleta when I was in it, being *al* the horizon, that watery perspective became my normal one as I set myself various boats as goals: "Bonita" the first, then "Estrella," "Irma la Dulce," the cold "Columba," "Lupita" . . .

[249]

Indifferent to men at last, the whole trauma came as a relief; it freed my will; I was no longer the enchanted audience dreaming at the shoreline but the actor plunging, watched, admired, indifferent. I claimed the water, the shore line, a few bodies that passed by which I scrutinized nakedly. I maintained a look between glaring and neutral offering of myself as model and potential ally when a gang of young girls with the same look observed me as I lay sprawled, legs spread so that margin of white, hair-sprinkled flesh near pussy showed! I willed them to be as nearly bare-tit and in shape as I was; but later on, when I was in my fourth round of ocean, I thought anything women do—if they're not into the body, fine—as long as they're not *ashamed,* not modest, let the white flesh hang out, let it hang out for all the world to see and not cross their goddamn legs or drape a towel between their legs when they lie on their side or wear underwear under their bathing suits—an unbelievable habit here. Vile.

I did a few dance steps on the shore making believe I was limbering up. Slapped my arms repeatedly behind my back which made my breasts—no longer tits—jump, but my Diana Nyad imitation fooled everyone as well as me. Of course I had to play the part so in I dashed again, falling into the water and then slicing off like a shark. Breaking free of land, I the sea's true daughter. Mother Mar spoke to me, words of easedom. Receiving me, bathing me, washing me free, clean, strong, lean.

Back at shore I jabbed my hard thighs with a finger, tested my metal, made an arm muscle, sucked in my fat hard waist and patted my stum.

At 1 I broke for two hours to eat cunt and fish: lapa (abalone) and seviche. I claimed the restaurant, my right to drink tequila, ask for coffee and write. Easy with the young waiters, one always is as Lily, so distressingly to me, concurs—we are all so un-unique—in tragedy. So attractive, strong, relaxed.

Back at 3:10 to water and surprising myself by going in repeatedly again, until the eighth, ninth, tenth time, everyone—the lifeguards, boatmen, the inner-tube renters—had noticed, and my muscles were actually sore.

With my eyes closed and drunk, it was the passive activity I long for—effortless life. Each time I swam out I didn't know whether it was to drown or to return.

Once, at about 4 P.M., that late-ish afternoon time, a ten- or twelve-year-old boy passed, nearly tripping on my legs which I, the dueña of the beach, had just then knifed out. I turned to see his reaction—he was with a young girl his age, his sister, sweetheart or both—expecting hostility and instead he flashed a practiced sophisticated social smile at me. A knifed-out artificial thing but quite neutral. He was, and would continue to be, a charming social being. He was as dark as so many of them are. Suddenly that darkness brought back Miguel, that sweet unending darkness that only faded a bit toward the lower turnip legs. The dark skin that is my mystery, that is a miracle for me. I thought too of staring at some Chinese black glossy hair on a subway six months ago or so and trying to solve the riddle of its fascination for me: an emblem of darkness, darkness as unsolvable origin, mystery; all this mud becoming Hegelian abstraction, sometimes the only translation. An emblem became a metaphor—a cliché that becomes felt experience: darkness, the emblem, is axiomatic and the cliché, that it equals, mystery is so deep-seated, so old, that one *feels* it, believes it, looking at that dark light of that brilliant Chinese hair on the subway, remembering Mexico, the untranslatable love one had for its physical characteristics, and finally back to Miguel, brought back by that boy. That darkness I once had in my grasp, at the beginning of my third month here when I was still at the stage of "mediated strangeness," when his gestures were fresh and his alone but Mexico's as well—*he* its emblem; when I loved his "¿sabes qué?" to "¿ya vistes?" and the upside-down question mark answered some question I hadn't yet formulated, was about to tell me something, answer, like God, some question that was so new it gave me a sense of being born again, religious—"this-is-what-we-live-for," this is why we're on the planet, that kind of feeling. Like the recurrent dream I used to have of the forest, always seen from the same angle, that slope, that contained all the answers and that I was always about to penetrate.

Miguel's darkness, that black hair, that irreducible, origin color, that impenetrable mystery, that forest, that going no further, that foundry of all color, that deepest pit that reflects itself back at you without answering you, that bottom when everything has to bounce back, that once I woke up to, that I stroked wonderingly and greedily, my private treasure, that once I *had*, and I had no longer. I huddled on the shore and once again the ocean poured out of my eyes and ran down my knees. The morning's cry was about losing beauty in general, and affection. The afternoon's, this darkness. I thought of Doris, and her hair. I have always, I will always long for it, that sleek black silk that tosses like a perfect dress.

I realized my own hair's attractiveness. When it is good, it is a rich jumble of color and shapes, it has the agility, the speed and grace, the straight line of winning race cars, with the hills of surrounding countryside. It is both straight and wavy, mobile and stable, and the color as well at least a double offering. But it is my offering, not what I want—another mystery. I appreciate my own but don't desire it.

Writing to you is like some embarrassing remake of *Waiting for Godot*. Why don't you jerk off on paper in my direction, as I've done.

I am so unhappy it's amusing.

Love,
M.

Ω

Dear E.,

The latest magic in my life is a beautiful Valkyrie; I am in a competition with her. Everything I am she negates. I am showing my clothes to a Swiss girl of exquisite taste. She, the German, talks in my room to a butch French Canadian about mushroom hassles with federales and ignores my show.

Each of the three exquisite and so young, the Valkyrie was the oldest at twenty-six, with such unblemished bodies. I remember their thighs, like drumsticks: no secret jiggle near the crotch, a smooth stretch up to pussy, no furtive index of decay.

That company of young unashamed thighs, legs apart, comfortably squatting, lying, lounging. And the young carefree minds, the certainty of being attractive to more than one man so that my elaborate nostalgia and ratiocinations seemed square to them. But especially to Brigitte. It was like being in a superintellectual new new wave French movie, say one by Rivette, in which a dark actress and a light one are dialectical antitheses, though our scene offered more authentic polarities than Rivette's (say Rivette's) often only visual opposites. But it did have that uncanny abstract oppositeness. I'd been feeling so rich about my theme—desire—and of all the experience that filled me to overflowing, she corroborated only one detail: that it's unpleasant to pay for a man—it makes you feel old.

I tried and tried to dominate, to *connect*. Neither worked. She was pure gaiety, pure energy. Traveling through all South America, all the world, with her female dog Sophie, a homey dog out of a Bonnard painting. A free-lance photographer who boogied in Brazil for two years, tried learning Chinese at the "Fac" in Paris.

Her French was better, my Spanish. I tried and tried and tried but she reduced my life to flatness. The best I could come up with in my attempt to integrate her was after the door had closed behind her and Esther, the French Canadian, was: being a woman made her an identifiable target—otherwise how could I have rejected her? In a word, I must forget Miguel is the message.

I just spoke with him. How I love his voice!

So I mulled the whole day over, how I must be realistic—time and men stop for no woman. . . .

As usual he was fuzzy on the hard-core data stuff: his present job, why he hasn't called. Said he got my two letters but there was no telephone number.

But his voice is reassuring. Why? Well, because . . . it is so kind, it is mama-kind, grandfather-kind, honey-kind. It is the sort of thing a child is good at being reassured by, despite words—it is a tone of acceptance. Yes, yes, the voice says, through the dark wire, it *is* me, I *am* here, I *do* know who you are, I *am* accepting this call (now that you are paying for it), I *do* feel pleasure. I am happy, I am more—I am content. Something deeply, and comfortably settles in me. The universe is stable, it offers an abiding affection, an affection that abides because your voice and mine are mutually agreeable.

If he calls, we're home free, you and I, in our darkness and our attraction to the deeper dark.

Once more I want to experience a recap of my antique desire for those wild slit eyes, that comical alegría, gaiety. It is, above all, what anchors me to him—his lawless sense of fun.

It hurts me to admit to myself that even if Miguel calls nothing can wipe off the stain of fear and cynicism of whore's self-doubt that assails me after tonight. I suppose I would be violent too if I were ugly and male. But Miguel? I doubt he ever needed to rape anyone. How awful to be heterosexual! To love assholes who say I don't care if your father is dying, shut up!

[253]

A = amour. M = Miguel, passion, beauty, beauty, beauty. He is my Jewess.

I am sad unto death as usual as it approaches zero hour. He said he'd call at 12 and it is 11:40. Mama E. will hear me asking him why he didn't call, where he works, etc. The fact is he *didn't* call so my theory was right: I told Lily he'd only come to Zi if I had rented a house. The thought of sharing rent did not appeal, the bastard. He thinks of me as a moderately well-to-do woman of leisure. From the first moment he saw me at the Casa Elvira, he said, he knew I was a writer because I had an air of not having to work for a living! True enough . . .

Perhaps another of my theories is right: that it really is dry season during the rainy season and it makes the men crazy. All these near-rapes and abductions of late. Or is it just me? If so, it is unavoidable. I drink to dance with abandon and the abandon will land me in hot water. There is nothing I can do either about my inability to tolerate boredom.

Why can't these assholes ever learn—I want to choose. Direct requests insulted me—now they amuse or exasperate me, bore me. I use them as reasons to dismiss men; I have my modest prides.

This is the scenario—he won't call but I'll go to Mexico City anyway in two or three days, or less, as I told him. I am beyond caring that he doesn't care enough to show he cares. I won't ever get that kind of affection again. He wrote me that love letter; I'll find some way of explaining his not doing anything else as weirdly, typically, Mexican. I want a lover in Mexico. I have chosen him, faute de mieux. But, he did warn me, he doesn't like one-sided pursuits on the part of women. Oh well. Even I know I'm playing badly. So that even if I "get" him, he won't be worth much·to me. I'll be dried out where he's concerned and gone, gone, gone with the wind.

Ugly women never sleep I think this morning, or last night. They are always wanting, alert. There is no time left for them; no opportunity must be missed.

Benito the fisherman doesn't come here anymore to Mama E's. Manuel doesn't go to the Flor. One after another my evil longing fills spaces vacated by men frightened of contamination. I hang over Zi like a plague cloud, the pestilential cunt.

Oh I ache in old and new ways.

What would I have done with a working Miguel—any adjustment in the machine of our relationship might've killed it. He all serious and early to bed, I sluttishly lolling? No, going to galleries and visiting the city and learning Spanish and writing.

No, he broke it to me gently, I can't go to Zihau. But, he said, and I can't remember whether he said are you planning to come to Mexico City or *can* you come to Mexico City. Where will I stay? I asked. Have you got a room for me? Eso es de lo menos. I think he said. A lovely gentle voice. Síii! Pleadingly, too. *Yessss, Doooo.* Very elongated. My beauty. Nah, you never get the prize winners, just the also-rans.

Also, he was preventing me from even looking at another Miguel lookalike. God the original has a voice that melts you down to your bones. It's like his soul shows when he talks. Wide open, the gate to his feelings through his voice.

Love,
M.

Ω

Dear E.,

Yes, Miguel did call a second time and spoke from god knows what unknown rip-off phone for a warm fifteen minutes. It was an awful strain. I had nothing to say—my one boast, prison, was impossible in Mama E.'s presence. Nor its corollary: my terrible, *specific* affection for him there. Instead, I manufactured Platonic affections; warm concurrences that I wanted to see him again. I stood at the phone mute, flattered, dull. Perhaps *I* bored myself in that conventional female demureness. Plus all the holes—why he'd gone to Huatla without me, why he hadn't written in Oaxaca, why my calls had been refused. And his awful, unbelievable, Platonic warmth. The whole thing a performance, an unreality.

One of the things it's too late to mention in this letter is that Miguel has always responded too late. If I'd found a letter from him when I returned to Oaxaca it would've killed the mala onda of Salina Cruz, it would have been in time to save me, despite the defection of his magical "cuidado." I could tolerate Eduardo's defection as a write-off of an inexplicable kind and Salina Cruz as a harmful but cute onda. Miguel, my true love (but always, I knew, faute de mieux)—but still, I did *choose* him over the one other applicant. I lost half my weight in energy and hopefulness and youth and replaced it with slack flesh acquired through a lethargy that barely got me to the pastry shops on time. Whatever food was at hand made do, often: chemical cakes in wrappers, dry tortillas, phony ice cream. I was dead and old and unbodied for months.

His love letter waits for me in Zi. I receive it August 1. I write him two quick letters filled with contact details. Two weeks and no reply. Once more the onda subsides. I call on a whim. He's in and warm and says he'll call. He doesn't. Once more the onda dies. He calls the next day and says it was mere accident he couldn't call the day before. But defection is defection—I know it will be his gifts at whim and nothing I can control or hold him responsible for. We speak for fifteen minutes, an absolutely abstract conversation.

I got bored with Castaneda toward the end—felt he abandoned, to disadvantage, his skepticism and with it any mediation between the real and the fantastic. And thus any credibility. i.e., he stopped being a translator and became a fantasy writer spinning off one (dull because unmediated) miracle after another. Finally, I felt the book was ultimately about a contest of wills which Castaneda lost without knowing it. Tired of fighting, intimidated, he succumbed to an iron irony and illogic.

Plus, I was, god knows, no longer a bruja. Plus I hadn't taken mushrooms. Plus the whole magic aura in which such things would've been possible because all of Mexico was a mystical, expanding metaphor for me, was dead. And—and—all this stuff was months ago. And was my appeal, as with Eduardo, that I could be the trippy companion few Mexican women are? The German was right—I *am* full of qualities, I am a rich store, but not of mushrooms.

Anyway, Sebastian, recovered from last night's vulgarity—he was with Benito and an asshole. I was with death. Sebastian insisted on my beauty and kept slobbering in the direction of my Rivette rival, about whom he said, "What a beautiful thing." Invited me to Manzanillo beach today, where he, I, and his organ would be alone together. Strange onda! He's well-educated, witty, an architect, but such a deep hostility to women, which manifests itself as a desire for a zipperless fuck.

Back to Miguel . . .

I rushed up to get a cigarette—death entitling me to death—and I realized I was killing myself or I was dying, because I'd had Miguel. I had had a perfect beauty, a passionate reciprocated love, an entry into the Mexican home, even a marriage proposal and

[256]

every other follow-up I requested: the two letters, the one, long phone call at his expense ... It was an intense experience—how could I ever care again as much about anyone else? Yes, of course, there were all of his lookalikes at those moments when they danced with such grace that I was my own serpent emblem: head touching tail in simultaneous desire and fulfillment, motion and stillness, the other's beauty and my own, a mutually experienced perfection.

I am, therefore, looking forward to seeing him again, his vulgarity and indifference having accomplished what nothing else could have—my relaxation. I hope he has money this time, and that we go dancing. Passion is not long possible for me outside the disco. I have never had ecstasies like those when I dance to music I love with a man whose beauty I love.

Same day, Aug. 15

I may be dying. I can't take breath. And I don't stop smoking. My lungs are knotted small with phlegm and I'm tired, tired. . . .

Can't sleep—excitement, booze, being thin. Miguel, even the anticipation of that darling boy. Fantasies take up squatter's residence in my head of moving him into New York apartment, a penniless, shiftless chavo! Idly wonder whether to risk asking him to pay own fare and half the rent.

Dark Miguel: last stop at Darkness. Baby M.

See ya.

Love,
M.

Ω

Dear E.,

Here I am in café # 3, no 4, black coffee-ing it before my half sober rendezvous with Miguel in a purported half hour. On my drunken guts I called from the desk at 3:30.

Next day, jueves the 18th of Aug.

Miguel did make his appearance a mere hour late. He was supposed to come by for me today but at 3:15 still hadn't shown. Left note he'd be back at 5, at the Washington desk, but it's 10 to 7 now. I don't think he'll show.

Awful to greet Miguel in that hole.

[257]

I was good and bombed when he came. So mostly I remember none of most of what I said. He'd cut his hair, but it looked good. I did not feel wild joy or gratitude but embarrassment which I buried in his neck so he wouldn't smell my boozy, ciggy, phlegmy breath. He said I was "flacita" (skinny). I said just for you, like these new espadrilles and this black bathing suit . . . I told him straight off I was drunk—it was the only way to be for a first meeting after such longing and fear. We went out and *he* bought a bottle of brandy, a half litre of the cheaper stuff. We drank and drank. All was a dizzy blur. Then I asked to go out for coffee (the concert was vetoed by him—didn't I just want to stay in and talk?). Same old routine. *He'd* come for our rendezvous, mind you, with a casual acquaintance he met in the streets.

He seemed bored with my prison tale, which I told badly in Spanish.

Fri, Aug. 19th.
I'm in Moorish Sanborn's. I'll pay 20 p's to sit here and tell you how I cannot leave Mexico and how again, though he won't show and I look good, I'm in love with Miguel.

I'd spent the day, having decided to stay at the Rioja, doing laundry, resuming exercises, sunning on the roof, putting my stuff neatly away in the tiny room. The golden light that filters through the strangely bubbled skylight of Sanborn's was present in spirit in the streets. An effortless passivity transformed by body into pure receptive unconscious. Weightless, I perceived I saw one not particularly attractive guy in a striped T-shirt cross the street but that's when it crystallized: that I was here in Mexico City where even the unattractive were slim and sharp.

It's of course 5:45 and the bitter tone of the last sentence reflects my being back in the hotel where nary a trace of Miguel ever having communicated. This is awful, awful, awful. I am being hideously pissed-on and rejected. The slut siempre en su casa.

On day 1, he was the reformed delinquent—working, clean-cut, naively proud of his rehabilitation. I was slim, dark, drunk, weary, world-traveled, and bored by him. I stroked his hair as a gesture to the past but found myself idly combing my fingers through my own later with greater pleasure. We made love three times, twice at night. All times were boring. He lay a dead heap on top of me. I was ill and claustrophobed and suffocated in the ugly room. Nevertheless, I let him sleep on my side of the bed and did not insist on my own pleasure.

[258]

"¡ Soy feliz!" he kept saying. Me too! Me too! I lied bleakly. "Te quiero," and "Me enamoré de ti" were others. We went for coffee to our "Café Popular" (where I consumed nineteen pastries our last night) and I clutched at him drunkenly at the counter. My chavo, world! That sort of evening—drunk, unconscious, bonhomie. I barely remember what we spilled out to each other. Only that it was strange hearing him talk again, using his Miguel language as if he were unaware of all the other Spanishes I'd heard in between. Once more his words were resurrected and assumed their previous opacity though I'd translated them all with men who succeeded him. It was as if I'd learned nothing, as if something in him somehow warred against my having an experience of Mexico or the language apart from him. He took no notice of any change in me or in my Spanish, for instance. And on day 2, when I forced the issue by reading my Eduardo words to him, he asked me if I knew just how old all that slang was.

I think I know now that he's not coming. Last night was bad. And no sex this morning either.

Last night I said I'm not beautiful, I have a deformada face, hoping deformada was considerably more neutral in tone than deformed, and Miguel said so what? But that, my sweetheart, we both know is why he's not sharing the rent. Forget beauty he says on day 2 when I say Oh baby you are so beautiful to me.

Anyway, day 1, you could say, was a fresa Miguel and a hip, stoned, bored chick me, with little interludes of public pash and mash in the café, in the store he bought liquor in. I nestled, I crunched, I buried, I hid shyly behind, I stroked, I leaned in, I caressed, I giggled, I opened wide eyes, I laughed, I cupped his knee. You, me, Hollywood.

Magic page! My birthdate. Really beyond discipline of patterning the past. Pure streaming present is all I can moisten this paper with.

Magic. Yes. That finally one more time again now I am away from a rational analytic consciousness, away from Lily and the whole world of understanding Mexico, of translating it, of finding words like "bruja" absurd ... and, perhaps because I'm alone, perhaps because it's been a long time since Lily, perhaps because I'm in love again, perhaps because I'm leaving soon unless I can help it, perhaps because Miguel refused—yes, this is it—that a vast continent of Mexico experience and language had occurred in me. How to put it—I can't explain it, refused to acknowledge that I had a consciousness, that I was loved and traveled—I *can't*. That worlds

[259]

of language united and separated us, that I'd heard his words after him. He thus effectively reduced my comprehension of them to when I was with him the first time—i.e., when I didn't understand them. Yes, that's it. Language is not a metaphor but the absolute literal cause of an emotion in this instance.

He is terribly self-involved. It is a bit a bore. I mean my mass displaces space, ¿verdad? So maybe an eyeball could roll in my direction occasionally?

Night # 2: like before, a reversal from need and tit-sucking. Tonight he is (i.e., was) *cunning*. Everything he's been with me has been a ploy. Marriage? Am I kidding?! He wants to be free! Why did he ask me, I ask? For cortejo, teasing, he answers, a lie.

The truth came earlier night # 2. Dig it, he says, you want to be in Mexico, I want to go to the States. What do you think is the solution?.

Everything on Mexico City trip # 1 was deception. It was all a rap, he said. Everything he'd said . . .

Do you believe the devil exists? he asks. Of course, I answer. He cries. I can't talk like this to anyone, he explains. I'm so alone. He continues disgustingly alone in his narcissistic banal self-discourse as I wonder where the mutual onda has fled. I'm deathly ill, understand, deathly tired, deathly, passionately in love, and this asshole's mushrooming solo. Oh men! I suffer silently.

You know, he says about the sierra, one is alone with oneself there, he says. Oh yeah? I say, pretending sympathetic interest as I ruefully remember him joining Monte Alban in my loins back yore.

So I chew cheek and call Miguel. He just left. Oh? Said he was going to see you, she said. Ho ho. Nothing about it to me, and no call from him that desk knows about. I think I've become the safe alibi . . .

I look so spiffo tonight. And I am so drunk. And he's gone. And not coming here. Even if he does, it absolutely no longer matters. I'm drunk again and polymorphous and bored again. I don't want him when I'm drunk.

I wanted him this afternoon when I was the mushroom WAC. So niftee!

I'm going out. Screw Miguel. Screw Mexico City. My clothes are better this year. I'll try to go it alone, grease a few palms.

Still Friday night. Miguel and I are in my room. The update on the economics? He paid for two nights, owes for two more. Brought no money to boogie with, borrowed ten to buy coffee (me) and Tehuacan (him) with. Left no tip.

Presently, he's working out his bill collector calculations at my table.

He came after all. Too late as usual. I was into my cups, madly telephoning discos to find out their address before hitting them. He hit first. All green and blue and yellow and clean and dark and my lover whom I loved. I collapsed into him publicly, as always, and then felt immediate boredom and resentment.

In my room an awful little masquerade on his part of how I'm exploiting him by asking him to split the rent. Who knew, he implored me, that he'd agara such a mala onda off me! You dig the usual male ploy. Stop doing that male projection ploy on me I screamed. How am I exploiting you by asking you to pay half the rent? Do you think I'm old and ugly? Well, sucker, I'm not, I said, parading my thin waist in front of the vanity mirror. I looked O.K., the tawny fullish hair on top of black shirt, black pants, white vest. He pursued. I pursued. We fucked.

Today, Saturday, August 20. About 11:40 A.M. What I meant about the two faces of Miguel, to tidy that up as the maid does my room and I sit here on the roof greased up under a cloudy sky: Miguel I was the reformed sinner whose three weeks of mushroom tripping revealed unto him the glowing onda of work. He was feliz, etc., arms in the night. Miguel II was the unregenerate mafioso. So nasty, quick, cynical. I seems slow; II was sharp, with it.

12:45.

He swore he'd be on time this time, between 12 and 12:30. I can't take the pain anymore. The dismal cynicism, the instant bitter aging. Every time I fall for it; then follow the excuses and lies. Yesterday he came *five* hours late—and weren't we supposed to eat together? I swear I've had it. Nothing is worth sacrificing my *life* to, my health.

As usual, for instance, I couldn't sleep with him in the bed. Woke up at 7 or so after four hours sleep, restive. He'd slept with his back to me all night. I lay and lay and lay there waiting for him to merely apply pressure with a part of his body on a part of mine that I could interpret as affection. At 9 I gave him till 10 to give me a sign on whether I should return to Mexico—for if not for him or more specifically for what he represents—why return? At about 9:34 a fairly unequivocal squeeze of my thigh occurred.

[261]

But this is *not* the first stage stuff at all. Te quiero, he explained the other night, could be used for shoes or cake. Whereas te amo, which he doesn't use, is the real thing. He is not in love with me and that's that. I'm a temporary buena onda. But last night he made me come with his hand, spent a long time on it and did it gently, letting me guide him. Sex was again fun. Again he wanted me to go down but didn't push my head down. I made him come with my hand, letting him show me how. Buena onda all around. So why this?

He talks fast and slangy, not caring if I understand or not. I lose big chunks of language with him. It takes 4 times before I hear a new word. He talks to himself, essentially, laughs at his quaintness, *looks* at me, of course, when he's doing it but there it ends.

We both feel something is missing, both wish we could smoke together again. How sweet it was gonna be! He was gonna pop in on me in his bill-collection rounds in the middle of the day and he'd buy me a Tehuacan! Or we'd have a meal. In a month he'd have an apartment and we could live together there, etc.

Something the French Canadian girl in Zi said stuck like a burr to my brain: she could never have a deep relationship with someone she couldn't explain herself fully to, which meant communicating in her own language.

I feel this enormous gap between us now of his Spanish, my English, his Mexicanness, my Americanness, not to mention the sex distinction. Perhaps because it's the end of the trip and I no longer have the forward impetus of the detective on a quest. He can teach me only what I will too rapidly forget at this point.

Ah, the elevator lurches—maybe Miguel will rescue me from my brooding emptiness. His sheer presence, not to even ask for affection, or a meal together.

I have nothing more to add. It's a quarter to 2; he vowed he'd be on time. He's not, he won't be. Again, I may never see him again. He took his hairbrush with him and brought, as usual, no change of clothes, or toiletries, here. The money request may have done it. He doesn't want to pay. Natural enough for a man not in love. . . .

With a Miguel, I can dispense with Miguels. Without, I can't. I need to be loved in order not to need to be loved. Oh Lord. I'm going.

Ciao,
Heartbroken

[262]

Ω

Dear Edith,

A knock on the door but not for me. How could he, with a daylight life, track this vampire operating on a magic frequency down? Oh babe—you see, no? What he saw? On booze I'm so *poetic*. So free and bitter and open and sweet and lovable and unafraid and siempre young.

Goodbye.

Isn't it nice to be drunk?

Love,
M.

Ω

Dear E.,

Mexico City is Paris with hot sauce. Cinque de Mayo might as well be the Boulevard St. Michel. The same pasty-faced middle-aged male bureaucrats sit in the Café Popular. Cars stream past. The waitresses are indifferent to my having eaten too much. The music is slick, lovely, corny, somehow tropical in its transparent manipulative schmaltz.

Only I, listening to the abstract alto drone of the stream of cars, the basso profundo to the sickly-sweet high juke box, am odd, odd, odd tonight. Mad again. As who wouldn't be, giving her soul and having it not recognized. Do you know what I mean? I said to M. Here, recognize me. I give you this data, and I love you. And he threw it down the toilet as an unintelligible tip.

Why is the street suddenly so weird? It won't physically harm me—and there's no way I can commit suicide from my room—but it is killing me just the same. Suddenly, every familiar corner is absent of Miguel. The Café Popular—he's never been there, it says. The disgusting ever-late afternoon light mockingly loans itself out to the abyss of a street. Miguel is off somewhere gay and normal and high and laughing at me. And I? If only I could cry. I am beyond that.

[263]

The light, the light, lending itself to empty downtown Saturday, but still the stupid insensate cars flush by oblivious to their stupidity, my silent plea.

It isn't Mexico. It's not Paris. It's a painting by Hopper come to life. I am trapped inside a dead thing. Language is impossible here, even in English. Who has the arrogance to say: I'm mad, this is my crazy view of things, help me.

I'm trapped in a silent world, a tableau of forty years ago. The walls are different, the tables, the heights of the ceiling and the chairs. I loom above this letter. The view past the rows of cakes in the plate glass window is unfamiliar. I am a ghost. There is nothing now between me and death. Death is the unfamiliarity of everything, the strangeness of the once familiar. The same spatial configurations only the light is hollow, sick.

I think I lack the energy to hit expensive discos which I don't know where they are to be rejected tonight. I look passable. My energy's low. I love to dance but despair is not a good muse.

This Mexico, babe. Men who don't love you but act wildly as if they do initially. Self-involved, narcissistic men . . . The men drink and philosophize about pain. The women live it solo and culturelessly. No one cries, except easily, sentimentally. The devil, therefore God, exists.

Oaxaca was a pushover compared to this. Pain had boundaries there.

Spare us big cities, oh lord!

M.

Ω

Monday, Aug. 22? 7 P.M.

Dear Edith,

Pussy's back on the page, not knowing where to start. Perhaps the stomach: everytime I wait for him I destroy my body. The list of consumed edibles today appraches the usual grotesque. Plus I'm tired. And I think I'm bored, as much with my Miguel life as with my own. For instance. I had a café con leche in a big restaurant across the street and I saw this semi-chic red-haired woman with her two kids. They seemed to be having a little outing. Other eaters were probably taking a welcome break after work. I was just in one

[264]

more café. The endless break. Doing nothing is awful after a while—I'm filled with a desert. My times with Miguel are slightly duller than before. We still don't go to the movies or dancing and I see nothing of his friends, and saw his family only once (at my suggestion). We went to scrape the kitchen bare.

So off, with my bottle of mescal, something he evidently felt he'd also paid for, for a drunken joy ride with R. patting my knee and telling me how linda I was—suicidal driving at 4:30 A.M. in nearly empty Mexico City. Hair-raising passing of the few cars there were, on my left, Miguel's gently and sadly smiling saintface on my right. Dark, kind, passive. Pure joy at the balance of danger and desire, recklessness and safe harbor. I the moll between two asshole chavos. But always more sober, and as usual, acting the gentle den mother, a role I loathe. But there it is with Miguel—I am his mama.

It was a very good thing all around I managed to go dancing at the best spot in town or I would've hated M.'s guts forever, but good. Also, he was, surprisingly, enormously jealous. Another macho feature is dog-in-the-manger. Even if he didn't want me, goddamn if anyone else could have me.

My earlier metaphor of bruja was appropriate for one's first experience of Mexico—the magic unknown, men mysteriously pursuing one; and it could have protected me to this day with its infectious power—viz., Eduardo, a better fish in every way than Miguel. (Shall I repeat: younger, a better teacher and lover, a lovely body, financially generous, a guide to Mexico, fascinating friends, a car, liked to take me dancing, better clothes.) To believe one is brilliant and beautiful is seductive, and to deal in magic metaphors—I was still, after prison, la gran muestra de hadas for E.'s political cousin Feliciano.

My second metaphor, begun in La Ventosa, was detective. I don't know the Spanish word for this which is a shame because my second persona just might impress Miguel anew. This too fascinated. It almost cancelled out Luisa's fine figure. Everyone was impressed by the existential/structural/phenomenological black Chandleresque combination. The forties sleuth, female snaking through the sewers of desire. The slut intellectual—the woman who'd found a way to justify her sexual curiosity, solitude, hard knocks. And everyone was intensely flattered that I wanted to solve their mystery. Me next! Research me next. Respect for this persona. Fat Mischkovsky the poet said oh so you're the detective. And, later, if you're really doing an investigation, then you have to hear

[265]

this too: this is a homosexual country. No, I don't want to hear it, I protested. Anyway, with the detective came the beginning of skepticism, detachment. Luisa's beauty confined to a pudgy pompous dropout engineer because she could no longer desire the dark beauties, knowing what lay behind.

I suppose the outcast has to be counted as a role I was forced into in Zi, that strange place where desire ebbed and flowed and Benito once more resumed his presence at Mama's tables and once more, now that the barque of possibility was safely lost at sea.

He asks me if my teeth are my own because they're even. Pues, sí, I say, amazed at a new Mexican concept. But my hand, I say, my hand is artificial. I take it off every night. We both laugh at the unstated, barely thought sexual innuendo—the night or several nights before he'd placed my hand on his erect prick. He actually tells me what he's doing in Zi, and proffers first interesting (though blatantly sexual) invitation. But there is affection and respect—trust intuition. I like him and he's thirty-two or thirty-three. And perhaps that's why I feel a rich and salty adultness with him.

Fascinating, no? the train of desire? the unpredictability of it. Neither you nor I suspected Sebastian, my "pretendiente," would finally make the grade. Because he wasn't my physical type. Good-looking, but not my type, period.

What danger can there be in inventing—his talk was all Platonic anyhow. He must've said: Live with me, oh please live with me. Must've promised once again he'd get me help in staying here longer. What are you thinking about he must've asked repeatedly it must have been on Sunday. Well, what to do with my modest life, I answered over and over, thinking how, how do I assimilate Mexico and Miguel with a career, and a book that can only be written in N.Y. on women and film, a great, rigorous book, my destiny. How does a feminist live with a macho hood and how does Maryse give up gentle Stan?

For I bought it all though it didn't jibe with the evidence. I don't know. I'd gone from being an unregarded dullard to a passionately desired savior. Who knew why. His awful weirdness on bleak Sunday. Emptiness snuck in on silent insect feet into my gray room. Outside, the world of others shone sunny and alive. We slept on and on and it must've been on Sunday he did his endless rap on desiring me. I wish I could produce the evidence—it might delude one or two members of the jury into believing I'd been loved. It is

[266]

nice to keep even false love letters after all. People can always think you're being modest and merely cynical when you deny their sincerity. Though it is of course mostly for my own records that I wish to remember the data. I wish the accumulation of all of it. Yet that my memory fails is appropriate, for it was all false, toda falsa. The onda is over. Even the romance of wooing him through ironic appreciation of his exploitation, even this is over.

And not to forget that after the densest syrup of love talk I've ever had held to my lips, the cock looked at other women on the subway on the way to his house. More, was nakedly, miserably aggressive. Asked a leprous student why his skin was peeling—as a guy whose hand I hadn't noticed wasn't there hid his new stump under his shirt. Miguel surfaced every deformity on the train. In the station he pushed two women out of his way. On the bus, it was cozy and I say, eyes closed, it's like we're on a plane, each of us, dreaming private dreams but joined by the darkness as we fly to some mutual destination. Hoping, hoping, to make him value me and not kick lamp poles, trees, women and lepers (out of the sheer indignity of proposing love to such as me).

He had heated the savory-baited chicken after laboriously preparing fresh tomato juice with squeezed lime and salt. There was tart green salsa with the chicken, cold and newly-made, and cold melon for dessert. Coffee and beer, then brandy. In that kitchen that will always always be a locus of desire for me and him in it, patiently at work among its ordered implements ...

Back to Sunday? His look, that look—pleased pussycat. Smug, pleased, happy grin. *His* family at sport, his party going fine. A lovely look ... A closed smile concealing missing tooth—you know how sweet-closed-mouth smiles are, no? Containing secret treasures. And the eyes happy with all it's been given as their pleasure by a quixotic god to survey in this given, chosen moment.

I won't call him. (Shall I call him I ask twenty-one-year-old woman who thought *I* was twenty. A vrai dire, she has more eye wrinkles than I—early marriage and pregnancy.)

Miguel. Sunday. We return "home"—he brings bag with change of clothes. You capish that I am happy, happy. Before we even hit his house we go to a señora who's converted her suburb ground floor into a tienda. He gets two beers on credit, first, and second, asks to rent her apartment. It's for yo and ella, he says, pointing to me. Afterwards, in the kitchen, he describes it. I am the fresh and

[267]

cherished sweetheart. But later, he'll tell me that the reason he told her it was for me as well was that that would make her rent it to him sooner than to single men.

Oh how false it rings, that glib Spanish, in this mean city, vicious, unmystical country understood more by a Third World lesbian separatist who doesn't speak Spanish than by me and my once inviolably rich research. And my tawny youth. Oh false Miguel, hungry country, pimply arrogance, sad grateful women. How can I write your epic? It isn't of desire but of economics, and how dull, how dull can you get? Oh rich pretentious German, only the bourgeois (who call themselves communists) have the pocket money for love. I *hate* economics. How awful and perfect that Sex and Money should turn out to be the title after all, the translation of "Translation."

And what does it matter if he shows up now? I'm stoned, again, alone in my room, writing away, wanting only not to be so drunk. Once more he'll take me to the Café Popular, where I'll pay for a café con leche and a cream puff and astound him with my bitter amusement. Ah! Intelligent, the cava. I don't want it anymore, lord help me. I've had it. The claustrophobia of los mismos lugares, if nada más.

Sunday night, I suppose, draws to a close. We get to bed too late and all night I hit the john, farting and shitting a bad stomach away. The mosquitoes bother him. All night, as all night and day Saturday and Sunday, he must've been finally warm. Held me all night, tried to make my tummy pains disappear, horribly, by laying a heavy hand on my stomach.

(He's here).

I won't look up.

Argument. He leaves.

Who cares?! I say, after slamming the door. I care.

Wed., Aug. 24, 4:30 P.M.

Yes, I care and I rush off after him and catch him in the elevator and drag him back.

More about that later.

Where were we?

I can't write.

It's raining and all my wet clothes are inside, being smoked. I'm tired and I want clothes and more clothes. He won't come today, of course, which is fine because I'm exhausted and the room is crowded. Besides, we should give each other time to desire each other.

I'm worried about this clothes business. It means a negation of Miguel. As soon as I wanted the lime green Mexico jacket with the embroidered felt dancers on the back, the feeling in my pussy, the memory of physical pleasure it was a miracle to feel again disappeared.

Sunday?

Monday? Oh yes. Monday was when he came all sober, at night, as usual these days without calling, all spiffed up. I was totally drunk and writing my letter to you. Right? You know dates better than I do at this point. Goddamn if I'm going to research my own letter. You're reading it a lot faster than I'm writing and your memory's good, right?

Miguel called. You gather I am slightly in love, god what a miracle. What an unbelievable miracle at my age. You know how I know? two things: the pussy feeling and that last night he made me come with his hand without my interposing my own. You dig that my anxiety about my crepy nine-years-older flesh, as well as my face, prevents me from relaxing for pleasure. One or two tokes of mescal, and the dark and ¡ya! Voilà.

Monday: ¿Qué más? (God what a sexy voice he has. Low, slow.) He could have anyone he wanted, and of course has, and of course will again when he has more dinero. But I go down on him and swallow the come. The lesbian-separatists should only know! At least I taught him the clit. I think one of the reasons—yes, the major one—I relaxed last night was I had the confirmed suspicion for the first time that he both regarded the clit as "natural" and at last *wanted* me to come first. Did not do it dutifully, suspiciously, paranoically (thinking something was wrong with me, or worse, him). And he gets hot getting me hot, the third sign of love, I suppose. How incredibly sweet it is.

Now that he's slimmer, I feel active desire for his body as well. Lovely, lovely shoulders. And that strange Indian hunchback that I adore. He looks dynamite in clothes now.

You're bella, he said on Monday, relax. Why keep checking in the mirror? Don't you know it? No, I said, I've never believed a man could love me. Why? he asked. Because of my face, I said.

[269]

You understand that there is nothing I don't say when I'm drunk. The horror is I need to be drunk with him. I am such a bore, he so fascinating. For one thing, his Spanish is superb—a rich medley of slang. And his equally rich, guttery, intellectual slum life.

Mon: what else did *I* supply? *My* onda. Money. What am I, chopped liver? I asked. Am I old and ugly that you free-ride me so?

He lapses into another love onda. The same absurd jealousy. He bores me. Does he? Yes, I sadly state, standing by the door so he can't get out, sometimes you do.

Amazing the things he lets me get away with! Of course my appeal is precisely this honesty, this mirror I hold up to him, that I can only supply when drunk and which has the ironic effect of making him, as well as you, the greater custodian of my reality than I am myself. Because I remember almost nothing. . . .

And the other trend? The privileged tourist, of course. His richness of language and experience is intimidating. Yo tengo el verbo, he boasts repeatedly. I have the word, the power of language. People respect this about me he says, pointing to his head. He will cry, later, when he talks about his deepest persona—he is a brujo who has helped many people. Transformed wayward lives on mushroom trips. People beg to trip with him because they know they'll only get good ondas off him. He is a prophet, a revealer, a genius, and a saint: so why is he collecting bills? I, throughout, feeling the utter square. I'd like to take mushrooms with you, he says.

Weds. he shows early—how could he not? Either Mon. explicitly angry, or Tues., implicitly loving—he'd gotten the message that to show responsibly was an act of love. And who wouldn't have loved after Tues., after he'd responsibly fulfilled the Maryse-onda obligation of going to a flick, having enjoyed it, having been gratefully and slavishly worshipped, having had his come swallowed sweetly by a deft and loving mouth?

So I fell in love again—I knew from Weds., visit-to-market, yesterday's cunt stirrings that it had happened, finally again. I felt not only (obviously, *manifestly*), sexual rejuvenation, the return of sensation in my body—oh lord, lord, lord I was physically alive again—but a tender secure expectation of further pleasure, for I had a lover, and not a one-night stand Luís.

Still, I planned to stand him up. It was such an *atypically* good onda with him. I was confident now, knew I was valuable, eager to prove myself on other men, eager to resume my onda—explorer, culture-seeker, vamp.

He showed early.

Let's end as friends, he says. I'll drop the money off tomorrow. I'm going to Acapulco, I say. Write and tell me where to send it, he says. I don't want to owe you anything. This too is typical. He drinks my booze, smokes my cigs, eats my oranges but has me keeping track of the room which he also won't pay. Anything he has paid for, he either steals back (if I'm correct) or borrows back. He paid 10 p's for the flick and borrowed 10 p's in the morning. I don't want to owe you, exploit you, he says, and does. I want to eat you, he says, and makes me eat him.

Look M., I say, if you're sincere about this "love," give me the gift of honesty. When have I ever lied? he asks. No phones in Mexico City three or four days in a row, I say, and one other innocuous thing—oh yes, that you'll return for me in the afternoon, that's why you're taking your overnight bag with you. He laughs appreciatively, but it makes no dif.

I poke him alert to me, desperate at his thick-skinned indifference, his englobulated guru-ishness, his shining transported eyes. . . .

And my dear, I was at the point last night—drunk—that I'm at tonight, no longer bothering to be the smart Jew lawyer, just blearily, beatifically nodding—but always resolving, on some forever-awake level, that tomorrow I'd produce a wide-awake evidence to Edith; justice never sleeps; tomorrow is another day.

M.

Ω

Dear E.,

Miguel—I didn't sufficiently communicate my intense repressed anxiety about his banality. In the dream—I mentioned it, no?—I lectured a freshman class of black students who were tough and competitive and thought they were hip because they read Hesse. I broke down and wailed "A cliché is shitty *by definition!*"

Weak, weak is one, under the barrage of wrong logic, wrong sequence, constant attack, perennial little red fish.

[271]

Why think all Chilangos are nasty? Who me? I exclaimed. I'm from the Big Apple—I always felt you and I shared a big city bond, always dug Chilangos, prick. Where'd you get that wrong idea? Some fishy twist about Mexicanos. Who cares? I'm off to a new, dull life. I learned what I had to.

Why return to Mexico indeed? Why learn M.'s lesson if not to be a rich mystery for them? Now that I know, know their impermeability to women—know it in a careful, precise researcher's way—what is left? Their darkness is a mirage, it reflects not depth of receptivity but opacity, reflection rather than profundity. I could've loved him well—I tried. I took the risk. I transcended fear (through booze, admittedly). I sought it—him—out. He sacrificed nothing being here. I would've sacrificed everything.

Lily's been asked to leave her room at Casa Rosita, because of A., apparently. Ah Mexico!

Love,
M.

Ω

E.,

Please dear god let me get the ms. out of the way so I can at last (at least?) begin to live, begin to finally appreciate Miguel, such as there is. It's too ghastly this writing business, I live to stall my body writing the few minutes I've lived. And once I chose to live—the first time with him. It was too rich to capture. Maybe that defines life—the too too too for words.

A few last second addenda.

I forgot to mention, or didn't elaborate, my sense of his jealousy at my independent experience (especially of Mexico). He rivaled my prison story with his—he had to be the expert on Mexican prisons. Awfully competitive guy. All that early generosity—listening to me appreciatively, digging intelligence in women—has been belied lately. They're just as bad as the homegrown product.

Today, this last realization—that I was *not* dull but was being actively impeded from being interesting.

One of his dicta last night was: be yourself, be simple (and *that* is the secret of winning the Mexican man's heart? I wondered to myself). My dream about idiots who didn't understand banality

[272]

must've touched that pronunciamento of his and tarnished its alchemical gold to lead. Leadenness. I felt a right fool, restored to definition, common sense, thirty-six years of life as I've lived and analyzed it in *my* context. . . .

Love,
M.

Ω

Dear Lily,*

Here I sit after six hours of anguished sleep (after four hours of smug sleep, à vrai dire, my last night in Acapulco). As disgusting as that onda was, it gave me a certain confianza—perhaps the most disorienting onda of all. I've been dreaming of not connecting up with Miguel or with a life-plan. And the two, alas, are not equivalent.

It's 7:45 A.M. Called him seven minutes ago. He'd salió'd already. The chavo is your typical hard-working Mexican—another reason the familia is not too anxious to chart my onda on their radar screen.

So I drink and smoke and write and feel anguish.

Outside Acapulco, we passed a field of corn I wanted to dig up with my teeth to get at the essence of Mexico. One onda I never sufficiently agara'ed was the campo. Smells of fresh cow manure and earth and vegetation swam in through the darkening windows and I thought: do I smoke to forget the smells of health and life, of connection with a "madre naturaleza" that would remind me too cunningly, too insidiously, that I'm aging and my life is in a shambles?

He was seventeen and I was gorgeous from Acap.—thin, dark, healthy. Christ—I floated upstairs with my bags, strode through the streets in forty-league boots. Did get an enormous shot of physical health there. Back in the city—booze, writing, cigs, no sun, no swimming, no dancing, and this old-making affair with Miguel.

---

* This letter was never sent to Lily. In mid-letter, the mode of address changes. It is then Edith who is being addressed in this, Maryse's last letter. The last part of the letter was never sent but was recovered by Stan from Maryse's effects in Mexico, around three months after her death.

Every time I call or expect him to and nada, I drink, so when he finally shows—calls, whatever, I'm too smashed to care. An O'Henry relationship—you-got-what-you-wanted-in-evil, indifferent spades too late. Always. Así es la vida, chica. And all I wanted was the dark.

It is a kind of heroism—guts—I took and take this risk. Three, unintended—perhaps the state that drug itself gives you—of confidence. Four—it makes weirdness (older women) natural.

The nightmare rages on. I haven't seen or spoken to him since my return two days ago—and I leave in three days!

My entire middle body is heavy with the food I ate last night in the Café Popular: my last supper, I thought ruefully, as I ordered a perennial fantasy: huevos rancheros, and two fat rolls, and two cream puffs, and two big cafés con leche. On top of the day's two or three c.c.l's, two queso de pays, one quesadilla and two tortas. Too tente.

A Chilango schmuck type who for some weird private idée fixe of his own missed the reality principle of my sluttishness and became my knight erroring, worshipping me as a chaste dispenser of la culture française. This has been my shtick for months now, that I am a franco-gringa—it saves me from a lot of abuse, fuck it, universal hatred.

We leave hotel. I understand none of his rich language. My anxiety level is at whatever the word is for atomic bombs about to explode or radioactive matter to emit or whatever that nifty metaphor would be.

Outside, the dozens of secret agents whistle like indigenous Mexico City birds to each other—a cute code in the metropolis—and speak in numbers. Only I, I said to the one who pursued me last night, would fail to appreciate the masquerade—dig this—of hundreds of "workers" sweeping sand back and forth across a perfectly healthy street.

So my date begins. I'm uptight, bored. He's all clean but with that awful hair style—long, shapeless, parted on the side and combed frontwards from the back as if to hide a bald spot, American style. A murderously crowded subway ride, a long wait in a light, radioactive rain. Finally, a cab. Another wait while he calls the friend and wife and kid with whom he lives. Too long. I think, Oh M., another setup, but cattle always go to slaughter—self-constitutiveness long bred out of them, they await only their fate, what they deserve. A day (a life) of total will-less-ness you understand. Like that last night in Acapulco.

[274]

Wind my sluggish way up to my room to hear "Señorita, señorita"—and turn around coldly and say "Mande?" in my curtest and most formal tone.

They apologize. They are agents. And all the night's paranoia about the gringa being set up instantly roosts ruefully in my brain. So I was right. I die a quiet, almost amused death, almost grateful to die (but annoyed at my stupidity).

They continue. Since the president is riding in a calvalcade tomorrow, they have been appointed to screen guests. Can they check my bag, por favor. I reach into the outside pocket of my bag and feel the hard lump of grass wrapped in newspaper. I clutch. They sense this, being good psychologists, and politely enquire if there is any problem and this translates in me as a wild experimental desire to play for all I'm worth before I go, to fool and foil and charm and outmaneuver and outmanipulate these three, then four, then five, assholes, who are men—the ultimate feminism, no? Five judiciales—FBI's—against one lone gringa female. Why not try, I venture to myself, with a courage, you can imagine, born of absolute knowledge that I, my stay in Mexico—that is, my life—was about to be gunned down for good. With such certainty of death, it was rather easy, rather fun, to play.

It was a matter of seconds. My hand had touched the stash. I seemed anxious. I was stoned (and wondering whether it was smellable) and drunk and therefore omnipotent, inventive, perceptive, cunning and *quick*. I saw that they noticed my uncertainty. So yes, I acknowledged that they were right: my first, I wish there was a word for it, un-mistake. Actually, I said, it's just that I have to pay 3 pesos in a café across the street. I didn't have enough money. I said I'd return within ten minutes.

This onda is fantastically successful: it established that I am honest, and a fresa, and a foreigner.

Three p's, they exclaim! Your tab was 3 p's. No, it was 18, I say, going on to provide unsolicited details.

Three p's, they expectorate. Sí, I concur, relinquishing, but fluently, the fresa onda, absurd, isn't it. It's not as if they don't know me—I've been going there for years. I'm a good customer, once or twice a day. But, they seemed suspicious. And, I ruefully added, así son los Americanas—honest fresas, guilt-ridden. You dig the modulation, but always in another key.

(Of course, this onda came not only from Miguel but from hundreds of mysteries—one big tip was never to tell an unnecessary

[275]

lie—it's hard to remember, and, mystically, truth is more believable.)

I forget the next modulation but I got us quickly—not too hard
in Mexico—onto the female-male onda. I acted what I in reality
was: the cynical, disheartened gringa who'd loved and lost a Mexicano. Yes, I adore Mexicanos, but god, I said, I'd never marry one.
Well, because they're free to onda all around while the poor wife
stays put in her casa. And, I said, they never call or come when they
say they will.

You dig I flatter these assholes in three subtle ways: 1. I desire
you and you reject me 2. I'm telling you about you. I forget 3. . . .

Several dozen more ondas transpire in forty minutes that only
an idiot or a vain Mexican male, or a vain male, or a male, would
fail to perceive as "Why should she be talking to me so long if she
had nothing to hide?"

I am exhausted by long truth-telling, flirtation, dialectic, flattery, battle of wits, terror, imminent doom, and success. It was a
superb performance.

293 mystery novels can't be wrong. Don't lie.

Ah shit, who the fuck needs mystery novels. Isn't it enough
being a woman? All those rides we hitched where we had to be
provocative enough to merit the ride and keep the driver awake yet
not too provocative to inspire the driver to rape? Had to *earn*,
unlike men, our passage, through a fine balance between provoca-
tion and temperance.

Oh M., will you ever, ever, ever understand the brilliance of
women's solutions, of their different, far more complicated and
oppressed situations in the world? Will you ever appreciate either
the suffering—or call it strain—and the cleverness? M., who when I
ask, knowing in advance his utter indifference, isn't it a crime
women can't go into cantinas, says yeah.

Oh M., M., M., I pleaded—do you dig how unjust it is? Yeah
sure, he said.

Shall we skip the shit and get right to M.?

Miguel is a brilliant witty actor: I am a brilliant, illiterate
analyst. He wins.

He masters tone and masters double-talk. The tone stuff is
interesting—he baby talks in a parodic way, he imitates a hood, the
archeologist of language unearths the latest and earliest ways of
saying the same thing.

He's quick, facile, gay, alive, smarter than anyone around him, into being worshipped, physically beautiful. The ugliness of his bod was a bad dream—so taut, hip, Italian did he look. But no. It's all *face* and the bod, fat or weird, sick Indian child's bod from the shoulders down. He is the most beautiful in his family. He, however, has a stunning beauty. All the bones went to him, and the dark skin. And the hair—which, actually, went to every last one of them, but which they curl or dye. He alone knows that straight Italian shag hair is exquisite. And the bones: a deep cut from the upper nose out to the ear = his cheekbone. The cheekbones take the burden of pleasure, tensed at the point of orgasm. There are two sleepy intelligent ironic laugh lines down his mouth. When he smiles, God does. He looks like Sara Moreno. tho no one but me knows, kindness and smartness and good will all wrapped up together when he smiles.

I his carbuncle moll. Real mafia style. (Him—standing there talking to guys while holding me close to him though not looking at me.) Geez, I thought, what the fuck am *I* doing with this whiz-o?! Too slick to believe. I knew it couldn't last. Alegre M. is harder to take than guru M.—genuinely hip, gorgeous, a leader, jes like he wants to be. And rattle rattle rattle of ceaseless rap . . .

M.'s supposed to come by at 9 and we're supposed to go dancing. This will be the last joke on me I suppose, the one that will pitch me off the roof.

I will not be restrained tonight if he doesn't show.

It is absolute sickness this relationship. The contempt! The incredible contempt for me, my intelligence, my pain, my time. He wasn't this way at the beginning—are they ever? Once I ordered him to show or else. What gave me the courage then?

Saturday night. I was absolutely exhausted but dragged myself out at 12:45, hailed a cab driver who wanted to fuck me and spent a fruitless hour and a half being rejected from every bar and disco in the Zona Rosa for being an unaccompanied woman.

I do think this is an important outrage, almost the most. If only Latin women who call themselves feminists weren't Marxists, who are anti-pleasure, or lesbians, who are anti either men, or more typically, sex. Because to prohibit a woman from going drinking or dancing alone is to deny her thousands of things that we are on the planet for: pleasure foremost, freedom, independence.

Look at it this way: say I lived with Miguel in Mexico City, with all the problems that would entail from my living in a country, a city, where he has family, language, friends, history, a job, connec-

[277]

tions and I have nothing—no resources or apoyos, where I am by myself in a social and cultural situation, and by living in essentially *his* apartment, a slave, a prisoner, rather, a dumb, still, gringa center surrounded by a cultural dance swirling around me. O.K.—he doesn't show one (two, three, a million) night. What can I do? I am not allowed to be on the streets alone, almost, or to drink publicly (or privately). I cannot seek solace or alliances in a cantina. I can't take my revenge or pleasure or alternative solution to my life in a bar or disco. I can't even *distract* myself from my pain. I am made to suffer on the cross for it, incarcerated in a home not even my own (in my case; though of course, ditto for many nonworking Mexican wives).

Even without this hypothetical situation. Take me, right now, or you. We are young (más o menos) or *old*, we want to meet men, we want to go dancing (I *live* for it for Christsake, it is my deporte, my exercise, my skill, my art, my research, my sophistication, my mysticism, my ecstasy, my youth, my body moving through space, my sexuality, my fucking health); we also want to choose among men.

And then a call, at 22 to 6. He'll be late. After my ultimatum: if you ever want to see me again in your life, be here at 6, or else, olvídate. Planning to stand him up. Unable to stop crying, vexed, in agony, exacerbatedly enraged, nerves, energy, hopes on fire—my last few days in Mexico and I've seen him once out of five days. He's ruined an entire weekend. The time he doesn't work, when we could be together, when the world celebrates—he's murdered my Friday night, my Saturday day, my Saturday night and I, killing him, killing myself, murdering the shreds of the weekend, give him a rendezvous when he calls at 2 P.M. not for Sunday day but for Sunday night—this is my heroism. To deprive myself of still more. He's taken it all; kill the dregs that remain so I can cry and hate and weep more and more and more with the incredible loss. Let the assassination be perfect, the pain, the rage almost unbearable to see how much I can take, how much I can punish and be punished because he's punished me so unbelievably already. Planning, too, to stand him up, of course, and the two other pricks who won't show at 6. After all this, all this, he calls to be late. "¿Vamos al cine?" he anxiously inquires. No, vamos a bailar, I say, knife in cheek, driving it through my face and his stupidity, that doesn't recognize my murderous irony—to mention dancing is to insure his nonappearnace, the fucking cocksucker. To mention anything he doesn't want to do. His stupid male Mexican asshole dumbness, not to know I am rejecting him, taunting him. And then I say O.K. and hang up abruptly. Weeping, moaning, enraged. . . .

I am not human. For me to say a feminist dictum that repels me in the States with its obviousness and insufficiency and timidity and stupidity: "Women are human beings"—would be a mind-blowing announcement here in Mexico. Men think we are, how to put it, a species apart, a saint species, a hole species, a species *meant*, *designed* to suffer. One does—I do—appreciate the dyke position after a Miguel.

The whole hotel knows my affair. The night clerk, a male, merrily conspired with me to screw Miguel. When I left at 1 I told him to tell M., if he should call or come by, that I'd left for Acapulco. When I returned, at 4:30 A.M., the clerk is all confidential and gay—Yeah! he came by at 2 and I told him you'd gone to Acap. And he didn't believe me—said where's her key then. Go up and check for yourself said the night clerk, which Miguel did, and sure enough I was out. Ho ho ho. What a gas!

At 2 A.M., after a good time with his friends, he came to fuck me, his sex machine. And there I am, dying to have danced with my chavo (you speak in the past tense a lot these days he says). How nice it could have been—the tense of the knife in the gut that only through cowardice does end up in his stomach, twisting away in mad, terrified delight, weeping horrendously at the same time.

He got it in first. Got bored before I properly had a chance to be. How strong I was after seeing you in Acap.! How "self-constitutive," as Kant would say (sorry, I really need that term). Self-defining, knowing my values, my priorities. Feeling attractive. Feeling, well, loved a bit because of our friendship. You know, valuable.

Stop deluding yourself, pussy : . . it's over. Time stopped. It needn't go on. You know what you need to know.

And there was so much, Lily and Edith, for of course this letter is to her—to you—as well, now you'll meet at last—strange, no? One really does write different things to different people. More sequential, logical, synoptic to one, more stream-of-consciouness to another.

No darkness, no charm, no place for women anywhere. Here I have a place—the suffering saint, and I cannot provoke them to physical violence. There, I could be loved, understood, free. But in a world of men that recognizes, finally, that we are their rivals and murder us in actuality as well as culturally. Freud, what do women

[279]

want? Why, you knew all along—to be men. Yet no, no, no. I'd like to be as physically strong as they are, but I like my female sensibility. Perhaps because we suffer, we're smarter, subtler, more able to feel ecstasy in love. And, mostly, we dance better. But boy would I like their looseness. To drink, and even smoke, without this heavy burden of guilt and secrecy and shame and distance from other women. To let 'im rip, sweetheart! Let it all hang out.

"Lies pollute love," I wrote Stan from Oaxaca—"so here's the lowdown on my sex life in Mexico." Yet Miguel pollutes and pollutes me. To lie to someone is ultimately—immediately—to hold them in contempt.

No woman is ugly for us in Mexico said the bus driver and salsa musician after telling me his aunt could cure my face (my face—one of the reasons it doesn't shock them is that it's a common product they think and get this, of anger or chili!). An ugly man, he said, and an ugly woman—can agara a very sweet pleasure. My commonplace intelligence returns, and my about-to-shock ugliness. But also my true worth. No longer will I be dumb cunt at least. Oh shit. I can't can't leave. Though I suffer. . . .

Sunday. Miguel appeared at 11:45 tonight and said he'd come back later said the desk clerk when I got back at 12:45. Oh god, I said, how that muchacho me lástima, and is a gigantesco pain in the ass. The night guy and I are now conspirators to con Miguel. I realize belatedly it is not because of me or jokes but because Miguel has probably abused him too, wounded his macho, made him feel stupid, or merely manipulated. So return the key to the desk, says he, so he'll think you're still out. Can't you just forbid him to come up to the room I ask. Sería muy necio, he says, a real ugly scene where Miguel would insist on going up to my room and he, night man, would have to call the policía. Oh yeah!?! I say, rubbing my hands together in glee, to the clerk's delight. Virtuous Woman does not triumph once again.

Oh Lord, for a new feminism! A sluttish, heterosexual one. One without virtue. But with pleasure and freedom and power and evil as its asuntos. Power and Pleasure . . .

It wasn't or was it—pride—but rage, absolute rage, that made me deny myself him even though I knew—I can't remember. Oh who cares, who the fuck cares about this evil country to women that the bus driver, Humberto, said wouldn't let me in alone because any woman alone was a whore.

Miguel thinks women are stupid.

[280]

He forced me to be rejected—like the crippled girl thing. How could I possibly go through with that? The alternative was to be without consciousness, an automaton waiting without affect in a rented room. A pure unthinking machine, a stopped watch. How can you say to your oppressor, you hurt me? How can a cow say to her slaughterer . . . the only correct, and *translating*, tone, is anger. But to be angry at men is to be fat. And to be fat is to lose not only the theme I'm best at but the thing you and I live for, desire.

Monday, 12:15.

Go downstairs to pick up my key—a note from M. who called at 9:10 to say he'd call at 12 or come by. And again hasn't and again that sensation of actual physiological decay, flesh sagging, stomach hanging down at the knees. Nausea, fear, the brain dragging behind in the wake of the body. An awful craziness that comes from the sky covering the city like a shroud. *Inertia*—that's closer to it, the body feeling its own weight, sucked down by gravity, and overhead, that screen of madness so that when the maids talk to me, the butchy one I like particularly, their voices come through a filter and their friendliness gives me no pleasure. Going back to New York will be a horror—I was looking forward to that country place, an all-over tan by the pond, cheap boozing and dancing, my garden, my vegetables, my herb garden, talking to Gloria in Spanish about machismo, living cheap—i.e., subletting the city place, getting healthy up there and finally doing the article, etc. Oh god. Christ, almost want to talk to Miguel as an escape from N.Y.—a *light* distraction from real life. Like he is now less important. If only my apartment weren't unrentable I'd stay on and on and on and back to Acap. to get thin and brown again and see you and stay in Mexico.

I give you my respetos that you can give rodeos, bullshit your way through a needle's eye, but don't pull that shit on me. (Of course, all this jive goes on in my increasingly N.Y. head and doesn't pass quite efficiently translated out of my illiterate Mexico City mouth. More and more I feel that until I master—dominate, as they say—the language, there is no hope of *any* relationship, including with women, here.)

It frustrates, pains, agonizes, bores me that he's not into my cultural shtick (which I also loathe, but at which I'm facile and which I also like). I can handle it just fine, and más. And it's fun, a game. A mental exercise. I'm even, and this is the disturbing part, interested in it. Disturbing because it brings back duty, obligation, the real world, at which I failed so perfectly. No, that's false. It's that culture is a different wave length which invalidates my present research into desire. Once more I can't handle all the choices. And I feel a dilettante. No, again it's more fundamental. It's like too many pretty clothes and not enough money. And the other thing— being dazzled out of my dark subterranean cave of passion—into this familiar light. Like I'll never get to live my tragic Jean Rhys cycle. Never get to be a complete slut or the compleat expatriate. Never get to define *my* own terms and make the world bow down to them. Why couldn't I say straight out to this guy tonight—look, you have 90 p's, I have 50. Why don't we ditch your friend, pick up my bottle, and go dancing? Why am I *ashamed* to insist on dancing? I passively await their passivity. Never, never, do they get it on and my frustration at my own inability to agara unto myself as well as them rechannels—sublimates—whatever the fucking word is—into behavior that isn't mine. . . .

And *none* of this he gave me. Nothing—nada. Like he wanted to keep me in the dark, wanted me a powerless pussy so all things should come from him. I loathe his thinking I'm stupid.

The usual fantasy of males—rape, humiliate, kill, pussies . . . I leave the theater bitterly knowing that this is a Spain flick, but still, knowing, this is it, no? In the guise of exposing male sadistic tendencies towards women, the director participates in them. After the flick, in the john, where women hang out, I agara'ed a blond gringa who said isn't it nice to be a woman. And she sits in cafés in the Zona Rosa and men send her cards or she drives in her car and they quickly dispatch vendored roses to her. Oh so that's why you're into the consciousness thing, she says to me, coz you're from N.Y. And thank god I'm into it I say so I have a way of handling my pain when I see a flick in which a woman gets raped, shorn, shot in the head. Men suffer too, she says. No, I say. I don't know of movies where women humiliate, torture, and kill men. Isn't it nice to be a woman, she says. Sure, I say, I just wish it were a little nicer, even a lot. Oh how dumb we pussies are. My latest line, I tentatively tested it out tonight, is that I'm a man (with a man's emotions and needs), only better (smarter, subtler). Anyway, I'm gonna try it on for size, you might say perfect fit, or unfit, in Mexico. But thank god in a way there's a model—a *precedent*—for me. I'm a "man" (and of course, Jeannie Rhys, better). And Colette. But the "man" line will have to serve for openers. How dare they prevent me from loosening up, choosing amongst them, defining what, who and how turns me on—and when we'll get it on. I mean *I* dug the schmuck, *I* picked *him* up—how dare he act as if I'm a passive dumb piece of shit he managed to conquer, that he can feel up publicly.

Thurs., 10:45 A.M.

The elevator outside my door lurches sickeningly inside my head. What was it I wanted to say about the latest stage of Miguel: that the world outside him is empty (but interesting) and reflects its emptiness back on him somehow. I mean these boys are so charming initially, everyone is. And full of invitations and promises to call and help me find work and help me with any problem, etc. Movies, fiestas. If I could trace last night's trajectory from my bored, cynical, sexually aggressive, dismayed and mariada approach to what's his name—ah, Juan. . . .

Ach lord, another day, another hangover. And the pens so quickly lose their fine points. Despite this life, I look younger these days—it's sleeping alone, no matter how little and in what condition. I like it. I don't need to wake up before him anxious, adoring.

The boys show me what he's like. Miguel. And what he lacks. The utter shallowness of their feeling for gringas, all this they teach me about Miguel.

Again and again he plays dumb, me for dumb, forces me to throw up the bitter food that's made me sodden and depressed. Your ring has turned black, he says. Por dolor, I answer, tears springing from my eyes at my verbal skill that makes me love myself and can't fail but make him love me in return. And did you suffer, too? I ask. He won't answer because I'll hurt him more. Discúlpame, he'd said and I'd said: why? I want to kill you, to hurt you more than you've hurt me. So he won't answer, won't give me more power. Again and again he has asked and will forever continue to ask, what has he done to me, digging the recital of pain, proof of *his* power, and also, waiting for me to forget, so he can lie his way out of responsibility. Change effect to cause. But he came—that was the broad point—because the night before I stood him up.

And oh honey, when I was jealous, was he ever remote and amused at my anger. But when he's jealous, I rush over and grab him and stroke him and plead, etc. And boy, mujeres, did that phone call ever break the ice for me with his family. Complete pitying condescension and friendliness after that. They couldn't do enough for the cuckolded gringa fool.

I should write about that close-to-perfect rainy Sunday.

His last promise was that we would speak with truth when he got back from Puebla. That we'd passed through a dark period but

[283]

now, once more would come the light. So it's 11:45 and it's ending, ending, in this slow trickle of time and cigarettes. And whether it's happening because I like onda-ing about on my own and picking up ondas here and there. I like discovering how to cope in my nabe, getting more physically oriented in the city, like walking in the street without somebody's goddamn arm imprisoning me, liked (alas) going to gallery openings, a cocktail party every night—getting the feel of the Zona Rosa, meeting the young artsy set and the old artsy set and the awful rich old güeros.

And all of this rich interaction, mastering my environment, winning discussions, attracting attractive professionals, representing the female position well to perhaps, finally, the more sympathetic waitresses—all of this accretion was somehow supposed to communicate itself to Miguel, make me richer, make him richer too. Complicate the relationship, make it adult, complex, accreting. I was alive and acquiring knowledge and experience. I liked charting my own course at the same time that I put all that under the heading of my rational, N.Y., self when what I wanted from Mexico was the dark and mysterious. Had wanted to be a prisoner of sex, as I think Miguel did. The world flushed out Miguel, flushed out love. It was both a relief and a sorrow that I could live without love. And also—and this I never got around to say because he caused me too much pain—I began to suspect that what I'd said half-theoretically and to hurt him weeks before—that I was too old to fall in love again—was true.

For that Thursday, twice, I knew I felt no passion. Chose to remember how I feared I'd never see his face again, know it, memorize it. And there it was! right next to me: dark, high Comanche-cheeked, that silken hair, that earlier superb performance in the soccer field of the natural punk leader—puro cotoreo, brilliant fluent ad-libs left and right—always the joke, the surprise, the slight boredom that hovers on the edge of alegría and flight—when will the plane alight. ... He was flying. And I was the grounded native enthralled and intimidated by the big silver bird in the sky.

He's a brilliant, hip young Italian hood and I am a lumpen stone, so knowing I couldn't hold him long (but realizing my own gifts too and therefore not depressed) I gave myself up to the moment. I resurrected my past desire—all the months and days of fear and longing, and the present intimidation—and I said to myself "Christ almighty, what a goddman miracle that here I am, in my thirtieth year, and once more it has been vouchsafed to me to stand in the doorway of a gentle, scandalized store in a foreign city next to a gorgeous young hood, dark, dark. . . . Forced myself to concentrate on his darkness as something once again *unfamiliar*—for yes, Lily, I too meditate—and plunged into him, contoured my entire self onto him, unto him, into him. I love you, I love you, I love you. You are perfect, I said soundlessly. I don't mind the rain, your cheapness, the boredom. I am not bored. I am here with you when I never again (once again) thought I would be. I will not forget past petitions for miracles. Will not normally, humanly, forget the miracle of petitions of the past in the all-too-boring actuality of the present familiarity.

So I leaned my lean figure into him completely and bathed his face in gratitude, young desire, old maternalism.

But, again the broad missed the boat, the big, initial point—all of this was conscious choice. Existential. I chose to construct passion. So it was a game and fácil, fácil. Besides, he's not the only actor in the family. Ah yes, it was the hip square chicano director I met in Oaxaca who figured me for either an eternal graduate student or an actress.

The second recognition of my unspontaneous desire came when we made out in his blacked-out kitchen and my cunt didn't throb. We kissed in my third big sex locale (after movie balconies and cars) and nada. He roughly nuzzled my ear and dough. I felt his cock, expanded like the dough. "¿Te gusta? he asked. Sí, sí, I said, feeling nothing. ¡Qué rico! he always says about my slathering cunt. But nada, you know, nada. When younger, Christ! Peter P. when I was 16, in Prospect Park on a cool spring night touched my nipple and worlds exploded.

So I was flirty and fun and a fan but I felt nothing. Just the cuteness of casi fucking in this dark kitchen with the rain outside and the relatives upstairs.

And why did I feel nothing. Because I'm older than he is and no one will ever want to again except, of course, an older man. I am afraid—all we older women are afraid—of repelling. So that in every sense all I can be is a rich receptacle—for his cock and his words. And his charm and his beauty. Though lord, his body is not and I therefore stood a chance. To stand a chance—what a lovely, meaningless modismo. To stand up against a chance—a hood—in a doorway.

But oh chica, once I merited blow jobs. After you and me and Hollywood in Zi, after Miguel's waking up to grin with immense smiling tenderness, all slit eyes and dark skin, in my bed in Mexico City (so that I thought—Jesus hijole Christ—this *can't* be happening to *me*). The blond pussy I met in Migración knew: love is like faith. And Oaxaca, natch—and Eduardo and all the others. When I thought my body and mind were beautiful! Now, all I can manage, catching sight of myself in unpredictable Zona Rosa mirrors is this: genuine ugliness, i.e., grotesqueness, but still thin, tough-looking, ugly, tough, with style and intelligence. O.K., I say to mirror. Live with it. Not too bad. Accept and therefore transcend it.

Across from me in the VIP's restaurant of the cineteca a woman who asked me for a light sits, plain but attractive, in tough, slightly grubby jeans and shirt and long unwashed hair. We both wonder, I suppose, whether we're dykes.

Friday 9:55 A.M.

So it's really over, after four hours sleep. I don't know his plan— it seems to be utter humiliation and rejection. I am never allowed revenge. Monday night I called him from the Zona Rosa and warmly and boozily insisted he come on over. I was very convincing because I really did want to see him. But then Juan invited me to some writer friend's house and I thought: great! (knowing I'd be stood up by Miguel). It turns out he came, twice, and finally went home at 12:45, after leaving me this note: Miguel ... no puedo esperar Adios Marys. The 45 p's he owes me—olvídate. And the dozens of broken promises.

Ah, well, Christ, what a disastrous mystery. The only reason I'm not out of my mind with grief is I have two more irons in the fire who haven't yet called.

Yea, I told Stan, weeping, I finally scored. He was the big one.

Mientras, I'm pregnant. It's been forty days since I got my period and I'm quite fat—116, 117. Bloated belly, big tits, and famished.

I'm gonna telegraph my bank for mon. Sent them a special delivery registered letter over two weeks ago but Mexico says no dinero, absurd.

P.P.S. Fíjate, Miguel, on Monday, when I summoned him, came at night and insisted on going up to my room because he'd paid for it. I'm dismayed and flattered and drunk and in love with Silvia, who says my varicose veins are nothing compared to your neighbor's, the profesora's, in room #50 ¿verdad? I flee this strange confidence with my drunkard's breath.

[286]

But what does it all matter anyway, in the long run of the short run of our lives.

The tension I started to feel only being with one person. . . .

Men looked at me hungrily on the metro and fell in from all sides.

I'm keeping it under close wraps—the switchblade, the feminism, the polymorphous perverse, even the flamboyant dancing. No abandon, no show of will, strength, independence, autonomy, *wildness*. Thrills at rest, the sleeping thrills, the soared and timid thrills.

Stan just called. He said we don't have a place in the country because.

Friday, almost 1 A.M.

When you read about the murder in the paper, if my albeit strange case ever reaches the States, you at least will know why.

If Miguel comes tonight, I would like to greet his disturbing my peace with an extended switchblade in his stomach. He'll come at 2 or 3 or 4, after going out with a novia, or to a fiesta, or out drinking with the boys. And I can't bear what I've done to my body tonight. I don't masturbate anymore. I must measure forty around the waist, now thicker than my broad rib cage and bust.

But what will make my body beautiful again? Somebody has to pay the price besides me.

I'm sick of Stan telling me don't come back unless you're thin. I'm nobody's fat smart darling anymore.

The Miguel thing is so polluted and sick and so are these awful schmucks I meet at gallery openings.

Sat. 12:44:07

I am visibly dying. Everyone sees it. I am no longer even bitter, just energyless and pitiable. I had a love nightmare. I was very plain, tall, with faded blond hair and the same color skin, and studying accounting in the shabby basement of some shoddy university. Miguel, my sadistic beautiful and dark young lover, who has been torturing me with his absence, bounds in on his way to bound out again. I clutch and whine and he throws me off him verbally with a loud, angry, pimp's (somehow) demand to know my real age. He proves I can't be twenty-seven: "Is your mother seventy-seven then?" he demands angrily. And were you seven when you went north to Chicago?" I'm thinking 1947, born in 1947—would that make me come out twenty-seven? I can't figure, I can't calculate quickly enough. I start to cry, hoping my anguish will be interpreted

[287]

as stemming from his cruelty and humiliation in public and obviate my need to answer, will mask the real source of pain. It seems he won't continue with me until I tell him the truth about my age and I know how angry he'll be, how duped he'll feel and how angry that he's been with an old bag all this time, more unattractive even than he suspected. Meanwhile, all my fellow students—all young beautiful dark boys—have witnessed this humiliation. I am spindly and whey-faced with this lank colorless short hair, a Midwest spinster. Miguel bounds off.

The dream is so awful I wake up at 4 A.M. The three Darvons on top of all the booze haven't killed me. A vrai dire, there's no place to move in my stomach. My headache, my vicious headache, is gone but it's clear nothing will ever make me sleep again. I start reading the third Castaneda. He doesn't bore me, though it was repugnance at agara-ing an exclusive male onda that I bought it, actual physical distaste and resentment. Bout of resentment at Mexico, I wanted to read American scene while still here, and something light. But then it felt like that was giving up on the country. on myself, and on cultivating my intelligence and knowledge. And much as the hallucinogenic hippy onda distressed and bored the old square, she chose once more to give Miguel. . . .

This morning I went to the market, which I always enjoy, and decided to be efficient, so took my rope bag along. I bought twenty kilos of stuff it felt like; but when I got home, there was a mess in the bag: the expensive tomatoes had burst, the detergent had spilled all over the vegetables and fruits and then onto my floor, and, looking for plastic bags to put these perishables in, in my room that has no surfaces and basically is big enough to contain the double bed and nada más, I discovered that either I, or the maid, had thrown out the paper bag that contained the pot, that expensive wad that put me through such terrors and that I had finally gotten around to wanting to smoke, hoping, that like mushrooms, it would yield an equanimous confidence. For I am hideously self-involved, self-pitying, incarcerated in a debilitating personal anguish I can't escape. My body, once beautiful, is a fat loathsome toad, rolls and rolls of flesh, thickness, inelegance, unagility. A fat object, and not an agile, live sensate being, alive grace and motion and feeling.

Those burst expensive tomatoes are an awful symbol of I-don't-know-what to me. The failure to secure a rich store of thinnables—

[288]

and at what expense!—the failure of the voyaged-for, expensive, healthy cherishables. Even the tomatoes burst. And the detergent spilled, and despite my best efforts, I'm worse off than before. Somehow, these tomatoes assure me, too, that I'm pregnant, that I should not delude myself that by providing myself with an inexhaustible (though unrefrigerated) supply of tomatoes, I will regain my thinness. They have burst, like my body, like my entrañable guts of love, and all is disorderly, diarrhea mess in my cramped cell.

I am in such pain. Every day now for days I begin the day with Emily Dickinson's lines: "After great pain a formal feeling comes." The poem continues to say that that pain is not raging fire but the cold stone of tombs. I am myself close to poetry now, so great is my pain, and so controlled.

Last night, when I came home sullied by propositions from inferior men who should've found me intimidating because of my wit, liveliness and attractiveness, I received M.'s note that he'd called at 9:10 and would call again at 10:30. And I was ruined, Edith, so completely physically ugly, stuffed to bursting, with this maddening Orestes headache, this buzzing pain that wouldn't stop its dervish round inside my head, and I knew he wouldn't call or come or if he did, it would be gothic horror too late—I would be lying bloated and immobile on my lumpy sarcophagus, dead, beyond recriminations. I had taken the last step—had killed my beauty.

I hadn't been able to bear walking home, carrying that load of rotting food in my belly. I took a cab and complained about the cost and leaned forward and poured out bored dry tears to the ugly young driver who charged me 20 centavos less because he couldn't bear to see pretty girls like me sad.

I bare my soul to everyone. It is cheap I know but have this subliminal hope that I can regain my entrancing person of chava abierta, that onda I had in initial Oaxaca.

No, it isn't yet great enough my pain to produce pain in the readers of my letters. For today's message from M. said he'd call at 3 and it is 1:42. Only oh god only oh god . . . now, now—after all the oh gods—even shorter a wait till magic, till love, till redemption, oh god, to live again—for I am so dead now, Edith, an awful fat ghost who's survived her own death and who can't remember ever having been loved, found charming. Only oh lord if he calls only less than an hour and twenty minutes.

So I got back and got his note and moaned aloud to myself even before I hit the elevator: I can't take it anymore, surprising the night man who does not like me and all the way up the elevator shaft Oh lord, I can't take it anymore, the classic words, the classic gut-twisting sick joke of the missed-again encounter, and the love that comes too late.

For I'd broken my resolve that no matter what else I did, I would not ruin my body again.

And the noise from the street deafens the ringing of the phone and consciousness. It will be difficult to write above the ceaseless rumble. But it is larger, higher-ceilinged. And I needed to escape the bad dream of all last night—staring up at the rusty, peeling, mottled ceiling, the leprous, sick ceiling, the low squat sickness of a room that when I smoked the air turned to stale garbage. And space, I said to Miguel, space—space for our minds to expand in, and our sexuality and our games—I squatting on him sitting in chair. Oooh! What kindergarten fun and games. Show and come. Tell and love. Expand the consciousness.

How can only I not know it's ended when all my correspondents do? How much romantic ugliness does it take to stop seeing reality written large and mean on a bare unfeeling wall? I hurt and hurt and hurt and hurt. It seems equally a dream, the positing of love of antes. It *was* love the first time. And not the second.

The Eduardo shtick is really for me a pure, encapsulated youth shtick, no matter how intelligently wielded.

I continued to monologue "How I could've been beautiful, how I cannot take this kind of life anymore, it is killing me. What have I done to him? This is destroying my body, my health, my energy, my will to will. Never has anything been worse." A gentle, firm tap comes on the wall, in the middle of my dry-heaved sobbing. "This is death," I refrain to myself, maybe seventy-five times. I chant it, in a lower voice, out my window to the cosmos: "This is death, this is death, this is death." I wake at 4 A.M. from the nightmare. Read Castaneda on impersonality. Go back to sleep. Never has or will he come. I wake again at 6, dry-mouthed, and eat three oranges and need to piss but am too lazy. And a stoic awful impossibility of happiness takes root, giving me a boring strength. I scratch in between my left toes madly, athlete's foot has given me a reason to live. It's such fun cleaning out the cheesy debris and scratching off loose itchy scaly skin! At 9 again I wake up, wondering what lack of guts it took not to burn myself to death with my droopy-lit 6 A.M.

[290]

cig. More Castaneda. His prose is limpid and English and the power game he describes is more or less universal, no? And the ever further remoteness of Miguel, let alone proposals, love, even sex, hammer their cold steel nails into my coffin of a feeling, hopeful mind. Of a young, sexual woman who wants love. Who once, through what scheme of his or magic of mine, had it. I am really dead—it was no illusion I wake up to. I am dead.

Or Juan, to whom I would rush up and apologize in the following manner: forgive me for being angry that you felt me up in the street the other day and allowed your friend to do the same. You see, I'm really a very nice and worthwhile person and I will of course let you feel me up if only you will recognize my worthiness.

I stood up taut and straight in my leotard like you, looking charmed by his recitals, and physically proud, a dancer, an athlete. The stupid scum ignores every onda of attractiveness and generosity and previous acquaintance, and status, wafted in his direction to say let's fuck in your room . . .

Pues qué onda now? I ask. Let's fuck, he says. Cojer? I ask in cynical mock-surprise. Ah, how dull indeed; think I'll pass. Pues, nos vemos, and I cordially shake his hand and he splits. Cute, no?

What shall I write you at a little after 8 P.M. except that I am totally drunk. I give, lista-ly, Miguel as an excuse for this but the truth is I love the confidence, the glamor, the liberty, that comes from booze.

It is after 8. Miguel is over five hours late in calling me back. But do I care?

I crunch glass underfoot—the broken half liter of 55 p. vodka, over two bucks. Earlier, I saw blood on my left hand, correlative of my intense suffering, but it disappeared, including its origin, as soon as I wiped it off, and so remains a disturbing fiction, false pain. I sweep up the glass debris with my hand, indifferent to cuts.

¿Quién sabe? I lurch out into the night, truly dizzy, to make a quick 500 p's whoring and then go boogying. Odd as it may seem to anyone but me, the big obstacle entre mí y whoredom is my compulsion to reveal all. I know I'll tell.

Whatever guilt I felt at transcending a frontier of authentic love/sexual feeling has been superseded by the easy charm of a quick and necessary 25 bucks American. I've earned nada in Mexico, and am truly broke, truly unloved.

And, natch, the impossibility of ever being loved. Though lord knows, Silvia said to me today: you are one of those persons one will miss. I suspect Silvia is a dyke, but no matter. I adore her, and Angela. We converse equally. They know me for an independent, physical, suffering, and critical female "fellow" soul.

It's nigh on 8:30 and no call. But do I care?

Already, in Lechuga's mirror, I'd ascertained that I was ugly, inescapably visibly weird on the left side, dewlapped and corrugated, but thin, all in black, hair pulled back, tough, alive, glamorous. And of course, I do occasionally (there are verbal testimonies to this) move well, excitingly . . .

At 7:30 I called M.'s and got T. and said let's boogie at Satellite, the disco suburb out of Mexico City. It's hard to tell her good will or honesty. I know I like her. She's the youngest sister, thirty-one, and acts young. I dig her, dig her being into good times and chic and talking sexual tastes with me and being dark.

Just called T. and got I. who said "Ya salió," you should call in the morning. T., like Miguel, gives this dumb punctilious gringa a bum rap. Absurd no? I am really so smashingly drunk and still limber, though dancing with J.-L. last night I panted from exertion, as I pant tonight from cigs. I adore J.-L. and pray he calls. Doubt he will since he neither fucked my rico cunt or offered me his.

E., I *am* good, was good. Qué joke! I am, after all, so objectively good at times. Why shouldn't I lead when the entire sitting audience is following my moves.

This, of course, happened. Even the evil frater chavos had to acknowledge that I was a boogier born I was. No longer am. My heart races now. I get tired quickly on the crowded Mexico City dance floor that can't let me do my moderate rhythmic, soul baby soul, folly.

But falta, no. A eso manuscrito falta la historia . . . pasado la religión. . . . Jueves más tarde perfecto. . . . Pero, soy escritora. El es mi experimento. No tengo . . . dentro de historica explosiva.

So what remains to be written before I depart?

Eduardo and his highs,

Perfect Thursday with Miguel,

Machistic manipulations.

And love to you, querida fellow woman—or are you one of the boys? . . .

Need to remember I'm human, in love, polymorphous. . . .

Ω

EPILOGUE
New York, 1977

August, and I am waiting for Maryse to come back from Mexico. I've pulled together a few pieces of my life since the last shattering separation from her, and I only need her return to get the peace, the confidence, the validation to be able to go on. The very clouds wait with me for her return—when they will assume luminescent and subtle shapes—"nuances des nuages." The sky will confirm me. There will be clouds with important numinous shapes—and sun. We will get a tan.

I keep calling Stan. Why doesn't she come? I have denied myself Maryse for almost a year. I had refused my love to her around her birthday, in October, 1976. I was saving it for a new lover whom I jealously hid from her. Then my life fell apart again and I hid like a wounded animal until I could repossess her. Now I'm ready. August moves into September. Finally Stan tells me she's disappeared from her hotel room. Walked out one night and didn't come back. As soon as he tells me, I know she's dead. Murdered.

It's not like Maryse to disappear. Her life is a drama played to an audience. If they're laughing and crying out there, it confirms her. She does not care enough about herself. Why can't she, my sister, my doppelganger, care more and I less? Why has she chosen me who always cares more about the other? Did she always know that about me?

The clouds remain flat, without significance. Now the rain. My tears are the rain. I walk the autumn streets in the rain sobbing and holding out my hands. They remain empty. She is dead, murdered. I refuse to get involved in the tracking-down. It does not matter to me who killed her. She created her own murder.

She used to ask me why I didn't kill my lover, the young poet who left me. She expressed no rancor, only curiosity.

"I don't want to go to the electric chair," I answered, preferring my anger to melt my brains into soup and turn my life dry. For Maryse, there was no electric chair. In the act of murder would occur one's own death as well.

But, for me, it was Maryse who gave my life shape, validation, élan. Now the tears that would have confirmed her are for me. If

[293]

only she were sitting in some unknown Mexican jail. I must hold on to the fact of her death, or I will start to see her where she isn't, as I have during one of our angry separations.

New York, 1959-1962

We met the year my mother died. We were students at Brooklyn College. We didn't find each other. We were introduced by someone who knew—knew that each of us had the qualities to Bobbsey-twin the other, as Maryse used to say.

Maryse was exotic. She had been born in France. She knew what was hip. She had a visible wound. I was trying to survive and to escape knowledge of myself. Maryse was creating an identity. She was in therapy with a psychoanalyst, a woman who gave her a sort of temporary identity by telling her that middle-class people didn't shoplift or run away or charge men for a quick feel in bars. She stopped doing those things. She never stopped looking for the mother she had lost when she was a child of two. The mother was always one who loved you more than you loved yourself and more than she loved herself.

Maryse's mother had been shot by the Germans in France in about 1943. Maryse did not regard her mother as a hero of the Resistance, as I did when she told me about it. She could only see that her mother had deserted her. She regarded her death as a kind of suicide and she thought that her mother had been trying to escape from her father. It was only in the sense that she was motherless that she regarded herself as a victim—she who was a child of the greatest systematized brutality the world has ever known until then. She maintained always the belief that people acted only by their own individual passions and desires. The most she conceded to society was that men oppressed women.

Maryse had been hidden by her father and her aunt with a Catholic family. Her father retrieved her and brought her to Paris immediately after the Liberation. He had been in Vichy. One night he went out, leaving Maryse alone in her cot; maybe he was seeking his wife, believing her still alive. A storm blew up, and he did not return that night. Maryse would talk about her father's deserting her. She believed her mother would not have left her if it had not been for intolerable personal pressures. She did not count the Nazi invasion as a pressure strong enough to wrench a mother from her

[294]

child. Only what she later thought she knew about her father—not understanding the care a father must take to avoid loving his daughter too much—could have caused her mother to get herself killed in the Resistance.

In any case, the cold she caught that night turned into mastoiditis. There was no penicillin in Paris then, not for civilian children. During the operation to leave a hole in her head where her ear had been, her facial nerve was cut. Her face was paralyzed on one side and slightly distorted. That fact, that pain, never left her. After about three weeks of knowing her, I had stopped noticing it. She would keep asking me to get on the side of her good ear, and I would forget that she had no insides to her left ear. She was unusually sensitive to music, as she was to all nuance, so why did I have to remember that she was deaf on one side. She did not ever let you forget, nor did she forget herself. I think it was because not remembering would have seemed to her like a loss of perception. She was afraid that the world would see her as dull.

She quantified perception. In the era when people used to say something was "too much" to show that they were hip, Maryse would say "too much and a half." We used to try to outdo each other in mots, japes, aperçus, epigrams. She would look at me with her soft eyes and say, "I've lost my wit." She needed constant reassurance that she was bright. To have told her that she was intelligent would have been an insult, however. You had to tell her that she "used to be bright." Her assumed ingenuousness was not perhaps so assumed. "Do you think I'm stupid?" she would ask over and over. It was the consciousness of a loss that never left her. The magnitude of that loss never did either, although the question was idiotic.

Maryse had the metaphoric appearance of a Mayan stone figure. She believed in being hard, so that although she weighed too much for most of the time I knew her, she was never flabby. She had enormous bones—gigantic hands and feet, but she was quite short, so that she had a look of being dwarfed, pressed down. Her face was Mayan, too, apart from its defects. Her enormous chic made it difficult to regard her as squat, but she was. She had grape-trampling flat feet, which she ignored, except when she wanted sympathy, when she would evoke them, but she usually wore fashionable shoes that obviously hurt.

The mass of unresolvable contradictions made Maryse herself. I

[295]

remember walking with her often by water—on a Staten Island beach in the winter, by the Hudson River in Fort Tryon Park. Swimming, always swimming. She was not supposed to get water in her ear, but she swam like a spaniel.

She wrote about Eliot's use of stone and bone imagery, equating the two. She herself was like stone—heavy, hard, and at the same time moist, molle. She died in the sun getting a tan. Drying herself out. Her eyes were liquid, but I can only remember seeing her cry once or twice—always as a performance.

Maryse knew there was a formula for everything. If you possessed the correct formula, you could be anything. She knew there were good, heavy, magical formulas and banal, cheesy formulas, and she did not make judgments as to their value or the value of what she would get by pronouncing the correct formulas. She was not an esthetician of camp or of tackiness, but it was important to her to be able to create the role of a working-class teenager, for instance, just to be able to do it. It gave her relief from having to create the role of a young critic and intellectual.

She lived in an institution called "The Girl's Club," a social work place for teenage girls from broken homes. Everyone was always having breakdowns and going to the hospital or having abortions and breakdowns and going to the hospital. Maryse, who was always slightly a stranger, an outsider, never had a real breakdown. She wanted to go to the hospital simply to conform to the prevailing culture and to have a breakdown so as to suffer maximally. She would tell me tentatively that she had pissed in her bed. She would say that she had allowed the house gorgons to know. It never worked. They never came and took her away, and she had to finish her paper or study for the exam or whatever. I never believed it either. I never knew whether she was telling me she had done it to get my response or whether she had forced herself to do it, the way we used to walk on copper pennies to give ourselves a fever so that we could be sent home from school.

She once appeared for a dinner party to which I had invited her with her wrists in bandages. "I suicided myself last night," she announced dramatically. I insisted on seeing the wounds. She appeared to have suicided herself with a blunt bobby pin. Her dramatic scenes of passion and angst were never quite believable, but they were always interesting.

When the time came for me to graduate from college, I asked Maryse, who had been there as long as I had, when she was graduating. She did not understand the question. She assumed that she would naturally be graduated, probably with a brass band, and probably about ten years thence. The idea that you had to apply to the dean and count your own credits for graduation appalled her. I applied her into graduate school and organized her into taking the proper exams. She won a major graduate fellowship at Cornell. She had all along received B's in courses without having cracked a single book. Why study when passion and angst were more fun?

When she was twenty-one, she became an American citizen. I tried to talk her out of it, thinking she had French nationality. How much more interesting to be French than from Brooklyn thought I. Being born in France does not confer citizenship, however. Maryse was stateless. The horror of that shook me. It was summer when we went to the naturalization board, I as her witness. The bright, banal New York summer beat down on us but could not erase the haunting. Maryse did not seem to notice that much. The word "stateless" reverberated for me with the taste of ashes. The investigator, utterly uninterested in her record of being a juvenile runaway, wanted to know if she was a communist. I regretted to tell him that her political beliefs were the opposite of communist. She was forte.

Maryse taught me to speak French by telling me to imitate how French people spoke—exaggeratedly, as though I were mocking. The formula worked. For years, I spoke almost as much French as English and thought in French, and always those thoughts were conversations in my head with Maryse. Maryse herself seemed quintessentially European, although her accent was American and assumed Brooklyn.

She wore clothes that were outlandish for being noticeably chic in an era when one did not dress to be seen, but to merge. She would wear uncomfortable shoes because they were beautiful—a heresy. She had a pair of green lizardskin shoes that were too small for her enormous peasant feet. She had gotten her boyfriend of the moment to pay an enormous sum for them. I chided her for buying shoes that didn't fit, but she said the store had only the one pair and she "had to have them."

Madison-Ithaca, 1963-1965

We quarreled before we departed from New York—she to Cornell and I to the University of Wisconsin. We quarreled so that

[297]

we would not have to face what our parting meant to us. We had boyfriends—roommates at Union Seminary. Each of us was in love with the other's love as well as with her own. It was terribly important to us to be caught up in intertwining relationships with men so that we would not have to deal with what we were to each other. I began to see Maryse in Madison—where she wasn't. That was so impossible to bear that we began to live through our letters to each other. Maryse wrote more than I did. She would write ten-page letters, sometimes twice a day.

We met at Christmas, 1963, in a Chinese restaurant in New York. The taste of the food was unutterably sensuous. We went to hear jazz. Coltrane played, and we were high on each other—high in a way that was impossible to sustain or to climax. There was no modus vivendi for us.

I visited her in Ithaca for a few weekends. Away from the natural oppression of New York life, Maryse entered the life of the seasons, of fields and animals. She would orient herself by the animals and was very generous in sharing them. She took me to visit a goat who was a close friend of hers. There was no need to be jealous, as she sometimes was with human friends. She hung out with the packs of dogs that roamed the streets of Ithaca, ownerless, but gentle, large, fat, soft, and loved. They belonged to everybody.

Our boyfriends, amid scenes of passion and angst, left us. Maryse had a succession of lovers. Each of them was special—extraordinarily beautiful or witty. Bob was sharp, hard, beautiful. He was witty and had the face of an angel and the soul of a saint. He was athletic, but had a crippled foot that gave him the cachet of suffering that Maryse liked in people. She did not let herself be loved by him or by anyone, particularly someone who did not find it hard to love and be loved.

Once, Maryse arranged an expedition for us to gather wild strawberries. She laughed at me for spending hours hulling them, but was extravagant in calling me "earth mother" to her friends. Maryse would always arrange for wonderful food—wild strawberries, meat, fish, and she would allow me to cook wonderful meals. I am a good cook, but I have never met anyone who could appreciate the sensuousness of food more than Maryse.

She nursed a pregnant cat for a summer with a devotion and lovingness to that ungainly splayfooted animal that she would only show toward something that was not hers and that she would have to give back to its owner at the end of a summer.

We swam naked in Beebe Lake at night. Drunk. We were always drunk together—sometimes on alcohol, mainly on each other. I accepted Maryse's not doing any work. She avoided finishing her graduate degree like the plague. She would talk about her instructors, but little about her actual work. She gave me a copy of Flaubert's L'Education sentimentale to read and praised my underlining, claiming I had seen the essence of the novel. She wanted to write her dissertation on Flaubert's acceptance of Frédéric without judgment.

Maryse could accept people without judging them, but she could never get the difference between judging and knowing what was going on. She thought that the love she gave would always be returned. When it wasn't, she did not accept that.

Paris, 1965-1966

Maryse spent a year in Paris in 1965-66. I was teaching in Ohio. Her letters by this time were more controlled. She was consciously writing not for me this time, but to create herself and to communicate with the world. We had an agreement to be each other's literary executors. It meant nothing to me. I withered in her absence. Her letters seemed like complaints. I could not understand why she endured the coldness of Paris, the emotional bleakness, the rejections she claimed to meet with on every side. For myself, I could not accept the level on which I missed her. By this time, I had no self left that was not part of Maryse. She had taught me everything—how to appreciate nuance, how to dress, how to eat, how to make love. But it was not a teaching that was like an imparting. It was as though all my actions were for Maryse. She owned me. Neither of us realized it. I sent her finally a suicide note. She replied, "Your letters make me want to die along with you. You are emptying me out gradually. I become a pure light—floating vessel. I was always what you put in me. (Must you believe my words as I believe yours?) Cheap terms are what I settle for and distraction of illusion of help from sex. Am floating lighter every day. I smoke incredibly. I don't care if I die—want to but floating off." We didn't realize where one of us left off and the other began. She wrote that on the envelope in which I had sent her the note—torn open. The words, and there were more of them, were hard to read. They were written over the address, the stamp. They covered both sides of the envelope.

When I left Ohio, defeated, I burned most of her letters. I repeated to myself as I burned them—"trash to the collectors, garbage to the pig feeders, paper to the incinerator." It was the litany of that place.

New York, 1967-1976

When Maryse returned from Paris, she had purple shoes, a job in a publishing house, an apartment—all the accoutrements of the young woman about town. She did not like her job which consisted of culling French quotations for an update of Bartlett's. Her sojourn in New York was interrupted by forays back to Ithaca. She spent months at a time in Ithaca.

Finally she resolved to give up her attempt to not get a Ph.D. from Cornell. She started trying to finish her degree at City University and teaching in the colleges of the City University system. We saw less of each other. I could no longer bear the violence with which we drew together and separated. I could never accept within myself how much I needed and cared for her because of the overt hostility she presented.

New York, 1970-1974

Maryse moved from West 80th Street, a relative slum, to 88th Street near Riverside Drive. Her apartment, in a brownstone, was a masterpiece. She had recognized it under its coats of paint, become lovers with the person who occupied it (one who had also recognized it), and her will to assume possession of it was stronger than his to retain it. She stripped the paint from the wood paneling. She installed dark green trees and a victorian sofa covered in faded mauve silk. When one passed her bow window from the street, the light or the intense darkness of her trees beckoned with a mysterious expression—welcoming and yet always a bit foreign. The paint on the walls was shaded in greens and mauves. The walls were a painting, not like anyone else's walls.

Maryse worked at teaching in the various colleges of The City University. She did not like publishing, and again, we passed each other. I returned to being an editor and she a teacher. She accepted the premise of the women's movement—that men oppressed women, but she never accepted her position as a member of a group. She was into individual protest. Her father had left New

[300]

York. *In some vague sense, he had anchored her a little. She maintained a relationship with a man, but they did not live together and he was, as Maryse used to say a "stone breast."*

As long as the teaching jobs held out, Maryse had a goal and a purpose, apart from the seeking of love. She fell in love with one of her students, a boy named Georges. I never believed in the reality, but her attachment to the idea was passionate. Georges eventually left the college, without anything substantial having taken place between them.

Maryse organized a film seminar for women's films. She was publishing film and art criticism in obscure feminist publications— but still, publishing. She felt that she was having some influence on her students. Sir Isaiah Berlin thanked her for having been his student and wrote a note praising her brilliance.

New York, 1975-1976

I had not seen Maryse for a long time. It was late fall. I had been going through a bad scene that lasted for years. Maryse gave me a gift. It was a poker game for women at her apartment. She would lovingly drop a social occasion at your feet the way a terrier drops a rat—without thinking about how the recipient would feel, but so pleased with the gift. Some of the players in the game spoke of literary things; Maryse, myself, and Edith spoke of fathers. I had not thought of my father or of Maryse's father for years. In that game, I lost my father.

Maryse had baked a pie. It was delicious and bespoke the essence of pie. It's effect was early American. She had made the crust with lard. It had a life of its own and an affect. Maryse seldom cooked, but when she did, it was to create the essence of each dish individually. Maryse was never a stone breast, but I was unable to suck at that time.

After a long winter of suffering, I called Maryse to ask if I could come for a cup of coffee. I was getting ready to move forward. Maryse had lost her job. The sunlight was brilliant in her apartment. She served café con leche with goat's milk. She was thin and tanned. She had been to Mexico. She did not speak much of her experiences there, but she exulted in her triumph. The trip had been a triumph and she expected that she would be renewed, in exactly the way she had been by coming back from Paris. We moved to the garden where Maryse lay back and stressed the

[301]

importance of getting a tan. My resolve strengthened. I found a new job in a couple of weeks. Again, we passed each other.

Maryse had an abortion. The next night we went, a bunch of us, to dance at The Midnight Special. The dancers were all very young, black. Maryse talked about the importance of dancing correctly. She was revolted by the way I danced, free-style. But the abortion she had had the previous day prevented her from dancing herself and prevented her from seeing the obvious fact that she would have been a sore thumb among the dancers, or a spectacle, but never one of them. Stan nursed her tenderly and maintained the bubble around her.

On July 4, 1976, we played poker all day, naked by the side of a pond in New Paltz. I won all the money. The moment was sunlit and golden for me, as Maryse wished it to be. She was envious, but the texture of her life was richer than that of mine, in any case. That was the last golden, sunlit moment for us. Maryse had been to Mexico and knew she could go back.

In October of that year, I had a birthday party for a friend. Maryse had been dragged away by the police a few weeks before at an opera performance in Central Park. She had been fighting for a space, a fight which erupted into a melee. She had some marijuana and an illegal switchblade which she had brought from Mexico. Although the D.A. would easily enough drop the marijuana charge, the Sullivan law violation is a serious thing in New York. The quarrel she had provoked that had led to the arrest was forgotten, but Maryse was at odds again. Although the memory of the police dragging her away was galling, she wanted more from the situation than it contained. She was eager to prove the lawyer I had recommended a fool. At the party, she was both quarrelsome, accusing one of the guests of wrongful sexual tastes, and demanding of love and attention. I threw her out.

My life fell apart again after that moment, and I hid like a wounded animal. She went back to Mexico. They found her body by the side of a road. Somebody had smashed her into silence. The post-mortem revealed no pregnancy.

They drain Beebe Lake, where we used to swim, once a year. My tears, if only she had been able to evoke them when she was alive, would have confirmed her; they would fill the lake again. She would have saved her life. But when she was alive, my tears were dry inside, and now they are for myself because she's gone.

—SELMA YAMPOLSKY